I0138794

The Charter Fragment
and
Pascon agan Arluth

CORPUS TEXTUUM CORNICORUM
Volume 1

CORPUS TEXTUUM CORNICORUM
Volume 1

The Charter Fragment
and
Pascon agan Arluth

Edited and translated by
Nicholas Williams

Palaeographic manuscript transcription and facsimile prepared by
Michael Everson

Introduction by
Alan M. Kent

evertype
2020

Published by Evertype, 19A Corso Street, Dundee, DD2 1DR, Scotland.
www.evertype.com.

A catalogue record for this book is available from the British Library.

ISBN-10 1-78201-182-X
ISBN-13 978-1-78201-182-8

Typeset in Baskerville, Chartour, Sancreed, and Bastarda Anglicana by Michael Everson.

Cover design by Michael Everson. Image from Harley MS 1782 *f.* 19v, lines 1811–1828. Courtesy of the British Library Board.

TABLE OF CONTENTS

ACKNOWLEDGEMENTS

We would like to thank Michelle Brown, Greg Buzwell, William Frame, Stephen Noble, Zoë Stansell, Claire Wotherspoon, and the staff at the British Library for their assistance in our consultation of the primary manuscripts, and in particular to Eleanor Jackson, Curator of Illuminated Manuscripts, and to Kathleen Doyle, Curator of Western Manuscripts, who arranged for the digitization of the entire manuscript for this edition. For permissions to print the facsimile we thank Rebecca Nuotio and Chris Rawlings for their generous assistance. We appreciate the efforts of Angela Broome of the Courtney Library, Royal Institution of Cornwall, and of David Thomas and Deborah Tritton of Kresen Kernow (formerly the Cornwall Records Office) for their help in the consultation of secondary sources. Our thanks are also due to Brian Murdoch and to Neil Kennedy for their observations about the texts as we prepared this edition, as they are to Laura Wideberg for her observations about the illustrations on folios 9r and 10r. We offer our thanks to Susanna Tavares Pedro and to Patrick H. Wynne for their review of the section on the palaeographic transcription. For the tireless assistance that Andrew C. West has offered in helping to compile the indexes with his BabelPad text editor[1] we are very grateful indeed.

1 https://web.archive.org/web/20200215180819/www.babelstone.co.uk /Software/BabelPad.html, retrieved 2020-02-18.

ABBREVIATIONS

ACB *Archæologia Cornu-Britannica*, Pryce 1790.
BB Bilbao MS, in Jenner 1925, 421–437.
BN William Bodinar, in Pool and Padel 1976, 231–234.
CF *Charter Fragment*.
CW *Creation of the World*, in Stokes 1864.
JB John Boson, in Padel 1975b, 52–53.
KS Kernowek Standard, Standard Cornish.
ME Middle English.
MS manuscript, *pl.* MSS.
NB Nicholas Boson, in Padel 1975b, 8–37.
OM *Origo Mundi*, in Norris 1968, 1:1–219.
PA *Pascon agan Arluth*.
PC *Passio Christi*, in Norris 1968, 1:221–479.
RD *Resurrexio Domini*, in Norris 1968, 2:1–199.
SA *Sacrament an Alter*, in Bice [1969], 38–43.
SWF Standard Written Form.
TH Tregear's Homilies, in Bice [1969], 1–38.
WR William Rowe (Wella Kerew), in Loth 1902, 173–200.

In Chapter 2, the following linguistic conventions are used:

⟨ ⟩ enclose graphemes, that is, written letters.
/ / enclose phonemic transcriptions.
[ ] enclose phonetic transcriptions.

See § 3.5 for the use of various brackets in palaeographic transcription.

1
INTRODUCTION

1.1 THE LITERARY CONTEXT

1.1.1 *The Charter Fragment*

The piece of Middle-Cornish writing now known as *The Charter Fragment* is the earliest surviving text written in Cornish. Although there are earlier glosses, vocabularies, and marginalia, as well as one text that might feasibly have once been constructed in Cornish, namely, John of Cornwall's *The Prophecy of Merlin c.* 1150[1]—*The Charter Fragment* stands at present as the first true piece of Cornish literature, which is why it is placed first in this volume, and first in the wider series of Evertype's comprehensive *Corpus Textuum Cornicorum*. Estimated to have been written sometime around 1380–1400, it is indeed an ancient and intriguing piece of literature constructing a "lost" Cornwall. We may label it "literature" because of its intricate poetic construction, and although it is rather short, it is clearly much more than just a quick note or scribble.

Since the text's discovery, general debate on it has straddled three main areas which may or may not be interlinked. First of all, the text is of interest because it has been seen by some as a *secular* work—one which seems to differ considerably from other surviving work in Cornish from the medieval period, which we may label "community verse dramas" with either biblical or hagiographical themes. Secondly, however, the work has been considered to be a surviving fragment of a larger work; its verse indicating that it was once possibly part of a longer poetic or dramatic text. Paradoxically, though, other observers have come to read it as a sacred piece of writing, extolling the virtues of celibacy. Finally, the text has been conceived as an epithalamion or a kind of wedding speech, either on its own, or as part of something grander, inviting harmony between both the bride and the groom in what Toorians has labelled "the making of a marriage in Medieval Cornwall".[2] The difficulty with this latter theory is that if it were simply a note written down on the back of a land charter for the purpose of an immediate speech, then why would the author go to such pains to construct it poetically? These are examples of some of the difficulties we

1 For examples, Kent and Saunders 2000, pp. 28–29, and 257–261. See also Curley 1982, pp. 217–219.

2 Toorians 1991.

face when trying to interpret *The Charter Fragment*. Its status, however, has gradually increased over the years since its discovery, and it has certainly prompted much debate; not only by linguists and Celticists,[3] but also recently by feminist and literary scholars.[4]

1.1.2 *Pascon agan Arluth*

Pascon agan Arluth[5] (in contemporary orthography *Passyon agan Arlùth*, known alternatively as *The Cornish Poem of the Passion* or as *Mount Calvary*) is the earliest lengthy text surviving in Cornish.[6] It is a narrative poem detailing the Passion of Christ, told in 259 stanzas, each consisting of eight lines. The poem is based n the narrative of the Gospels, but also integrates other legendaria and motifs of medieval Gothic mysticism. Written in Middle Cornish, the poem dates from around the same period as *The Charter Fragment* (roughly 1400–1450), but almost certainly predates the dramatic trilogy known as the *Ordinalia*.[7] Indeed, there is strong evidence that the second play of the *Ordinalia*, *Passio Christi* ('*The Passion of Christ*'), and the third play of the trilogy, *Resurrexio Domini* ('*The Resurrection of the Lord*') directly and indirectly incorporate much material from *Pascon agan Arluth*, and that they are an adaptation of it.

Although the status of the poem and the achievement its author has not always been asserted or even realized by Celtic scholars outside Cornwall,[8] the reputation of *Pascon agan Arluth* has grown in recent years and has been subject to further investigation and scrutiny.[9] Connections and similarities have been made to Passion poems from elsewhere in Britain and Ireland (such as the *Northern* and *Southern Passion Poems*), and to elsewhere in Europe.[10] The poem has a powerful metaphorical base, as well as a striking, if rather macabre, beauty, demonstrating much of the quality of Cornish writing during this period. The poem's couplet structure means that the verse was intended to be heard rather than read silently. The repetitive rhythm of the seven-syllable line contributes to the sense of inevitability in the narrative.

---

3 See Price 1984, p. 139; Williams 2006, pp. 90–92.

4 Kent 1999, pp. 8–9; Kent 2000, p. 35.

5 [ˈpæʃən ˈægən ˈɑɹlʊθ].

6 Gilbert 1826; Edwards 1993; Woodhouse 2002.

7 See Norris 1969; Kent 2005.

8 See, for example, Maclean 1908, p. 249. Cornish literature is however, generally ignored by Celtic Studies. See Williams 1971.

9 A leading scholar in this field has been Brian Murdoch. See Murdoch 1979.

10 See Edwards 1993; Murdoch 1979b.

Murdoch has suggested that the poem is about "the underlining of the Redemption in narrative terms".[11] The narrative leads us from Christ's temptation in the wilderness, through his betrayal, arrest, trial, and crucifixion, to his death and eventual resurrection. *Pascon agan Arluth* exhibits many of the same themes of the community based and popular dramas elsewhere in Middle Cornish literature; its masterful poetic structure shows us that rather different forms of native verse were available to Middle Cornish poets. Indeed, the style of verse seems to evoke the sort of verse practised by earlier poets—perhaps suggestive of the survival of the native Celtic poetic tradition. The line of seven syllables, unusual in Breton verse, is reminiscent of the Welsh *cywydd*.

1.2 NAMING AND PLACING

1.2.1 *The Charter Fragment*

The Charter Fragment has not always been known as such. Henry Jenner (1848–1934), who discovered the text in 1915, labelled it "the charter endorsement". The more common term, *The Charter Fragment*, suggests that the text was part of a longer, work and that its brevity is due to its fragmentary status. Jenner's name for the text might be considered reasonable, since the text is found on the back of an earlier land charter from the mid-Cornwall parish of St Stephen-in-Brannel; on the other hand, since the term "endorsement" has the sense of "recommendation" or "emendation" today (the definition "something written on the back of a document" is decidedly old-fashioned), we have preferred the term "fragment".[12]

The parish of St Stephen-in-Brannel lies about nine kilometres inland from the coastal town of St Austell, lying on the southern side of the Hensbarrow upland district.[13] The area is noted for its surviving Iron Age hill-forts which follow the route of the River Fal.[14] It is an area which has been mined for tin since the medieval period, and since the eighteenth century has been subject to extraction of uranium and china clay. In terms of literary continuities forward in time, the parish was also the birthplace of Silas, Joseph, and Salome Hocking—the best-selling nineteenth-century novelists who defined populist historical novels in that period—and the Anglo-Cornish poet and novelist Jack Clemo.[15] Both the Hockings and

11 Murdoch 1979b, p. 1.

12 The manuscript is reproduced in colour facsimile, Plates 1–3, pp. 101–103 below.

13 For a useful history see Olver [n.d].

14 Weatherhill 1985, p.120.

15 See Kent 2002; Clemo 1988.

Clemo may be deemed Christian writers so there may be a long continuity here if we judge *The Charter Fragment* to be essentially a Christian text.

1.2.2 *Pascon agan Arluth*

The various names for *Pascon agan Arluth* derive from its publishing history. Like *The Charter Fragment*, the work is untitled in the earliest manuscript but was given the name *Mount Calvary* by Davies Gilbert in a translation published in 1826 (though to be fair, he probably took this from one of the manuscript titles he studied).[16] Gilbert's somewhat flawed translation may also have been named from the reference to Calvary in stanza 162. Though *Pascon agan Arluth* was the first of the longer canonical Cornish manuscripts to be published in the modern period, it was known earlier by still other names. In 1695, Edmund Gibson (1669–1748), in his English-language edition of William Camden's *Britannica*, refers to it as "The History of the Passion of Our Saviour",[17] while in 1680, William Scawen (1600–1689) used the name "Passio Christi" for this text alone,[18] rather than for the second play of the *Ordinalia*.

The name *Mount Calvary* stood for a while however, until 1861 when Whitley Stokes published a corrected translation which he titled *The Passion: A Middle-Cornish Poem.*[19] The more commonly used title *Pascon agan Arluth* ['*The Passion of our Lord*'] seems to have been applied by Robert Morton Nance in numbers of *Kernow* magazine issued between 1934 and 1936, when sections of the poem were published at the end of each number.[20] It was edited by both A. S. D. Smith and Nance, though it appears Nance himself determined what the title should be.[21] This name for the text has stood more or less consistently for the rest of the twentieth century, with various groups in the revival of Cornish spelling this differently. Observers such as Herriman and Murdoch have more recently reverted to calling it *The Cornish Poem of the Passion.*[22]

A number of manuscript copies of *Pascon agan Arluth* have been made, most fragmentary, although all seem to derive from one fifteenth-century

16 See Gilbert 1826.

17 See Piggot and Walters 1971 [1695], col. 17.

18 Scawen 1979, p. 15. For background to Scawen, see Spriggs 2005. See also Whetter 2017.

19 Stokes, 1861.

20 These were eventually collated. See Hooper 1972.

21 The phrase "*passyon agan Arlùth ker*" 'the passion of our dear Lord' appears on line 1822 as *pascon̄ agan arluth ker* and is reproduced on the front cover of this book.

22 See Herriman 1984; Murdoch 1993, pp. 19–40.

manuscript now held in the British Library.[23] That manuscript was probably the one once owned by William Scawen; it is described by him as "an ancient manuscript... written upon rough old vellum".[24] The Harleian catalogue describes this manuscript as having been donated by John Antis (1669–1744) though it was previously owned by one John Robyn. The exact process of transmission from Scawen is still unknown. The catalogue also notes that Antis "procured this Poem to be translated into English, and that he lent the same Translation to Mr. Lhwyd,[25] who did not return it". Another important manuscript copy is found in the papers of William Gwavas (1674–1741) which suggests a place of origin for the text.[26] Gwavas had transcribed the poem from a manuscript found in *Sancret* Church that had been corrected and translated by the historian William Hals (1655–1737). Sancreed is a parish in West Penwith.

Spatially, this is as far back as we can go with this text. The text's position at Sancreed is interesting however, since we are bound to make a connection between the church and Saint Credan of Evesham (d. 780), a saint in the calendar of the pre-Reformation Church, who is also known in Latin as Credus and Credanus. Credan has been associated with the founding of the church at Sancreed, though we must be careful of making too much of this association, for there were other Cornish saints of this name who might be confused with him.[27] A possible candidate might be Credan who is said to have "killed by misfortune his own father, with which he was so moved as abandoning the world he became a hogherd, and lived so exemplary as he was after esteemed a saint". This legend is now embellished by a small, modern statue showing the saint holding a piglet held in the porch of the church. Certainly the "Age of Saints" was past long before the manuscript was written, but something of the spirituality of the saint may well have survived the passage of time. This is perhaps also seen in the two highly-decorated and distinctive wheel-headed stone crosses found in Sancreed churchyard both carrying knotwork and figures of Christ triumphant.[28] We know from *plen-an-gwary* evidence in Sancreed that sacred dramas were performed there until relatively late. A connection is, in my opinion, possible.[29]

23 British Library, Harley MS 1782.

24 Scawen 1979.

25 Edward Lhuyd (1660–1709).

26 British Library, Additional MS 28554, Nr. 7.

27 See John 2001, p. 74.

28 Langdon 1997, pp. 81–82.

29 Kent 2010, pp. 274–275.

This geographical indication of the manuscript's origin is fascinating because, as is shown below, the text of *Passio Christi* of the *Ordinalia*, was profoundly influenced by *Pascon agan Arluth*, and yet from internal place-name evidence it appears that the trilogy's geography is much more centred around the River Fal (and thus possibly Glasney College itself).[30] Therefore either the text or a scholar would have had to travel at some point. We may speculate, of course, that both *Pascon agan Arluth* and *Passio Christi* were at some point housed in the same institution, or in close proximity.

Scawen noted the illustrations accompanying the text, observing that "by the rude pictures set out therewith, it may seem to be before the art of painting became better amongst us".[31] The Harley manuscript does contain ten line-drawings with a coloured wash, though this manuscript may well be copy of an earlier version—itself with illustrations. The surviving illustrations are of interest in part because they are unique in accompanying Cornish text in a manuscript. They can be seen in the lower half of some folios of the Harley manuscript.[32] Space seems to have been left for other illustrations, which suggests perhaps that the illustration of the manuscript was incomplete. Scawen's observation on their lack of sophistication is perhaps a little harsh. There is, in fact, a naïve beauty to the illustrations, which impose a late medieval world view onto the gospel narrative. For example, the soldiers who capture Christ are shown to be wearing armour as though medieval knights,[33] and those who are scourging Christ are likewise dressed in medieval clothing.[34] Michael Everson has provided a description of the illustrations in § 5.2.1 below, basing some of his observations on the text as presented on the illustrated page itself. Among the most immediately recognizable though, are Adam and Eve in the Garden of Eden,[35] and Christ carrying the cross (this latter image has been used on the cover of many published texts associated with the poem).[36]

---

30 See Bakere 1980, pp. 12–39; Whetter 1988. Whetter offers useful thoughts on literary production in Cornwall during this phase. However, see the alternative view offered in Frost 2003, pp. 291–307.

31 Scawen 1979.

32 The manuscript is reproduced in colour facsimile (Plates 4–45, pp. 105–146 below) and the ten illustrations are described and shown in greater detail (Plates 46–55, pp. 150–154 below).

33 Folio 6v, Plate 15, p.. 116 below.

34 Folio 11v, Plate 25, p.. 126 below.

35 Folio 1v, Plate 5, p.. 106 below.

36 Folio 14v, Plate 31, p.. 132 below.

1.3 SOURCES

1.3.1 *The Charter Fragment*

There is only one source for *The Charter Fragment* text, which is now held in the British Library. The manuscript is composed of a single piece of parchment, which is dirty and blotted; upon the *verso* can be made out the forty-one lines of the text.[37] The manuscript itself measures about 30cm by 15cm, and is marked by a vertical fold in the parchment. The script is an Anglicana Book hand consistent with a late-fourteenth-century date. The catalogue description of the charter reads:

> 19491 Indenture of Final Concord at Westminster. Michaelmas Term. 14 Edw. III [1340]. before John de Stonore, William de Shareshall, and others. whereas Thomas Leghe of Rosagon and Margery. his wife. grant to Nicholas. son of John of Menkeden. messuages. etc.. in Menleder. [co. Cornwall]. *Latin.*
>
> [*added in another hand*] Cornish poem on the back[38]

There is no Menleder on present maps, although the name may perhaps be related to Meledor in the north-east of St Stephen-in-Brannel parish, an area which has been more recently altered out of all recognition by the china clay industry. The date of the land charter itself, coupled with the hand, gives us the approximate date of 1380–1400 for the work. The fact that there is strong evidence for a *plen-an-gwary* site in St Stephen-in-Brannel is one element supporting the suggestion that the fragment was from a play. The evidence has been considered by Henderson and by Kent, who conclude that the original site may well have been in the centre of the village, once occupied by the Primary School and now converted into industrial units.[39] The round would have been close to the parish church and in the centre of the parish.

Scholarship on the sources of the narrative and its themes, however, is very thin indeed. Edwards has suggested some basic similarities to *The Canterbury Tales* by Geoffrey Chaucer (begun in 1380),[40] but this could be applied to much European literature of the same period. He also notes some similarities to the Spanish text of *Libro de Buen Amor* ['*The Book of Good Love*'].[41] This was a semi-biographical account of romantic adventures by

37 British Library, MS Add. Chart. 19491.
38 British Library, MS. Add. Chart. 19491.
39 See Henderson 1915; Kent, 2010, p. 163.
40 Edwards 1995, pp. 17–20.
41 Edwards 1995.

Juan Ruiz, the Archpriest of Hit, dating initially from 1330, but completed with revisions and expansions in 1343. The work is considered as the best piece of the medieval genre known as *Mester de Clarecía* ['*Ministry of Clergy*'].[42] The genre gave advice on how to find good and appropriate love and there could certainly be echoes of that in *The Charter Fragment* text. Edwards notes Ruiz's use of an old woman called "Trotaconventos" who acts as a go-between, going to convents and seeking lovers for him. Certainly, the speaker of *The Charter Fragment* has the feel of fulfilling such a role. Applicability of this interpretation of our text here is dependent on some of the precise translation: for example, in line 9 where the Cornish reads "*â, tanha y*"—this might mean 'go, take her' or 'go, seduce her'. Such a pan-European theme may at first seem far removed from the peripheral location of Cornwall and the parish of St Stephen-in-Brannel, yet as Murdoch has proven with later Cornish texts, we often find unexpected pan-European connections—showing transnational narrative exchange and adaptation.[43] Cornish Tristana also travelled across Europe to distant locations so there is no reason to assume that European narratives did not enter Cornwall as well.[44]

1.3.2 *Pascon agan Arluth*

Much research has been completed on the sources of *Pascon agan Arluth*. Comparative studies have also provided useful contextual material. The Gospels of Matthew, Mark, Luke, and John help provide the foundation of the text here, with the poet selecting his own perspective on the narrative. Murdoch has noted three other strands at work within the text.[45] He considers these to be "a) exegetical", where interjected comments are made by the speaker about "the literal understanding of the narrative"; "b) echoes of devotional works", which he considers to show clear "links with post-Bernardine cross-mysticism or devotion to the virgin"; and finally "c) legends". By legends, he refers to additional material such as the apocryphal gospels, for example, the Gospel of Nicodemus. These sources supply rather superficial additions to the gospel narrative. There may also be in the text further additions from the comprehensive collections of Peter Comoster's *Historica Scholastica* or Jacob de Voragine's *Legenda Aurea*. These works were known and read throughout Europe and suggest again that such knowledge, debate, and literary creation were not unknown in medieval Cornwall.

42 This is mainly a traditional Castilian literature, written by learned poets.

43 Murdoch 1996, pp. 45–63.

44 See Hale, Kent, and Saunders 2000, p. 14. See also Grimbert 1995.

45 Murdoch 1979b, p. 1.

1.4 PUBLISHING HISTORY AND LITERARY CRITICISM

1.4.1 *The Charter Fragment*

The year 1877 marked the centenary of the death of one of the last speakers of traditional Cornish—Dolly Pentreath (1692–1777) of Mousehole.[46] Henry Jenner discovered and published *The Charter Endorsement* in the same year. Indeed, Jenner's discovery of the text is embedded in the folklore of the revival of Cornish.[47] The text's published history begins when Jenner was employed in the British Museum cataloguing Additional and Egerton manuscripts and charters which had been acquired into the Museum's collection between 1845 and 1874.[48] Jenner's task was to write descriptions of these manuscripts and charters. Among these were some 37 grants of land from St Stephen-in-Brannel which had been presented by Sir Charles Trevelyan in 1872.[49] They had been drafted during the reigns of Edward III and Edward IV.

As can be seen from the charter itself, the Brannel documentation had been drawn up in 1340; Edward III remained on the throne until 1377. We therefore have excellent evidence here that the Cornish language persisted in mid-Cornwall during this period. Jenner had already been intrigued by fragments of Cornish still existing in West Penwith in the late nineteenth century, but the discovery of *The Charter Fragment* set him on a path which culminated in his *A Handbook of the Cornish Language* in 1904—the first modern text which provided a grammar and history of the language and its literature.[50]

Jenner set about translating the text and provided a copy for publication in the *Athenaeum* on 1 December 1877.[51] He apparently then sent a copy of this to Whitley Stokes, who had already been working on Cornish texts including *Beunans Meriasek*. Stokes completed his own translation for publication in *Revue Celtique* 1879/80.[52] Stokes found Jenner's version helpful, but

46 See Kent and Saunders 2000, p. 318.

47 Williams 2004, p. 29. For background on Jenner at the British Museum, see Everett 2011, pp. 140–158.

48 The Egerton Collection is a collection of historical manuscripts held in the British Library. The core of the collection comprises sixty-seven manuscripts bequeathed to the British Museum in 1829 by Francis Henry Egerton, 8th Earl of Bridgewater. Further manuscripts were then added to the collection.

49 Sir Charles Edward Trevelyan, 1st Baronet, (1807–1886) was a British civil servant and colonial administrator in India and Ireland.

50 Jenner 1904; second edition 2010.

51 Jenner 1877.

52 Stokes 1880, pp. 258–262.

offered a different translation of the piece, commenting that "Mr Jenner's readings seem to be, in some cases, completely wrong". However, other interpretations of this moment have also been made. Edwards, reading Enrico Campanile,[53] suggests that Stokes had already obtained a photographic reproduction of the text from the Reverend Robert Williams (1810–1881) at Rhydycroesau, commencing his work independently from Jenner.[54]

Over time, a consensus arose with regard to the reading of the text, with Jenner completing another translation for the *Journal of the Royal Institution of Cornwall* in 1915,[55] and Robert Morton Nance (1873–1959) providing a version in Unified Cornish orthography for *Old Cornwall* magazine in 1932.[56] Nance reconsidered the text again in *Old Cornwall* in the 1943–1951 series in an article titled "New Light on Cornish" where he sought again, to understand the context of the text.[57] Although *The Charter Fragment* remained in the consciousness of the Cornish revival, no further published commentaries were made until Enrico Campanile's examination of the text published in 1963.[58] Campanile's version was problematic; being written in Italian it would perforce have had a rather restricted readership. Because it was published, however, in the learned journal *Studi e saggi linguistici*, this reignited European-wide interest in text, coinciding with pan-Celtic cultural nationalism of the decade to follow. Just over ten years later, the work was examined once more in Peter Berresford Ellis' *The Cornish Language and its Literature*—a seminal text in terms of asserting the significance of Cornish in the history of the islands of Britain and Ireland. Ellis reprinted Stokes' translation and this has remained one of the most readily accessible versions to date.[59] Cursory attention was also given to the text in Crysten Fudge's *The Life of Cornish* (1982),[60] but discussion of its literary significance was limited.

Detailed discussion and re-evaluation of *The Charter Fragment* only really came in 1991, with two editions emerging in that year. These were Lauran Toorians' *The Middle Cornish Charter Endorsement: The Making of a Marriage in Medieval Cornwall* and Ray Edwards' *The Charter Fragment*.[61] Toorians' edition became the standard work for a number of years, having a glossary and

53 Edwards 1995. See also Campanile 1963.
54 Williams 2013, pp. 53–62.
55 Jenner 1921, pp. 41–48.
56 Nance 1932, pp. 34–36.
57 Nance 1951, pp. 214–216.
58 Campanile 1963.
59 Ellis 1974, pp. 42–43.
60 Fudge 1982, p. 13.
61 Toorians 1991; Edwards 1991.

commentary, as well as a description of the manuscript (completed by J. P. M. Jansen). If anything however, it was somewhat light on the text's literary content. Edwards' edition, meanwhile, was generally more accessible and included much about the text's discovery by Jenner. In a way, both seem to be a reaction to the limited way the text had been dealt with in the past—and acted as an important corrective.

The year 1993 also marked an important year for the development of studies of *The Charter Fragment*. The medievalist Brian Murdoch examined the text within the wider framework of traditional and revived writing in Cornish in his volume *Cornish Literature*.[62] He discusses *The Charter Fragment* in a chapter which considers literary possibilities of the past. In 1995 Edwards also showed the significance of the work in *The Celtic Pen*—a popular magazine devoted to Celtic literature.[63] In 2000, Kent and Saunders published a new translation of the text in their reader of Cornish literature, *Looking at the Mermaid*.[64] Readers were here able to trace *The Charter Fragment*'s place in the history of writing in Cornish. *The Charter Fragment* was considered again by Kent in 2000, when he examined the internal continuities of Cornish Literature, and again in 2010, when the fragment was explored as a possible dramatic text in the larger history of the theatrical culture of Cornwall.[65]

It is perhaps worth noting that the British Library was, in fact, originally a department of the British Museum and *The Charter Fragment* was originally housed in the famous circular British Museum Reading Room. The two entities became legally separate in 1973 and by 1997 the British Library had moved into its new purpose-built building at St Pancras, London. Both *The Charter Fragment* and *Pascon agan Arluth* were moved there.

1.4.2 *Pascon agan Arluth*

The publishing and manuscript history of *Pascon agan Arluth* is a good deal more complex than that of *The Charter Fragment*, not least from the fact that there are perhaps twelve extant manuscript versions. We have established that the Harley manuscript[66] (Stokes' "A" manuscript, the one used by Michael Everson in his palaeographic text in this edition) may well not be the original, but the remaining manuscripts are probably related to this one in some way. In the Bodleian Library one manuscript is found in the Richard Gough (1735–1809) collection which offers the Cornish text and

62 Murdoch 1979b; Murdoch 1993.
63 Edwards 1991; Edwards 1995.
64 Kent and Saunders 2000, pp. 30–31.
65 Kent 2000; Kent 2010.
66 British Library, Harley MS 1782. (MS "A").

English translation under the title *Mount Calvary; or the history of the passion, death, and resurrection, of our lord and saviour Jesus Christ. Written in Cornish (as it may be conjectured) some centuries past. Interpreted in the English tongue, in the year 1682, by John Keigwin, Gent.*[67] Stokes labels this as manuscript "C" in his work; this manuscript would seem to be the text on which Davies Gilbert based his edition. Also in the Gough collection is another manuscript which contains an untitled Cornish text, along with Keigwin's translation and introduction, but not in his hand.[68] Curiously, on folio 57 is the statement, "Protestation of the Bishops of Briten to Augustine… in the year 600" as well as the first chapter of Genesis in Cornish. Both of these are noted in Gilbert's edition of the text.[69] Stokes viewed this as source "B", and it was probably used by both Stokes and Gilbert for comparison.

A fourth manuscript is to be found in Lambeth Palace Library, London.[70] Presumably this was the version that Stokes referred to in 1861/2 as being "lately in the possession of Mr. Hotton of Piccadilly". Designated by him as manuscript "D", it was also known by Jenner who knew of the manuscript being in private hands. E. G. Retallack Hooper assumed that this was the version used by Keigwin and then published by Gilbert, an assumption which is far from certain. As noted above, it appears that Gilbert used manuscript "C". How "D" found its way to Lambeth Palace is at present unknown.

The British Library's collection of Gwavas' papers contains a fifth copy of the manuscript, together with a translation by William Hals.[71] In my view the presence of this copy among Gwavas' papers is indicative of a connection back to Sancreed.[72] This text is incomplete, however, finishing up at stanza 200, and so omitting the final 59 stanzas of the Harley original.[73] Another incomplete version is also found in the British Library,

67 Bodleian Library, Gough Cornwall 3 17853. (MS "C").

68 Bodleian Library, Gough Cornwall 4 17854. (MS "B").

69 Gilbert 1826.

70 Lambeth Palace Library, MS 806, ff. 40r–82v. (MS "D"). For more details, see Murdoch 1979b, p. 6.

71 British Library, Additional MS 28554, Nr 7, folios 51r–58v. We designate this fragment as MS "E".

72 At the beginning of the text Gwavas writes the following:

> Mount Calvary or the History of the Incarnation pafsion death and Refurrection of our Lord and Saviour Jefus christ written originally in Kernewish verse by an unknown Author before printing and found in Sacret church in this County translated into Englifh by W. H. 1679 and 1680 wherein the obliterations of that ancient manufcript and the errors of the fcribe are in the following Difcourfe alfo amended and corrected by W. H.

in a manuscript comprised of papers relating to the Welsh scholar Lewis Morris (1700–1765).[74] This manuscript contains only stanzas 65–80, in Cornish with an English translation.[75] Related to MS "E" and "F" is "G". a set of letters of Lewis Morris containing the another transcript of stanzas 65–80 found in his letters to Evan Evans (1731–1739). These are to be found in Aberystwyth.[76]

Three additional partial copies of *Pascon agan Arluth* are found in Truro. The first is in the Kresen Kernow Fortescue Collection. This is another manuscript from the Scawen collection, but is not in his hand.[77] The Fortescue manuscript (MS "H") is actually comprised of four individual manuscripts. These are in a different hand than that of Scawen and have

---

73 The differences between the Gwavas manuscript and the Harley manuscript are considerable, in ways which go well beyond copying errors. Compare the transcription of Gwavas' stanzas 1, 65, and 197 with the corresponding Harley stanzas below: 1, page 160; 65, page 202; 197, page 290.

> Tays, hag mab, hag Sperifsans why ⌜vyth⌝ abys a leun Golon
> rewronte the uge ras, ha whans the. Glewas an Bafcon
> Hag thymmo ras, ha [whan] skyans the therevas pare Lavarow
> May tho the Thu. the worthyans. ha Sylwans. the agan eneowe.
>
> Pan deus ve theth yn tyller may e chrift ve Befy
> Lowene thys vester yn meath Joudas an brathky
> thotho y fekyll chare hag y ame Trewefy
> ef a vynne ober gull kynys del dys wythy
>
> Re the [ch]grist levery aberth Grows pan ef effe ve
> Mar fos chrift mab a davy rag vy keth therl Grous heb pystege
> ha nye agris thy vestry hag fynfy le rag meste2 neffre
> me on Mab du yredy chrift aleveris thethe.

74 British Library, Additional MS 14934, folios 167v–170r. We designate this fragment as MS "F".

75 The differences between the Morris and the Harley manuscripts are also quite considerable. Compare the transcription of Morris' stanza 65 with the Gwavas transcription in note 73 above, and with corresponding Harley stanza on page 202 below.

> Pan dothyans bys yn tyller a thefe Chrest ow Pefy
> lowene thys a vester yn meth Judas an brathky
> thotho y rug fe kyl cher hag y ame trewefy
> ef a vynne an ober gul ken ys del dysroythy.

76 National Library of Wales MS 2039D (Panton 74, 1), "Letters to 'Ieuan Fardd', etc.". We designate this fragment as MS "G".

77 Kresen Kernow Fortescue Collection, MS F/2/39. We designate this fragment as MS "H". This is called informally "the Scawen manuscript" by the staff of Kresen Kernow.

been looked over and annotated by William Borlase. Much of the manuscript is composed of long album-style sheets of different sizes. The handwriting would suggest that they are all from the late seventeenth century. The third part of this manuscript contains 228 stanzas of *Pascon Agan Arluth*, which are translated by the copyist into both a literal translation into English, followed by a poetic translation. It would appear that the copyist had plans to complete the poem (for there is designated space) and finish the remaining stanzas, but ultimately this was not completed (stanzas 229–259 are missing). The Cornish of the poem appears to be rendered into the Cornish of this period, and ignores the conventions of the earlier Medieval version (now held in the British Library) used in this edition.

In the Royal Institution of Cornwall's Courtney Library, a manuscript called "Notes connected with the observations of William Scawen" contains part of the poem in Cornish and in English.[78] This manuscript, "J", is connected to MS "H", as it would appear at points to have the same copyist, though it is again not Scawen himself. In 1975, Oliver Padel commented that *Pascon agan Arluth* is contained in both of these manuscripts,[79] but the extant poem is really only found in the Fortescue manuscript (MS "H') that contains the 228 stanzas with translations. The Royal Institution of Cornwall manuscript appears to have a few quotations from the Fortescue manuscript to illustrate particular points, but nothing more than this. Sometimes these are marginal notes or insertions. Observers such as Padel who believe that MS "J" contains a lengthy copy and English translation of *Pascon agan Arluth* are mistaken. Small sections of the poem are only used as illustrative examples of "ancient" Cornish. In sixteen key points, Scawen explains the retreat of Cornish and its replacement by English. He also notes what needs to be done in order to save Cornish from extinction, including the wider circulation of Cornish literary texts, such as *Pascon agan Arluth*.

Also at the Courtney Library, within a collection of Nance's papers, are to be found the manuscripts of Nance and Smith's work on the poem.[80] They clearly had access to the Harley manuscript. Perhaps surprisingly, the Gatley Papers at the Courtney Library (a transcript of the Gwavas Papers by John Gatley (1845–1936)) do not contain anything from the poem. Expanded versions of these manuscript details are offered by Brian Murdoch and by Andrew Hawke.[81] In 1982, Hawke said that he also

78 Courtney Library, Royal Institution of Cornwall, Truro. We designate this fragment as MS "J". It appears to be in the same hand as MS "H".

79 Padel 1975, pp. 5–6.

80 Nance papers, in the Courtney Library, Royal Institution of Cornwall, Truro. We designate this fragment as MS "K".

believed that an additional manuscript of *Pascon agan Arluth* might also be found in lost Borlase or Tonkin manuscripts.[82]

We have already noted the importance of Gilbert's edition, and Stokes' edition of *Pascon agan Arluth*, not to mention the publication of the text by Nance and Smith of the text in *Kernow* between 1934 and 1936. The text was not to be published again until the post-war period. This was in the magazine *An Lef Kernewek*, edited by E. G. R. Hooper, which published the text in Cornish in 29 parts between the years 1963 and 1968. In 1971 Hooper was to offer a final version of the text, mainly based on the earlier work of Nance and Smith. This was published in Unified Cornish under the title *Passyon agan Arluth: Cornish Poem of the Passion*.[83]

In the late twentieth century the poem received little critical attention overall from Medievalists or Celticists. Some exceptions were David C. Fowler, who used it to examine the dating of the *Ordinalia*. Publishing in *Medieval Studies*, the unconventional Fowler took a controversial line by arguing that in fact, the *Ordinalia* predated *Pascon agan Arluth*, basing his case on just six sequences.[84] Few readers have agreed with this, most taking the view that the evidence presented is not substantial enough to make the case. As he did for *The Charter Fragment*, Peter Berresford Ellis extolled the virtues of *Pascon agan Arluth* in his *The Cornish Language and its Literature*, but remains surprisingly brief on the content of the poem.[85] It was really left to Murdoch, and later to Herriman, to interpret this text in more detail. Murdoch read a paper titled "The Literary Position of the Cornish Passion-Poem: A Comparative Approach" at the Seventh International Congress of Celtic Studies held in Galway in 1979,[86] and this kind of interpretation of the text was later refined by the researches of Herriman in his 1984 M.A. dissertation, *Pascon agan Arluth: A Critical Study of the Cornish Passion Poem*. Here, Herriman offered an in-depth study of the work that had been lacking in Ellis, coupled with the first analysis of the illustrations and their relationship to the text.[87] Both works were milestones in the critical appreciation of the poem.

81 Murdoch 1979b; Hawke 1982, pp. 23–28.
82 Hawke 1982, pp. 26–27.
83 See Hooper 1972.
84 Fowler 1961, pp. 91–125. Fowler's position on the *Ordinalia* can also be seen in Fowler 1995, p. 241–247.
85 Ellis 1974, pp. 43–45.
86 Murdoch 1979a. This has become the basis of Murdoch's approach to his later work on *Pascon agan Arluth*. See Murdoch 1993.
87 Herriman 1984.

Towards the end of the twentieth century, new figures were beginning to reconsider the text again. The Breton scholar Goulven Pennaod published a version in 1980 with a preface in Breton.[88] He had drawn his work from the translation of Stokes which he had found in the Bibliothèque Nationale in Paris. This version gradually filtered its way towards a new generation of Celtic scholars; among them, Ray Edwards, who in co-ordinating his *Kernewek dre Lyther* programme of correspondence course Cornish lessons, set about producing a new edition of *Pascon agan Arluth* which emerged in 1993.[89] Although useful in many ways (particularly in exploring how Smith and Nance had used *Pascon agan Arluth* in their structuring of the textbook *Cornish Simplified*), the edition did not have high production values, though its low price did make the text available to a new generation of learners, speakers, and readers.

Kent's explorations of *Pascon agan Arluth* kept it on the cultural agenda; he treats it as a key text in Cornwall's literary history, linking it not only to texts in the past but also showing it to be an indicator of what was to follow. Kent argued that *Pascon agan Arluth* was a core text in terms of literary "continuity" within Cornwall, and that it offered insights into a lost world of Cornish poetics, which had, because of other literary and theatrical criticism, come to be dominated by studies of the verse dramas alone.[90] The anthologization of the poem in *Looking at the Mermaid* again took the work to a wider readership beyond those solely concerned with the Cornish Revival and the learning of the language.[91]

In 2002, Harry Woodhouse published a useful greyscale facsimile of the text (with Cornish and an English translation), funded by Gorseth Kernow.[92] It has been Edwards' and Woodhouse's editions which have sustained interest in the text over the last quarter of a century. It may be worth observing that the Cornish Language Partnership (commonly known as *Maga*) have consistently promoted and developed workshops and educational opportunities on the verse dramas developed in the same period.[93] They have been remarkably quiet on using and developing responses to *Pascon agan Arluth*, although perhaps this may be because of the intensity of its Christian message. In 2017, Graham Sandercock published a brief review of the history of scholarship on the poem, with a short comparison of the poem with other Passion literature.[94]

88 Pennaod 1978.

89 Edwards 1993.

90 Kent 2000, p. 42.

91 Kent and Saunders 2000, pp. 102–117.

92 Woodhouse 2002.

93 See Stewart 2012.

1.5 THE TEXT AND ITS INTERPRETATION

1.5.1 *The Charter Fragment*

There are various interpretations of *The Charter Fragment*, some of which will be addressed here. First of all, let us clarify the structure of the text. The piece, although commonly divided by most observers into two sections, it seems rather to have three distinct units of dialogue. In lines 1–24 the anonymous speaker addresses a young man. At this point in the text, the girl is offered as being suitable as a wife and she is being complimented. The speech here begins urgently with the young man being asked to listen, and the speaker desiring him to stand close. This could be so that the lines do not have to be shouted, but rather said in confidence. In lines 25–26, the speaker now addresses the young man and the girl, as we can see from the plural verbs. We assume that the girl has been standing close by. The speaker has already said that no one is her equal this side of the River Tamar, which not only asserts her value and good heart, but also offers a territorial definition of Cornwall. The notion that she is still a "*flogh*" 'child' may be nothing more serious than a view of her inexperience or virginity, though nowadays we are bound to read it somewhat warily. Could this be part of a marriage arranged when the girl was still quite young? It is hard to say. There is also an imperative of speedy union, which may imply that the speaker (evidently a friend of both) is aware that their union may not be approved of by others. The third and final section of the text (lines 27–41) indicates another change in who is being addressed. The speaker seems to turn to the girl now, and although she is expected to follow her husband's commands, she should also realize that he is courteous and gentle. This suggests that the line 9 "*â, tanha hy*" is not suggestive of ill intent.

Of the three people in the text, it is the speaker who is of most interest to us. Little is revealed of the speaker's background or place in society, though he (perhaps more likely than *she*) is presented as caring and kind. The speaker appears to know both the young man and the girl whom he addresses, and knows their particular circumstances and perhaps their reasons for a union. Certainly he seems a more experienced member of the society, and we are bound to think of him as possibly a priest or elder of the community.

The text's status as play, poem, or speech began as far back as Jenner's observations in his *Handbook of the Cornish Language*, where he was to comment that:

94 Sandercock 2017, pp. 5–9.

> The speaker (it may be a part in some play) offers a lady to some other person as a wife, praises her virtues, and then gives the lady some rather amusing advice as to her behaviour to her future husband, and how to acquire the position attributed in Cornish folklore to the influence of the well of St Keyne and St Michael's Chair.[95]

Jenner's reference to the well of St Keyne reminds us of the famous story attached to it which is partially relayed in Richard Carew's *Survey of Cornwall* (1602), in which a man and a woman marry and take advantage of the water in the well of St Keyne to acquire dominance in the marriage.[96] One core story pervades: the well offered mastery over one's marriage partner if one were to drink from it immediately after the ceremony. The groom therefore swiftly made his way to the well and imbibed of its waters thinking he would surely have mastery over his wife. However, the bride had already secured a bottle of the water from the well which she drank soon after the ceremony without having to trek to the well, thus assuring her mastery over her husband.

The legend of St Michael's Chair is a more obscure piece of folklore but is embodied in the poem *St Michael's Chair* by Robert Southey (1774–1843).[97] Southey recounts the story from St Michael's Mount, where the wife, here named Rebecca, tries to gain mastery over her husband Richard Penlake by sitting in the chair, but dies in the process. Jenner, of course, was not merely a linguist, but also a folklorist,[98] so this link to *The Charter Fragment* was perhaps too difficult to resist. Perhaps there may be some residual truth in a folkloric obsession with control in a marriage, though the link is still somewhat tenuous.

Interpretation of the text as part of a lost play continued to be considered. In 1915–1916, Jenner made the same assertion again, pointing out his interpretation of the secular nature of the text:

> If it is part of a play, it seems, unlike the rest of the Cornish dramatic literature, to be part of a non-religious one. Such a drama is unusual, not only in Cornish but in medieval literature generally.[99]

---

95 Jenner 2010 [1904], p. 25.

96 Halliday 1953, p. 203.

97 See Southey 1879, pp. 20–21.

98 See Jenner's contribution to Evans-Wentz 2010 [1911].

99 Jenner 1921.

Toorians takes a different line and describes this as "wishful thinking" on Jenner's behalf. He sees the same problem with Nance's interpretation that the text is "obviously the copied out part of one performer in some lost Cornish play"[100] Nance does make an important point here, however. In early dramatic performance across Britain, scripts were rarely compiled as a whole. Instead, performers learnt their parts only—sometimes without knowledge of what the rest of the text would be composed of. The play would then be assembled by the performers in chronological order.

This seems all well and good, but there is a problem with this interpretation. Most medieval actors learnt their parts orally and in most cases would have been illiterate. Supposing that this is the case, then it is more likely that the text comprises the words of the *ordinale* (the prompter) who would whisper them to the actor before they were declaimed.[101] We know this is part of the tradition in Cornwall because the more theatrically-modern Carew gives a sceptical account of it in his *Survey*.[102] But Toorians dismisses the theory that the piece is part of a larger, lost dramatic text.[103]

Toorians' assertions that *The Charter Fragment* should be reconsidered arise from several factors. The first is that Cornish literature does not necessarily have to be verse drama alone (this being a preconception of both Nance and Jenner). In 1991 when his work was published, this argument may have been tentative, but by 2000, upon the discovery of *Bewnans Ke* ['*The Life of St Kea*'], it became clear that other literary forms had constituted part of the Cornish literary tradition. There, the character of King Arthur mentions the fact that his guests would be entertained with rhyming triplets (Cornish *eglynnyon*).[104] To insist that *The Charter Fragment* must have to have been part of a larger dramatic text might be unwarranted. Toorians' central argument however, was that the text needed to be reinterpreted as "an independent entity" and that it was "perfectly understandable as it stands".[105] In that case, the poem could stand alone as a piece of native secular poetry about match-making and how to maintain a healthy marriage.

Still, Toorians was keen to assert the possibility of *The Charter Fragment* having dramatic potential, but merely warned that the play-text theory should not be taken to be definitive. Developing this strand of thought, Toorians offers one other suggestion in support of the poem working

100 Toorians 1991, pp. 13–14.

101 For contexts of performance, see Kent 2000, pp. 149–328.

102 See Halliday 1953, p. 145.

103 Toorians 1991.

104 Thomas and Williams 2007, pp. 206–207.

105 Toorians 1991.

independently, making a comparison with Breton and Welsh secular poetry, which, like *The Charter Fragment*, have a high use of internal rhyme. Toorians does not provide any comparative examples, though the argument may have some merit. Toorians also makes the assertion that a comparison to *Pascon agan Arluth* can be made: "in general it can be described as having end rhyme and a fixed number of syllables in each line (often seven). For *Pascon agan Arluth*, which is closest in time to the endorsement, this is the rule without exception".[106]

The case for interpreting the text as part of a play has been considered in detail in Kent (2010), and I remain open-minded; particularly in the light of other emergent contextual material such as *Bewnans Ke*, and my earlier observations on the intensity (meaning Cornwall's dense and extensive theatrical culture of this period) and non-religious dramas that may have been presented in early Cornwall.[107] Nicholas Williams (for whose linguistic notes on *The Charter Fragment*, see p. 41 below) is a committed exponent of the view that the fragment is a portion of an otherwise lost text. He observed that "I don't believe for an instant that this fragment is anything other than a portion of a missing play. An older man is cynically suggesting to a young couple how they should behave when married. I take it that the young man doesn't actually want to marry, and does not. Rather, like Meriasek, he goes on to be a celibate saint, the hero of the lost play."[108] This supports Campanile's general reading—that the married state was inferior to celibacy, and that a sacred play might therefore encourage young people not to marry and to enter religious orders.[109] Such a view is an appealing one, since it refines the original view of the text as a drama, and positions it within a dramatic context. This then relocates the play as actually being religious rather than secular. That the text is a portion of a play is, of course, supported by the knowledge of a *plen-an-gwary* within the parish.

Murdoch, writing on the text in 1993, notes that "The first twenty-six lines appear to be a speech in which someone is offering in marriage to a friend or companion (*coweth*) a girl who is praised highly and commended as a good housewife. She is, however, also described as a child, and the

106 Toorians 1991. In fact, the metre of *The Charter Fragment* is not so regular and a comparison with *Pascon agan Arluth* does not indicate a similarity. The metre of *Pascon agan Arluth* in manuscript "A" is nearly, but not entirely, perfect in its seven syllables per line, though the normalized text given in this volume has corrected this minor defect.

107 Kent 2010, pp. 162–163.

108 Personal communication, March 2014.

109 Campanile 1963.

speaker assures the friend that she will do his bidding."[110] He believes that the second half of the text is more difficult. Here, he argues that "the lines are from a different speaker, and a woman is being told how to control a man… However, the woman is also assured that the man is of such gentility that he will not force her."[111] He cannot however, offer a convincing interpretation one way or the other because the contextual evidence is so scant. Play, poem, or speech? It is, at present, impossible to tell, though the first of these seems most likely.

1.5.2 *Pascon agan Arluth*

Pascon agan Arluth is a major piece of writing in Cornish, though in the past criticism about its achievement was somewhat dismissive. Indeed this can be said about many approaches made to the whole corpus of writing in Cornish. The general criticism of literature in Cornish was that there was not enough of it, and that what there was, although "Celtic" in terms of vocabulary and form, was not necessarily "Celtic" in terms of subject matter or theme. Early criticism was also intolerant and dismissive towards the dramatic base of writing in Cornish, based on an implicit assumption that epic poetry or narrative were more impressive literary forms. This attitude, as I have argued elsewhere,[112] needs to be revised radically. If we are viewing the texts in terms of consumption, then we must recognize that the dramatic medium is the one most likely to have reached a larger number of contemporary consumers of the text than, say, poetry or narrative could have. Thus Cornish literature, in general, has had a much wider base of consumption than found in other territories. *Pascon agan Arluth*, as a text, may stand somewhere between the two poles of verse drama and the more confined readership of verse alone. A poem like it may well have been presented to audiences at public readings, to which an audience would listen. The storytelling style of the speaker and his use of the narrative would very much suit this style of delivery.[113] It may be that the poem had a place during the church's year when it was deemed appropriate to "perform". Alternatively, might it even be possible that *Pascon agan Arluth* operated as a developmental text in an eventually more fully operational dramatic culture in Cornwall. Perhaps still images of some of the scenes might have been performed as a form of tableaux while the

110 Murdoch 1993, p. 11. As noted on p. 17 above, we believe the plural verbs in lines 25–26 suggest a change of stage direction (or focus).

111 Murdoch 1993, pp. 11–12.

112 Kent 2000.

113 For some contextual comparisons to Wales and Ireland, see Pryce 1998.

reading took place. The text's illustrations would then have operated as a guide to what the images should look like.

One of the chief difficulties of interpreting *Pascon agan Arluth* is the tension between elements of the gospel narrative the poet uses and those additional elements from outside that narrative which he incorporates into his work. A more thorough examination of the narrative will be helpful to explore this here. Adam and Eve's inclusion at the start of the poem (stanzas 6–7) are important for contextual purposes. Christ in the poem, as in the *Ordinalia*, is presented as the "second Adam". The narrative begins with the Fall of Man (stanzas 6–8), and in consequence God's intention to reverse the Fall with his plan of salvation—which is at the heart of the text. Throughout the poem, Christ offers himself as the Redeemer. His temptation by the Devil is given rather cursory treatment (stanza 22), and we are soon following his triumphant entry into Jerusalem on Palm Sunday (stanzas 28–31). We note that his three years of ministry are compressed in the narrative here, being described in only four stanzas (23–26). Considering the importance of these events in Christ's ministry, this seems a curious omission, though it is probable that the poet wished to press on with the essential matter of the crucifixion. We are, however, shown a scene in which the Jews become angry with him (stanzas 91–93, 107–109), and considerable time is given over to Judas' betrayal of Jesus (stanza 104–106).

The rest of the text moves through more standard descriptions of the Last Supper (stanzas 42–59), Christ's trial (stanzas 92–101), crucifixion (stanzas 178–185), and resurrection (stanzas 253–259), and there are extended scenes showing his scourging and crucifixion. As argued above, there is a macabre quality to these sequences, and they seem to have been included by the poet to emphasize the horror of the Passion. The detail here is remarkable—for example, the description of ropes to pull Christ's arms so they reach the holes in the cross, as well as the apocryphal figures of the blacksmith and his wife.

The legendary material added to the text often comes in the small details offered by the poet. These seem to have been more widely-known motifs at the time of the poem's composition, and we should perhaps not thank solely the poet for them, but also the culture of his time for their material inclusion in the work. There is not room in an introduction of this length to discuss all these, but some are worth brief mention here. In stanza 106, an allusion is made to the inability of Judas' soul to escape through his mouth after he had hanged himself. Stanza 162 contains material related to the Legend of the Rood, which tells that a seed planted into the mouth of Adam eventually becomes the cross on which Christ is crucified. The message here is that the cause of the Fall (the forbidden fruit) will eventually contribute to the redemption of mankind.[114]

Stanzas 154–160 give the tale of the Smith who refuses to make the nails and of his wife takes it upon herself to do it. This is an interesting sequence which is found in Northern English and French Passion plays, which suggests that the motif was known throughout Europe. The wife is an important and noteworthy character because she is effectively the only unsympathetic woman mentioned in the poem. Another female figure appears in stanza 177; she is unnamed but the narrative sequence matches what we know about Veronica, who wraps Jesus in a garment to cover him.[115]

In stanza 186, the poet does not name the two thieves crucified alongside Jesus; they are, of course, not named in either Mark or Matthew. Here *Pascon agan Arluth* differs from *Passio Christi*, which names the two thieves Dismas and Jesmas—names deriving from Dismas and Gestas found in the Gospel of Nicodemus.[116] Another motif here (stanzas 212–213) is the Harrowing of Hell, a theme widely used within the medieval period and found in the Gospel of Nicodemus.[117] The poet also chooses to incorporate the name of the soldier who pierced Jesus' side. He is not named in the canonical gospels but is named, again in the Gospel of Nicodemus, Longinus, which name appears in the poem as Longys in stanzas 217–218.

In stanza 225 there is a curious mention of Mary shedding three tears of blood, something neither found in the gospels nor, it seeems, in medieval folklore. The three Marys—well attested in medieval legend though not named in the gospels—are mentioned by the poet in stanza 230. Much of the resurrection material either enhances or develops the standard gospel narrative. The activity of the soldiers outside Christ's tomb in stanzas 241–251 permits listeners or readers to step back from the forward movement of the narrative for more reflection on the impact of the story on humanity.

114 This is part of the overall Legend of the Rood strand of the text. For more, see Halliday 1954.

115 In popular tradition, Veronica gives Jesus her veil to wipe his forehead as he was carrying his cross to Golgotha. After he held it to his face, its image was impressed upon it.

116 Gesmas was the name given in Jacobus de Varagine's popular (even by medieval standards) *Golden Legend*, compiled c. 1260.

117 Audiences and readers were fully aware of the concept of the Harrowing of Hell in medieval Cornwall. In Lanivet church is a small wall painting detailing this moment. It is known locally as "The Whale". In fact, it is a Hell-mouth depicting the Harrowing of Hell. The clause *descendit ad inveros* 'he descended into hell' occurs in both the Apostles' Creed and the Athanasian Creed.

Again, toward the end of the poem, in stanza 252, the three Marys return to visit the tomb.

Now that we have examined some of the non-gospel narrative sources included in the poem, it may well be useful here to take a look at a full overview of the text and its interpretation. As the poem opens, the poet's voice is distinctive; he addresses the audience directly. He tells of his reasons for writing the poem, and makes a comparison between Christ and a hunted deer. This is a striking image which forms the pretext for the work: the reader is encouraged to think of Christ as continually being pursued by a pack of hounds—images which are visualized later on in the narrative when Christ is scourged and crucified:

2 Seul a vynno bos selwys
golsowens ow lavarow
a Jesu dell veu helhys
wàr an bÿs avell carow;
ragon menowgh rebukys
ha dysprêsys yn harow,
i'n grows gans kentrow fastys,
painys bys pàn veu marow.

2 Whoever wishes to be saved,
let him listen to my words,
of Jesus how he was hunted
on the earth like a stag;
often reproached for us
and cruelly disparaged,
fixed upon the cross with nails,
tormented until he died.

As the opening section of the poem develops, the poet steps back somewhat, and allows the narrative to proceed more naturally. There is no nativity—a feature echoed in the extant *Ordinalia*.[118] The poem begins midway through the life of Christ. A central idea is that unlike Adam, Christ is able to resist temptation; which is why the illustration of Adam and Eve is given here (folio 1v) in the manuscript. The poem then moves to Christ's coming of age and experiences in the wilderness, being tempted by the Devil. The poet ably presents the drama of the Devil's persuasive

118 There is some textual evidence in the *Ordinalia* that a "childhood" play may have once existed. See notes in Kent 2006, pp. 3–4.

tone, while the illustration on folio 2r shows Christ's divinity through his gesture. Christ is offered gold, silver, grass, and trees—all temptations offsetting the hardships he experiences in the desert—but Christ resists and commands the Devil to be gone (stanzas 10–11). As an opening sequence for the narrative, this is highly effective, placing Christ strongly in the minds of the audience. Next follows a short sequence about Christ's ministries; these are not developed in much detail at all. Presumably they were taken as read, and did not require expansion. At the same time, however, the jealousy of the Jews is noted. Although we see commonplace medieval antisemitism, we learn that "*rag henna an vuscogyon orto a borthas avy*" 'in consequence the mad ones bore resentment towards him' (lines 205–206), which might suggest that it is not all Jews, but rather only some of them, who were resentful.

Four stanzas then follow which are devoted to Palm Sunday—a key moment in Christ's life (stanzas 27–30). The wickedness and anger of others is emphasized. There is a diversion at this point—the story of a woman who has committed adultery, serving to highlight Christ's compassion—before a major sequence devoted to Judas and the ointment. The drama continues with Christ's betrayal and leads into what is effectively Maundy Thursday.

The poem becomes easier to interpret now, with the poet following the key events of the Passion. These include the Last Supper, the washing of the feet, Judas and Christ, and Christ speaking to the disciples. Christ's arrest follows, along with the confusion over the severing of Malchus' ear by Simon Peter (stanzas 70–72).[119] The gospel narrative continues as Christ is tried before Annas and Caiaphas, linking poetically to Peter's denial. The dovetailing effect then leads to Christ being presented before Pilate. The drama is interrupted by the news that Judas has hanged himself, with the image of his soul being unable to leave his body through the mouth that had kissed Christ. This is the emotional climax to this part of the poem. The poet presents a macabre sense of resignation and despair.

The deer-hunting theme established at the start of the poem is continued further in the next sequence, when Christ is sent first before Herod and then returned to Pilate. The abuse of Christ begins here; the poet subtly includes the remarks of Pilate, who admires Christ's resilience and faith. A short sequence follows devoted to Pilate's wife though this is much more developed in the *Ordinalia* as it is in other dramas of the medieval period.[120] Pilate continues to plead for Christ's innocence but the poet is already

119 Malchus is not named in the text, and Simon Peter is called Peter.
120 See Murdoch 1993, p. 30.

building a picture of the inevitability of the Redeemer's ultimate death. Some time is then given to Christ's plea about his divinity (stanzas 111–114). In the description of the torture of Christ, he poet makes much of the way the thorns pierce Christ's brain, and it is such detail which adds to the shocking realism of the piece.

Pilate sees Christ for the last time. He washes his hands, symbolically making the Jews responsible for the death of Christ. Much poetic energy (stanzas 154–173) describes the crucifixion itself which includes a number of additional motifs (some of which have been mentioned above). The most striking of these is the refusal of the Smith to make the nails, this task being undertaken by his wife in his stead. There is also the grim detail of stretching Christ on the cross and jolting him into position. Here, the poet succeeds in creating the horror of the crucifixion even to the smallest details (stanzas 167–182). Some attention is given to the story of Veronica though this is not greatly expanded. Her presence helps reinforce the sorrow of the situation being shown so graphically in the poet's so graphic depiction. The events of the crucifixion are described with the usual imagery of earthquakes and thunder which create another climax to the narrative.

After the crucifixion, events are dealt with more speedily by the poet (at least in comparison to the way in which they are treated in the later *Resurrexio Domini*). These events include the Harrowing of Hell and Joseph of Arimathea's taking of Christ's body to be laid in the sepulchre. We also learn of the healing of the blind Roman soldier Longinus and of the sorrows of the Virgin Mary. The poet then follows the narrative of the gospels more closely, depicting the grief of the three Marys (stanzas 164–172), followed by the shock of the soldiers who report to Pilate that Christ has risen; Pilate's response to them is to advise them to say that robbers stole the body. The poet concludes with the narration of Christ's resurrection and appearance in Galilee. As in the opening of the poem, the writer's own voice enters with a poetically masterful evocation of the achievement of Christ and a celebration of the Passion:

259 Dell sevys Mab Duw a'y vedh
i'n eur-na dhe'n tressa dëdh,
indella oll ny a sev
dëdh breus, drog ha dâ inwedh.
Obereth dremas a dëv;
i'n eur-na rych ev a vëdh;
drog-dhen i'n jÿdh-na goev!
Dhe Grist y fÿdh a'n barth cledh.

259 As the Son of God rose from the tomb
at that time on the third day,
so we all shall rise
on the day of judgement, evil and good also.
The works of a good man will grow;
at that hour he will be rich;
woe betide the wicked man on that day!
He will be on the left side of Christ.

In the poem, a number of levels of interpretation may be distinguished. First of all, we see the poet neatly interweaving both gospel and apocryphal material with the principal aim of showing the humanity of Christ, and the fact that he is sinless and effectively a "Second Adam". The poem also has a homiletic tone and is intended to convert unbelievers.[121] It is written in a Brythonic Celtic language but it has a pan-European theme—and is part of a wider medieval framework of literary activity. The strand of the Holy Rood lurks in the background of the poem—it is perhaps not as explicitly present as in the *Ordinalia*, but the poet is clearly aware of the connection—especially with the Adamic material. Throughout, the poet makes many interesting observations on the nature of wickedness and how the audience ought to follow a righteous path. The most extreme example is, of course, Judas, whose unhappy end is ably demonstrated. It is not the task of this introduction to discuss all of the comparable texts (including *The Southern Passion*) which have similar sequences to *Pascon agan Arluth*, although should the reader be interested, these are discussed in detail elsewhere.[122]

1.6 THE POETRY

1.6.1 *The Charter Fragment*

The earliest researchers looking at *The Charter Fragment* argued about its proper translation, but all were in agreement that it had a poetic dimension. The nature of that poetry and its implications for our understanding of the text has not led to a uniform consensus, however. Campanile gives a syllable count and an analysis of the rhyme scheme,[123] but because of its irregularity he suggests that a more standard beat and rhythm might have existed in an earlier variant of the text.

Murdoch attempts to compare the poetry of *The Charter Fragment* with other Cornish poetry, stating that "the fragment may be divided into

121 Seemingly a noticeable strand within Cornish-language literature, and reaching maturity within the work of John Tregear.

122 See Murdoch 1993.

123 Campanile 1963.

strophic units which are not unlike (though not exactly parallel to) those found in the major works of medieval Cornish".[124] Murdoch interprets the verse structure in the following way: "An initial strophe (based on sense division) has 12 lines varying between four and six syllables, rhyming *aabbbbccdccd*."[125] This does not seem to be correct; in *bbbb* for instance the first and last *b*'s rhyme in /ˈɔwɔs/ and the middle two *b*'s rhyme in /eːz/—and attempts to "redeem" inconsistencies in the text are unnecessary.

Toorians divides the text into five stanzas,[126] but does not explain how his divisions make sense; nor does he discuss the rhymes or the metre in the same way for each verse, and the argument is hard to follow. The section on metre ends wondering whether "our poet was perhaps a survivor of a Cornish bardic order, which [had] already fallen apart in the fourteenth century?"[127] This is wishful thinking; *The Charter Fragment* isn't a work of Cornish genius. And there's nothing wrong with that.

While working on the palaeographic transcription of the poem, Michael Everson drew up the following simple description:

Stanza 1 consists of lines 1–12, has the rhyme scheme *aabccbddedde*, and the metre is 5-4-6 5-5-6 5-5-4 5-5-5.

Stanza 2 consists of lines 13–16, has the rhyme scheme *abab*, and the metre is 6-5 6-5.

Stanza 3 consists of lines 17–26, has the rhyme scheme *aabbccddee* and the metre is 7-7 4-7 7-7 7-8 7-8.

Stanza 4 consists of lines 27–30, has the rhyme scheme *abcb*, and the metre is 8-4 7-4.

Stanza 5 consists of lines 31–36, has the rhyme scheme *aabbcc*, and the metre is 7-8 8-9 9-9.

Stanza 6 consists of lines 37–41, has the rhyme scheme *abcbc*, and the metre is 8 7-5 7-8.

All three of the editors of this book believe that what the structure does and does not do here tells a good deal about the nature of the fragment. The poet was writing drama, which is why there are rhymes. Audiences expected their drama to rhyme. That the metre is erratic indicates that metrical perfection was not the dramatist's primary interest. Reading the text aloud, as rhyming conversational dialogue, was sufficient. Metrical uniformity is not achieved in this piece—perhaps written in haste on the

124 Murdoch 1993, p. 12.

125 Murdoch 1993.

126 Toorians 1991, pp. 15–16.

127 Toorians 1991, pp. 16.

back of an available charter to give lines to a specific actor—because metrical uniformity was not the author's goal.

It has been suggested that the dialogue in *The Charter Fragment* is secular in nature and deals with the making of a marriage in medieval Cornwall. This is highly unlikely, since what we have of Middle Cornish drama is never secular but rather exclusively religious in content. It is much more likely that the fragment is an early portion of a saint's life in dramatic form. The older man encourages the younger one to take the young and amenable girl as wife, while at the same time advising the prospective bride to ensure that she herself be the dominant partner in the marriage. The young man is most probably the saint whose life forms the subject of the play. In the section following the fragment it is likely that the young man refuses to be betrothed to the girl on the grounds that he is determined not to marry at all. He intends rather to remain celibate and to receive holy orders. There is a very obvious parallel for such a narrative. In the complete play *Beunans Meriasek*, the King of Armorica comes with his nobles to the house of Meriasek's father, a Breton duke, in the hope of concluding a marriage between Meriasek and a royal princess. Meriasek however is resolutely opposed to such an idea, saying that he wishes to remain unmarried, to be ordained priest and thus to devote himself entirely to God. We have no way of knowing how the lost play develops after the dialogue in the fragment. It is highly likely, however, that it contains a repudiation of marriage by the young man and the consequent consternation of his advisors, exactly as is the case in *Beunans Meriasek*.

1.6.2 *Pascon agan Arluth*

In considering the poetry of *Pascon agan Arluth* we need to look again at the Harley manuscript. Here, the lines are laid out in stanzas of four lines, but each line contains two lines of verse. This layout, of course, saves space in the manuscript. It was followed long ago in Gilbert's edition,[128] as well as more recently in Woodhouse's facsimile.[129] Most published versions have presented the poem in eight-line stanzas composed of seven syllables.[130] Eight-line stanzas have also been used in this edition, since this better shows

128 Gilbert 1826.

129 Woodhouse 2002.

130 The manuscript text of the poem occasionally has fewer than seven syllables or more than seven syllables in a line, but we consider this to reflect copying errors, since the metre is otherwise so consistent. See the translator's note on p. 41 below. In addition, stanza 208 has ten lines, not eight.

the rhyme scheme. The four-line format is presented in Michael Everson's palaeographic readings.

A further point should be noted about the poetic quality of *Pascon agan Arluth*. Although the poem follows a strict metre throughout, and in so doing, covers a large amount of narrative, it has an adept efficiency in the way in which particular moments of Christ's story are delivered. This quite masterful and succinct style is found throughout but is perhaps most noticeable at the crucifixion itself and in the deft way that more minor figures (such as Simon the Leper or Veronica) are swiftly woven into the narrative (stanzas 174–177). Centurion Longinus is give four stanzas describing his use of the spear to pierce Christ's side (stanzas 217–220); it is interesting to note the dramatist who wrote *Passio Christi* developed the character further, giving him plenty of time on stage. The strictness of metre is only compromised at a few points in the poem; the most noticeable is the addition of an extra line at 1665 in the description of Christ's death. It may be that this was not accidental, but rather deliberate; the poet delaying and reiterating the moment when Christ gives up the ghost. His poetic achievement in this work is considerable.

1.7 THE CONTINUUM OF WRITING IN CORNISH

1.7.1 *The Charter Fragment*

With *The Charter Fragment* it is hard to see any direct connection to other surviving literary texts in Cornish. In trying to decipher *The Charter Fragment*, Murdoch wonders whether it is a fragment of a religious work, perhaps something like "the apocryphal betrothal scenes of Joseph with the Virgin that we find in the English N-Town plays", but even he admits this is "hard to fit".[131] Such a scene is not even part of the extant *Ordinalia*. Murdoch suggests that the only surviving scenes which bear any similarity to *The Charter Fragment* are those found in *Origo Mundi* when "a butler [is] offering to get a girl for one of his mates" (lines 2067–2072) and perhaps the "conversations between soldiers".[132] Apart from this, it can be hard to see any further connections to the surviving dramas. Perhaps something of *The Charter Fragment*'s pithy guidance is echoed in later works, such as the two poems of advice by James Jenkins of Alverton, Penzance, circa 1700, or even in Nicholas Boson's moralistic fable *John of Chyanhor* from around the same time.[133] These are thematic continuities across the centuries, perhaps indicating the inherited concerns of the Cornish as a group—or perhaps just expressions of the human condition.

131 Murdoch 1993, p. 12.

132 Murdoch 1993, p. 12.

133 Kent and Saunders 2000, pp. 230–231 and pp. 312–319.

1.7.2 *Pascon agan Arluth*

When we come to compare *Pascon agan Arluth* with the *Ordinalia*, we find that several elements are pertinent for consideration. Both texts address the themes of Adam and the Rood, where the seed of the apple tree is planted in Adam's mouth, resulting in a tree whose wood is later used for Christ's cross. These twin themes run through both *Pascon agan Arluth* and also throughout *Origo Mundi*, *Passio Christi*, and *Resurrexio Domini*, connecting all of them along thematic, metaphorical, and structural lines. However, there is a third, deeper layer to this connection: close scrutiny of *Pascon agan Arluth* and *Passio Christi* show that it is clear that six stanzas of the poem are of the same metre as similar sequences in the play. There are also a further three stanzas which appear to have been adapted and reworked for the play, with some of the closest parallels are to be found in stanza 12. Some other issues are worth noting here. Like *Pascon agan Arluth*, *Passio Christi* has no nativity sequence, and both begin in the desert with Christ being tempted by the Devil.

There has, to a degree, always been some confusion among Celticists due the labelling of both *Pascon agan Arluth* and *Passio Christi* as "the *Passion*". It is my view that the poem was written before the play, and that the dramatist was familiar with it. David Fowler has argued[134] that the debt is the other way around, and that the play influenced the poem, but overall, the evidence would seem to point to the contrary. Given their similarities, there is a surprising dearth of detailed scholarly comparison of the two texts. In part, this is because critical work on *Pascon agan Arluth* is still in its infancy, though there have been more major studies of the *Ordinalia*, and on aspects of that trilogy.[135] Still however, comparative analysis is somewhat incomplete. The only initial early studies were completed by Phyllis Pier Harris (now held in the Courtney Library of the Royal Institution of Cornwall) who by way of work actually on *Origo Mundi* observed that "these and other discoverable distinctions may prove of some significance".[136] Murdoch argues against Fowler by asserting that "the relevant strophes in the play are padded by repetitions and gratuitous assertions, and, more significantly, one passage of objective exegetical explanation is placed by the dramatist into the mouth of Christ".[137] These additions are the most convincing evidence that the play was influenced by the poem. Murdoch continues his position by stating that

134 Fowler 1961.

135 Bakere 1980; Kent 2010; Longsworth 1967; Murdoch 1994; Higgins 2013.

136 Phyllis Pier Harris archive in Courtney Library, Royal Institution of Cornwall, Truro.

137 Murdoch 1994, p. 217.

> [a]lthough actual verbal correspondences are not numerous, the Passio Christi contains a good number of exegetical and additional apocryphal motifs found in the poem, including several that are not common elsewhere, so that if the influence is not direct, then a shared source is likely.[138]

As Jane A. Bakere notes, there are other examples in the European tradition where poems did influence plays.[139] These include the *Passion des Jongleurs* which is known to have influenced the Old French plays *Passion de Palatinus* and the *St Genevieve Passion*. In the English tradition, we also know that the *Northern Passion* influenced the play texts of the York and Townley Cycles. There is then, a general pattern of influence of poem into play, which may also have been the case in Cornwall.

When we see similarities between the play and the poem, this may well be down to wider apocryphal or gospel knowledge than to a specific link between the two texts. This is where it becomes difficult. Several key moments may show this. One is the narrative moment when Judas' soul is unable to leave his body through his mouth because his lips had kissed Christ (stanzas 103–106). The presentation of the Smith and his wife is also similar in both texts (stanzas 154–159). Another is the way in which Christ is stretched on the cross (stanzas 178–184). A further similarity of both texts is the way in which the Harrowing of Hell is presented (stanzas 212–215). Such material is generally apocryphal, but there is also much similarity in the way that the gospels are used. Bakere has given this thought, alongside numerous examples, but in the end, as she concludes, it is really a matter of degree of usage.[140] One text may omit a particular image, while the other may include it, and vice versa. An example of such similarity may be found in the opening of each text. *Pascon agan Arluth* has the following lines:

12 Dre worthyp Crist i'n eur-na
lemmyn ny a yll gweles
lavar Duw maga dell wra
neb a vynno y glêwes. 96

12 By Christ's answer at that time
now we can see
how the word of God nourishes
him who is prepared to hear it. 96

138 Murdoch 1994.
139 Bakere 1980, p. 104.
140 Bakere 1980, pp. 104–106.

These appear to be echoed in *Passio Christi*. Even if they are not linguistically identical, a similar argument is offered:

> Ow dyskyblyon, dre henna
> lemmyn why a yll gweles
> lavar Duw maga dell wra
> neb a yll y gemeres
>
> My disciples, by this
> now you can see
> how the word of God feeds
> him who can receive it.

As Bakere contends, one way of approaching these similarities is to imagine that the dramatist is using the poem as an inspiring starting point.[141] As the text of the drama proceeds, the influence is far less noticeable. Presumably therefore, the base material helped to structure the work, and then the respective poet and dramatist took the text in the direction he preferred. In this sense *Pascon agan Arluth* may have worked as a "guide track" for the development of the play. Alternatively, the play might be seen as a kind of stage adaptation of the poem. Another passage where such similarities may be discerned is when Peter is talking to Christ in both *Passio Christi* and in *Pascon agan Arluth*. The two sections are similar but they are not identical. It is reasonable to assert that such similarities may be derived from late-medieval preconceptions and source material, rather than from textual integration or intertextuality.

Attention has already been paid to suggestions for some of the poem's sources. It would certainly appear that the playwright or playwrights of the *Ordinalia* either a) had access to similar sources as the poet, b) had access to the poem itself, or c) had access to a combination of similar sources and the poem. The issue of the geography of this has been touched on above, and there will be on-going debate about where and when the transfer of such material took place. It may have been within individual institutions, parishes and churches, but also it may have happened at Glasney College at Penryn, which in many ways appears to have been a processing centre for much literary activity in Cornwall during this period.[142] Perhaps clerical students would have constructed poems or plays centred around either their own hagiographic legends (as in the case with *Beunans Meriasek* and

141 Bakere 1980, p. 104–106.

142 Whetter 1988, pp. 102–114.

Bewnans Ke),[143] or drawn on wider Biblical elements (as with *Pascon agan Arluth* and the *Ordinalia*). Such texts may well have been originally constructed at Glasney and then taken back to the parishes for performance there. As documented by a number of observers these performances were highly stylized and community oriented; the last traces of these were watched by observers such as Richard Carew.[144] Murdoch suggested that perhaps the individual reading of the poem might guarantee a certain period of pardon,[145] but given the low levels of literacy, it appears more likely perhaps that listening to such a work might have offered the same opportunity. Although it appears the poem probably influenced the play in some way, there is no other documentary material to support or shed light on the question. What is more certain is that both the poet and the playwright had an excellent grasp of their themes, and used the chosen genres with verve and sophistication.

1.8 CONCLUSIONS

1.8.1 *The Charter Fragment*

We may never know the truth behind the production and consumption of the text now known as *The Charter Fragment*. It has an elusive nature, but the compelling interest it gives to us as readers is unlikely to diminish over the coming years. It still stands, however, as the earliest complete text known within the canon of Cornish-language literature. It may be that as further discoveries of manuscripts occur (as was the case with *Bewnans Ke* in 2000), then these may help to shed more light on the cultural geography behind this text. The fact that it emerged from the mid-Cornwall parish of St Stephen-in-Brannel remains of interest, since during successive centuries that parish witnessed a flourishing of literary activity. As Andrew Symons noted perceptively in an article in 1999,[146] might this literary ignition be because of mid-Cornwall's unique position of being caught between two internal oral and literary cultures—that of residual Cornish and emergent English? This, he believed, had a long-term impact on literary production in that area of Cornwall.

1.8.2 *Pascon agan Arluth*

Pascon agan Arluth remains a substantial literary achievement, which Cornwall ought to celebrate more vigorously. The text is a masterful piece of poetry, comparable with other high-points in late medieval Celtic and

143 See Stokes 1872; Thomas and Williams 2007.

144 Halliday 1953.

145 Murdoch 1994, p. 40.

146 Symons 1999.

European literature.[147] Although some might be repelled by its macabre realism and vivid depiction of the Passion, its capacity to express humanity and sympathy for the "hunted" Christ show what could be achieved in Cornwall's literary past. Although Cornish literature has been dismissed by some Celticists and Medievalists alike, the picture is rapidly changing, and works like *Pascon agan Arluth* ably demonstrate how the wider world was imagined in the West of Britain.[148] If the poem's origins were truly in Sancreed, then put together with remaining material culture (in the form of stone crosses and in the remains of a "playing place" amphitheatre in the locale) the whole suggests a vibrant Celto-Christian landscape in which literary production was central. Murdoch noted in 1993 that the Harley manuscript of *The Northern Passion* promised 100 days indulgence for reading it.[149] He suggests that the purpose of *Pascon agan Arluth* might be the same.

A linguist who has specialized in writing systems and orthographies, Michael Everson here provides a first-class, typeset palaeographic version of the original Cornish manuscripts. He designed the special characters used in the palaeographic transcription (after having written proposals to encode them many years ago). Everson has skilfully reproduced the look of the text in its original form, a feature absent from previous editions. Together with this, the new translations of these two texts offered by Nicholas Williams capture much of the new confidence felt by scholars of Cornish about the importance of this literature and the language it was written in. Williams has worked fastidiously, looking afresh through the palaeographic transcriptions, correcting previous errors, and offering new suggestions as to how the texts ought to be read. We have therefore, for the first time, the core texts in their original spelling alongside a robust English translation together with the Cornish text sensibly and accurately rendered into Standard Cornish orthography. Everson and Williams are to be congratulated on their achievement here. As part of a series of volumes devoted to documenting and presenting before the general reader, the core texts of Cornish-language literature, this is a major step forward in asserting their global significance.

Alan M. Kent

147 See texts under discussion in Fulton 2005.

148 For a context of this change, see Kent 2012.

149 Murdoch 1994.

1.9 SOURCES AND EDITIONS

1.9.1 *The Charter Fragment*

British Library:

MS Add. Charter 19491.

Edwards 1993.

Jenner 1877.

Stokes 1880.

Toorians 1991.

Woodhouse 2002, pp. 102–103.

1.9.2 *Pascon agan Arluth*

British Library:

Harley MS 1782. (MS "A").

Additional MS 28554, Nr. 7, folios 51r–58v. (MS "E").

Additional MS 14934, folios 167v–170r. (MS "F").

Bodleian Library:

Gough Cornwall 3 17853. (MS "C").

Gough Cornwall 4 17854. (MS "B").

Lambeth Palace Library:

MS 806, ff. 40r–82v. (MS "D").

Cornwall County Records Office Fortescue Collection:

MS F/2/39. (MS "H").

Courtney Library, Royal Institution of Cornwall, Truro:

"Notes connected with the observations of William Scawen". (MS "J").

Nance Papers. (MS "K").

National Library of Wales:

MS 2039D (Panton 74, 1). (MS "G").

Edwards 1993.

Gilbert 1826.

Hooper 1972.

Woodhouse 2002.

1.10 BIBLIOGRAPHY AND REFERENCES

Bakere, Jane A. 1980. *The Cornish Ordinalia: A Critical Study*. Cardiff: University of Wales Press. ISBN 0-7083-0745-0.

Bice, Christopher. [1969]. *The Tregear Manuscript: Homelyes xiii in Cornysche*. [n.p.]: privately cyclostyled text. Reprint, *The Tregear Homilies*, Sutton Coldfield: Cornish Language Board, 1994. ISBN 0-907064-46-9. See also: http://wikisource.org/wiki/Homelyes_XIII_in_Cornysche, retrieved 2020-02-18.

Borlase, William. 1769. *Antiquities, Historical and Monumental, of the County of Cornwall, consisting of Several Essays on the First Inhabitants, Druid-superstition, Customs, and Remains of the most*

Remote Antiquity in Britain, and the British Isles, Exemplified and proved my Monuments now extant in Cornwall and the Scilly Islands, with a Vocabulary of the Cornu-British Language. London: W. Nower and J. Nichols.

Butler, Charles. 1634. *The English Grammar: or, The Institution of Letters, Syllables, and Words, in the English tongue: Whereunto is annexed An Index of Words Like and Unlike*. Oxford: William Turner. Reprinted in Eicher 1910.

Campanile, Enrico. 1963. "Un frammento scenico medio-cornico" in *Studi e saggi linguistici* 4, pp. 60–80.

Clemo, Jack. 1988. *Selected Poems*. Newcastle upon Tyne: Bloodaxe. ISBN 1-85224-052-0.

Curley, Michael J. (ed.). 1982. "A New Edition of John of Cornwall's *Prophetia Merlin*" in *Speculum* 57, pp. 217–219.

Deacon, Bernard. 2007. *Cornwall: A Concise History*. Cardiff: University of Wales Press. ISBN 978-0-7083-2032-7.

Derolez, Albert. 2003. *The Palaeography of Gothic Manuscript Books: From the Twelfth to the Early Sixteenth Century*. Cambridge: Cambridge University Press. ISBN 0-521-68690-3.

Edwards, Ray (ed. and tr.). 1991. *The Charter Fragment*. Sutton Coldfield: Kernewek dre Lyther.

—— (ed. and tr.). 1993. *Pascon agan Arluth*. Sutton Coldfield: Kernewek dre Lyther.

—— 1995. "The Charter Fragment: Play or Poem?" in *The Celtic Pen*, Vol. 3, № 1, pp. 17–20.

Eicher, A. 1910. *Charles Butler's English Grammar (1634)*. (Neudrucke frühneuenglischer Grammatiken; 4,1) Halle: Max Niemeyer.

Elliot-Binns, L. E. 1955. *Medieval Cornwall*. London: Methuen.

Ellis, Peter Berresford. 1974. *The Cornish Language and its Literature*. London and Boston: Routledge and Kegan Paul. ISBN 0-7100-7928-2

Evans-Wentz, Walter Yeeling. 1911. *The Fairy Faith in Celtic Countries*. Reprint, Glastonbury: The Lost Library, 2010. ISBN 978-1-906621-10-0.

Everett, David. 2011. "Henry Jenner and the British Museum" in Philip Payton (ed.). *Cornish Studies: Nineteen*, Exeter: University of Exeter Press, pp. 140–158. ISBN 978-0-85989-866-9.

Everson, Michael. 2017a. "Proposal to add LATIN LETTER ANGLICANA W to the UCS". https://web.archive.org/web/20190615142416/www.unicode.org/wg2/docs/n4838-anglicana-w.pdf, retrieved 2020-02-18.

—— 2017b "Proposal to add one punctuation character for medieval Cornish to the UCS". https://web.archive.org/web/20190615142717/www.unicode.org/wg2/docs/n4906-medieval-cornish-punct.pdf, retrieved 2020-02-18.

Fowler, David C. 1961. "The Date of the Cornish Ordinalia" in *Medieval Studies* 23, pp. 91–125.

—— 1995. *The Life and Times of John Trevisa, Medieval Scholar*. Seattle and London: University of Washington Press. ISBN 0-295-97427-3.

Frost, D. H. 2003. "Sacrament an Alter: A Tudor Cornish Patristic *Catena*" in Philip Payton (ed.), *Cornish Studies: Eleven*, Exeter: University of Exeter Press, pp. 291–307. ISBN 978-0-85989-747-1.

Fudge, Crysten. 1982. *The Life of Cornish*. Redruth: Dyllansow Truran. ISBN 0-907566-24-3.

Fulton, Helen (ed.). 2005. *Medieval Celtic Literature and Society*. Dublin: Four Courts Press. ISBN 1-85182-928-8.

Gilbert, Davies (ed.). 1826. *Mount Calvary; or the history of the passion, death, and resurrection, of our lord and saviour Jesus Christ. Written in Cornish (as it may be conjectured) some centuries past. Interpreted in the English tongue, in the year 1682, by John Keigwin, Gent.* London: Nichols.

Grimbert Joan Tasker (ed.). 1995. *Tristan and Isolde: A Casebook*. New York and London: Garland. ISBN 0-8153-0654-7.

Hale, Amy, Alan M. Kent, and Tim Saunders (eds. and trs.). 2000. *Inside Merlin's Cave: A Cornish Arthurian Reader 1000–2000*. London: Francis Boutle. ISBN 1-903427-04-5.

Halliday, F. E. (ed.). 1953. *Richard Carew: The Survey of Cornwall*. London: Melrose.

—— 1954. *The Legend of the Rood*, London: Gerald Duckworth.

Hatcher, John. 1970. *Rural Economy and Society in the Duchy of Cornwall 1300-1500*. Cambridge: Cambridge University Press. ISBN 0-521-07660-9.

Hawke, Andrew. 1982. "The Manuscripts of the Cornish Passion Poem" in Charles Thomas (ed.), *Cornish Studies: Journal of the Institute of Cornish Studies / Studhyansow Kernewek: Lyver-Termyn an Fundyans rak Studhyans Kerenwek*. Redruth: Institute of Cornish Studies, pp. 23–28.

Hays, Rosalind Conklin, and McGee, C. E. (Dorset) and Joyce, Sally L. and Newlyn, Evelyn S. (Cornwall) (eds.). 1999. *Records of Early English Drama: Dorset / Cornwall*. Toronto: University of Toronto and Brepols. ISBN 0-8020-4379-8.

Henderson, Charles. 1915. *Parochial Antiquities*, vol 5. MSS in Charles Henderson Collection, Courtney Library, Royal Institution of Cornwall, Truro.

Herriman, Mark. 1984. *Pascon agan Arluth: A Critical Study of the Cornish Passion Poem*. Diss. MA, Exeter.

Higgins, Sydney. 2013. *Theatre in the Round: The Staging of Cornish Medieval Drama*. North Charleston: Alldrama. ISBN 978-1-4849-4705-0.

Hooper, E. G. Retallack (ed.). 1972. *Passyon agan Arluth: Cornish Poem of the Passion in Unified Cornish by R. Morton Nance and A. S. D. Smith*. [Plymouth]: Kesva an Tavas Kernewek.

Jago, Fred. W. P. 1887. *An English-Cornish Dictionary, compiled from the best sources*. London: Simpkin, Marshall, & Co.; Plymouth: W. H. Luke.

Jenner, Henry. 1877. "An Early Cornish Fragment" in *The Athenaeum*, 1 December 1877.

—— 1904. *A Handbook of the Cornish Language*. London: David Nutt.

—— 1921. "The Fourteenth-Century Charter Endorsement" in *Journal of the Royal Institution of Cornwall*, № 20, 1915–1921, pp. 41–48.

—— 1925. "The Cornish Manuscript in the provincial library at Bilbao, Spain", in *Journal of the Royal Institution of Cornwall* 21 (1924-25): 421-37.

—— 2010. *Henry Jenner's Handbook of the Cornish Language: Revised by Michael Everson and including three early articles on Cornish by Jenner*. Cathair na Mart: Evertype. ISBN 978-1-904808-37-4.

John, Catherine Rachel. 2001. *The Saints of Cornwall: 100 Years of Christian Landscape*. Padstow: Tabb House. ISBN 1-873951-39-6.

Johnson, Charles, and Hilary Jenkinson. 1915. *English Court Hand A.D. 1066 to 1500, illustrated chiefly from the public records*. Reprint, New York: Frederick Ungar, 1967.

Kent, Alan M. 1999. *Wives, Mothers and Sisters: Feminism, Literature and Women Writers of Cornwall*. Newmill: Patten Press. ISBN 1-872229-33-6.

—— 2000. *The Literature of Cornwall: Identity, Continuity, Difference 1000–2000*. Bristol: Redcliffe. ISBN 1-900178-28-1.

—— 2002. *Pulp Methodism: The Lives and Literature of Silas, Joseph and Salome Hocking*. St Austell: Cornish Hillside. ISBN 1-900147-25-4.

—— 2005. *Ordinalia: The Cornish Mystery Play Cycle—A Verse Translation*. London: Francis Boutle. ISBN 1-903427-27-4.

—— 2006. *Nativitas Christi / The Nativity: A New Cornish Mystery Play*. London: Francis Boutle. ISBN 1-903427-31-2.

—— 2010. *The Theatre of Cornwall: Space, Place, Performance*. Bristol: Redcliffe. ISBN 978-1-904537-99-1.

—— 2012. "Mending the Gap in Medieval, Modern and Post-Modern in New Cornish Studies: Celtic materialism and potential of presentism" in Philip Payton (ed.), *Cornish Studies: Twenty*, Exeter: University of Exeter Press, pp. 13–31. ISBN 978-0-85989-874-4.

—— and Tim Saunders (eds. and trs.). 2000. *Looking at the Mermaid: A Reader in Cornish Literature*. London: Francis Boutle. ISBN 1-903427-01-0.

Langdon, Andrew. 1997. *Stone Crosses in West Penwith*. [St Austell]: The Federation of Old Cornwall Societies. ISBN 0-902660-25-X.

Le Braz, Anatole. 1905. *Le Théatre Celtique*. Paris: Calmann-Lévy.

Longsworth, Robert. 1967. *The Cornish Ordinalia: Religion and Dramaturgy*. Cambridge: Harvard University Press.

Loth, Joseph. 1902. "Textes inedits en cornique moderne," *Revue Celtique* 23:173-200.

Maclean, Magnus. 1908. *The Literature of the Celts*. London: Blackie and Son.

Murdoch, Brian. 1979a. "The Literary Position of the Cornish Passion-Poem: A Comparative Approach". Paper presented at the Seventh International Congress of Celtic Studies held in Galway in 1979.

—— 1979b. *The Medieval Cornish Poem of the Passion: Special Bibliography No. 5*. Redruth: Institute of Cornish Studies.

—— 1993. *Cornish Literature*. Cambridge: D. S. Brewer. ISBN 0-85991-364-3.

—— 1994. "The Cornish medieval drama" in Richard Beadle (ed.). *The Cambridge Companion to Medieval English Theatre*. Cambridge: Cambridge University Press, pp. 211–239. ISBN 978-0-521-68254-1.

—— 1996. "Is *John of Chyanhor* Really a 'Cornish *Ruodlieb*'?" in Philip Payton (ed.), *Cornish Studies: Four*, Exeter: University of Exeter Press, pp. 45–63. ISBN 978-0-85989-523-1.

Nance, Robert Morton. 1932. "The Charter Endorsement in Cornish" in *Old Cornwall*, pp. 34–36.

—— 1951. "New Light on Cornish" in *Old Cornwall*, 1943–1951, pp. 214–216.

Norris, Edwin (ed. and tr.). 1859. *The Ancient Cornish Drama*. Oxford: Oxford University Press. 2 vols. Reprint, New York and London: Benjamin Blom, 1968.

Olver, T. J. [n.d.] *An Account of the History of St Stephen-in-Brannel*. St Stephen-in-Brannel: St Stephen-in-Brannel Church Publication.

Padel, Oliver. 1975a. *Exhibition of Manuscripts and Printed Books on the Cornish Language (15th C.–1904)*. Truro: Royal Institution of Cornwall.

—— 1975b. *The Cornish Writings of the Bosun Family*. Redruth: Institute of Cornish Studies. ISBN 0-903686-09-0.

Parkes, M. B. 1979. *English Cursive Book Hands 1250–1500*. Ilkley: Scolar Press. ISBN 0-85967-535-1.

Pennaod, Goulven (ed. and tr.). 1978. "Passyon agan Arluth: Passion hon Aotrou. Barzhoneg kernevek eus ar 15. kantved" in *Preder*, pp. 232–234.

Piggot, Stuart, and Gwyn Walters (eds.). 1971. *Camden's Britannia 1695: A facsimile of the 1695 edition published by Edward Gibson*. Newton Abbot: David and Charles. ISBN 0-7153-5101-X.

Pool, P. A. S., and O. J. Padel. 1976. "William Bodinar's letter, 1776," in *Journal of the Royal Institution of Cornwall*, New Series 8, part 3 (1975-76): 231-34.

Price, Glanville. 1984. *The Languages of Britain*. London: Edward Arnold. ISBN 0-7131-6452-2.

Pryce, Huw (ed.). 1998. *Literacy in Medieval Celtic Societies*. Cambridge: Cambridge University Press. ISBN 0-521-57039-5.

Pryce, William. 1790. *Archaeologia Cornu-Britannica*. Sherborne: W. Cruttwell. Reprint, Menston, Yorkshire: Scolar Press, 1972. ISBN 0-85417-888-0.

Russell, Paul. 1995. *An Introduction to the Celtic Languages*. London and New York: Longman. ISBN 0-582-10081-X.

Sandercock, Graham. 2017. "Pashyon Agan Arluth" in *An Gannas* № 492, pp. 5–9.

Scawen, William. 1993. "Observations on an Ancient Cornish Manuscript entitled *Passio Christi*". Cited in Murdoch 1993.

Southey, Robert, 1879. "St Michael's Mount: St Michael's Chair" in Henry Wadsworth Longfellow (ed.) *Poems of Places: An Anthology in 31 Volumes*, vols. 1–4, 1876–1879, pp. 20–21.

Spriggs, Matthew, 2005. "William Scawen (1600–1680)—A Neglected Cornish Patriot and Father of the Cornish Language Revival" in Philip Payton (ed.). *Cornish Studies: Thirteen*, Exeter: University of Exeter Press, pp. 98–125. ISBN 978-0-85989-771-6.

Stewart, Elizabeth. 2012. *Drama Kernewek: Cornish Medieval Drama—A Resource and Activity Pack.* Truro: Cornish Language Partnership. ISBN 978-1-903798-85-0.

Stokes, Whitley. 1861. "The Passion: A Middle Cornish Poem" in *Transactions of the Philological Society*, 1860–1861, Appendix 1–100.

—— (ed. and tr.). 1872. *The Life of St Meriasek: Bishop and Confessor—A Cornish Drama.* London: Trübner and Co.

—— (ed. and tr.). 1864. *Gwreans an Bys: The Creation of the World, A Cornish Mystery*. London: Williams and Norgate. Reprint, Whitefish, Montana: Kessinger Publishing 1987. ISBN 0-7661-8009-3.

—— (as "W. S."). 1880. "Cornica IV: The Fragments of a Drama in Add. Ch. 19. 491, Mus. Brit." in *Revue Celtique*, 1879–1880, pp. 258–262.

Symons, Andrew. 1999. "Models of Language Transfer" in James Whetter (ed.), *An Baner Kernewek / The Cornish Banner*, № 96, pp. 6–9.

Thomas, Graham, and Nicholas Williams (eds. and trs.). 2006. *Bewnans Ke: The Life of St Kea. A Critical Edition with Translation.* Exeter: University of Exeter Press. ISBN 978-0-85989-800-3.

Thomas, Peter, and Derek R. Williams (eds.). 2007. *Setting Cornwall on its Feet: Robert Morton Nance 1873–1959*. London: Francis Boutle. ISBN 978-1-903427-34-7.

Toorians, Lauran (ed. and tr.). 1991. *The Middle Cornish Charter Endorsement: The Making of a Marriage in Medieval Cornwall.* Innsbruck: Institut für Sprachwissenschaft der Universität Innsbruck. ISBN 3-8512-4622-5.

Wakelin, Martyn F. 1974. *Language and History in Cornwall.* Leicester: Leicester University Press. ISBN 0-7185-1124-7.

Weatherhill, Craig. 1985. *Cornovia: Ancient Sites of Cornwall and Scilly*. Penzance: Alison Hodge. ISBN 0-906720-12-5.

Whetter, James. 1988. *The History of Glasney College.* Padstow: Tabb House. ISBN 0-907018-42-4.

—— 2017. "William Scawen of Molenick" in *An Baner Kernewek / The Cornish Banner*, № 168, pp. 7–14.

Williams, Derek R. (ed.). 2004. *Henry and Katharine Jenner: A Celebration of Cornwall's Culture, Language and Identity*. London: Francis Boutle. ISBN 1-903427-19-3.

—— 2013. *Williams, the Llawnt – Robert Williams: A Neglected Celtic Scholar.* Talybont: Y Lolfa.

Williams, J. E. Caerwyn (ed.). 1971. *Literature in Celtic Countries*. Cardiff: University of Wales Press. ISBN 978-1-84771-667-5.

Williams, Nicholas. 2006. *Cornish Today*. Third edition. Cathair na Mart: Evertype. ISBN 1-904808-07-7.

Wilson, R. M. 1952. *The Lost Literature of Medieval England.* London: Methuen.

Woodhouse, Harry (ed. and tr.). 2002. *The Cornish Passion Poem in Facsimile*. Cornwall: Gorseth Kernow. ISBN 1-903668-02-6.

Wright, C. E. 1960. *English Vernacular Hands from the Twelfth to the Fifteenth Centuries.* Oxford: Clarendon Press.

2
LINGUISTIC NOTES

2.1 *THE CHARTER FRAGMENT*

The Charter Fragment, which is almost certainly part of a larger dramatic work, consists of forty-one lines. The entire piece appears to be spoken by the same character, who seems to be an older man talking first to a young prospective groom and thereafter to his proposed bride. The speaker tells the young man that the girl is beautiful, very young and obedient, and will do as her husband wishes. He then turns to the girl, and presumably out of earshot of the groom, assures her that she should start her marriage as she intends to continue. She should refuse to do her husband's bidding and then he will acknowledge her to be the authority in the marriage.

Attempts have been made to explain the endorsement as a document that is complete in itself. Given the obviously incomplete nature of the text, this is unlikely. It is much more probable that the endorsement has come from a longer dramatic work, quite probably a dramatized saint's life on the model of *Beunans Meriasek* or *Bewnans Ke*. It seems reasonable to assume that the young man addressed first is the subject of the play. It is also probable that the narrative after the fragment proceeds when the young man tells his mentor that he has no intention of marrying, but rather wishes to remain unmarried so that he may be ordained priest, in exactly the same way that Meriasek rejects the marriage his parents have arranged for him with the daughter of King Conan. Whether the mutually contradictory advice given to the two young people is an added incentive to the young saint to reject the marriage is impossible to say. At all events it is clear that the text is incomplete, and for that reason calling it *The Charter Fragment* is quite legitimate.

From the point of view of metre *The Charter Fragment* is curious. Many of the lines at the beginning are of four syllables, a length found elsewhere in Cornish verse. Other lines contain five and six syllables, and in the later section eight and nine syllables. Such line lengths are without parallel elsewhere in Middle Cornish. For further discussion see p. 28 above.

The author's spelling has certain distinctive features. He uses yogh for both voiced and voiceless sounds, e.g. *coweȝ* 'companion' (line 1) and *hy a vyȝ* 'she will be' (line 13). He also uses *-g* in final position where *-gh* might be expected, e.g. *flog* for **flogh* 'child' (line 23), *ymmyug* 'kiss!' (plural imperative) for **ymmyugh* (line 25), *eug* 'go!' (plural imperative), for **eugh* (line 26), *fystynyug* 'hurry!' (plural imperative) for **fystynyugh* (line 126), *maraȝ herg ȝys* 'if he bid you' for **maraȝ ergh ȝys* (line 31). He even uses *-oug* for *-ow* in the opening line of the fragment *golsoug ty coweȝ* 'listen, thou companion' for **golsow ty coweȝ* (line 1). He also writes *gwreg ty* 'wife, housewife' (line 13); this is usually *gwregh ty* in other texts. He omits initial *h-* for *hag* in *ag ol ȝe voȝ* 'and all thy will' (line 22). On the other hand he places an unnecessary *h-* at the beginning of *herg* 'bid' (line 31) and *harluȝes* 'lady' (line 36).

The author or scribe uses *hedyr* for 'while' rather than *hedre* customary elsewhere. Indeed *hedyr* 'while' seems to have no parallel apart from *dirr* in *dirr vo an enef in kigg mab deane* 'while the soul is in the flesh of mankind' in SA 60a. The verb *y'm bus* 'I have' has in the text already become confused with *bos* 'to be', as can be seen in *ha ty a vyȝ hy* 'and thou shalt have her' (line 12).

There are a few borrowings from Middle English in the text: *sconye* 'to shun, to refuse' (line 11), *mekya* 'pretend' (line 11), *meystres* 'mistress' (line 35), *curtes* 'courteous' line 38, *deboner* 'debonair' (line 38), *danger* 'authority' (line 40).

2.2 *PASCON AGAN ARLUTH*

Pascon Agan Arluth is the only verse text in Middle Cornish which is not dramatic in form. The poem consists of 259 eight-lined stanzas of seven syllables each rhyming *abababab*. This metre is used elsewhere in Middle Cornish in solemn and declamatory passages, for example, at the beginning of *Origo Mundi*, when God the Father is creating the heavens and the earth (OM 1–80), and at the end of *Resurrexio Domini* when the ascended Christ is recounting his passion (RD 2571–602). In the manuscript some lines have one syllable too many. Others have one syllable too few. In each case in the normalized text the line has been emended to give seven syllables. It is unlikely that the poet's autograph was imperfect since very few lines require amendment of this kind.

Pascon Agan Arluth is also, as far as the date of composition is concerned, the oldest complete composition in Middle Cornish. The text as we have it, however, is not from the hand of the author. The scribe writes *adam hag evef* 'Adam and Eve' at PA 213a,[1] where the scribe has mistakenly written the name *ef* as a disyllable by hypercorrection. This makes it unlikely that the scribe and the author were one and the same.

1 References with the letters -a through -e appended are to stanza numbers; thus, for instance, stanza 213a contains both lines 1699 and 1700, stanza 213b contains both lines 1701 and 1702, etc.; see p. 301 below. Stanza 208 is unique in having ten lines rather than eight.

Pascon Agan Arluth is also earlier than *Passio Christi*, the second and longest of the three plays of the *Ordinalia*. This is apparent from a comparison of the temptation of Christ in the two texts. In PA Jesus, despite his great hunger, resists Satan's temptation to turn stones into bread and cites Deuteronomy 8:3 as his reason. The poet continues:

12 dre worȝyp crist yn vr-na
lemmyn ny a yll gwelas
lauar du maga del wra
neb a vynno y glewas 96

12 By Christ's answer at that time
now we can see
how the word of God nourishes
him who is prepared to hear it. 96
PA 12cd.

In *Passio Christi* on the other hand Jesus resists the Devil's tempting words and then, according to the stage direction, speaks *ad discipulos* 'to the disciples', and says:

ow dyscyblyon dre henna
leman why a yl gueles
laver dev maga del wra
neb a yl y kemeres

my disciples by that
now you can see
that the word of God nourishes
him who wishes to receive it
PC 69–72.

It clear that the passage in PC derives from PA, since PA follows the gospel narrative, but PC does violence to it. In the gospels Christ is driven into the wilderness to be tempted and he is alone. Moreover he has not yet chosen his disciples. In the second and third temptations in PA Christ is still alone; in PC, on the other hand, he discusses the temptations with his disciples—further evidence that PC is based on PA, not *vice versa*.

2.2.1 Archaic features in *Pascon agan Arluth*

Linguistically PA is also archaic. It contains the only known example in Cornish of a *t*-preterite:

3 Du sur dre virtu an tas
ȝyn ny a ȝyttyas gweras
En mab dre y skyans bras
pan **gemert** kyg a werhas

3 God indeed by the Father's power
provided for us assistance:
the Son by his great wisdom
when he assumed the flesh of the Virgin,
PA 3ab.

There is no doubt that *gemert* < *kemert* (for **kemerth* 'took') is correct, since the disyllable is guaranteed by the metre.

PA is also archaic in that it is the only Middle Cornish text in which the pluperfect functions as a pluperfect, rather than, as in the later language, as a conditional only.

It also seems that ⟨oy⟩ still represented a diphthong in PA. Although the scribe sometimes writes /oː/ as ⟨oy⟩, he rhymes ⟨oy⟩, the reflex of Old Cornish /ui/, in stanzas 10 and 45, for example, only with itself, but never with /oː/.

The rhymes in stanza 21 are noteworthy, since *dry* 'to bring' rhymes there with *gans otry* 'outrageously' (for *gans *outray*), *pray* 'prey', and *ioy* 'joy'. This shows that the vowel in *dry* was already at the time of composition pronounced with a diphthong [əi] or [ei], an indication that the author's dialect had undergone the Prosodic Shift.

2.2.2 More modern features in *Pascon agan Arluth*

On the other hand there are a number of features in PA that show affinities with Late Cornish. I will list several here:

i) The pronominal preposition *genama* 'with me' occurs at 193d. This is the only attested example in Middle Cornish, but is the predecessor of Late Cornish *gennam* 'with me'.

ii) In *dre an nerth may tensons hy* 'by the strength with which they pulled it' 182a and *arluth prag y hysta vy* 'Lord, why hast thou forsaken me?' 201c, the object pronoun is not infixed but follows its verb. This is reminiscent of the syntax seen in late Middle Cornish and Late Cornish, e.g. in *ny a ra eff gowak* 'we make him mendacious' (TH 8); *te a wore henna, fatell caraff ve ge* 'you know that, that I love you' (TH

43); *me a wra ge dean a bry* 'I make you, O man, of clay' (CW 345) and *An hagar-breeve a thullas ve* 'the evil serpent deceived me' (WR).

iii) The opening lines of stanza 73 read: *Hag a pe yn della ve neffre ny vean fethys* 'And were it thus, I, never would I be overcome'. Here the pronoun 'I' is *ve* rather than *me* or *my*. This is immediately reminiscent of Late Cornish *ve*, *vee* 'I', for example, in *Vee o gwrege ha flehes* 'I my wife and children' (BB).

iv) The phrase *kynyuer tra* 'everything' occurs at 208b. This is reminiscent of Late Cornish, e.g. *kanifer tra* in John Boson's translation of Genesis 1 (JB).

v) At 123a we read *Thy gour hy a ȝanonas* 'she sent word to her husband'. The omission of *-v-* in the word for 'to send' is reminiscent of Late Cornish: *Danen rag meele kentrow* 'Send for a thousand nails' (BB), *Danen rag teese tha trehe gorra* 'Send for men to cut hay' (ACB: F f 2). This may simply be an error, since *danvon* occurs elsewhere in the text. On the other hand, this form may perhaps reflect the language of the scribe, rather than of the author; if so, it is suggestive of a form found widely in Late Cornish.

vi) Although this may also simply reflect the language of the scribe rather than that of the author, it should be noted that the diphthong *ew* is often rounded to *ow* in PA, e.g. *dowȝek* 'twelve' 47a, 61a; *y a gowsys* 'they uttered' 50d; *war/ȝe ben dowlyn* 'on bended knee' 137a, 171c, 220b. This rounding of *ew* > *ow* is not found in the *Ordinalia*.

vii) At line 33b the reading of the manuscript *I thesa an venyn gansa* must be emended to *Thesa an venyn gansa* in order to give seven syllables. The loss of the vowel of the particle *yth/ith* before a following vowel is usually considered a late feature; cf. *thera Trigaz en St. Levan* (N. Boson) and *Thera vee dean boadjack an poscas* (BN).[2]

2.2.3 Middle English borrowings

Pascon agan Arluth is the earliest surviving long text in Middle Cornish. It does nonetheless exhibit a remarkably high proportion of borrowings from Middle English. This would seem to suggest that English loanwords were a distinctive feature of Middle Cornish from the earliest period. I list below a number of such borrowings, citing both the place where the word occurs and where necessary the Middle English form from which the etymon derives. There are 486 wordforms. which constitute 0.048% of the 10,204 wordforms in the text. Unmutated citation forms and verbal nouns unattested in the text preceded by *asterisks in the lists below.

2 See also note 1 on page 65 below.

2.2.3.1 Substantives

acheson 141b, 187a 'occasion, reason' (ME *achesoun*)
angus 221d, 224a 'anguish' (ME *angusse*)
bazon 45c 'basin'
belyny 20b, 82d, 96b, 162d, 146b, **bylyny** 83a, 188a, **velyny** 80d, 127b, 166d, **vylyny** 216a 'wickedness' (ME *vileinie*)
boclers 74b 'bucklers'
box 35a, 36b 'box, recepticle'
box 81b, *pl.* **boxow** 120d, **buxow** 138c 'blow to head'
burges 214a 'citizen'
cher (in **fekyl-cher**) 65c 'mood, behaviour' (ME *chere*)
cheryta 45b, **cheryte** 35a, **geryte** 38a 'charity'
chyffar 40b 'bargain' (ME *cheffare*)
confort 22b, 199d, 225b 'comfort'
contrary 146d 'enemy, opponent'
***covaytys** (as **govaytys**) 15d, 62d 'covetousness' (ME *coveitise*)
coyntys 109c, **goyntys** 19a, 125a 'novelty, craftiness' (ME *queintise*, *cointise*)
creatur 151b 'creature'
cry 117a, 208a 'cry'
cyte 28d, 127d, 189c, 210c, 214a 'city'
dyfout 192c 'fault, defect'
***dyscyplys** (as **ȝyscyplys**) 52b, 55c 'disciples'
***dyspyt** (as **dyspyth**) 139b 'contempt'
envy 90c, 107a, 126a, 127a 'envy, hatred'
fas 59b, 196c, **feth** 'face' 200c, 216c
florys 29d 'flowers'
frut 153c, 153d 'fruit'
fylte 47b, **fyltye** 23c, wickedness' (ME *vilte*, *filte*)
garlont 133a, **arlont** 134b, 205c 'garland, crown'
greff 162d, 204a 'grief, affliction'
harlot 38c, 81c 'scoundrel'
hast 159b, 202a, 202d 'haste'
ioy 21d, 30a, 226a, 251b, 258c 'joy'
iunctys 181d 'joints of the body'
iucter (in pl. **iucters**) 156a, as **iutter** 76d 'justice, justiciar'
iustys 81d, 92a, 98a, 107b, 113b, 114c, 119a, 124c, 143c, 163d, 215a, 239a, 247b, 248a 'justice, judge'
laha 99c, 143a, **lahys** 182d, **lays** 32c, 75a, 78c, 79b, 80a, 121c 'law'
lasch 138b 'lash, blow'
lewte 116c, 157c, 175c 'loyalty'
lybell 189a 'document, writing'
lycour (in **tebell-lycour**) 202b 'liquid, drink'
maner 13b, 15c, 100c, 124c, 173b, 199c, **vaner** 104a, 185b, 232b 'manner, custom'
mester 60d, 89a, 92a, 111d, 122d, 197c, 215a 'master'
mestry 144c, 145a, **vestry** 17d, 57b, 91c, 188c, 194c, 197c, 240d 'dominance, domination'
mowys 95c, 196a 'grimaces' (ME *moues*)
natur 208c, 211c 'nature'
nyscyte 185c 'silliness, ignorance'
onour 136c 'honour
otry (**ganso try** *written for* **gans otry**) 21a 'misdeed, sinfulness' (ME *outraie*)
oynment 235b, 252c, **vnment** 234 'ointment, unguent'
paradis 193d 'paradise'
pascon 228b 'passion, suffering' (ME *pascioun*)
payn 55a, 59d, 134a, 135c, 135d, 172d, **peyn** 21d, **bayn** 137d, **paynys** 3d, 139b, **peynys** 2d, 6a, 59d, 66d, 86c, 221d, 223d, 251c, **baynys** 70d, 182c, **beynys** 9b, 56b, 203c, **faynys** 166b, **feynys** 168d, 226a 'pain, pains'
penans 10b, **benans** 60b 'penance'
pencon 38b 'pension, money'
post 130b 'post, stake'
pray 21c 'prey'

pryson 124a, 124d, **breson** 24c, 213a 'prison'
prins 77c, 78a, 88a, **fryns** 76d, **princys** 64a, **pryncys** 97b 'prince, princes'
***pris** 'price' *in phrase* **a brys** 190b, 217b, **y breys** 255c 'of value, of worth' (ME *of pris*)
pyte 98c, 203a, **byte** 132c, 134d, **pyteth** 164b, **pytet** 177b, 223b, 223c 'pity'
reson 7a, 56d, 117d, 120b, 121b, 128b, 128d, **resons** 100b, 118b 'reason, reasons'
scherewes 213d, **scherewys** 31a, 203d 'scoundrels, villains' (ME *shreue*)
scherewneth 19a, 52d 'wickedness' (ME *shreunes*)
scorgye 130c, **scorgijs** 131a 'scourge, scourges (n.)'
scyle 116c, 125d, 142d, 175b, 187c, 211c 'cause, reason' (ME *skil*, *scile*)
sendall 232c 'cendal, linen'
sentury 208a 'centurion' (ME *centurie* for *centurioun*)
seruys 15b, 19c, 49a, 67b, 237c 'service'
sleyneth 212b 'wisdom, cleverness' (ME *sleighnesse*)
soget 211d 'subjects' (ME *sogette*)
soper 42b 'supper'
spong 202c 'sponge'
spycys 234d, 236a 'spices'
spykys 159d 'spikes' pl.
strekys 227b 'stripes'
strocosow 174c, **strokosow** 173b 'strokes, buffets' (ME *strokes*)
stryff 160d 'strife, dispute'
tempel 91b, **tempell** 193d, **tempyll** 209c, **templys** 30c 'temple, temples'
toche 158b 'touch, bit'
tormont 66b, 213d, **dormont** 132d 'torture'
traytour 98c, **treytour** 119c, 240a, **trayteur** 121a, **treytours** 157a, **thraytor** 61c 'traitor, traitors'
treson 42c, **dreyson** 74b, 124b 'treason'
tretury 194d 'treachery' (ME *tretherie*)
trystans 222c 'sorrow' (ME *tristenes*)
venions 122d, 123d, 149b, 149c 'vengeance'
veyll 209c 'veil'
virtu 3a, 23b, 33d, 68a 'virtue, power'

2.2.3.2 Adjectives and adverbs

apert 79a, 92b, 210a, 243c, 255c, 258b 'open, clear'
***bold** (as **voldh**) 78b 'bold'
cleyr 243c, 252b 'clear'
dyboner 129d 'debonaire, untroubled'
fekyl (in **fekyl-cher**) 65c 'false' (ME *fikel* 'false, treacherous')
rych 35a, 100b, 136a, 161a, 232c, 259c 'rich'
seruabyll 19c 'obedient, compliant'
specyall 110d 'special, specially'
veyll 156a, 165a, 177b, 220c 'vile, vilely'
vylen 112c, **velen** 183b 'savage, savagely'
vylle 176d 'viler'

2.2.3.3 Verbs

acordye 40d 'to agree'
amontye 40b, 59c 'to count up'
***ancombra** as **ancombrys** 34a 'to bewilder' (ME *encombren*)
angre 195c 'to anger'
aspye 241c 'to watch, to observe' (ME *aspien*)
attamye 153d 'to broach' (ME *attamen*)

*__attendie__ as **attendijs** 202d 'to pay attention to'

batayles 51a 'to do battle' (ME *bataillen*)

confortye 35c, 55d, **gomfortye** 58b, **gonfortye** 18c, **homfortye** 167a, **confortys** 257a 'to comfort'

*__convyctya__ as **convyctys** 18b 'to prove guilty' (ME *convicten*)

crakye 139a, **grakye** 164b 'to crack'

dampnye 32c, 94d, 99d, 107b, 116d, **dampne** 108c, **dampnyaf** 34d, **dampnowgh** 99c, **dampnys** 142d, 151a, 163a, 187b **dapnys** 128b, **thampnye** 110c, **ȝamnye** 98d 'to condemn' (ME *dampnen*)

*__decevya__ as **desevijs** 5c 'to deceive'

*__defendye__ as **defendys** 188b 'to prohibit'

delyffre 150a, **delyrf** 126b, 127d, **delyrfsens** 102b, **delyffrys**, 124d, 125c, 144d, 184b, **dylyr** 57c, **thelyffras** 150d, 213a, **ȝelyffra** 145d, **ȝelyffre** 203c 'to deliver'

*__desyrya__ as **theseryas** 9d, **ȝeserya** 4a 'to desire'

dropye 59b, **ȝroppye** 173c 'to drop'

*__dyghtye__ as **dyȝgthtya** 7d, **dygtye** 199d, **dygtyas** 130d, **dyȝgtyas** 235d, **dyȝgthtyas** 71d, **dygtys** 165a, 177b, **dyȝgtys** 141d, 153a, 163a, 202a, 219d, **dyȝgthtys** 133a, **ȝygtye** 164a, **ȝyttyas** 3a 'to provide, to arrange, to treat' (ME *dighten*)

*__dysconfortye__ as **dysconfortys** 255a, **dygonfortys** 58a 'to discomfort, distress'

*__dyspresya__ as **dyspresijs** 2c, **dyspresys** 44c, **dyspresyas** 104d 'to slander, to disparage' (ME *dispreisen*)

dyssaytye 194d 'to deceive' (ME *deceite*)

faste 180a, **fasteys** 184a 'to fasten'

fecle 40c 'to dissemble' (ME *fikelen*)

*__gorthye__ as **gorȝye** 226b, **gorthijs** 28d, **gorȝijs** 228b, **worȝye** 29b, 137c, 148c 'to venerate, to honour' (ME *worthien*)

grevye 132b, 176c, 205c, 231c, **grevijs** 58c, 61b, 211d 'to afflict'

*__grontye__ as **wronte** 1b, **growntyas** 75c, **rontyas** 230b, **grontys** 9d, 70b, 215c, **grontijs** 113d 'to grant'

*__growndye__ as **growndys** 118b 'to base, to ground'

*__gwarnye__ as **warnyas**, 42c, **gwarnys** 86d, **guarnys** 101b 'to warn'

honore 15b, 16d, 115d, **onore** 199c, **honorys** 31a 'to honour'

*__iuggye__ as **ivggye** 118d, **iudgye**, 116a, **iuggyas** 150c, **iuggijs** 160d 'to judge'

*__metye__ as **vetye** 20b 'to meet'

*__mevye__ as **mevijs** 4b 'to move'

notye 214d, 249c, **notya** 234b, **notyas** 251d, **notijs** 31b 'to take note, to mention, to make known' (ME *noten*)

ordna, 7b, **ordnys** 24b, 151b, 152c, 176a 'to order, to provide'

*__pechye__ as **bechye** 218c 'to thrust, to stab' (ME *picchen*)

peyne 90b, **peynye** 74c, **peynys** 185a, 211c 'to pain'

plentye 33c 'to make complaint'

plynchye 130b 'to move suddenly'

*__praysye__ as **praysys** 109b 'to praise'

*__prysonye__ as **prysonys** 24c, 124b 'to imprison'

pyltye 112c 'to strike' (ME *pilten*)

*__rebukye__ as **rebukys** 156a, **rebekys** 2c, **rebukyas** 112a 'to rebuke'

receve 233b, **rysseve** 103b 'to receive'

redye 187c, 189b, **redijs** 189d, **redyn** 204c, 206b 'to read'

sackye 195b 'to shake'

scolchye 74b 'to skulk'

sconye 174d, **sconyas** 46a, 174c, **sconyth** 120d 'to shun, to avoid, refuse'

scorgye 130c, **scorgyas** 130c 'to flog, to scourge'

scornye 83b, 114a, 137a, 194a, 208d, **scornyas** 70b, 95c, 112c 'to mock'
seruye 180d 'to serve, to be of use'
***settye** as **settyas** 71c, 117a, **syttys** 138d 'to set'
sewye 116b, **sywye** 175b, **syw** 226c, **sewyas** 52b, 108d, 213c, **sewijs** 73d 'to follow' (ME *seuen*)
sopye 41c 'to sup'
spedye 39b, 63b, **spedyas** 42b 'to succeed'
***speyna** as **speynas** 10c 'to spend' (ME *spenen*)
***storvye** as **storuys** 177d 'to die of cold'
***strechye** as **strechyaff** 158c 'to delay'
strevye 73d, 248c 'to strive' (ME *striven*)
syndye 74c, 97d, 107a, **syndys** 62d, 223a 'to ruin' (ME *shenden*)
***tackye** as **tackys** 179b 'to attach' (ME *takken*)
temptye 15a**, demptya** 13b, **demptye** 11a, 14a, 20d, **temtijs** 52d, **temptijs** 22a 'to tempt'
***tochye** as **dochye** 14c 'to touch'
***tormontye** as **tormont** 66b, **dormontye** 97a 'to torture'
vntye 35b 'to anoint'(ME *ointe*, *uinte*)
vsye 161a, 205b, **vsijs** 223b 'to use, to wear'

The borrowed verb *dyssaytya* 'to deceive' occurs at 194d, but is unattested elsewhere. The verb *rebukya* occurs three times in PA (2c, 112a, 156a) and is elsewhere the verb is known only from TH.

Nicholas Williams

3
ORTHOGRAPHIC NOTES

3.1 GENERAL COMMENTS

One of the most difficult discussions within the Cornish Revival has been ongoing argument about the most suitable orthography for representing the language. Unified Cornish attempted to use the most common graphs Nance's analysis could establish. Common Cornish posited an unlikely phonology and a mechanism for marking vowel length which is reminiscent of the Middle English *Ormulum*. A variety of Revived Late Cornish orthographies were based variously on the texts of the last writers of Cornish, or on the phonetic orthographic practices of Edward Lhuyd. Unified Cornish Revised implemented changes to Unified Cornish chiefly increasing the number of voiced consonants in final position in stressed monosyllables, and adding variety in the use of the letters **i** and **y**. The Standard Written Form (SWF) built on the work of the group Udn Form Screfys in implementing a robust reliable mechanism for indicating vowel length while retaining many of the reconstructed preferences of Common Cornish. *Kernowek Standard* (KS) or Standard Cornish, devised by the group Spellyans, removed errors and ambiguities in the SWF and has been used in dozens of books. In the *Corpus Textuum Cornicorum*, KS is used as the normalized orthography for Cornish of all periods.

Many of us have argued at length about the relative importance of authenticity when choosing spellings for the revived language. And almost everybody has argued on the basis of either originally transcribed nineteenth-century editions or of revivalist orthographies based on those, or based on non-Cornish orthographic theory. But few if any of those arguing have actually seen genuine Cornish literary orthography as written by literate native speakers. In *Pascon agan Arluth* itself we find *gorrys* 'put, set, placed' written as *gorrys*, *goꝛꝛys*, *gorrꝭ*, *gorys*, and *gurrꝭ*. One *r*? Two? What to make of this **r**-rotunda (**ꝛ**)? Or of the character **-ꝭ** (*-is*, *-ys*)? (The alternation *gor-* ~ *gur-* is not so unusual.) A variety of scribal conventions common throughout medieval and Tudor Britain are used in Cornish manuscripts, and the palaeographic text given in this series presents them in typeset form so that the original orthography can be seen.

It is probable that most readers of this book will be more interested in the text and translation than in the palaeographic transcription, but the presentation of such transcriptions in this series will perhaps be found useful to some scholars now and in future. Since this series is, as Henry Jenner would have wished, for modern Cornishmen and Cornishwomen as well as for Celticists and medievalists, some of the commentary in the present chapter constitutes a sort of tutorial on palaeography and transcription.

Why is a palaeographic transcription of interest? It shows in typographic form the letterforms and abbreviations used by the scribe. His mistakes can be seen, of course, but importantly his knowledge of the basic or underlying wordforms behind his abbreviations can be compared with those same words that he writes out in full—and this sometimes helps with the reading of the text, and has contributed to our understanding of medieval Cornish since the texts began to be read in the modern era.[1]

In this volume the palaeographic transcription can be compared with the colour facsimile. In § 3.4 below I give a list of the letters and special characters used in the texts here. By "special characters" I mean letters, abbreviation letters, superscript letters, and diacritical marks outside the Latin letters **A** to **Z**. Sometimes in the descriptions below I use, in SMALL CAPITALS, the formal character names of the letters as encoded in the Universal Character Set (Unicode and ISO/IEC 10646).

It seems clear that the scriptorium at Glasney influenced Cornish orthography greatly from *Pascon agan Arluth* until *The Creation of the World*.[2] Thereafter traditional Cornish came to be written on the basis of contemporary English orthography, or of adaptations of Edward Lhuyd's phonetic transcription. Comparison of the orthographic practices in the manuscripts through time shows a gradual attenuation of adherence to the scribal tradition of Glasney—but the influence of that tradition is generally discernable nevertheless.

3.2 *THE CHARTER FRAGMENT*

The script of the late fourteenth-century MS Add. Charter 19491 is an Anglicana Book hand.[3] It is not particularly tidy, but then the metre and rhyme scheme is nowhere near as perfect as that of *Pascon agan Arluth*, either. The text looks to have been penned quickly by a hand well-used to writing. Speed—and not calligraphy—must have been the writer's main concern.

---

1 For example at line 1053 in *Pascon agan Arluth* the scribe writes *tā*, which one would normally expand as *tam* or *tan*. But here the sense requires *tra*, which he might write in abbreviated form as *tr̃*. In this case it appears that he wrote *ta* rather than *tr*, and just put a mark over it even though he hadn't written the word in the usual way.

2 The orthography of *The Charter Fragment* has a decidedly archaic flavour.

3 See Parkes 1979 and Johnson and Jenkinson 1915 in the bibliography above.

3.2.1 Letterforms

The hand of *The Charter Fragment* uses a two-compartment **a** (ɑ), **d** with a strong diagonal (ꝺ), figure-8 **g** (g),[4] and rounded Anglicana **w** (ꝡ).[5] Both **f** and long-**s** (**ſ**) have long descenders (f ſ); final **s** is sigmoid in shape (ꜱ).[6] A long descender is also found on **r**, which is strongly vertical with a wispy shoulder (r), in final position with a flourished form **r̂** (r̂) in all but two cases (where *kymmerr y* (line 10) and *mar mennyȝ* (line 33) are run together). The **r**-rotunda (**ꝛ**) is used (ꝛ). Both yogh **ȝ** and **z** have a similar shape with a round right-swinging descender (ȝ).[7] The letter **i** is written without a dot (ı); the letter **y** is usually written with dot above or an inverted breve (ẏ y̑).[8] Both the letters **n** and **u** are written identically (u u).

Two distinct shapes for **e** are found, though without phonetic distinction; the shape more familiar to us (e) was common throughout the thirteenth century but from just before the middle of the fourteenth century and continuing to the end of the fifteenth century the crossbar of the *e* is formed from its tail at the end of a continuous loop (ɘ).[9] In the transcription below these are distinguished as **e** and **ɘ**. The letter **ɘ** appears nine times in word-final position, and once internally in *worȝɘſy*.

The letterforms **r** and **r**-rotunda, and **s** and long-**s** have also been distinguished: even if **ꝛ** and **ſ** do not indicate any phonetic distinction, they are important letter variants which in some texts are often regularly distinguished positionally from **r** and **s**, and so are of general palaeographic interest. The **ꝛ** is found only after **o** (*boꝛȝ*, *poꝛȝo*, *toꝛn*), although **r** can also

4 Johnson and Jenkinson 1915:2–3 (**a**), 11–12 (**d**), 19–21 (**g**).

5 The Anglicana **w** (typographically **ꝡ**) has a variety of glyph shapes in Middle English and Middle Cornish and appears to be an original ligature of two letters used for Middle Welsh (ỽ, typographically **ỽ**); our modern **w** is a ligature of two ordinary **v**'s (v w). See Everson 2017a.

6 Johnson and Jenkinson 1915:17–18, (**f**), 44–45 (**ſ**, **s**).

7 Johnson and Jenkinson 1915:40–42 (**r**, **ꝛ**), 55 (**z**), 57 (**ȝ**).

8 Although both the COMBINING DOT ABOVE ◌̇ and the COMBINING INVERTED BREVE ◌̑ over **y** are found in *The Charter Fragment*, neither is a diacritical mark bearing any meaning; it is plain to see that *my* ~ *mẏ* 'I', *ty̑* ~ *ty̑* 'you', *ȝys* ~ *ȝẏs* ~ *ȝy̑s* 'to you' and the like are the same words. In this series, for consistency, these marks are generally not transcribed; **i** is more legible than **ı**, and the mark on **y̑** could be mistaken for a genuine nasal abbreviation. Historically the form **ẏ** was used in English manuscripts to distinguish **y** from thorn **þ** since the glyphs for the two had often become indistinguishable (ẏ y)—but **þ** is not much relevant in Cornish after the *Old Cornish Vocabulary* (it appears in some English-language stage directions in *Beunans Meriasek*, for instance). In this transcription, because of the text's antiquity and brevity, both ◌̇ and ◌̑ have been retained, for flavour.

9 Johnson and Jenkinson 1915:14–15 (**e**, **ɘ**).

found in the same position (*worty*, *worȝ9ſy*). Texts which use both **ſ** and **s** typically use the former generally and the latter in final position. In *The Charter Fragment*—short as it is—exceptions to that practice are found: *aſ*, *sens*, *sconya*, *senſ9*, and *soȝ* are found, rather than the expected spellings *as*, *ſens*, *ſconya*, *ſenſ9*, and *ſoȝ*.

Capital letters in *The Charter Fragment* are used regularly though they seem not to have been previously described. I identify **G** (G), **H** (H), **L** (L), **D** (D), M (M), **R** (R) at the beginnings of stanzas, and **C** (C) at line 38.

3.2.2 Abbreviations

Two combining abbreviations are used, in t̃ where COMBINING LATIN SMALL LETTER FLATTENED OPEN A ABOVE ◌ᷓ indicates *ra*, and in *debon᷎* where COMBINING ZIGZAG ABOVE ◌᷎ indicates *er*. An otiose COMBINING OVERLINE ◌̅ appears once, through the **l** in *alema* and evidently in the capital **L** in *Lemen*.[10]

3.2.3 Punctuation

Punctuation is not used in *The Charter Fragment*. Some ruling is used to link the lines of stanzas, as is common in texts of this period, but it is very faint, and in any case is an indication of layout, not punctuation *per se*.

3.3 *PASCON AGAN ARLUTH*

The script of the late fourteenth-century Harley MS 1782 is likewise an Anglicana Book hand. Twenty-seven special characters are used, of which 11 are letters, 2 are superscript letters, and 14 are diacritical marks.

3.3.1 Letterforms

The hand uses a looped **a** (a), looped **d** (d), a cursive **e** (e), and a rather modern-looking **g** (g). A typical shape is used for **v** (v) and **w** (w); the Anglicana **w** (w) also occurs.[11] Both **f** and long-**s** (**ſ**) have long descenders (f, ſ); final **s** is sigmoid in shape (s). A long descender is also found on **r**, which, as in *The Charter Fragment*, is strongly vertical with a wispy shoulder (r); the **r**-rotunda (ꝛ) is also used (ꝛ). The yogh **ȝ** and **z** are identical, and have a somewhat unusual shape with a vertical descender (ȝ).[12]

In *Pascon agan Arluth* **i** is dotless (ı); the letterform **j** (j) is used only positionally after the letter **i** as a swash allograph of it, as in the Roman numeral (*ij* = *2*) or to represent what is otherwise a letter **y**, as in the adjectival ending *-ijs* ~ *-ys*. The letter **j** as distinct from the letter **i** did not exist in English until Charles Butler's seventeenth-century *English Grammar*,[13] and

10 See note 19 below.

11 Johnson and Jenkinson 1915:50–51 (**v**), 51–52 (**w**, **ꝡ**). See notes 4 and 9 above.

12 Johnson and Jenkinson 1915:55 (**z**), 57 (**ȝ**).

13 Butler 1634; Eichler 1910:2, 17.

was not distinctive in fourteenth-century Cornish either. The graph used for initial capital **I** in *Pascon agan Arluth* looks rather like our capital **J** (ꝗ), but since there is no distinction between capital **I** and capital **J** at this period, **I** has been used in the transcription here, whether it represents /i/ (40 times) or /dʒ/ (179 times).

Of the 29 instances of **ij** in the text, 25 are marked with the COMBINING ACUTE ACCENT ◌́, **íj** (ıȷ́). Although the acute accent is not a meaningful diacritical mark, but rather of the same nature as the minim-distinguishing dot (discussed in note 8 above), this feature is given in the transcription since the accents are mostly reasonably obvious as written, and since retaining them provides insight into what the scribe was doing.

As with *The Charter Fragment*, the letterforms **r** and **ꝛ**, and **s** and **ſ**, are recorded for those interested in positional use, or in the feel of the scribal hand as far as this orthographic choice goes. At line 316 **chyffaꝛꝛ* appears to be written, but really the second **ꝛ** is an erroneous duplicate where **aꝛ** has been overwritten by **aꝛ** with an enlarged **ꝛ** (aꝛ);[14] the duplicate has not been recorded here and the word has been transcribed *chyffaꝛ*. See the end of § 3.3.2.2 below for further comments about the letter **r**.

The letter yogh **ȝ** is used quite regularly for the sounds /ð/ and /θ/ and also thrice for /z/; as noted above, the shape of **ȝ** and **z** is identical in the manuscript (ȝ). In the transcription I distinguish the two; not to do so would be inconsistent practice, since both **n** and **u** are also identical throughout and they are of course transcribed distinctly.

Capital letters in *Pascon agan Arluth* are used regularly at the beginnings of stanzas, and nearly the entire alphabet is represented.[15] Some letters have more than one shape, within a range of forms which can be dated to a the period from the mid-fourteenth to the mid-fifteenth century. **A** 𝔄, **B** 𝔅, **C** ℭ, **D** 𝔇, **E** 𝔈, **F** ꝼꝼ (identical to two lowercase f's), **G** 𝔊, **H** ℌ, **I** ꝗ, **K** 𝔎, **L** 𝔏, **M** 𝔐, **N** 𝔑, **O** 𝔒, **P** 𝔓, **R** ℜ, **S** 𝔖, **T** 𝔗, **V** 𝔙, **W** 𝔚, and **Y** 𝔜 are the most typical forms, though a few letters have some variants. Of these, the two most striking are the insular **T** Ꞇ (less frequent than 𝔗, but also appearing in the ornamented initial capital at the beginning of the poem; see p. 105 below) and the Anglicana **W** 𝔚.

3.3.2 Abbreviations

Both letter-based and diacritical approaches to abbreviation are found in *Pascon agan Arluth*.

14 The overwriting may have been contemporary or later; see the second paragraph in § 5.2 below. The facsimile is on *f.* 4v; see page 112 above.

15 **Q**, **X**, and **Ȝ/Z** are not; **J** did not yet exist, and **V** is used for both capital **u** and **v**. Lowercase **u** does not occur in initial position.

3.3.2.1 Letter-based abbreviations

The letters used come in a number of categories. The first type is comprised of regular Latin-alphabet letters with some glyphic modification. One of these is LATIN SMALL LETTER DUM **ꝱ** (ꝱ), which was originally used for Latin syllables like *dum* but here is used for /d/ (×2, perhaps in error), for /ð/ (×4) and /θ/ (once). Others are LATIN SMALL LETTER P WITH STROKE THROUGH DESCENDER **ꝑ** (ꝑ), LATIN SMALL LETTER P WITH FLOURISH **ꝓ** (ꝓ), and LATIN SMALL LETTER LONG S WITH DIAGONAL STROKE **ẜ** (ẜ); the uses of these three characters are given in § 3.4 below.[16]

The scribe also uses two conventional abbreviation letters, namely LATIN SMALL LETTER IS **ꝭ** (ꝭ) which means *is* or *ys*, and LATIN SMALL LETTER CON **ꝯ** (ꝯ) which is used for *os* or *us*, typically used in final position.[17] Spacing superscript Latin letters ᵍ and ᵗ are also used (ᵍ, ᵗ).

3.3.2.2 Diacritical abbreviations

The non-spacing diacritical letters ◌ᷣ, ◌ᷔ, ◌ͥ, and ◌ᷦ (◌ᷣ, ◌ᷔ, ◌ͥ, ◌ᷦ) are used for a variety of abbreviations detailed below in § 3.4. As in *The Charter Fragment*, the COMBINING ZIGZAG ABOVE ◌͛ (◌͛) is used, as well as the COMBINING UR ABOVE ◌᷒ (◌᷒), also discussed below.[18] In line 922 a mark which looks like ◌̑ has been read as *d* since Stokes' 1861 edition; I have retained this reading as ◌ͩ (◌ͩ) though it is a bit anomalous.

By far the most frequently occurring diacritical mark is the COMBINING OVERLINE ◌̅ (◌̅), which has several uses in the text.[19] It is used non-phonetically with single **h**, **u**, and **l** to indicate contractions like *ih̄us*, *ihūs* 'Jesus', and *ierl̄m* 'Jerusalem' (both words having a number of spellings).

The COMBINING OVERLINE is also used inconsistently over (or through) one or both of the letters in the digraphs **gh**, **ll**, and **th**. It appears to be nothing more than a graphic device, but it has been transcribed here as **gh̄**, **l̄l̄**, and **t̄h̄**. In general, when used in this way, the overline is found in final position. One word which appears to have been extraordinarily difficult for our scribe to spell is *dyghtys* [ˈdɪçtɪs] 'prepared, treated', an English borrowing, which has a variety of spellings, in one place even *dyȝgt̄h̄tys*.

In general the COMBINING OVERLINE ◌̅ and the COMBINING FERMATA ◌͒ (◌͒), and the less frequent COMBINING INVERTED BREVE ◌̑ (◌̑, best considered a dotless FERMATA) and COMBINING TILDE ◌̃ (◌̃, best considered a swash variant of the OVERLINE) are placed atop a vowel preceding an **m** or **n**, as in **e͒m**

16 Johnson and Jenkinson 1915:68 (**ꝱ**), 64–65 (**ꝑ**), 65 (**ꝓ**), 67 (**ẜ**).

17 Johnson and Jenkinson 1915:63 (**ꝭ**), 60 (**ꝯ**, in the section "*Con*"); Wright 1960:xvii (**ꝯ**).

18 Johnson and Jenkinson 1915:3–4 (◌᷒), 59 (◌͛), 64 (◌᷒).

19 Johnson and Jenkinson 1915:57–58 (◌̅).

(for *emm*) or **e͒n** (for *enn*). The diacritic need not represent the same consonant that follows: compare *dēma* for *denma* ‘this man’ and *hēma* for *hemma* ‘this one’. Often in *Pascon agan Arluth* the ◌̄ or ◌͒ is written more or less between the two letters (as **e͒m** or **e͒n**); in such a case the diacritic has been transcribed as being placed over the vowel. In two instances the FERMATA (when indicating a nasal consonant) is written over the following consonant: *kym͒ys*, *fyn͒e* (lines 1080 and 1942). This would appear to be accidental; certainly in a searchable database it would be more convenient to normalize to over-the-vowel placement, and such normalization has been applied here: *ky͒mys*, *fy͒ne*. At line 1138 *ȝy̅nny* is written; evidently *ȝy̅ny* or *ȝynny* was the intended spelling; in the expanded text *ȝynn ny* is the form given.

In the alphabetical lists in § 3.4 and § 7.2 below, ◌̃, ◌͒, ◌̄, and ◌̑ are sorted together as a *separate letter* between **m** and **n** when they indicate a nasal consonant (because one cannot tell which letter it signifies), but they are ignored in sorting when used to indicate a contraction as in *ih̄us* or *ihȗs*, as is the “decorative” ◌̄ in *pegh̄*. (The index verborum in § 7.2 has been handtailored to produce this result.)

Along with these four, an additional diacritical mark, a COMBINING OVERCURL ◌᷎ (◌᷎), was identified while the transcription was being prepared.[20] This appears quite commonly in word-final and occasionally in medial position.[21] Like the COMBINING OVERLINE ◌̄, sometimes it is meaningful, indicating **m** or **n**, but very often it is otiose, having no meaning at all—when combined with **r** (**r᷎**), it often indicates a following **e** (as in Middle English); **e᷎** and **n᷎** where it has the readings **w** and **s** are also found. The OVERCURL is not a glyph variant of INVERTED BREVE, which reliably represents a nasal consonant.[22] The mark can also be supplemented with a COMBINING DOT ABOVE ◌̇, as in *bafco᷎n* (line 4). This is not a glyph variant of the FERMATA, though it’s likely the dot was added by habit since the shape

20 I am certainly not the first to identify the OVERCURL as a text element. It has been remarked upon many times, in particular in Middle English, where it typically represents **e** or is otiose.

21 Of the 1614 marks of this kind in *Pascon agan Arluth*, the COMBINING OVERLINE ◌̄ comprises 72% of them, the COMBINING OVERCURL ◌᷎ comprises 20%, the COMBINING FERMATA ◌͒ just over 6%, the COMBINING INVERTED BREVE ◌̑ about 1%, and the COMBINING TILDE ABOVE ◌̃ something less than 1%.

22 Parkes 1979:xxix describes his use of the apostrophe **’** for *any* otiose sign, while giving expansions where the signs are meaningful. Examples: *angur᷎* → *angur’*, *multiplicar᷎* → *multiplicare*; *and* → *and’*, *abstinend* → *abstinendum*; *all̄* → *all’*, *al̄* → *aliter*. Expansion, however, differs from palaeography. The OVERCURL is also found in Middle Scots: in Murdoch Nisbet’s 1520 translation of the New Testament, it is used typically to represent **m** or **n**, in both medial and final positions, alongside marks like ◌̄ and ◌̑; it also means **e** or nothing.

of ꝏ and ꝏ̂ are somewhat similar. A purely decorative swash n̂ is found in *yn* (line 14), *Pehadozyon* (line 37), and *Iowan* (line 1587); these decorations were not retained in the expanded transcription (since *-nn* would be unwarranted), and in the palaeographic transcription I have ignored them.

In final position, the letter **r** presents some difficulty to the transcriber. To judge from the way the letter typically ligates with following minims, it is reasonable to say that the basic character shape has a minimal arm (ꝛ). It often has a curl when ligated with a following **e** (ꝛ), with the circle looking like the top of that letter (e); a similar curl on **d** and **t** indicates the COMBINING ZIGZAG ABOVE: d᷏ (d᷏) *der*, t᷏ (t᷏) *ter*. But the final **r** very often has a swash tail (ꝛ) which cannot be identified with COMBINING ZIGZAG ABOVE, as there is a normal form for that, r᷏ (r᷏); with the OVERCURL, r̂ is often to be read *re* (as in *dr̂* for *dre*, lines 38, 298, 475, 994, 1070). The OVERCURL is ordered with the other nasalizing marks, as a separate letter between **m** and **n** (even though it may represent **e** or nothing).

3.3.3 Punctuation

Punctuation is used very rarely in *Pascon agan Arluth*, though as in *The Charter Fragment* ruling is used to link the lines of stanzas. Each line in the manuscript contains two metrical lines; in the first line of the poem, the two lines are divided by a mark, perhaps unique to the Cornish scribal tradition, ⁒, which is called CORNISH VERSE DIVIDER.[23] All the other lines are divided by a solidus /; a bullet • has been used editorially to indicate the division where the solidus was not written in the manuscript.[24] A dot is used at the end of the second metrical line in five places in the text (lines 976, 1572, 1580, 1582, 1586); this doesn't seem to be meaningful. The close proximity of four of the could mean anything: even scribal fatigue.

3.4 TABLE OF CHARACTERS[25]

A	*A*	–	A	a squarer form A is also found.
a	*a*	a	a	

23 This mark ⁒ is used very clearly in *Beunans Meriasek*, and is found elsewhere in the corpus, sometimes in attenuated forms like ·/·/·, ·//·, |:|, and //, particularly as the distance from the scribal tradition increases. Scribes seemed to know "I need to separate the verses with dots and slashes" but the strength of the tradition weakened through time. See Everson 2017b.

24 After line 1701 the scribe writes two together: //.

25 Roman, *italic*, CF, and PA forms are shown in this table. Examples give a line number from PA, generally the first one given in the word's entry in the index verborum, though there are exceptions for polyvalent signs like ꝏ̃. Citations from *The Charter Fragment* are marked "CF".

ꝛ̃	*ꝛ̃*	ꝛ̃	ꝛ̃	1) for *a* (*m̃ꝛth* "marth" 1326, *dr̃* "dra" 785, *bꝛ̃s* "bras" 1993). 2) for *ar* (as in *m̃th* "marth" 953). 3) for *ra* (as in *t̃* "tra" CF 34).
B	*B*	–	B	the vertical line is rubricated.
b	*b*	b	b	
C	*C*	C	C	the *C* is only slightly larger than most letters (CF 38).
c	*c*	c	c	
D	*D*	D	D	the *D* is only slightly larger than *d* (CF 27).
d	*d*	d	d	
ꝛᵈ	*ꝛᵈ*	–	ꝛ̃	for *d* (as in *iꝛᵈgye* "iudgye" 922).
ꝺ	*ꝺ*	–	ꝺ	originally used for Latin *-dum*, this character (whose glyph contrasts with that of *d* d) has various uses: 1) for ordinary *d* (*acoꝛꝺ* "acord" 60, *volꝺ* "vold" 619). 2) for *th* [ð] (*harꝺ* "harth" 1869; at line 979 *keꝛꝺ delma* "kerth delma" has been emended to "kettel-ma"). 3) for *th* [θ] (*orꝺ* "orth" 636).
E	*E*	–	E	a squarer form E is also found.
e	*e*	e	e	
ꝛᵉ	*ꝛᵉ*	–	ꝛᵉ	for *re* (as in *ſꝛᵉfys* "screfys" 1503).
ɘ	*ɘ*	ɘ	–	used in medial and final positions in CF.
F	*F*	–	ff	the glyph for the capital *F* is identical to that for *ff* and so is distinguished positionally and by sense.
f	*f*	f	f	
G	*G*	G	G	
g	*g*	g	g	
ᵍ	*ᵍ*	–	ᵍ	for *ag* (as in *ꝛᵍ* "rag" 284).
H	*H*	H	H	the unusual form H at line 1417 may have begun with an erroneous stroke, similar to that of the capital V *V* in the preceding stanza.
h	*h*	h	h	
I	*I*	–	I	used for both /i/ and /dʒ/
i	*i*	ı	ı	
ꝛⁱ	*ꝛⁱ*	–	ꝛⁱ	1) for *ir* (as in *vⁱtu* "virtu" 17). 2) for *ri* (as in *cⁱſt* "crist" 28, *gⁱſt* "grist" 644, *pⁱncꝭ* "princys" 505).
j	*j*	–	j	a glyph variant of *i*, used only following an *i* in *-ijs* or *-íjs* alongside the past participle ending *-ys*, and as the final part of Roman numerals *íj* '2' and *íij* '3'.

K	*K*	–	K	
k	*k*	k	k	
L	*L*	L	L	the *L* has a lower bowl as well as OVERLINE (CF 17).
l	*l*	l	l	
M	*M*	M	M	the downcurl on *M* is probable but debatable (CF 31).
m	*m*	m	m	
◌̃	◌̃	–	◌̃	1) a contraction mark (as in *Ihũs* "Ihesus" 129). 2) for *-m* (as in *oỹmet͛* "oynment" 2015).
◌̂	◌̂	–	◌̂	1) for *-m* (as in *âme* "amme" 503, *lêmyn* "lemmyn" 483, *ancôbꝛrys* "ancombrys" 266, *ʒŷmo* "thymmo" 1029). 2) for *-n* (as in *hâ* "han" 1, *pê* "pen" 2029, *hōbꝛôkyas* "hombronkyas" 121, *chûgſyons* "chungsyons" 208, *nŷg* "nyng" 269).
◌̄	◌̄	◌̄	◌̄	1) a contraction mark (as in *iħu* "Ihesu" 141, *iꝛłem* "Ierusalem" 853). 2) a graphic stroke with no meaning, often used in final position (as in *pegħ* "pegh" 61, *arałł* "arall" 670, *aꝛluth̄* "arluth" 127). 3) for *-m* (as in *dāpnyaf* "dampnyaf" 271, *lēmyn͛* "lemmyn" 43, *hōbꝛôkyas* "hombronkyas" 121, *rū* "rum" 926, *ʒȳmo* "thymmo" 5). 4) for *-n* (as in *whās* "whans" 3, *hēna* "henna" 39, *cōvyctíjs* "convyctijs" 139, *leū* "leun" 691, *vȳno* "vynno" 9). 5) for *-r-* (as in *tā* "tra" in line 1053, likely a correction after writing *ta* rather than *tr*).
◌̂	◌̂	◌̂	◌̂	1) a contraction mark (as in *Iħus* "Ihesus" 337. 2) for *-m* (as in *gŷmys* "gymmys" 1445). 3) for *-n* (as in *pê* "pen" 1507, *nŷg* "nyng" 1225). 4) a meaningless decoration on the letter *y* in CF.
◌͛	◌͛	◌͛	◌͛	1) a contraction mark (as in *ihus͛* "Ihesus" 976, *ihu͛* "Ihesu" 11). 2) for *-e* (as in *dr͛* "dre" 38). 3) for *-m* (as in *ʒu͛* "thum" 440). 4) for *-n* (as in *pora͛* "poran" 526, *de͛* "den" 49, *ſpyr͛* "spyrn" 1633, *leu͛* "leun" 21, *t͛my͛* "termyn" 528, *y͛tre* "yntre" 1672). 5) for *-nt* (as in *oỹmet͛* "oynment" 1877, *t͛mot͛* "tormont" 524). 6) for *-s* (as in *ꝛeſon͛* "resons" 939, perhaps unusually). 7) for *-w* (as in *de͛* "dew" 2040, perhaps unusually).

8) a meaningless decoration (as in *palm̄* “palm” 231, *dreyſon̄* “dreyson” 987, *pehadur̄* “pehadur” 59).

a glyph variant of the above, basically an OVERCURL having the same dot as the FERMATA (as in *tenewē* “tenewen” 1885, *baſcon̄* “bascon” 4, *leū* “leun” 69).

N *N* –

n *n* n n

O *O* –

o *o* o o

P *P* –

p *p* p p

ꝑ *ꝑ* – 1) for *par* (as in *padſ* “paradis” 1544, *ꝑna* “parna” 31, *ꝑys* “parys” 141).

2) for *per* (as in *gweſꝑ* “gwesper” 1836, *ꝑnys* “pernys” 349, *ſꝑn* “spern” 1058).

ꝓ *ꝓ* – 1) for *per* (as in *ſoꝓ* “soper” 332; probably an error for *ſoꝑ*).

2) for *pro* (as in *ꝓvas* “provas” 48; this is the usual meaning of *ꝓ*).

q *q* –

R *R* in CF 37 the *R* is unusual but clearly neither *r* nor ꝛ.

r *r* generally used initially, medially, and finally.

ꝛ ꝛ r-rotunda, generally used initially, medially, and finally; in other languages this letterform originally followed *o* and never occurred in initial position. There is no phonetic distinction between *rag* and *ꝛag*.

superscript r-rotunda has various uses:

1) for *ar* (as in *mᷣ* “mar” 44, *kepᷣ* “kepar” 310, *wᷣ* “war” 101).

2) for *er* (as in *aſkemᷣ ha* at line 1800; the editor has emended this to “a’s kemeras”).

3) for *ur* (as in *creatᷣ* “creatur” 1204, *natᷣ* “natur” 1662).

originally used for Latin -*er*, the zigzag has various uses:

1) for *ar* (as in *m͛nas* “marnas” 656, *dyn͛* “dynar” 282, *lau͛* “lauar” 618).

2) for *e* (as in *hono͛* “honore” 128, *d͛* “dre” 238).

3) for *er* (as in *lad͛* “lader” 302, *hag͛* “hager” 374, *m͛wel* “merwel” 560, *man͛* “maner” 100, *t͛myn* “termyn” 381, *myg͛tn* “mygtern” 813, *Iuc͛ts* “ju[s]ters” 1241).

				4) for *re* (as in *p̑derſ* "prederys" 148, *p̑goth* "pregoth" 179, *p̑ſon̄* "preson" 985, in *ynt̑* "yntre" 1370). 5) for *ry* (as in *meſt̑nges* "meystrynges" 810). 6) in error for otiose ◌̑ (as in *owȓ*, recte *owȓ* "owr" 124).
ȣ̃	ȣ̃	–	ȣ̃	originally used for Latin *-ur*, this character has various uses: 1) for *ar* (as in *p̃* "par" 'by' 356). 2) for *eur* (as in *m̃* "meur" 33, *ṽ* "veur" 61). 3) for *or* (as in *g̃ʒyn* "gorthyn" 39, *l̃o* "loor" 'moon' 1684, *p̃rſ* "porrys" 1649, *t̃mont* "tormont" 1706, *w̃th* "worth" 108, *w̃ʒye* "worthye" 228). 4) for *our* (as in *tꝛeyt̃* "treytour" 1915). 5) for *r* (as in *dõ* "dor" 'earth' 262). 6) for *ur* (as in *l̃e* "leur" 63, 1138, *traytẽ* "trayteur" 962, *gõ* "gour" 525, *tebeṫt-lycõ* "tebel-lycour" 1611, *p̃* "pur" 'truly' 57, *p̃pur* "purpur" 1282, *p̃re* "purre" 720, *s̃* "sur" *traytõ* "traitour" 782, *treytõs* "treytours" 1250). 7) for *wr* (as in *dõ* "dowr" 357, *l̃o* "lowr" 'enough' 407).
S	*S*	–	S	
s	*s*	ſ	s	generally used at the ends of words, sometimes of morphemes, accidentally elsewhere; at line 1464 we have corrected *crowspꝛen* with the expected *crowſpꝛen*.
ſ	*ſ*	ſ	ſ	long-s, generally used initially and medially.
ꞩ	*ꞩ*	–	ꞩ	1) for *ser* (as in *ꞩuabyṫt* "seruabyll" 150, *ꞩuye* "seruye" 1440, *ꞩuys* "seruys" 115). 2) for *spe* (as in *ꞩꝛys* "sperys" at line 137; likely an error; the MS does not otherwise have *ſp* or other ligatures).
T	*T*	–	T	
t	*t*	τ	t	
ᵗ	*ᵗ*	–	ᵗ	for *yth* (as in *vᵗ* "vyth" 385); a common English abbreviation was *wᵗ* "with".
Ꞇ	*Ꞇ*	–	Ꞇ	the insular form of T.
u	*u*	u	u	does not occur in initial position in either text.
V	*V*	–	V	serves as the capital of both *u* and *v*.
v	*v*	v	v	
Ỽ	*Ỽ*	Ỽ	–	Middle Welsh *v*, (as in *ỽyꝩy* "vywy" CF 36).
W	*W*	–	W	
w	*w*	–	w	
Ꝩ	*Ꝩ*	–	Ꝩ	Anglicana *W*, used in free variation with *W*.
ꝩ	*ꝩ*	ꝩ	ꝩ	Anglicana *w*, used in free variation with *w*.

x	*x*	–		
Y	*Y*	–		
y	*y*			
ʒ	*ʒ*			yogh, used in Middle English for [ç], [ɣ], [j], [w], and [x]; in later Middle English and Middle Scots the glyphs for *ʒ* and *z* fell together, as they did in Cornish. 1) for *th* [ð] (as in *eſeʒa* "esetha" 102, *ʒoʒo* "thotho" 72). 2) for *th* [θ] (as in *coweʒe* "cowethe" 324; *w̃ʒyp* "worthyp" 93, *yʒo* "ytho" 790; note *ʒeʒorhas* "thethorhas" [ðəˈθɔrhəs] 1941). 3) as a learned spelling in the Middle English loanword "dyght-", which in PA is written *dygt-* ×4, *dyʒgt-* ×6, *dyʒgtht-* ×3, *dyʒgt̃ht-* ×1; *dyſk-* at line 1082 is an error for *dyʒgt-*.
z	*z*			the glyph is identical with that of *ʒ*; used in *greyz* CF 18, *bazon* 'basin' 357, *nazare*, *nazary* 'Nazareth' 549, 2037.
ꝭ	*ꝭ*	–		"is", originally used for Latin *-is*, this character has various uses: 1) for *-as* (as in *agꝭ* "agas" 295). 2) for *-es* (as in *drꝭ* "dres" 186). 3) for *-is* (as in *padꝭ* "paradis" 1544, *ʒꝭ* "this" 86). 4) for *-ys* (as in *florꝭ* "florys" 231, *leverꝭ* "leverys" 113).
ꝯ	*ꝯ*	–		originally used for Latin *con* (a similar raised character ꝰ was used for *-us*) this character came to be used in Britain for *-us*; it has two uses: 1) for *-os* (as in *gallꝯ* "gallos" 556). 2) for *-us* (as in *angꝯ* "angus" 1788, *dꝯ* "dus" 673, *Nycodemꝯ* "Nycodemus" 1868, *tꝯ* "tus" 795).

3.5 TRANSCRIPTION CONVENTIONS

There are three kinds of transcriptions in this book. A close palaeographic transcription is found in Chapter 4. At the top of the left-hand pages in Chapter 6 is the normalized text in Standard Cornish; at the bottom of the pages in Chapter 6, the expanded or quotable transcription is given, where abbreviations and special characters are written out in full (so *aſdyeꝛbȳnyas* becomes *as dyerbynnyas*, *ſc̓ꝭꝭ* becomes *scrifys*, and *t̃moƀ* becomes *tormont*). Various brackets are used in the two transcriptions to show words which have been emended editorially for sense. In Chapter 4, word division is as in the manuscript, but in Chapter 6 word division is given according to our understanding of Cornish morphology and grammar, and follows the modern spelling in Standard Cornish. In the indexes in Chapter 7, words are written in the palaeographic spelling but following the corrected expanded text.

In the transcription I have modified slightly the conventions suggested by M. B. Parkes (1979:xxviii–xxix) and used the symbols listed below.

⌜ ⌝ *top half brackets* enclose ⌜words and letters⌝ which have been inserted by the scribe either between the lines, or in the margin.

⌞ ⌟ *bottom half brackets* enclose ⌞words and letters⌟ which have been inserted by someone other than the principal scribe either between the lines, or in the margin.

[ ] *square brackets* enclose [words and letters] which have been deleted by the scribe by means of crossing out, erasure, or expunctuation (the use of a dot below a letter to show its deletion).

⁅ ⁆ *square brackets with quill* enclose ⁅words and letters⁆ which appear to have been deleted by someone other than the principal scribe.

⟦ ⟧ *white square brackets* enclose erroneous ⟦words and letters⟧ which should be deleted though they have not been deleted by the principal scribe. These are deleted in the expanded text.

⟬ ⟭ *white tortoise shell brackets* enclose erroneous ⟬words and letters⟭ which should be replaced by a corrected text. These are replaced by items within ⸨double parentheses⸩ in the expanded text.

⟨ ⟩ *angle brackets* enclose ⟨words and letters⟩ which have been supplied in the transcription where the manuscript is deficient through damage, where letters have been hidden by the binding, or where blots have obscured the letters. Where traces of the letter are still visible in the manuscript, the supplied letter has been printed in roman type. Where no traces of the letter remain, the supplied letter has been printed in *italic* type. Where it has not been possible to determine the nature of the missing letters from the context, dots have been supplied to indicate the approximate number of letters which would fit into the space available.

《 》 *double angle brackets* enclose 《words and letters》 which have been supplied either where the scribe has omitted them by mistake or where he has omitted them on purpose but has failed to use the appropriate mark of abbreviation.

⸨ ⸩ *double parentheses* enclose ⸨words and letters⸩ which replace evident errors in the text itself. In the palaeographic transcription the uncorrected text is given within ⟬white tortoise shell brackets⟭.

⟅ ⟆ *white parentheses* enclose ⟅words and letters⟆ which have been supplied by someone other than the principal scribe, even by someone non-contemporaneous. When this cannot be read clearly, an attempt is given in italic type.

{ } *curly brackets* enclose {notes or stage directions} written by the principal scribe (typically in Latin or English).

⦃ ⦄ *white curly brackets* enclose ⦃notes or stage directions⦄ added by someone other than the principal scribe, or similar notes added by the editors in the translation.

| *vertical line* used where a word or line of verse is divided between two folios.

Parkes offers the following note on palaeographical terms:

> A *script* is the model which the scribe has in his mind's eye when he writes, whereas a *hand* is what he actually puts down on the page. The *duct* of a hand is the distinctive manner in which strokes are traced upon the writing surface: it represents the combination of such factors as the angle at which the pen was held in relation to the way in which it was cut, the degree of pressure applied to it, and the direction in which it was moved. A *stroke* is a single trace made by the pen on the page; if the stroke has no sudden change of direction, it is made in a single *movement*. A *broken stroke* is made in more than one movement, the direction of the pen being changed suddenly without its being lifted from the page. A *minim stroke* is the shortest and simplest stroke: that used to form the letters **i**, **m**, **n**, **u**. An *otiose stroke* is a superfluous stroke, one which does not form part of a letter, and which does not indicate an abbreviation. *Biting* occurs when two adjacent contrary curved strokes coalesce, as when **b** is closely followed by **o**. The terms used when describing letter forms are best elucidated by examples: the letter **b** comprises a *stem* or mainstroke which rises above the general level of the other letters (*ascender*) and a *lobe* made with a curved stroke to the right of the stem; the letter **p** a *descender* and a lobe; the letter **h** an ascender and a *limb*; the letter **t** a *shaft* and a *headstroke*. The *body* of a letter form is that part which does not include an ascender or descender. (Parkes 1979:xxvi)

Duct is more commonly called *ductus*. The example of "biting"—which Derolez (2003:xx) calls "fusion"—described here would be **bo**. The general level above which an ascender ranges is known in typography as *x-height*.

Michael Everson

4
PALAEOGRAPHIC TRANSCRIPTIONS

The palaeographic transcription differs from the expanded, quotable text in a few ways. The most common of these differences has to do with word division. What is now considered a single word was often written as two (MS *a ȝesempys* → *aȝesempys*); the opposite also holds true (*resteffo* → *res teffo*). The scribe often fused verbal particles with the verb differently from the way in which we do it following modern analysis (*mar sos* → *mars os*; *may then* → *mayth en*; *may ȝese* → *mayȝ ese*; *y ȝesa* → *yȝ esa*; *nŷngo* → *nyng o*; *nŷ io* → *nyni o*.[1] Alterations like these have been made silently in the expanded text, unless a word division changes a medial long *ſ* into a final *s*, for instance. Hyphenation of the particles *-ma* and *-na* and other hyphenation such as that in *a-ugh* and other compounds has also been made silently in the expanded text. Apostrophes, such as those which change *ay* to *a'y*, have not been introduced into the expanded text.

Alterations which are marked in the text generally have to do with corrections of errors in the manuscript, which chiefly means words omitted, words repeated (leading to constructions with too few or too many syllables) or other errors, such as places where the rhyme is defective, where the letters represent the wrong tense, etc. Many of these corrections have been made by previous editors of the text. In the palaeographic text here in Chapter 4, our own additions are given between ⟨angle brackets⟩ (marked the same in the expanded text in Chapter 6); things the scribe should have added are marked with 《double angle brackets》 (marked the same in the expanded text); things the scribe should have omitted are marked with ⟦white square brackets⟧ (deleted silently in the expanded text); other more serious errors are marked in the palaeographic text with ⟬white tortoise shell brackets⟭ (marked with ⸨double parentheses⸩ in the expanded text). Thus *glot⟦e⟧ny* → *glotny* is left unmarked (line 97), but *fa⟬ſe⟭* → *fa⸨s⸩* is marked (line 758), ⟬*kuȝytt*⟭ → ⸨*kull*⸩ is marked (line 764, ⟬*y ny a*⟭ → ⸨*ethow ny*⸩ is marked (line 791), and *woȝye《s》* → *woȝye《s》* is marked (line 803).

1 A noteworthy example is at line 259, where the scribe has written *I ȝeſa*, which we would analyse now as *Yth esa*; the metre requires two syllables only, so we know this must have been read as what we would now write as *Th'esa*—an early indication of the reduction of /ə'θɛzə/ to /'θɛzə/.

Where possible the expansions use full or similar spellings already in the manuscript.

4.1 *THE CHARTER FRAGMENT*

The layout of *The Charter Fragment* has brackets connecting most of the paired verses; the first 12 lines have tail-rhymes which are shown here by indentation. The rest of the lines are paired except for lines 13–16, 27–30, and 38–39, which are run on; I have used the bullet to show the division between those. Stanza division is given as in the edition though only stanza 2 is set off by extra space in the manuscript. For the edition, see p. 156 below. For the facsimile, see p. 101 below.

Darn an Chartour

1 Golfoug tŷ coweʒ [1v]
bŷʒ na boꝛʒ meʒ
  d⟨y⟩ŷſkẏn ha po⸢wes⸣
ha ʒymo dus nes
mar͛ coʒes ʒe les
  ha ʒys ŷ rof mowe⸢s⸣
ha feſt onan dek
genes mar͛ a plek
  ha tanha ẏ
kŷmmerry ʒoʒ wrek
sconye ʒy⟨s *n*y vek⟩
  ha tŷ a vŷʒ hy

2 Hŷ a vŷʒ gwreg tŷ da • ʒŷs ʒe ſŷnſŷ⟦chy⟧
pur͛ wŷr͛ a lauara • ha govŷn worty

3 Ƚemen ẏʒ toꝛn mŷ af rɔ
ha war͛ en greẏz mŷ an tɔ
nag vs ŷ far͛
an barʒma ʒɔ pons tamar͛
⟦ad⟧ mẏ ad pes wortẏ bŷʒ da
ag ol ʒɔ voʒ hŷ a wra
rag flog yw ha genſŷ doʒ
ha⟦ gaffŷ⟧ ʒɔ gafus ŷ boʒ
kenes mos ʒŷmmo ŷmmẏug
eug aƚema ha fŷſtŷnŷug

4 Dallaʒ a var᷑ infreʒ dar᷑war᷑ • oun ma ⸢poꝛʒo⸣
ef emſettẏꝯ worʒꝯ⟦ſẏ⟧ • kam na veʒo

5 Mar᷑ aʒherg ʒŷs gul nep tra
lauar᷑ ʒe ſẏ bẏʒ nŷ venna
lauar᷑ ʒoʒo gwra marmennŷʒ
awos a gallo na wra t̄ vẏʒ
in vrna yʒ sens ʒꝯ ves meŷſtres
hedẏr᷑ bywy hag arluʒes

6 Ras o ganſo rꝯ⟦ n⟧offeren
Curtes ẏw ha debon᷑ • ʒŷs dregŷn ny ⸢wra⸣
mar᷑ an kefẏʒ in danger᷑
sen⟦ſ⟧ꝯ faſt in della

4.2 *PASCON AGAN ARLUTH*

The layout of *Pascon agan Arluth* has brackets connecting the four-line stanzas, but nothing indicates the rhymes per se. Each line in the manuscript contains two metrical lines; the lines are divided by a verse divider ⁒ (see § 3.3.3 above) or solidus /; a bullet • has been used editorially to indicate the division where the solidus was not written in the manuscript. For the edition, see p. 160 below. For the facsimile, see p. 104 below.

Pascon agan Arluth

1 Ꞇays ha mab hâ ſpeꝛis ſans ⁒ wy abys a levn̄ golon [1r]
Re wꝛonte ʒeugh̄ gꝛas ha whās / ʒe wolſowas y baſcon̄
Ha ʒȳmo gꝛas ha ſkyans • the ʒerevas par᷑ ⟦lauarow⟧
may ſo ʒe thu ʒe woꝛʒyans / ha ſylwans ʒe̋ ⟦enevow⟧

2 Suel a vȳno bos ſylwys / golſowens ow lauarow
a ihū del ve helheys / war᷑ an bys avel carow
Ragon̄ menough̄ rebekꝭ / ha dyſpꝭſijs yn harow
yn gꝛowys gans kentrow faſtꝭ / peynys bys pā ve marow

3 Du ſur᷑ dre v̇tu an tas / ʒȳny a ʒyttyas gweꝛas
En mab dre y ſkyans bꝛas / pan gemeꝛt kyg a weꝛhas
han ſpeꝛys ſans leū a ꝛas / dre y ʒadđ may fe gurꝭ
Goʒaff paynys pā vŷnas / neb na ylly gull peghes

4 **A**n dus vas a ʒeſerya / ʒeʒe gulas nef o kyllys
gans aga gaꝛm hag olua / ih̄us ċſt a ve mevijs
may ſȳnas díjſkȳna / yn gweꝛhas ha bos genys
gans y gyk agan ꝑna / Aꝛluth̄ du gwyn agan bys

5 **I**hũ ċſt m̃ gerenſe / ʒe vab den a ʒyſweʒas
an vgheld᷍ may ʒeſe / ʒⓔ bys pan deyſkȳnas
Pehadoꝛyon ꝛag ꝑna / o deſevíjs dꝛ̃ ſatnas [1v]
ꝛag hēna g̃ʒyn neffra / ih̄us neb agā ꝑnas

6 **A** peynys a wotheuys / ny ve ꝛagtho y honā
lēmyn ꝛag pobyll̄ an bys / pā vons y keffꝰ m̃ wan
an ioull̄ ʒe adam kewſys / an avel te kem̂ ta⟦m⟧
a vell̄ du y fethyth̄ gurys / pā yn ꝓvas nŷ io mā

7 **W**ꝛ lyꝛgh̄ mab dⓔ ʒe begha / ꝛeſon pꝛag y ſe prȳnys
yw ih̄us ċſt ʒe oꝛdna / yn neff y vonas tregys
y vos kyllys ny vȳna / y doull̄ ganſo o tewlys
ꝛag hēna ʒe bob dyʒgthtya / foꝛth̄ a rug ʒe vos ſylwys

8 **K**yn na goff den ſkentyll̄ p̃ / parꝰ del won lauaraff ʒys
yn tre du ha pehadurꝰ / acoꝛd del ve kemeꝛys
ꝛag bonas gôn pegh̄ m̃ v̂ / mayn yn treʒe a ve gurys
eff o ċſt a theth̄ ʒⓔ lē / mab du ha den yw kyffrꝭ

9 **R**agon y peſys y das / oll̄ y ſoꝛ may fe gevys
gans y goꝛff dre beynys bꝛas / agā pegh may ſo prēnys
mab marea leũ a ꝛas / oll̄ y voth a ve clewys
ha kȳmys a theſeꝛyas / ʒoʒo eff a ve gꝛontꝭ

10 **I** vam pan yn drehevys / hay vos deueʒꝭ ʒe oys
gull̄ penans ef a peſys / hēna gāſo nŷ io poys
⟨*dew vgons*⟩ dyth̄ ow penys / y ſpeynas y gyk hay woys [2r]
⟨*ha*⟩ woteweth ꝛag denſys / eff an geve awell̄ boys

11 ⟨**H**⟩an ioull̄ hēna pan glewas / y demptye a brederys
⟨h⟩a ʒoʒo y tysqueʒas / cals meyn hay leueꝛys
Maꝛ⟦ ſ⟧os mab du leũ a ꝛas / an veyn ma guꝛa baꝛa ʒꝭ
ih̄c ċſt parꝰ del vȳnas / ʒoʒo ef a w̃thebys

12 **M**ab dē heb ken ys baꝛa / nȳ geuas oll̄ y vewnas
lēmē yn lauarow da / a the ȝe w̃th an dremas 92
dre w̃ȝyp ċſt yn vꝛna / lēmyn ny a yll̄ gwelas
lauaꝛ du maga del wꝛa / neb a vȳno y glewas 96

13 **G**ans glot⟦e⟧ny ef pan welas / cam na ylly y dolla
en tebell̄ el a vȳnas / yn ken mañ y dēptya 100
wᵗ penakyll̄ yn goꝛas / dyantell̄ ȝe efeȝa
a vgh̄ eglos tek yn wlas / an yſetva y ȝeſa 104

14 **A**n ioul ȝe gryſt a gewſys / ẏ delma ꝛag y dēptye
a hanas y thew ſċfys / bos eleth̄ w̃th ȝe wyȝe 108
ꝛag own y⟦w⟧ ȝom deſevys / ȝe droys woꝛth meyn ȝe dochye
mᵈ⟦ ſ⟧os mab du a v̑ brys / díjſkyn ha ȝē dor ke 112

15 **I**h̄us ċſt a leuerſ / ȝe thu ny goth thys tēptye
yn neb ehan a ꝑuys / lēmyn ꝑſt y honore 116
Ha whath an Ioul a dewlys / towll̄ ken mañ m⟨ᶜa⟩lle [2v]
dꝛe neb foꝛth̄ a govaytſ / guȝyll̄ ȝy gowſys tryle 120

16 **A** lene yn hōbꝛōkyas / vghell̄ waꝛ ben vn meneth̄
ha ȝoȝo y tyſquethas / owr hag aꝛghans gwels ha gwe⟨*th̄*⟩ 124
ha kȳmys yn bys vs vas / yn meth̄ an ioul te a feth̄
ha me ad wꝛa aꝛluth̄ bꝛas / ow honor maꝛ mȳnyth̄ 128

17 **I**hūs ċſt a leuerſ / y vos ſcryſys yn lyffꝛow
yn pub gwythres ycoth̄ thys / goꝛȝye ȝe ȝu hay hanow 132
Ke ȝe ves omſcumvnys / ȝe ȝyveyth ⟦veth̄⟧ yn tewolgow
the veſtry a vyth̄ leȝys / neffre wᵗ an enevow 136

18 **A**n ioul a trylyas ꝑꝛys / hag eth ȝy tylleꝛ tythy
teꝛgweyth̄ y fe cōvyctíjs / evn yw ȝyn y voleythy 140
ȝe ih̄u may fons pys / ȝy gōfoꝛtye yredy
an neff y fe danvenys / ȝe w̃th an tas eleth dy 144

19 **H**a ſatnas gans y antell̄ / hay ſcherewneth̄ hay goȳtſ
ċſt mab an aꝛluth vghell̄ / y dēptye pan ꝑderſ 148
beſy yw ȝys bos vuell̄ / ha ꝑuabyll̄ yth ꝑuys
m⟦ā⟧no allo an tebell̄ / ogas ȝys bonas trylys 152

20 **R**ag y hylleꝛ eꝛvyꝛ̄ / hay welas yn ſuredy
y vos ꝑſt w̃th ȝe vetye / ȝe veth ȝys ha belyny
⟨T⟩e na yllyth̄ omweȝe / vn pꝛes yn geyth̄ na peghy [3r]
pan omſettyas ȝe dēptye / guȝyll̄ pegh̄ neb na ylly

21 **D**el yw ſc̍fys ꝑſt yma / adꝛo ȝȳny gan⟦ſo⟧try
maꝛa kyll̄ ȝe woꝛth an da / ȝe weȝyll̄ drok agan dry
folle yn ta y whela / ys del wꝛa lyon̄ y pꝛay
drey de̅ yn peyn a calla / neffre ny vnſa moy ioy

22 **G**ans an ioul kyn ſy temptíjs / anoȝo na ro dŷme
ꝛag cô̂foꝛt yw hēna ȝys / ſc̍fys yw ȳ leas le
yt allos y vos goꝛꝛys / kyffrꝭ ſeuell̄ ha cothe
ha ganſo kŷfes tewlys / te a yll̄ ſeuel aꝛte

23 **I**hu̅ c̍ſt ŷ pow a dro / pub eꝛoll̄ pꝛegoth a wre
han v̍tu an ꝑgoth o / mab de̅ ȝe aſe peghe
ha gevys may fe ȝoȝo / kyffrys y begh̄ hay fyltye
degꝭ na ve ȝe woꝛto / gulas nef a roys ȝe gen re

24 **B**enegas yw neb a gaꝛ̄ / du drꝭ pub tꝛa vs yn bys
hag a woȝaffo yn whaꝛ̄ / ȝoȝo kȳmys vs oꝛdnys
bo clevas bo peth keſcaꝛ̄ / po dre breſon ꝑſonys
ol en da han drok kepar / ȝe ih̄u beȝēs gꝛaffys

25 **I**h̄u c̍ſt yn pow may the / eff a ſawye an glevyon
dal na boȝaꝛ ny aſe / nag omlauaꝛ̄ na gonon
na claff vyth ow crowethe / m̄ peſy a leu̅ golon
whare ſawijs y feȝe / del vȳna c̍ſt y honon

26 **P**an welas en ethewon / bos c̍ſt au cuthyll̄ meyſtry [3v]
ow care eȝomogyon̄ / hag a neȝe na wre vry
ꝛag hêna an vuſcogyon / oꝛto a boꝛȝas avy
dre vꝛaſt̄ bꝛas yn golon / y chûgſyons y ȝeſtrewy

27 **D**evſull̄ blegyow pan eſe / yn myſk y abeſtely
y wreg ȝe re a neȝe / mos ȝen dre ha degylmy
an aſen ha dry ganſe / ha leuerell̄ yredy
m̄ teffa tus ha gweȝe / bos ȝe ȝu ȝe wull̄ gŷſy

28 **D**el yꝛghys ihūs ȝeȝe / y a rug a ȝeſympys
ol y voth ef del vӯne / an aſen a ve keꝛghys
warᷣ neȝy ⟦ꝛag⟧ eſeȝe / dyllas pan a ve gorrys
ꝛag morogeth̄ a vӯne / ȝe Cyte ȝe vos goꝛthijs

29 **M**u⟦ꝛ̄⟧ a dus ha benenas / a ieꝛl̄m yn dre
eꝛbӯ ċſt ꝛag y welas / y eth ha ꝛag y w̃ȝye
wᶻ an foꝛth̄ dyllas a les / a ve gurrſ ȝe ꝛagthe
palm ha florſ kekyffirſ / eꝛ y byn degſ a ve

30 **I** helwys a leu golon / gans m̃ ioy ha lowene
yn hanow du yn treȝon / benegas yw neb a the
ċſt a gafas goꝛkorian / yn templys a beꝛth̄ ŷ drᷣ
ef a rug ȝeȝe y ſcon / monas yn mes a lene[2]

31 **E**n ſcheꝛewys a ſoꝛꝛas / ꝛag bonas ċſt honorſ
Ha bos y obeꝛ m̃ vꝛas / ha drſ an bys ol̄l notijs
gruſſons cuſyl̄l na go vas / ꝛag may ſo ihūs dyſwrſ
Ha kӯmys y an cablas / may ſe an dre ⟨*crehyllys*⟩ [4r]

32 **E**n gusyl o may ſe drſ / ȝe ꝛag ċſt peha⟨*dures*⟩
ol ȝy voth may rollo bres / a neȝy del ve ȝe gr⟨*es*⟩
ꝛag an lays ȝӯny es / a vyn y dampnye poꝛres
ym meȝēs y[o] foꝛth nӯ ges / may hallo bos deflam gurſ

33 **T**hen tylleꝛ ċſt re dethye / hâ eȝevꝫon o dygnas
⟦I ⟧ȝeſa an veny ganſe / parſ ens ȝy huhuȝas
hedre vons y ov plentye / ih̄us yn dō̃ a ſcryſas
ha dre v̇tu an ſċſe / peb ȝe ves a ōdēnas

34 **P**an eȝons ol̄l ȝe wary / ancôbꝛys y rebea
pema y meth ċſt ȝyȝy / neb a vӯ ȝe guhuȝa
denvyth̄ nŷ ges yn meȝy / ih̄us a gewſys aꝛta
me nyth dāpnyaf yredy / ha na wꝛa na moy pegha

---

2 ⌊{the five laſt lynes engliſhed inſerted}⌋
⌊Chriſt found ydle fooliſh, in the temple w^th^in the town
and he made them, ym̄idiatly, to goe out from thence
The [...*ſchen y..s*] ⟦*ſcribes* ~ ~⟧ was wrathfull, be cauſe ⌜Chriſt⌝ was honored
and becauſe his worke was ſoe great, and through ye world ⌜now⟨*n*⟩⌝
they tooke counſell y^t^ was ⌜not⌝ good, that Ieſus ſhould be undo⌜ne⌝⌋

35 Benyn dyr̾ v̾ cheꝛyte / y box ꝛych⟦e⟧ leu̾ a yly
a vgh̄ c̓ſt ꝛag y vntye / hy a vȳnas y derry
coꝛf ihūs ꝛag cōfoꝛtye / gures p̃ ſur̾ o yredy
Iudas ſcharyoth a⟦ſ⟧cable / ha gans m̃ a falſury

36 Iudas fals a leueꝛys / trehans dyn̾ a vone
en box oll̄ beʒens gweꝛthys / a vos de̾ ꝛg y rāne
the vohoſogyon̄ yn bys / gwel vya ys y ſcolye
ih̄us c̓ſt a w̃thebys / y gowſys ef a woʒye

37 Na thegough̄ foꝛ yn golon̄ / w̓ neb a vȳ ow ſawye
ow theꝛmyn̄ a the yn ſcon̄ / genough̄ me nvm byth trege
Wy a gyff bohoſogyon̄ / pub er̾ w̓nough̄ ow caꝛme
pan vynnough̄ agſ̓ honon̄ / wy a yll̄ gull̄ da ʒeʒe

38 W⟨hare y ſo⟩ꝛas Iudas / ny gewſy dr̾ geryte [4v]
⟨l*emyn*⟩ ꝛag cafos ꝛan vꝛas / an pencon̄ maꝛ a calle
⟨ef *o* h⟩aꝛlot tebel was / woteweth lad̾ vye
ʒe̾ eʒewon̄ y ponyas / c̓ſt y aꝛluth ⟦ꝛag⟧ gweꝛʒe

39 Eff a leverſ̓ ʒeʒe / pyth a vȳnough why ʒe ry
ha me a ꝛa ʒeugh ſpedye / ow cafos c̓ſt yredy
yfons vnveꝛ ȳ treʒe / kep̓ ha del wovyny
⟦xxx⟧ a vone / yn vn payment y wrens ry

40 Aꝛte Iudas ow tryle / gwan wecoꝛ nȳ geve p̓
ny yl den vyth amontye / myns a gollas ȳ chyffaꝛ
⟦woꝛth⟧ ih̄u ef a fecle / kep̓ ha pā ve hegaꝛ
yn deweth ny acoꝛdye / y golon gans y lauaꝛ

41 Gans iudas del o tewlys / drey ihūs fur̾ del vŷne
gās c̓ſt y tho cowethys / byth nȳ gens y coweʒe
en [d]gyth o deyow hablys / may fēne ihūs ſopye
gans an re yn y ꝑuys / w̓ an bys reʒeweſſe

42 Dew ʒe̾ c̓ſt a ʒanvonas / ʒe beꝛna boys ha dewas
an keth rena a ſpedyas / han ſoꝑ a ve parſ̓
c̓ſt w̃th an goyn a waꝛnyas / dre onan bos treſon gurſ̓
aꝛluth du y a aꝛmas / pv a yl hêna bonas

43 **I**hûs cᷓſt a woꝛȝebys / ow tybbry genē yma
pub onan ol a ylwys / aꝛluth du yv me hena
ha ihūs a woꝛȝebys / am ſcudel dybbry a wꝛa
gwef vyth̄ pan ve⟦va⟧ genys / a doꝛ y vam ȝē by⟦ſ⟧ma

44 **D**u a ſonas an baꝛa / ȝe ꝛag y abeſtely
ow hoꝛf a ve yw hēma / yn meth cᷓſt ſur ꝛagough wy
ꝑnys a beꝛth yn by⟦ſ⟧ma / dyſpꝛeſys haneth a vyth̄
an deppro gans cregyans da / gobeꝛ tek eff an geuyth [5r]

45 **H**an gwyn eſa wᷓ en foys / ef a rānas yn treȝa
yn meth cᷓſt ⟦hema yw⟧ goys / evough why ꝑ̃ cheryta
gans dõ gorrꝭ yn bazon • y wolhas aga garrow
⟦hyſſeas⟧ ys gureḡh ꝑ̃ wyn / del vȳna du caradow

46 **H**ēna pedyꝛ a ſconyas / ihûs ȝe wolhy y dreys
taw pedyꝛ te ny woȝas / yn meth cᷓſt pan dꝛa ꝛaf ȝys
mᷓ nyth wolhaff dre ow gras / yn nef ny veȝyth tregꝭ
ȳmeth pedyꝛ ȝym na as / troys na leyff na vo golhys

47 **I**hūs cᷓſt leū a bete / a leuerꝭ ȝē dowȝek
wy yv glan a bub fylte / mas nȳ iouḡh ol da na whek
bos Iudas ef a woȝye • ꝑ̃ hagᷓ ha moloȝek
an ioul ȳno re drecſe / may ȝo gweth agꝭ cronek

48 **I**n delma cᷓſt pan wreſſe / ȝe iudas y leuerꝭ
te ke yn vn fyſtene / ȝe voth may ſo colenwys
ꝛag an ᷓtmyn re deve / may ſyth an begel k⟦yll⟧ys
ha chechys yn tre dewle / han deves ȝe ves fijs

49 **K**yn fallens ol me a vᵗ / yn meth pedyꝛ yth ꝑuys
yn meth cᷓſt yn nos haneth / kȳs ys boys colyek clewys
pedᷓ te am naḡh ᷓtgweth • bythqueth aꝛluth na vef ȝys
yn meth pedᷓ tan ow feth / nyth nahaff kȳ fen leȝys

50 **I**n meth cᷓſt a ban rug ȝeugh / ᷓtnoyth fernoth ow holye
daveꝛ vyth wy ny ȝecſyuḡh / ȝe worre trevyth ȳne
betegyns wy ny woȝough / pā dra eȝom a⟦y⟧an be
aꝛluth guyꝛ a leūſouḡh / y a gowſys yn treȝe

51 Mas lẽmyn ꝛys yv porrꝭ / batayles kyns ys coſke [5v]
an geffo pows as gwyꝛꝛȝy̅s / ha ȝoȝo ꝑn⟪a̅⟫s cleȝe
fur͛ y ma ⟦dew ȝyn⟧ parys / y a leuerꝭ whare
hen yw lõ na moy ny rys / du a leuerꝭ aꝛte

52 Mab marya leū a ꝛas / ȝe͛ meneth olyff y ȝeth̄
hay ȝyſcyplys an ſewyas / yn meth ċſt yn nos haneth
golyough ha peſough ow ȝas / may hallough mos ȝy aſeth
na veȝough̄ temtíjs dygnas / ga̅s gow ha ga̅s ſcherewneth

53 Pet͛ androw ha Iowan / yn meth ċſt deugh holyough ve
bys yn meneth ha me gwan / tryſty̅s vs w̃th ow bluȝye
ȝe woꝛte vn lam beghan / y ȝeth peſy may halle
ȝy ȝas ⟦ŷ⟧ weth vgy a van / hag ef ꝛag own ow cre̅ne

54 Mab marya m̃ a beyn͛ / a woȝevy yn vꝛna
ꝛag ef a woȝya yn feyn / han kyg ny vy̅na he̅na
mes y ȝenſys o m̓ feyn / pub vr͛ ⟦an trylya ȝeȝa⟧
may ȝeth w̓ ben y ȝewleyn / ha peſy yn ketelma

55 Maꝛa ſew ȝe voth ow ȝas / guꝛa ȝe͛ payn ma ow gaſa
Mes beȝe̅s gurꝭ ȝe vy̅nas / aꝛluth du ȝe voth del ve
ȝy ȝyſcyplys y trylyas / y⟦f⟧cafas ol ow coſke
y̅meth ċſt vn pols golyas • ny yllough̄ ȝu͛ co̅foꝛtye

56 Ena ċſt fur as gaſas / hag eth aꝛta ȝe beſy
w̓ ben gleyn ȝe w̃th y das • del lauaꝛſa ꝛagon ny
y beynys o cref ha bꝛas / w̓noȝo heb y dylly
ꝛeſon o ꝛag ol an wlas / ef a woȝye y veꝛwy

57 In meth ċſt o du ha den / aꝛte ȝy abeſtely
golyough ha peſough yn ven / ꝛag own an ioul hay veſtry
C̄reſſe gwyth hag ef yn cren / y peſys du dylyꝛ⟪f⟫ vy [6r]
aꝛluth m̓ ny yl bos ken / beȝens kep̓ del vy̅ny

58 Ihu̅s ċſt dygonfoꝛtys / w̓ ben dewlyn͛ pan eſe
an nef y fe danuenys / el ȝoȝo ȝy gomfoꝛtye
mab du o ky̅mys grevíjs / ꝛag tomd͛ ef a weſe
dowr͛ ha goys yn kemeſkys / weys ċſt ꝛag ȝe geꝛe̅ſe

59 Cryſt kẙmys payn yn geve / angus tyn ha galaꝛow
mateth angoys ha dropye / wͭ y fas an caꝛadow
Den vyth ny yl amontye / na leueꝛell wͭ anow
oll myns peynys an geve / kyns ys y vonas maꝛow

60 Lēmyn ny a yl gwelas / hag eꝛvyr feſt yn ta
cryſt ʒe woʒaff dꝛ ʒēſys / M̃ a benans yn by⟦ſ⟧ma
ef ny ylly dre ʒewſys / goʒaff na nyll drok na da
ꝛag meſt o wͭ an bys / hag ol myns vs ef a ꝛa

61 Pan o y beſadow gurꝭ / ʒe dowʒek y leueꝛys
koſcough lēmyn mͥ⟦ ſ⟧ew pꝛys / powʒeſough wy yv grevíjs
tus vs ʒym ow tevones / yv gās ow thraytoꝛ dyſkꝭ
fatel dons thov hemeꝛes / ha del veʒaff hombꝛonkꝭ

62 Kepͥ du del leueꝛys / pan eſa ċſt ow peſy
Iudas eth yn y negꝭ / en ioul yv en hombꝛōky
ʒe eʒewan dyrryvys / del o y fynas fynſy
ſyndꝭ ve dre govaytꝭ / yn della yw leas huny

63 Then eʒewon pan doʒye / ⟦y leuys⟧ hag y[o] ov tos
me a grꝭ yn ta ſpedye / om negꝭ haneth yn nos
deugh geneff ha holyough ve / gothveʒough na rellough tros
Ha me a ꝛa the ċſt āme / may hallough y aſſwonvos

64 An pncꝭ eſa yn pow / gans Iudas a thanvonas [6v]
tus ven gweſkꝭ yn aꝛvow / kepͥ ha del ens ʒe gas
ganſe y a thuk golow / nos o ny welons ẙ fas
bys yn Ihus caꝛadow / y eth del dyſkas Iudas

65 Pan doʒyans bys yn tylleꝛ / may ʒeſe ċſt ow peſy
lowene ʒys a veſt / yn meth Iudas an bꝛathky
ʒoʒo y rug fekyl cheꝛ / hag y āme treweſy
ef a vẙne yn obeꝛ / gul ken ys del dyſwyʒy

66 Ihus a gewſys p̃ dek / Iudas ow ry te a vyn
dre ʒe vay a reyth mͥ whek / ʒe neb am t̃mot mͥ dyn
moll⟪a⟫ʒ den ha gõ ha gwrek / a ʒe poꝛa eꝛʒebyn
peynys ad wꝛa moꝛeʒek / yn yffaꝛn down pub t̃my

67 Ihūs cͥſt a wovŷnys / w̃th an bobyƚƚ a ȝeth dy
gans an fals yn y ꝑuys / pandꝛa yw a vŷnough wy
en rena a w̃ȝebys / ihūs yw an caff⟦ans⟧ ny
en aꝛluth a w̃ȝebys / me yw hȇna yredy

68 Puꝛ wyꝛ̂ drefen an vͥtu / an lauaꝛ cͥſt pan gowſas
neb a wheleugh why me yw / ȝe ves y a omdēnas
ꝛag own̄ y a gangyes lyw / ꝛag gwand̄ y a goȝas
yn trevᵗ y nȳ gens gyw / ȝe weȝyƚƚ drꝭ y vȳnas

69 Cryſt a wovynys aꝛte / oꝛth an eȝewon woky
agꝭ negꝭ pyth ywe / pv yw neb a weleugh wy
ih̄us cͥſt a⟦n⟧ nazare / an rena a w̃ȝeby
yn meth ih̄us me ywe / lȇmyn̄ gureugh̄ agꝭ meyſtry

70 Whare y an kemeres / hag an ſenſys yn treȝe [7r]
gans lauarow an ſcoꝛnyas / gallꝯ o gꝛōtꝭ ȝeȝe
ȝe weȝyƚƚ aga mȳnas / yn della ef a vȳne
may halle dre baynys bꝛas / m̃wel ꝛag ȝe gerēſe

71 Pedyꝛ an ⟦n⟧eyl tenewen / yn mes a dēnas cleȝe
hag a dꝛohas ryb an pē / ſcoveꝛn onā aneȝe
cͥſt a ſettyas yn tyen / an ſcoveꝛn aꝛte ȝe dre
hag an dyȝgthtyas p̃ lowen / maga tek del rebye

72 ⟦Goꝛ ȝe gleȝe ȳ y goyn⟧ / ȝe pedyꝛ cͥſt a yꝛghys
ꝛag dre gleȝe a veughe / dꝛ̂ gleȝe yfyth leȝys
dewȝek lygyon yn vn ꝛo / vye an nef danuenys
ha moy a mȳnē ȝȳmo / peſy ow ȝas p̃ baꝛys

73 Hag a pe yn della ve / neffre ny vean̄ fethys
yn vꝛna fateƚƚ vye / am bewnās del yw ſcͥfys
yn lyffrow yn leas le / dre brofuſy leuerys
ꝛeys yw porrꝭ heb ſtrevye / both ow ȝas ȝe vos ſewíjs

74 Ih̄us a gewſys aꝛte / why a theth ȝym yn aꝛvow
dre dreyſon yn vn ſcolchye / gans bocleꝛs ha cleȝyȝyow
thom kemeꝛes ȝom ſyndye / ⟪ha⟫ ȝom peynye bys yn crow
kep̃ ha ⟦del⟧ vena ve / an purra lad̄ yn pow

75 In agſ myſk pan eſen / lays du ȝeugh ow tyſky
gallꝰ nȳ geſe kême • ȝō cara na ȝom ſenſy
lēmyn deve ken t͛myn / ow ȝas rom growntyas ȝewy
lew͞ a beghas ny won͞ ken / ȝe weȝyll agſ meyſtry

76 In vꝛna y a colmas / y ȝefregh̄ faſt gans crono⟨w⟩ [7v]
en goys yn mes may taꝛȝas / del faſtſens en colmēn⟨*ow*⟩
ganſa y an hombꝛōkyas / yn pꝛys hant͛ nos heb wow
bys yn aga fryns annas / o vn Iutt͛ bꝛas ȳ pow

77 Tus c͛ſt ȝe ves a fyas / peb aydu p̃ voreȝek
ſaw ped͛ c͛ſt a holyas / abell avel vn ownek
ȝe dylleꝛ an p̄ns annas / ene y ȝeſe ſethek
oꝛto ef ⟦y a⟧ ſethas / may clewo leff ih̄us whek

78 En p̄ns ſcon a leueꝛis / te c͛ſt lau͛ ȝym plema
ȝe dus maꝛ vold re ȝyſſys / pꝛag na ȝons genas ôma
an lays a bregowthys / lēmyn dyſwe m͛ ⟦ ſ⟧yns da
ha ih̄us a woꝛȝebys / ef del vȳna yn vꝛna

79 Pur͛ apeꝛt hag yn golow / y leuerſ ow dyſkas
ow lays haw lauaꝛow / ſuel a vȳna y⟪s⟫ clewas
yn le may then yn trevow / yn ſplan me a⟦ſ⟧derevas
ny gowſyn yn tewolgow / a dryff tus yn vn hanas

80 Pan dr̃ a wovente ſe / ȝe w̃ȝaff ve ham lays
m͛ a mŷnyth gov⟦ŷ⟧ny / oꝛd en keth re as clewas
an rena ⟦a⟧ yl ȝe ȝyſky / yn della y re ȝyſkas
yn delma heb velyny / oꝛto Ih̄us a gowſas

81 Gans henna an eȝewon / onan yn ban a ſevys
hag a ꝛos ryb an ſcoveꝛn / box ȝe g͛ſt a ȝeſympys
ha ȝe Ihūs y honon / an haꝛlot a leueꝛys
pu a woꝛas yt colon / cows yn delma w̃th iuſtſ

82 In meth̄ ihūs yn vꝛna / m͛ a kewſys falſury [8r]
ha na blek genas hēna / ha fals te dok duſtuny
mes maꝛa kewſys yn ta / han gwreoneth y ſynſy
pꝛag omgwyſketh̄ ȳ delma / nȳ gyw m̃nas belyny

83 Ena m̃ a vylyny / ped̃ ȝe gryſt a welas
y ſcoꝛnye hay voxſcuſy / trewe yn y ȝewlagas
hag ef ꝛag own̄ ny ylly / gans ihũ kewſel geꝛ̃ vas
⟦hēna⟧ o poynt a falſury / deȝewys heb koweꝛas

84 Vn venȳ haꝛd a ȳnyas / ⟦w̃⟧ ped̃ y vos tregꝰ
gans ihũs ef a naghas / y aꝛluth a ȝeſympys
taw gans c̍ſt me ad welas / gurek arall a leuerꝰ
ped̃ aꝛta agowſas / bythqueth me nȳ aſwonys

85 M̂ a dꝯ a leueꝛys / ny dayl ȝys cam y naghe
dre ȝe gows y ȝew p̃uys / ȝe vos den a galyle
ef a doys a ȝeſympys / maga town ty del woȝye
gans c̍ſt na vye tregꝰ / na bythquetħ ef nan quelſe

86 Gans hēma ef a clewas / en colyek ſcon ow cane
ha c̍ſt w̃to a wetras / an peynys bꝛas may ȝeſe
pedyꝛ ſuꝛ̃ a omdēnas / ŷ vꝛna del ꝛebeghſe
ow nagha du leū a ꝛas / hag ef gwaꝛnyys del vye

87 Whaꝛ̃ yn mes y trylyas / hay golon nā na dorre
ꝛag y aꝛluth leū a ꝛas / m̃ ȝynas ef ȝy nahe
dybbry boys ef ny vŷnas / lȳmyn pub eꝛol ole
ȝoȝo bys pan danvonas / c̍ſt y to ȝe galyle

88 Ihūs a ve danvenys / ⟦h⟧a ȝe woꝛth an p̍ns annas
gans tus ven a ȝeſympys / bys an ebſcob cayphas
Dꝛeȝo c̍ſt may fe bꝛeſys / ol ȝy voth ha ȝy vŷnas [8v]
m̃ a dus o cūtullys / eꝛ ybȳ ȝy guhuȝas

89 Rag y vos w̃ bꝛonteryon / meſt̃ bꝛas a beꝛtħ ŷ wlas
gurrꝰ ve ŷ y golon / yn delma gul may cowſas
ꝛys yw porrꝰ ȝe onō / m̃wel ꝛag pobyl an wlas
pobyl ihũs y honon / na vons tregꝰ gans ſatnas

90 En eȝewon̄ yn treȝe / a whelas duſtuneow
ꝛag peyne c̍ſt ha⟪y⟫ ſŷdye / ny gewſ⟦y⟧s ȝe blegadow
ſaw w̃ thu y a vŷne / dre envy leuerell gow
a dus fals y redoȝye / an p̃re laddron ȳ pow

91 Ha dew a thuk duſtuny / yn clewſons ow leuereƚƚ
p̃ wyr̄ y fēne t̃ry / an tempel cref hay wuȝeƚƚ
w᷑ lyꝛgh̄ hēna dre veſtry / yn treſſa dyth heb fylleƚƚ
dre neꝛth bꝛas yn drehevy / bytqueth̄ ef na vye gweƚƚ

92 Neb o meſt̃ ha Iuſtꝭ / w̃th ihūs ef a gowſas
myns vs ōma cūtullys / pur̄ a peꝛt y ret flamyas
ha te geꝛ vyth ny gewſys / ōweyth lēmyn m̄ coȝas
ol Ihūs an goȝevys / hay woꝛȝeby ny vŷnas

93 Kayphas aꝛta a gewſys / yn hanow du te lavaꝛ
m̄⟦ ſ⟧os du del danvanſys / me yw yn meth c̍ſt ȳ whar̄
yn nef y feȝaff tregꝭ / an baꝛth dyghow gans am car
yn fur thu ow tevones / wy am gwylvyth heb neb m̄

94 Kayphas pur wyr̄ a ſoꝛꝛas / hag eth p̃ fol yn vꝛna
hag a ſqueꝛdyas y ȝyllas / pan gowſas c̍ſt yn della
⟦yt⟧terevys dre ſoꝛ bꝛas / duſteneow drok na da
ny ꝛeys ȝȳny ȝe welas / awos dampnye an dēma

95 Ol ow cows why an clewas / leueꝛough m̄ pyth ſawys [9r]
ol w᷑beꝛth y a aꝛmas / gweff yw ȝe vonas leȝys
gans mowys y anſcoꝛnyas / yn y fa⟦ſe⟧ y a drewys
ty yv mab du leu̅ a ꝛas / yn ges y a leuerys

96 Gans queth y ben y queȝens / guelas bāna na ylly
ȝe ihūs c̍ſt betegyns / ow ⟦kuȝyƚƚ⟧ drok ha belyny
avel brathken aga dyns / oꝛto y a theſkeꝛny
eꝛaga ſyn betegyns / c̍ſt vn ger ny leueꝛy

97 Hag y woꝛth y doꝛmontye / y cuȝens y ben gans queth
han dꝯ eſa ol yn dre / ha pryncꝭ yn pow yn weth̄
ha m̄ a bobyƚƚ ganſe / a ȝyghow fur̄ hag a gleth
the gryſt y tons ȝy ſyndye / ha ȝe dry ȝ͡e dor̄ gās meth

98 I eth ha Ihūs ganſe / bys yn pylat o Iuſtꝭ
a noȝo bres may rolle / dre y vres may fo leȝys
lavaꝛſons y heb pyte / agan traytõ yw keſys
ꝛys yw ȝeſo y ȝānye / ȝe m̄nans a ȝeſympys

99 In meth pylat pā⟦ a⟧dr̃ / a ȳnyough̄ wy w͛noȝo
na ve bos fals an dēma / nȳ droſſen ny bys deſo
y leueꝛys dre laha / ha why dāpnowgha yȝo
yn meȝēs ⟦y ny a⟧ wꝛa / dāpnye dē lad͛ kyn ſo

100 Hēna pylat pan welas / kȳmys cawſys eꝛ y byn
rowtoꝛs ha tꝰ ⟦kyche⟧ ȳ wlas / reſons m̃ fol ha m̃ dyn
pylat oꝛto govȳnas / yn keth̄ van͛ ma govyn
oſe mab du leu͡ a ꝛas / lemyn gwyꝛ ⟪te⟫ lauaꝛ ȝyn

101 In meth̄ c̓ſt an kveff colon / pur͛ wyr͛ te ꝛe leuerys [9v]
te a woȝye⟪s⟫ ȝe honon / pe dre gen re ves guaꝛnys
pylat a gewſys yn ſcon / te a ve ȝym danvenys
lauaꝛ ȝȳmo ȝe honon / pyth yw en dꝛok rewruſſys

102 In meth Ihūs nyn gvgy / ow meſt͛nges yn by⟦ſ⟧ma
hag a pe ow thus ȝewy / ny⟦n⟧ delyꝛſſens yn delma
ytho mygt͛n ote ſe / yn meth pylat yn eꝛna
gwyr͛ re gweſys yredy / ȳ meth c̓ſt mygt͛n oma

103 Hêna Iudas pan welas / c̓ſt an bewnans na ſawye
an aꝛghās a gemeꝛas / ꝛag coꝛf c̓ſt ȝe ryſſeve
ef a⟦ſ⟧tewlys dre ſoꝛ bꝛas / ȝe͡ eȝewon͡ yn treȝe
dremas yw ef leu͡ a ꝛas / neb re weꝛȝys yn meȝe

104 Iudas ſcaryoth a gewſys / ŷ keth van͛ma aꝛte
feſt yn creff me re beghas / ihūs ȝe wy ov queꝛȝe
da y won y vos a ꝛas / gevyons me nvm byth neffr⟨*e*⟩
moy pegh̄ o pan dyſpreſyas / ys delo pā ŷ gueꝛȝe

105 Han eȝewon a gewſys / pan drew hēna ȝȳny ny
ny an ꝑnas ȝe w̃ȝys / ha ad pes pur͛ yredy
Iudas eth a ȝ⟦ê⟧ſympys / a neyl tu ȝe omgregy
cafas daffaꝛ p̃ paꝛys / lovan cryff ꝛag y ſenſy

106 Eneff iudas ny allas / dos ŷ mes waꝛ y anow
ꝛag y anow a āmas / ȝe ihu͡ leu͡ a ꝛaſow
dywolow yfaꝛn ⟦a⟧ ſqueꝛdyas / coꝛf iudas ol ȝe ȝaꝛnow
hag a notho a geꝛhas / y eneff ȝe dewolgoꝫ

107 En ethewon dre envy / a gewſys cͥſt ꝛag ſyndye [10r]
pylat Iuſtꝭ oteſe / Ihūs goꝛweyth y dampnye
a iꝛl̄em thȳny / ef a thueth̄ a galyle
lays nowyth ov teſky / leas ganſo ov tryle

108 Ganſe pylat pan glewas / bos Ih̄us a galyle
bos heꝛodes w͛ an wlas / mygt̄n pylat a woȝye
Rag henna y tāuonas / cͥſt ȝoȝo ef mayn dāpne
ꝛuth̄ veyꝛ a dꝯ an ſewyas / pub eyꝛ͛ parꝭ ȝy vlamye

109 I eth bys yn heꝛodes / ha cͥſt ganſe faſt kylmys
ef a gaꝛa cͥſt gwelas / ꝛag kȳmys y ȝo pꝛayſys
ganſo mͥ callo clewas / whelth̄ nowyth a vo coyntꝭ
mͥ callo trylye ȝe hes / laŭ cͥſt pan vo clewys

110 Ꞇhe heꝛodes y theſa / p̃ wyꝛ͛ w̃th pylat ſoꝛ bꝛas
y welas ef ny gaꝛa / na boys yn y goweȝas
ȝoȝo Ihūs ȝy thampnye / pylat bys pan danvonas
yn vꝛna keſkeweȝa / y a ve ha ſpecyall̄ bꝛas

111 Heꝛodes a wovȳnys / oꝛth Ih̄us cͥſt leas tꝛa
ha trevyth ny woꝛȝebys / man geve mͥth a hēna
an eȝewon a gewſys / doyn thyn duſtuny a wꝛa
mygt̄n yſyn bos ſynſys / ha meſt͛ bꝛas yn by[[ſ]]ma

112 Kȳmys tꝛa a lavaꝛſa / ena y an rebukyas
the ꝛag an try may ȝeſa / annas pylat ha cayhas
Puꝛ͛ vylen y an pyltye / hag yn ſpytꝭ an ſcoꝛnyas [10v]
moygha ȝoȝo drok a wre / hēna veȝa[[a]]n guella gwas

113 Heꝛodes a leueꝛys / ȝe eȝewon eugh̄ yn ſen
ȝe bylat agꝭ Iuſtꝭ / ꝛag me an ſyns p̃ ȝe len
ha leueꝛough̄ bos gevys / ol ow ſoꝛ beȝens lowen
ham gallꝯ y vos gꝛontíjs / ȝoȝo ȝe vruſy an den

114 I a wyſkꝭ cryſt gans gwyn / avel fol y an ſcoꝛnye
hag an gweſka feſt yn tyn / betegyns geꝛ͛ ny gewſy
hag an hombꝛonkyas bys yn / pylat o Iuſtꝭ ȝeȝe
may caffons y aga gwayn / w͛ Ihūs cͥſt ȝy laȝe

115 Then iouł m̃ neb o tus keth / ȝe belat a leuerſ
lowēna gwelha ȝe feth̄ / heꝛodes reth tenyꝛghys
yn y golen faſt regeth / m̃ a geꝛenſe w̃ȝys
hag ef a dalvyth ȝſ wheth̄ / y honore del wruffys

116 Ha ȝeſo y tanvonas / y allꝯ ċſt ꝛag iuͩgye
ha ny ad cuſyll̄ na as / lemyn̄ y voth heb ſewye
yn meth pylat ſcyle vas / me ny gafe rū lewte
na byth moy ef ny gaffas / pꝛag may ſe ꝛys y dâpnye

117 Oꝛth pylat ol y ſetſans / ha wͬnoȝo a rug cry
ꝛag Ihuſ ċſt ȝe͡ m̃nās / y a vȳne poꝛꝛys dry
yn meth pylat w̃th an mȳs / an peg̅h̅ peuas rſ yv ry
me ny gafa moy《 e》s kyns / ꝛeſon̄ gans gwyr̄ ȝy vꝛvſy

118 En eȝewon̄ a vȳne / poꝛꝛys y vonas leȝys
ꝛeſon̄ y a rey ꝛagthe / mes waꝛ fals y ȝens growndys
hēna pylat a woȝye / ꝛag hêna a ȝeſympys
⟨b⟩ys yn cayphas ȝy ⟦ȝe⟧I⟦ y⟧vggye / ef a rug may ſe goꝛꝛys [11r]

119 Kayphas an droys aꝛte / ȝe pylat o pen Iuſtſ
hag ef eth ȝy guſulye / ih̄us ċſt may ſe leȝys
en eȝewon̄ a aꝛme / treytõ pur y vos keffys
hag ol drok ſuel awreſſe / ha gow bꝛas ganſo clewys

120 In meth pylat m̃th am bes / kȳmes drok a woȝevyth
ha te reſon̄ vyth a dres / eꝛaga fyn na gewſyth
a na wylta ol myns es / oꝛth ȝe vlamye yn ſoweth̄
hag ov ry ȝys boxow tres / betegyns te ny ſconyth̄

121 In meth pylat me ny won̄ / ȝe͡ traytē eſa ganſo
yn ċſt cafos byth reſon̄ / m̃well̄ pꝛag y reys ȝoȝo
y hylwys en eȝewon̄ / lays es yn pow a dro
may rys y laȝe ȳ ſcon / mygt̄n neb a omwrello

122 Own̄ boys ċſt mab du ⟦a̅⟧ neff / an tebel el an geve
ꝛag hēna ſcon y ȝeth ef / ȝe wrek pylat may ȝeſe
han tebel el hag̃ bref / yn y holon a worre
wͬ y meſt̃ vēions cref / y to ihuſ m̃ laȝe.

123 Chy gõ hy a ȝanonas / a ċſt kep² del welſe
yn ke⸨ꝛdꝭ d⸩elma dre gânas / nŷ gew ꝛagos ſe laȝe
Cryſt yv ſynſys m̃ dremas / ȝe ȝ《ē》vyth̄ a wos plegye
ꝛag haneth me re welas / yto v《ē》ions had laȝe

124 Onon̄ eſa yn p̑ſon̄ / baꝛabas ytho gylwys
p̑ſonys o ⟦ef⟧ dre dreyſon̄ / ha ꝛag den lath kekyffrꝭ
man̄ o ȝe eȝewon̄ / w² dyth paſch̄ woꝛth an Iuſtꝭ
an p̑ſon̄ govyn onon̄ / ha bos hêna delyffrys

125 Pylat a vynſſe gwyȝe / bewnans Ihūs dȓ goŷtꝭ [11v]
hag a leueꝛys ȝeȝe / yn delma del yw ſċffꝭ
lēmyn meꝛough̄ ⸨pe nyle / an dus⸩ a vᵗ delyffrꝭ
po cryſt leueꝛough̄ ſcyle / po baꝛabas den blamys

126 En eȝewon̄ a aꝛmas / dre buȓ envy me a grꝭ
dyly⸨veꝛ⸩ ȝŷny baꝛabas / ha hēna ⸨ol ny⸩ a bys
Pylat aꝛte a gowſas / a Ihūs pyth a vᵗ gurꝭ
y havꝺlſons gans golon̄ vꝛas / ȝe m̑nans beȝens gurrꝭ

127 Pylat yn ta a woȝye / y ȝe guſel dre envy
ꝛag hēna ef a vynſe / gweȝe ċſt heb velyny
hag a leuerꝭ ȝeȝe / m² mȳnough̄ me an chaſty
ol w² baꝛth 《ȳ》nycyte / hag an delyꝛf ȝe wary

128 I helwys en eȝewon̄ / beȝēs ef yn crows gorrꝭ
yn meth pylat me ny won̄ / ꝛeſon̄ pꝛag y ſyt d《ā》pnys
y hawlſons gans moy colon̄ / beȝēs ef yn crow《s》 leȝys
yn meth pylat byth ꝛeſon̄ / ȝe laȝe nyn ges keffys

129 Ha pylat ȝe w² bred̑ / a leuerꝭ ȝe Ih̄u
ol an du⸨ſ⸩ma a leȗ / ȝe vos cregꝭ te yv gyw
laȗ gwyȓ ȝŷmo vn geȓ / m²⸨ ſ⸩ota mab den ha du
cryſt a gewſys dybon̄ / te a leȗys del yw

130 Whaȓ y an dyſtryppyas / m² noyth genys del vye
hag ⸨w̃th⸩ poſt faſt an colmas / vnwyth̄ na ylly plȳchye
hag ena ⸨íj⸩ an ſcoꝛgyas / yn tebel gans ⸨íj⸩ ſcoꝛgye
ha hag̑ feſt an dygtyas / coꝛf ha pen treys ha dewle

131 In ſcoꝛgíjs prenyeꝛ eſe / yn dewle an ⸨íj⸩ ethovꞵ [12r]
hag yn faſt kelmys ȝeȝe / keꝛdȳ gweȝȳ ⟦ŷ⟧ meſk cronovꞵ
may fons hyblyth̄ ȝe gronkye / hag a ꝛag gurꝭ colmēnovꞵ
gans pub colmⓔ may ȝelle / paⓐ wyſkens ȳ mes an crow

132 Han ȝewna bys pan vons ſquyth̄ / wꝫ ċſt y fons ov crôkye
⸨māna⸩ geve goth̄ na leyth̄ / na geſa woꝛth y grevye
na wꝫ y goꝛff wek tā vyth̄ / p̃ wyr͛ ⸨hêna⸩ o m̃ byte
ha whath moy wy a glewyth / a doꝛmoⓣ ċſt del whaꝛfe

133 In treȝe avel tꝯ fol / gaꝛlont ſꝑn⟦e⟧ a ve dyȝgth̄tys
ha dre aga huſyll ol / wꝫ y bⓔ a ve gorꝭ
may ȝo ſquaꝛdíjs a dro ol / ay ben y oys o ſcolijs
hag ȳno feſt luhas tol / gans an dreyn a ve tellys

134 Gans dⓔ ſcyntyll a woȝye / me a glewas leuerell
an aꝛlont y ȝe dēne / waꝛ y ben gans kŷmys nell
ma teth̄ an dreyn ha cropye / ȝⓔ ⟦n⟧ēpŷnyoⓝ dr͛ an tell
hēno payⓝ a ṽ byte / eſa ċſt ovꞵ coȝevell

135 A vyne gwaꝛȝe y ben / wꝫ y goꝛff bys ŷ y droys
ſquaꝛdíjs oll o y grohen / hag ef cuȝys yn y woys
m̃ o an payn 《a》daꝛ ken / ȝe vab du m̃ y alloys
del leu͛ ȝyn an levaꝛ / kŷmys payn ny ve ay oys

136 I a wyſkꝭ ċſt gans queth̄ / ⟦h⟧an purpuꝛ ꝛych̄ o dy⸨ſk⸩ꝭ
ꝛag y thry ȝⓔ dor͛ gans meth̄ / yn ges y a leuerꝭ
m̃ a onour͛ te aſyth / te yw myg͛tn cvrvnys
hag yn y leff ȝyghow ŷ weth̄ / gwelⓔ wȳ a ve gorꝭ

137 Hag y thens ȝe ben dowlyn • hag y kewſens ȝe ſcoꝛnye [12v]
hag a gāma aga meyn / pub onoⓝ ꝛag y eyſye
lowene ȝys te yw ȝeyn / myg͛tn ꝛys yw ȝe woꝛȝye
hen o ȝoȝo m̃ a bayn / may ȝe⸨r⸩ens woꝛth y ꝛanne

138 Onô gans an keth welen / yn leyff ċſt a ve gorꝭ
an gwyſkꝭ laſch̄⟦e⟧ wꝫ an pen / buⓦ pur͛ gewꝫ deſeȝys
ha buxow leas hep ken / ha tūmaſow kekyffrꝭ
ȝe gryſt a dro ȝⓔ ȝewen / gans neꝛth bꝛas a ve ſyttꝭ

139 Colon den a yꝉꝉ crakye / a vynha ꝓſt ꝓdery
an paynys bꝛas an geve / han dyſpyth̄ heb y dylly
hag ol ꝛag ȝe geꝛenſe / ihūs c̓ſt as goȝevy
lȳmyn goꝛqvyth̄ y gare / ha gweyth denat̓ na vy

140 Pylat eth yn mes ay heꝉꝉ / yn vn lowaꝛth an gevo
ogas o nȳ geſa peꝉꝉ / hag a worras c̓ſt ganſo
ena w̃to ꝛag kewſeꝉꝉ / queth eſa a dro ȝoȝo
ꝓſt an eȝewon̄ debel / ȝe Ihūs eſens a dro

141 Ena pylat a gewſys / yn delma ȝ℮ eȝewon
me ny won̄ bonas kyſys / yn dēma byth acheſon
may rys y vonas leȝys / gothveȝough̄ ketoponon
del yw an dēma dyȝgtꝭ / myꝛough yn agꝭ colon

142 Pan yn caffſons yn treȝe / ol w̓baꝛth y a ylwys
te pylat laȝe laȝe / m̑nans an grows deſympys
Pylat a gewſys aꝛte / dreȝough̄ why beȝēs leȝys
Rag ȳ̂no me ny gaffe / ſcyle vas may ſo dāpnys

143 An debel dus a gewſys / ȝȳnny s̃ yma laha [13r]
may rys y vonas leȝys / ꝛag mab du eff a omwꝛa
own̄ a gachyas an Iuſtꝭ / pan glewas cows yn della
ꝛag hēna a ȝeſympys / y trylyas thy aſethva

144 Oꝛth c̓ſt ef a wovȳnys / te ȝ℮ able ota gy
ȝy gows c̓ſt ny w̃ȝebys / ȳmeth pylat yredy
goꝛȝeby te ny vynſys / a ny woȝas ow meſtry
bos ȝȳmo may fes leȝys / bo delyffrꝭ ȝe wary

145 In meth̄ Ihūs yn vꝛna / meſtry vyth te ny vea
w̓⟪n⟫aff ve drok vyth na da / ken onā ȝys nā rolla
byth moy ys eȝow ȳ̂ ta / a beghas oꝛth ov ȝrayta
pylat pan glewas hēna / a whelas y ȝelyffra

146 Han eȝewon̄ oꝉꝉ a dro / ȝe belat a leuery
kerenſe ſeſaꝛ ytho / ny⟦ ȝe⟧ lēman belyny
m̓ ny wreth dyffry doȝo / a beꝛveth yn crows cregy
ꝛag mygt̑n a omwrello / ȝe ſeſaꝛ yw contrary

147 Ena pylat pā glewas / an lauarow na ganſe
Ihūs ef a ʒyſweʒas / pur evn̄ yn cres yn treʒe
a watta ef a gowſas / agꝭ mygᵗᵉn ple meve
ol wᶦ baꝛth I an naghas / hag a yꝛghys y laʒe

148 In meth̄ pylat why a vyn / drys pub tra me ʒy laʒe
agꝭ mygᵗᵉn̄ meth yw ʒyn / na veʒens clewys neffre
yn meʒens y nȳ goꝛʒyn / na ny goth̄ thyn y woꝛʒye
Na Ken mygᵗᵉn ny venyn / ys Ceſaꝛ caffos neffre

149 Y thewleff pylat a wolhas / hag a leuerys ʒeʒe [13v]
glan off a wos an dremas / ꝛag ay woys vēions a ʒe
ol wᶦbaꝛth y a aꝛmas / mᶦ te v⟪ē⟫ions ha cothe
wᶦ agan flehys ŷ fꝛas / ha wᶦnan beʒās neffre

150 Camē pylat pan welas / na ylly ċſt delyffre
manan geffo ef foꝛ bꝛas / ʒe woꝛth oll̄ an goweʒe
ꝛag hēna ef ⟦a⟧ Iuggyas / Ihūs ʒeʒe ʒy laʒe
the ves y a thelyffꝛas / baꝛabas quyth̄ may ʒelle

151 Pan o Ihūs cryſt dāpnys / abeꝛth yn crows may faꝛwe
haccra meꝛnās vyth̄ oꝛdnys / ʒe creatᶻ ny vye
en grows whath nȳ io ꝑys / ⟦n⟧ā eʒewon̄ ny woʒye
an ꝑnnyeꝛ py fens keffꝭ / ʒe wuʒyll̄ crous a neʒe

152 Vn ethow a bredeꝛys / hag a leuerys theʒe
bonas pren yn dō tewlys / a⟪y⟫ vs yn houl na vye
ꝛag an grous y ʒo oꝛdnys / han ⟦hu⟧thewon ny woʒye
hag an avell̄ deveʒys / dreʒy adam may pegh⟦fe⟧

153 En prŷnerᵖ a ve keꝛhys / en grows ſcon̄ dyʒgtꝭ may fe
hag ȳny bonas gorys / ꝛagon̄ ny cryſt a vȳne
ha waꝛ an pren frut degꝭ / may fe ſur ʒagā ſawye
may teth frut may fen kellys • ꝛag adam ʒe attamye

154 Whath kentrow ʒeʒe nŷgo / Ihūs yn crows ꝛag ſynſy
y h⟦wa⟧lſons ol a dro / mᶦ caffons goff yredy
onan a welſons eno / hag y ʒeʒons ʒy beſy
Hag y lauaꝛſons thoʒo / te gura ⟦íĳ⟧ kentᵉ ʒŷny

155 In meth̅ an goyff me ny wꝛaff / p̃ wyr̃ kentrow ȝewy vyth̅ [14r]
yn meȝens mͣ omwreyth̅ claff / goꝛꝛȝewyth̅ te an p̑nvyth̅
awos guthyll̅ wheyll̅ mͣ ſcaff / yn ethom ȝyn mͣ fyllyth
y w̃ȝebys ny vânaff / aga guȝyll̅ war ow fyth

156 Gans m̃ a Iuct̑s yn wlas / ef a ve veyll̅ rebukſ
kavanſkſ ef a whelas / ꝛag own̑ y vonas leȝys
ẙ meth̅ angoff clevas bꝛas / es omdewleff deveȝys
towyll̅ vyth ny allaff ẙ fas / ȳno ſenſy ȝe wonys

157 Reys o ȝoȝo dyſqueȝas / ȝe p̃ treytôs a ȝewle
wͥneȝe gwelſons clevas / bytegȳs byth nȳ geſe
yn meth̅ y wrek m̃ ⟦a⟧ vaꝛth bꝛas / yv hēna ȝym rȗ lewte
heȝow pan eȝys yn mes / cleves vyth nyth kem̑ſe

158 In meth̅ gurek an goff ȝeȝe / kentrow ȝewy why ny fyll̅
a wos bos claff y ȝewle / toche vyth gonys ef na yll̅
del won̑ ŷ vn fyſtene / me a⟦ſ⟧gura ny ſtrechyaff pell̅
a ban na ges a wothſe / ȝeugh̅ parſ as gurelle gwell̅

159 En debell̅ wrek caſadow / gans m̃ a doth eth yn chy
wͭ haſt ȝe weȝyll̅ kentrow / may fens creff ha treweſy
⟦íj⟧ droys Ih̅us caꝛadow / hay ⟦íj⟧ leyff y a delly
ꝛag an ſpykſ o gaꝛow / pan vons gwyſkſ ȝy ſenſy

160 Pan o an kentrow lēmys / hy as duk ȝe eȝewon̑
crows Ihūs nav̄⟦y⟧o parſ / y eth ȝy laȝe yn ſcon
breſell̅ creff a ve ſoꝛdíjs / en grows pu elle ȝy don
Dre ṽ ſtryff y ſe Iuggíjs / ys degy c̍ſt y honon

161 An queth̅ tek a ve dyſkſ / han p̃pur ꝛych⟦e⟧ a vſye [14v]
hay bow⟦y⟧s y honon̑ gurrſ / a dro ȝoȝo hy a ve
gans y vam y ſye gurſ / hag ef genſy ow tene
kep̑ Ihûs del devys / yn della an bows a wre

162 Oll̅ monas y a vȳne / bys yn mont a galvary
a veſt ȝe dre y ȝeſe / meneth vghell̅ yredy
an grows I a rug gorre / wͭ ſcoth Ihūs ȝy don ȝy
ȝe Ihūs c̍ſt may teffe / ol an greff han belyny

163 Dew lad͛ drevs o dāpnys / a ve dyʒgtꝭ gans Ihū
ganſo ef may fens cregꝭ / onon ʒoʒo a bub tu
Ihūs a ve hombꝛonkꝭ / ha wͥ y lyꝛgh m̃ a lu
dre vold͛ tebel Iuſtꝭ / ꝛag y chaſye kyn ʒo du

164 I vam whegol a welas / del efons w͠th y ʒygtye
pyteth m̃ a⟦ſ⟧kemeras / y holon nam na grakye
dre vn ſcochfoꝛth y ponyas / cafos y mab mᷓ calle
I woꝛtos hy a vy̅nas / guelas Ihūs a gare

165 Pan welas y mab dygtꝭ / gans an eʒewon mᷓ veyƚƚ
hay vos gans ſpn͡ curunys / ha peb ʒoʒo ow cuƚƚ geyƚƚ
hag yn y goꝛf bos gorrꝭ / goleow pals leas myƚƚ
heb cows ger y clamderꝭ / y cothas wͥ bol y hyƚƚ

166 Ena pan ſevys yn ban / hy a gewſys del ylly
nŷ gew ow faynys beghan / vs lemyn ⟦wͥ⟧ ow ſenſy
ow holon yn tre myƚƚ daꝛn / m̃ꝛth yw gene na ſquaꝛdhy
pan welaff ow mab mᷓ wan / ow town͡ kemys velyny

167 Genſy p͛ſt ⟦íj⟧ venyn len / efa w͠th y homfoꝛtye [15r]
Maꝛya magdalenen / ha marya cleophe
y a fyſtena yn fen / aꝛte ʒy dyeꝛbyne
ꝛag kerenſa ny̅ io ken / y welas y a vy̅ne

168 Benenas p͛ſt a holyas / Ihū͡ c̍ſt ŷ vn gaꝛme
Ihus w͠to a veras / hag a leuerꝭ ʒeʒe
Flehys m̃ ha benenas / a ierl̄m͡ y̅ dre
a wor bos ov feynys bꝛas / ꝛagoff na wheleugh̄ ole

169 Olough̄ ꝛag agꝭ fleghys / ha ꝛagough̄ agꝭ honon͡
en deʒyow a vyth guelys / hag a ʒe ſur yntꝛeʒon
may ſyth torrow benegꝭ / bythqueth na allas ⟦e⟧ʒon͡
han benenas kekyffrys / na ve ʒeʒe denys bꝛon

170 In eꝛna ʒe͡ menyʒyow / why a eꝛgh wͥnough coʒe
y̅ ketella an nanſſow / wy a bys ꝛagaſ cuthe
del lavare wͥ anow / wͥ an pren glays mᷓ a te
yn pre͡ ſeygh ha caſadow / ſur yn eꝛna ſatel ve

171 I vam whek marya wyn / pub vrᷓ fyſtene a wre
may halle doys wˀ y byn / y mab kēmys a gare
Rag gwandᷓ wˀ ben dowlyn / hy an guelas ow coʒe
han wlos a⟦ſ⟧kemeꝛas mᷓ dyn / may clamderas hy arte

172 Ena hy a ve ſeuys / yn ban ynᷓ benenas
aꝛluth hy a leuerſ / ow holon y ma genas
kepˀ ha te hy ʒew gurſ • yn anken w̃th ʒe welas
bytqueth den ny woʒevys / payn ella ʒy golon̄ nes

173 En golyas ha ſowt dybbry / a woʒevys Ihūs ker
han ſtrokoſow treweſy / warᷓ y goꝛff drſ pub manᷓ
goys ay ben hay yſely / a ʒroppye wˀ y ʒew verᷓ
ꝛag doʒo ef na ylly / don̄ an grows ꝛag gwandᷓ

174 Vn den̄ a⟦ſ⟧dyeꝛbŷnas / Sŷmon o ay own̄ hanow
y leueꝛys ʒoʒo guas / te a ʒek an grows heb wow
⟪a⟫y don ſymon̄ a ſconyas / ef an geve ſtrocoſow
na moy ſconye ny vŷnas / ꝛag own̄ caſos y ancow
[15v]

175 Ef a thuk an grous ganſe / p̃ wyrᷓ hēno ay anvoth̄
ny wrens y na hen ſcyle / lymyn ſywye aga both
pub erᷓ te ʒe gura lewte / beva de yonk bo de coth
oꝛʒaff mᷓ mȳnyth̄ cole / neffre gans an fals na ſoth

176 I eth ŷ vn fyſtene / ʒe tyller ⟦ganſo⟧ o oꝛdnys
pan doʒyans ʒy yn treʒe / pows Ihūs a ve dyſkſ
y dyſky mᷓ an grevye / woꝛto faſt navngo glenys
whath bytqueth claff ny vee / vylle ys dello dyſkſ

177 Vn̄ veny̅ da a welas / dello Ihūs dyſtryppíjs
pytet mᷓ a⟦ſ⟧kemeras / ꝛag y vos mᷓ veyll̄ dygtſ
vn̄ queth tek hy a drylyas / adro ʒoʒo deſympys
ha wˀnās hy an quuthas / ꝛag gwyʒe na ve ſtoꝛuys

178 Heys cᷓſt y a gemeras / an ⟦n⟧eyll̄ lef bys yn y ben
w̃th an les y a dollas / ⟦íj⟧ doll̄ yn ⟪an⟫ grows heb ken
may ʒello an kentrow bꝛas / dre y ʒewleff bys ŷ p⟪r⟫en
ꝛag y dreys y a vȳnas / telly ʒy worre ⟦ynt⟧ten

179 **G**anſe ċſt a ve tewlys / wˀ an grows ȝe wroweȝe
hay yƚƚ leff a ve tackꝭ / oꝛd en grows faſt may ȝeſe 1428
hay yƚƚ troys a ve gorꝛꝭ / poꝛan wˀ ben e gele
woꝛth an grows yfons laȝíȷ́s / gans kenꝰ guyſkꝭ dreȝe 1432

180 **T**hen levff araƚƚ pan doȝyans / w̃th an grovs ꝛᵍ y faſte [16r]
y fylly moy ys treſheys / ȝꝯ tol gurꝭ hy na heȝe 1436
En eȝewon̄ betegyns / gul tol araƚƚ ny vŷne
lemyn an tol re wrussens / y a vyne ȝe ꝑuye 1440

181 **G**anſe w̃th levff ċſt loven / faſt yn ſcon a ve kelmys
Hag yn tre an eȝewon̄ / an grovs faſt a ve ſenſys 1444
gans re a gŷmys colon̄ / en loven a ve tēnys
y iūctꝭ ketoponon̄ / oƚƚ wˀbaꝛth may ȝens ſquaꝛdꝭ 1448

182 **P**an deth̄ levff ċſt wˀ en toƚƚ / dre an neꝛth̄ may tenſons hy
vn ethow aveƚƚ pyth̄ foƚƚ / a wyſkꝭ kenꝰ ynhy 1452
lēmyn me agꝭ pys oƚƚ / a baynys ċſt ꝑdery
ha na vo geſys ȝe goƚƚ / an lahys a rug ȝŷny 1456

183 **S**ċfys yw yn furedy / ha kꝯ me nȳ lauaꝛſen
coꝛff Ihūs hay aſely / y ȝe dēna mͣ velen 1460
neb a vŷna a ylly / neueꝛa oƚƚ y yſcren
hay ſkēnys kyc ha gwyȝy / pan eſa ŷ crow⟦s⟧pꝛen 1464

184 **H**an grous a ve drehevys / ha Ihūs faſteys ŷny
han pen golas delyffrys / yn tol o tellys ꝛygthy 1468
ena hy a ve geſys / ȝe goȝa mͣ ankynſy
ȝe ċſt may fe crehyllys / oƚƚ y goꝛf hay eſely 1472

185 **H**a ċſt yn delma peynys / a beꝛth yn crows pan eſe
yn ⟨*va*⟩ñma y peſys / ꝛag an keth re ꝛen crowſe 1476
ow ȝas whek beȝēs gevys / ȝꝯ rema ⟦a⟧ga nyſcyte
ꝛag ⟦me ny won̄⟧ py gȳmys / y mons y s̃ ow peghe 1480

186 **A**n ethewon a gꝛogas / ladꝰ ȝe gryſt an baꝛth̄ cleth̄ [16v]
hag a ȝyghow ladꝰ bꝛas / cregy a ruſſons yn weth̄ 1484
ha ċſt yn cres leū a ꝛas / levn̄ y golon a voꝛeth̄
gans laddron y teweȝas / del yw ſċfys ay ȝeweth 1488

187 Pylat a vȳnas ſc̍ſe / a vewnans c̍ſt acheſon
pꝛaga dāpnys rebee / hag an ſc̍ſas y honon
pan eth pylat ʒy redye / ſcyle nȳ io na gonon
ꝑſt y keffy pā vyre / ⟦hēma⟧ yw mygꝛn eʒewon

188 En ethewon a gowſys / hēna yw ʒyn bylyny
beʒēs ʒe ves defendꝰ / y vonas mygꝛn ʒynny
ha beʒens ena gorrꝰ / y fenſe bos dre veſtry
han pyth̄ a ſc̍ſys ſc̍ſys / ȳ meth pylat ʒeʒe y

189 En lybell a ve tackꝰ / woꝛth en grous faſt may ʒeſe
hag a vgh̄ pē c̍ſt goꝛꝛys / may hylly peb y redye
ꝛag bos Ihūs c̍ſt crowſys / ogas ʒe foꝛth̄ an cyte
gans leas yſe ꝛedíjs / y vonas mygꝛn ʒethe

190 Dyllas c̍ſt a ve rȳnys / pedaꝛ ran gurꝰ a neʒe
gās peſwar maꝛꝛeg a brys / ʒe bub m̄ꝛeg ꝛan ⟦n⟧ay⟦ſ⟧e
y bous ef o m̄ dek gurꝰ / y ny vynſans y ꝛāne
wꝫ nethy pꝛen be tewlys / oll an bows pyv an gyffe

191 An baꝛth̄ cleyth̄ neb o cregꝰ / dyveth̄ o ha lad pur
yn ges ef a leuerys / te c̍ſt m̄⟦ ſ⟧ota m̄ fur
wꝫ an bys del omwreffys / lēmyn dyſwa ha gura cur
ha ſaw te ha me kyffrꝰ / agan bewnans may fen ſur

192 In meth̄ an lad arall / drok ʒe os kep del ves
ny ʒowtyth̄ du te yw dall / ꝛag gene cregꝰ neb es
den glan yw a begh̄ heb fall / ȳno eff dyfout nȳ ges
agan cregy ny yv mall / ꝛag ny ꝛebe laddron dres [17r]

193 An lad an baꝛth dyghow / a beſys yn ketelma
aꝛluth pā dyffy ʒet pow / predery a hanaff guꝛa
c̍ſt puꝛ wek an caꝛadow / an goꝛʒebys yn vꝛna
te a vᵗ yn keth golow / yn padꝰ genama

194 An eʒewon a gewſy / a Ihūs ꝛag y ſcoꝛnye
kyns yn ta ef a ylly / tꝰ a bub drok ol ſawye
lēmyn gans ol y veſtry / ꝛagon ny w̃ omweʒe
na gans oll y tretury / ny yll agan dyſſaytye

195 **W**ᵃaga dewlyn y ȝe / ⟦p⟧e ꝛag Ihūs re erell̄
aga fen y a ſackye[s] • hag a gewſy p̃ debell̄ 1556
w̃th Ihūs ꝛag y angre / a wott⟦a⟧ ōma neb ⟪a⟫ yll̄
tempell̄ du dowſtoll̄ ſquaꝛdye / ha ȝe voth y ȝrehevell̄ 1560

196 **H**ag y ee ȝe ben dewlyn / ha hagꝰ mowys a wre
gweȝe goȝyans aga meyn / oꝛth Ih̄us a ōgame 1564
hag ef moygha yn y beyn / yn y fas y a drewe
heno ȝoȝo calys feyn / agan pegh̄ ny ow prēne 1568

197 **R**e ȝe gryſt a leuery / a beꝛth yn crows pan eſe
m̃ꝛ⟦ ſ⟧oge ċſt mab dauy / des an grows heb pyſtege. 1572
ha ny a grys ȝe veſtry / hag ad ſyns meſtꝰ neffre
me yw mab du yredy / ċſt a leuerʃ thethe 1576

198 **A** baꝛth̄ dyghow y ȝeſe / ȝe gryſt y vam marya
hay vam ef neb a gare / an baꝛth arall̄ magata. 1580
deſo benyn yn meȝa / Iowan ȝe vab me a wra.
na byth moy ken mā neffre / es hyhy te na whela 1584

199 **W**ᵃlyꝛgh̄ ċſt enef ȝe ry / pub onan oll̄ ȝy gele.
Iowan y vam a ſenſy / marya ċſt del aꝛſe 1588 [17v]
yn pub manꝰ may hylly / y vam p̃ſt a⟦ſ⟧onore
yn delma cōfoꝛt ȝyȝy / y map a vy̅nas dygtye 1592

200 **N**evngo deuethys an pꝛys / may ȝo ogas ȝy ȝeweth
yn eꝛna y fe doꝛgʃ / ha drʃ ol an bys ef eth̄ 1596
tewolgow bꝛas a ve gurʃ / an houll̄ a gollas y feth̄
ha moy m̃ȝus me a grʃ / ys an rena ve yn weth 1600

201 **I**n della hy a begyas / bys hantꝰ dyth̄ yredy
yn eꝛna ċſt a vy̅nas / leuerell̄ ely ely 1604
ȝe ſtrirya yw a gowſas / aꝛluth̄ pꝛagh y hyſta vy
mas re wᶾ gryſt a ynnyas / y ȝo dewas a yꝛghy 1608

202 **G**ans an eȝewon̄ wᶾ haſt / drok ȝewas a ve dyȝgtys
tebell̄ lycō m̄ y laſt / eyſyll̄ beſtyll̄ kemyſkʃ 1612
yn ⟪vn⟫ ſpong oꝛth gwele̅ ſaſt / ȝe gryſt hy a ve heȝys
gonys oll̄ a wrens yn ⟦ſ⟧aſt / ꝛag na go ċſt attendíjs 1616

203 Re an eʒewon̄ tebell̄ • a leuerys heb pyte
a wottenſe ow kelwell̄ / hely ʒoʒo ʒy wyʒe
myꝛugh̄ m̄ te drehevell̄ / ay beynys ʒy ʒelyffre
han ſcherewys p̄ſt a bell̄ / ʒe woꝛth an gwyr̄ aſye

204 I beyn̄ o m̄ greff ha tyn / caman na ylly bewe
heb daſcoꝛ y eneff gwyn / bytqueth yn lan revewſe
c̄ſt a beſys del redyn / yn delma yn luas le
ow eneff me a gymyn / aꝛluth yn tre ʒe ʒewle

205 Rag gwan ſpyr̄ hag ef yn ten / caman na ylly gwyʒe
w̄ nans na boſſe y ben / ꝛag an aꝛlont a vſye
m̄ poſſe ⟦a⟧ neyll̄ tenewen / ꝛag y ſcoth hy an grevye
Ha whath gweth a wre an pren / w̄ ʒellaꝛgh̄ m̄ an gorre

206 Na w̄ ꝛag ef ny ylly / poſe ꝛag own̄ bos megẜ [18r]
yn eꝛna del redyn ny / ⟪y̅⟫ lyffrow y ʒew ſc̄fys
ʒe ⟦n⟧eʒyn gwyls ꝛag nyeʒy / tellyryow eſa parẜ
the c̄ſt y ben py ſenſy / telleꝛ vyth ny̑ go keẜẜ

207 Rag p̄rẜ ꝛys o ʒoʒo / gaſe y ben ʒegregy
ꝛag galſe glan ʒe w̃to / y woys bewe ny ylly
w̄ tu hay vam an pewo / y ben a vy̅nas ſynſy
hay eneff eth a noʒo / gans gaꝛm eyn hag vghel gry

208 Ryp crous Ihu̅s y ʒeſe / vn den henwys ſentury
a veꝛnans c̄ſt pan welſe / kynyu̅ tra m̄thuſy
han enef del daſcoꝛſe / eꝛbyn nat gans vn cry
y leuerys heb ſcoꝛnye / ⟦hēma⟧ yw mab du yredy
ha leas ganſo ene / doʒo a ʒuk duſtuny

209 Nango hant dyth yn wlas • po moy del yma ſcryẜẜ
doꝛgẜ eſa ha lughas / han tewolgow kekyffrys
veyll̄ an tempyll̄ a ſquaꝛdyas / y̅tre dew ʒe dor coʒys
ena yn weth y torras / en veyn o creff ha calys

210 En beʒow yn loweꝛ le / a peꝛt a ve egerys
han coꝛfow eſa y̅ne / a ve yn ban drehevys
hag eth poꝛan ʒe cyte / gans luas y fons gwelys
en gwyr̄ ʒe ʒuſtvnee / bos mab du neb o leʒys

211 Dowȓ ha ler ha tan ha gwy̅s / houl ha lȏ ha ſteyȓ kyffrꝭ 1684
a gryſt ow coȝaff m̑nās / anken y a woȝevys
natuꝛ ſcyle me a ſyns / aꝛluth da mᵃ pyth peynys 1688
ol y ſoget⟦e⟧ ky̑ fons ſyns / ꝛag y beyn ȝe vos grevíjs

212 Enaff c̓ſt ȝe yffaꝛn eth̄ / hag a dorras an poꝛȝow 1692
dre y neꝛth bꝛas hay ſleyneth / ena golmas dewolow
lucyfeꝛ kelmys yv whath / puȓ faſt yn y golmēnow 1696
Hag ef a dryk heb ſynweth̄ / yn yffaꝛn yn tewolgow

213 Ena c̓ſt a thelyffꝛas / a bꝛeſon adam hag ⟦ev⟧ef 1700 [18v]
ſuel a wreſſa both y das // man geffo tregva y̑ nef
pan eth yn mes yn ſewyas / en dꝰ vas del vy̅ne ef 1704
an ſcheꝛewes a dregas / yn yffaꝛn yn t̑mont creff

214 Vn buꝛges Ioſep hynwys / a ⦅h⦆aꝛamat̄ an cyte 1708
yn m̑nans c̓ſt a gewſys / bytqueth dremas re bee
ol y doul ef o tewlys / ganſo yn nef ꝛag trege 1712
Ihūs ganſo o kerꝭ / ha ny̅ io haꝛd ȝy notye

215 Ioſep eth bys yn Iuſtꝭ / ȝe bylat meſt̑ treus o 1716
ha p̃ haꝛd a wovy̅nys / coꝛf Ihūs w̃to yn ꝛo
ꝛag bos Ioſep den kerꝭ / grontꝭ ef a ve ȝoȝo 1720
pylat a woꝛomy̅nys / meꝛas c̓ſt marow mᵃ⦅ ſ⦆o

216 En eȝewon ſkyntyll̄ keth / re⦅ſ⦆teffo m̃ vylyny 1724
ȝe veꝛas w̃th c̓ſt y eth̄ / hag ef yn crous ow cregy
y a welas ⦅wᵃ⦆ y feth / y vos marow yredy 1728
⦅yt⦆taſefffons oll̄ yn weth / dre an golon y delly

217 ⦅In a⦆ga heꝛwyth y ȝeſe / vn mᵃreg longꝭ hynwys 1732
dal o ny wely banna / ef rebea dē a brys
gew a ve yn y ȝewle / gans an eȝewon̄ gorrꝭ 1736
ha pē lym ꝛag y wane / ȝe golon Ihūs ⦅h⦆ynwys

218 Longꝭ fuȓ an baꝛth dyghow / ȝe grous Ih̄us y ȝeſe 1740
ȝē marreg w̃th y hanow / y a yꝛhys may whane
yn coꝛf Ihūs caradow / en gew lym ef a bechye 1744
p̃ ewn̄ yn dan an aſow / dre an golon may ȝe⦅ſ⦆e

219 **A**n golon y ȝeth ſtret bꝛas / dõ ha goys yn kemeſkꝭ
ha ꝛyp an gyw a refas / ȝe ȝewle neb an gwyſkꝭ
y wholhas y ȝewlagas / gans y eyll̄ leyff o goſys
dre ꝛas an goys y whelas / Ihūs c̍ſt dell̄ o dyȝgtꝭ

220 **E**ddrek m̃ an kemeꝛas / ꝛag an obeꝛ re wreſſe [19r]
ȝy ben dowlyn y coȝas / aꝛluth gevyans yn meȝe
dall̄ en ny welyn yn fas / ow bos m̃ veyll̄ ow pewe
Ihūs ȝoȝo a avas / pan welas y edrege

221 **M**am Ihūs maꝛya wyn / heꝛdya an gyw pā welas
yn y mab yn tenewyn / dre an golon may refas
ha ȝ͛ doꝛ͛ an goys han lyn / an noȝo dell̄ deveras
angus bꝛas ha peynys tyn / ha gloys creff a⟦ſ⟧kemeres

222 **F**eſt yn tyn hy a wole / ȝe wheꝛȝyn ny⟦ſ⟧teva whans
hay dagrow a ȝevere / ⟦h⟧ay dew lagas puꝛ͛ ȝewhans
hay holon whek a rāne / me a leu͛ ꝛag tryſtans
ꝛag an graytħ yn hy eſe / nas gweȝe an ſpyꝛys ſans

223 **D**re y holon y ȝeth ſeth / y mab ſyndꝭ pan welſe
moꝛeth an ſeth ha pytet / natureth a ha denſetħ
han pen arall̄ o pytet / tackꝭ faſt gans kerenſe
ny woȝevys d͛ bythquetħ / kȳmys peynys ow pewe

224 **A**n ſeth yw ꝛag leuerꝭ / as gwyſkꝭ ⟦tyn⟧ gans m̃ angꝰ
w͛ hy holon may crunys / dre neꝛth an bū fynt͛ woys
ha hy a wolas kȳmys / gans m̃ veꝛ͛ neꝛth ha galloys
an fȳten may trehevys / ꝛan yn ban du drok a loys

225 **A**n goy⟦ſ⟧na dagrennow try / dre y ⟦íj⟧ lagas y ȝetħ
n⟪ȳ⟫ go cōfoꝛt na yly / a wrello y holon huetħ
hay veynys m̃ drewefy / ⟦aſkem̃ ha⟧ kȳmys cuetħ
yn oll̄ an bys ny ylly / den cafos kȳmys anfuetħ

226 **I** feynys o bꝛas ha creff / yn ioy ȝeȝy trylys yw
ꝛag mygt͛nas yw yn nef / ȝe vos g̃ȝíjs hy yv gyw
Eleth ȝe rygthy a feff / leas myll̄ y both a ſyw
hay mab as goꝛtħ del vȳ ef / tecke ys houl yv y lyw

227 In corff Ihūs y ʒeſe / hag ef yn crows ow cregy 1812 [19v]
pymp myꝉꝉ ſtrekꝭ del iove / ha pedeꝛgwyth̄ cans goly
ha tryvgons moy ganſe / ha py̅ʒek p̃ wyr̃ ens y 1816
hag ol ꝛag p̃ geꝛenſe / w̃th mab den ys goʒevy

228 Pub teʒoꝉꝉ neb a vy̅ne / leuerel py̅ʒek pat̃ 1820
a leū golon̄ ꝛag g̃ʒye / paſcon̄ agan aꝛluth ker
yn blyʒe̅ y a vye / ha bederow keneū̃ 1824
hag a ⟦ow⟧leow eſe / yn coꝛf Ihūs w̃th neū̃

229 En eʒewon̄ ny vy̅ne / bos an laddron ow cregy 1828
t̃nos ꝛag paſch o ʒeʒe / dyth vghel y a ſenſy
an eʒewon̄ yn treʒe / a rug may wrellons t̃ry 1832
aga moꝛʒoſow whare / hag a lena aga dry

230 Eꝛbyn bonas hēna gurꝭ / nan⟦ſ⟧o prys gweſp yn wlas 1836
yn eꝛna yn weth kemeas / ʒe Ioſep y a rontyas
hag an grou⟦s ⟧«pren» del o pꝛys / coꝛf Ihūs a gemeꝛas 1840
tyr̃ marya me a grys / pur̃ ylwys an gwereſas

231 Mam Ihūs c̉ſt a āme / coꝛf y mab p̃ dreweſy 1844
hay daggrow a ʒevere / a noʒo pan predery
han anken m̃ a⟦ſ⟧grevye / pan vyre w̃th y woly 1848
yn tenewe̅ y ʒeſe / dre an golon a⟦ſ⟧tylly

232 Ioſep ʒe gryſt a ⟦vy̅⟧nas / y aꝛꝛow hay ʒeffregh whek 1852
yn van̄ «ef» del ⟦yn wh⟧as / hag as yſtynnas p̃ dek
a dro ʒy goꝛff y trylyas / ſendaꝉꝉ rych̄ y̅ luas pleg 1856
ha maꝛya leū a ꝛas / ganſo treſt ha moꝛeʒek

233 Ena vn lowaꝛth eſe / ha ynno ⟦ny̅ io⟧ pys 1860
den marow ꝛag receve / newyth ⟦prys⟧ ny̅ io vſijs
coꝛff Ihūs c̉ſt yn treʒe / ʒe̅ logeꝉꝉ a ve degys 1864
Hag a heys ʒe wꝛoweʒe / y̅no eff a ve geſys

234 Vn den da «c̉»ſt a gaꝛa / Nycodemꝰ y hanow 1868 [20r]
eff ny̑ io hardꝭ ʒy notya / ꝛag own̄ caſos y ankow
dwoꝛennos yn pur̃ brena / ef eth ʒe̅ coꝛff o maꝛow 1872
gans v̑ment ʒoʒo eſa / ha ſpycꝭ a v̑ ꝛaſow

235 Nycodemꝰ a vras / coꝛff Ihūs hay eſely
oȳmet̄ o a gŷmys ꝛas / may weʒe coꝛf heb pedry
nagonō ef ny aſas / heb vre ay eſely
yn del⟦m⟧a ef an dyʒgtyas / mey eȳ ſur̄ o y wely

236 ⟦Ha⟧ ſpycſ leas ehen / ef a worras yn y veth̄
ʒe gꝛyſt a bub tenewē / hag a ʒyghow hag a gleth̄
w̃th y dreys ha w̃th y bē / ha ⟦w͛⟧ ol y goꝛf yn weth
dyſqueʒyens w͛ lyꝛgh̄ ankē / beʒe myg͛n yn deweth

237 Han eʒewon̄ a w̃ras / a vgh̄ Ihūs c͛ſt vn men
ledē o ha poys ha bꝛas / moy agſ gauel tredden
Ganſo drys nos y ⟦ʒ⟧olyas / yn y ꝑuys neb o len
an no⟦ſ⟧na a dremenas / hag oll y drok hay anken

238 Teꝛnoys y ſoꝛdyas breſel / gās an eʒewon̄ goky
lauarow tyn hag vghel / feſt yn foll̄ y a gewſy
may ⟦ʒ⟧ens y paꝛys ʒē well̄ / ny woʒyens y ʒyſtrowy
ꝛag Ihūs ʒe leuerell̄ / yn treſſa dyth y ſevy

239 In vn̄ ſtevya oll̄ y eth̄ / bys yn pylat o Iuſtſ
vn eʒow ʒoʒo ŷ freth̄ / yn delma a leuerys
ny a yll̄ yn nos haneth̄ / feſt dyſtough̄ bonas kellys
ha may ſo dŷny ʒe weth̄ • ꝛag bonas Ihūs leʒys

240 Rag an tꝛeyt̃ a gewſys / ha ʒe ꝛag leas huny [20v]
w͛ l⟨yꝛ⟩gh̄ y vonas leʒys / ʒē treſſa dyth̄ y ſeuy
maꝛs maꝛa peʒa degſ / gans y dus nã caffan ny
yn vꝛna byth leuerys / ef ʒe ſevell̄ dre veſtry

241 Pylat a yꝛghys ʒeʒe / w͛ beyn kylly an bewnans
monas ʒē coꝛf ʒy weʒe / n⟦â⟧ kemeꝛꝛe ⟦y⟧ yſkeꝛans
hag yn nos oll̄ aſpye / ha gwyʒe tam na guſkens
y eth yn vn fyſtene / peſwaꝛ marrek yꝛvys ens

242 Pan deʒens y bys yn beth̄ / y ʒeth vn maꝛꝛek ʒy ben
hag aꝛall̄ ʒy dreys ŷ weth / yꝛvys faſt bys yn ʒewen
hag a ʒyghow hag a gleth̄ / onon a bub tenewen
boſt a wrens tyn ha deveth / yn gweʒens w̃th̄ y ehen

243 En vaꝛogyon̄ a guſkas / myttyn han gyth̄ ow taꝛʒe
ha Ihûs a ʒeʒo⟦ꝛ⟧as / hag eth̄ yn le may ſŷne
Deu a peꝛt ha m̃ y ꝛas / golow cleyꝛ ow tewŷnye
ef a wre oll̄ y vŷnas / y ny yllens y weʒe

244 Pan o p̃ holeꝛgh̄ an gyth̄ / y tefenas vn marrek
del deth an nef wꝰ y fyth / ef a welas golow tek
han meyn vmhelys yn weth̄ / eſe a vgh̄ Ih̄us whek
ha wꝰnoʒo a⟪y⟫ yſeth̄ / ell̄ benegas lowenek

245 En maꝛꝛek na a ſevys / oll̄ yn ban y goweʒe
ha ʒeʒe a leuerys / a Ihūs fatell̄ vye
an dēma re drehevys / gallas ny woʒā pele
lêman na ven⟪ n⟫y leʒys / nŷ ges foꝛth̄ ʒe ōweʒe

246 Maꝛꝛak aꝛall̄ a gowſas / gony vyth̄ pā veŷ genys
tru a thu elhas elhas / gans vn huȳ re ben tullys
an bewnās ny re gollas / hag yn weth agan fleghys
om ʒyghtyn truſſen anwlas / fyan na ven⟪ n⟫y kefys

247 ⟨*An* p⟩eſwoꝛe a gewſys / na whelyn gwevye an pow [21r]
⟨*k*⟩epꝰ del ve ʒe Iuſtꝭ / dū leueryn wꝰ anow
ay veth̄ del yw drehevys / na leueꝛyn vn gerꝰ gow
y a ꝛuge a ʒeſympys / oll̄ wꝰ lyꝛgh̄ y aꝛhadow

248 I eth̄ yn vn fyſtene / ʒe pylat aga Iuſtꝭ
en deſkyens ⟪y⟫ del vye / ha ʒoʒo a leuerys
ꝛe ſaffe c̓ſt heb ſtrevye / ol ⟦ʒ⟧y voth̄ gans golowys
ha na yllens y gwyʒe / y voth na vo colenwys

249 Ena pylat pan glewas / yn delma y ʒe gewſell̄
predeꝛow an kemeꝛas / ꝛag own̄ y ʒe leuerell̄
ha ʒy notye drys an wlas / furꝰ a ogas hag a bell̄
may teffe tꝯ gans neꝛth bꝛ̃s / ⟦eꝛbyn⟧ ꝛg guſtle bell̄

250 Rag hēna pylat a ꝛos / ʒe voꝛogyon̄ aga ꝛo
may lavaꝛſans hadolos / ŷ pub tylleꝛ drꝭ an vꝛo
ʒe vos tus yꝛvys yn nos / wꝰneʒe kŷmys a dro
na gens y haꝛd꜌ ʒe w̃tos / lême oll̄ monas ʒe fo

251 En vaꝛogyon pan glewas / pylat ov cows ŷ della
m̃ a ioy a⟦ſ⟧kemeꝛas / y ʒe ʒeank yn della
an peynys o creff ha bꝛas / ha cafos ꝛohow mᷓ ʒa
both pylat y a notyas / yn le may ʒens ꝛag hēna

252 In keth gythna ꝑ̃ avaꝛ / han houl̄l nowyth̄ drehevys
tyꝛ̑ marea cleyꝛ ha whar / a ʒeth̄ ʒe beth leuerys
ha ganſe oy̆met heb ꝑᷓ / ꝛag coꝛf Ih̄us o ꝑ̑nnys
whath yn eꝛna nŷ gens war / bonas mab du drehevys

253 Pan o an tyꝛ̑ maꝛya • ogas ʒē beth deueth⟨ys⟩ [21v]
an meyn eſa a wᷓʒa / y an guelas drehevys
en benenas yn delma / yn treʒe a leueꝛys
ʒe woꝛth an beth an meȳma / ʒȳny pu an ōmelys

254 En benenas leu a ꝛas / gans an beth faſt poweſſês
ŵth an pê y a welas / ʒe beth yw leuerꝭ kens
vn flough̄ yonk gwȳ y ʒyllas / eyl̄l o ha y ny woʒyens
ſcruth own m̃ a⟦ſ⟧kemeꝛas / ꝛag an mᷓthus re welſens

255 En eyll a gewſys ʒeʒe / na veʒough̄ dyſcōfoꝛtꝭ
Ih̄us ċſt a nazary / del welſough̄ a ve lethys
ſevys gallas ʒe gen le / de a peꝛt ha m̃ y breys
a wott⟦a⟧ an le may ʒeſe / v̄ma nȳ gew ef tregꝭ

256 Eugh̄ yn fen ʒy ʒyſchyblon / ha leuerough wy ʒeʒe
ha ʒe pedyꝛ dos yn ſcon / ⟦eꝛbyn⟧ ʒe alyle
ena ċſt an kuf colon / wy an kyff yn lowene
del leuerys y honon / yn kyg yn goys ow pewe

257 Gans hēna y a drylyas / confoꝛtꝭ ha lowenek
hag eth̄ tus ċſt ꝛag whelas / hag as cafos moreʒek
y lauaꝛſons ol an cas / y ʒeʒons yn vn tonek
bys ⟦yn⟧ galyle ʒy whelas / ha ʒe gows ŵth Ih̄us wek

258 Pan deʒons ʒe alyle / Ihūs ċſt y a welas
yn y ʒenſys ow pewe / deu apeꝛt ha m̃ y ꝛas
ol y beyn yntremenſe / ha trylys ens yn ioy bꝛas
hag a vyth̄ ʒȳny neffre / mᷓ a creſyn ha bos vas

259 Del ſevys mab du ay veth̄ / yn eꝛna ȝe treſſa dyth̄
yn della ol ny a ſeff / deth brues drok ha da yn weth̄
obereth̄ dremas a dyff / yn eꝛna ꝛych̄ ef a vyth̄
drok ȝe yn gythna goef • ȝe gryſt y fyth̄ anbaꝛth cleth

5
FACSIMILES

5.1 *THE CHARTER FRAGMENT*

MS Add. Charter 19491 is a piece of vellum about 165 mm tall and 325 mm wide. On the recto is part of a land-grant, written in Latin; the verso is divided distinctly into two columns, with *The Charter Fragment* verse taking up most of the left-hand column.

There is plenty of room on the page—the writer keeps very strictly to the first column, even writing the parts of lines 3 and 6 above the line rather than intruding into the second column. It may very well have been that the author anticipated needing all of the space. This accords with our view that the text was part of a drama.

Reproduction of these images was made possible by the generosity of the British Library. Photographs by Michael Everson.

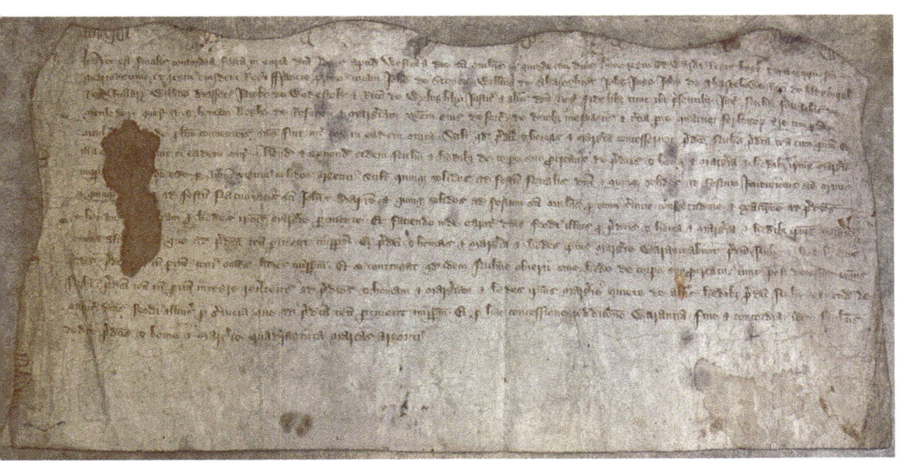

Plate 1. The recto of MS Add. Charter 19491.

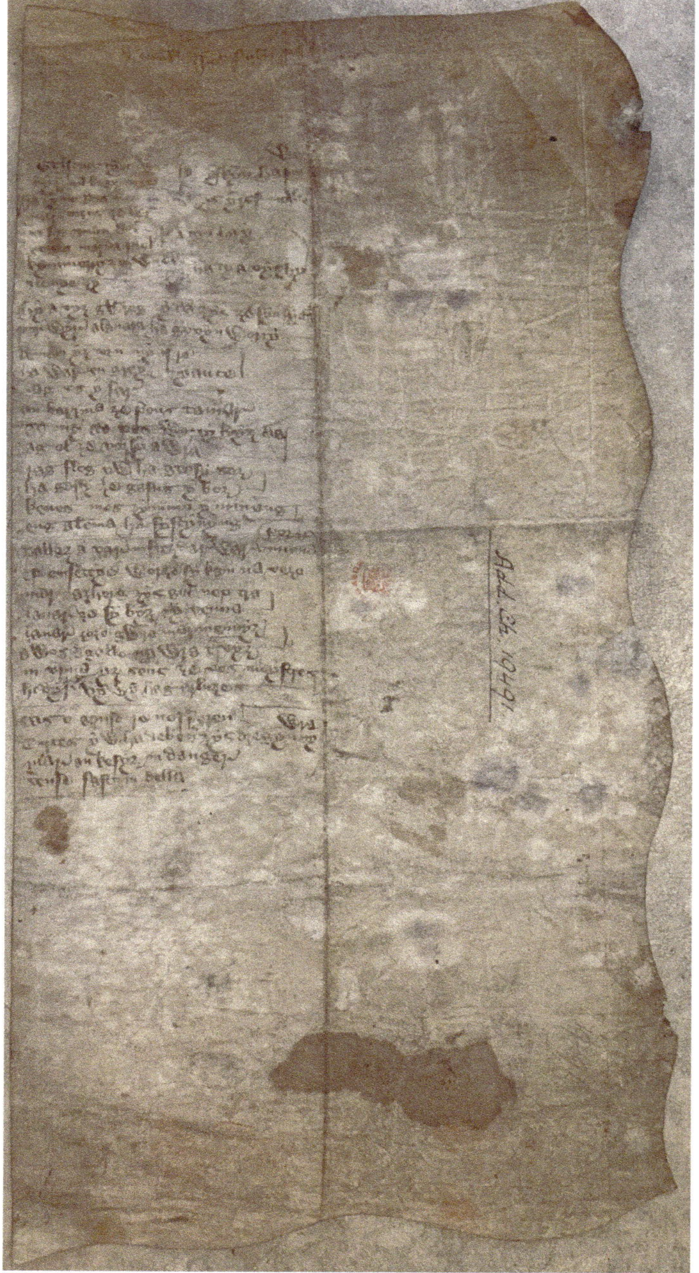

Plate 2. The verso of MS Add. Charter 19491.

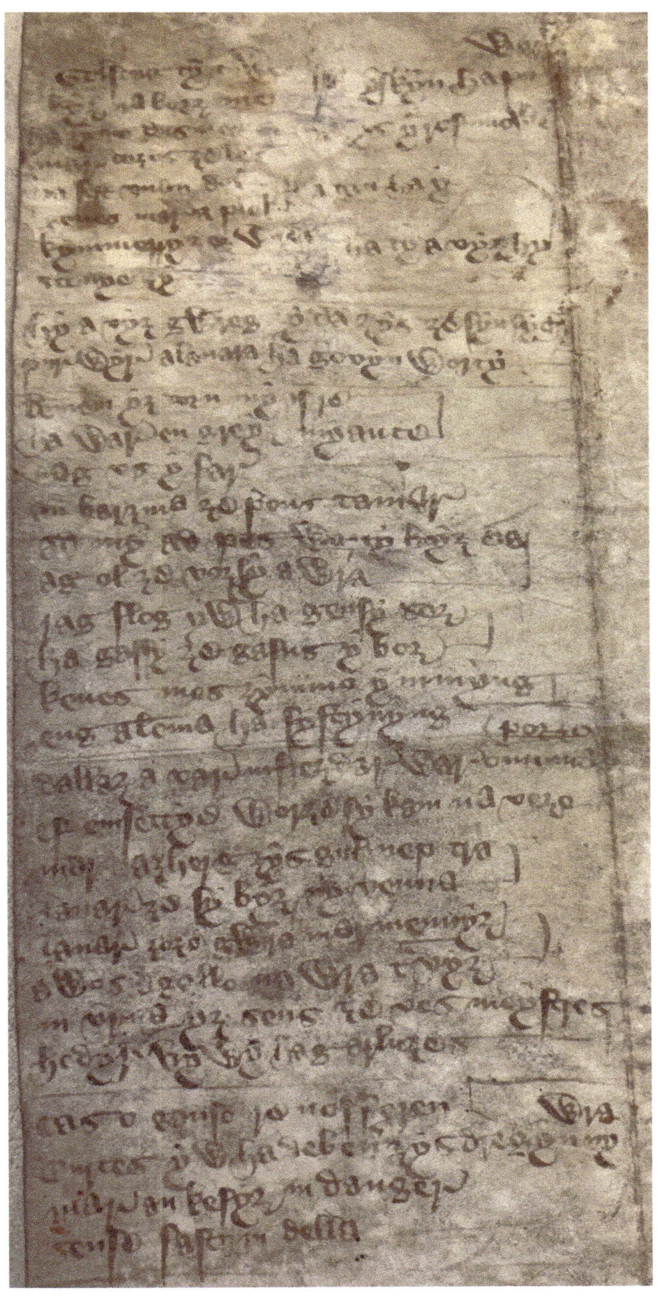

Plate 3. The text of *The Charter Fragment*.

5.2 *PASCON AGAN ARLUTH*

Harley MS 1782 is parchment codex about 170 mm tall and 120 mm wide. The text block measures about 130 mm by 100 mm. There are 10 drawings in the lower margins of folios 1r, 1v, 2r, 6v, 7v, 9r, 10r, 11v, 14v, and 15v, with colour wash in green, red, a brownish yellow representing gold, and dark blue. An initial capital insular T in red with yellow-washed penwork decoration appears on folio 1r. Initials, typically in the first line of a stanza (lines 5 and 1587 are exceptions), are highlighted in red; other letters have extensions of various kinds. In both the palaeographic and expanded transcriptions these have been coloured red as the scribe clearly intended, though on some of the folios the rubrication ranges from very faint brown to quite invisible. Brackets connect the verses in stanzas throughout.

In places on various folios the text has been overwritten, as at the top of folios 3v and 4r, 20r, and a fair few other places. Evidently this was done to strengthen or restore a faded or blurred text, and it does not appear that this has affected the reading of the text. Unfortunately we do not have evidence as to when or by whom the overwriting was made. An exhaustive discussion of this did not seem to be useful for this edition, however, apart from the note 1 on page 147, which is relevant to an obscured word in the English translation. It is likely we are fortunate to have the overwriting.

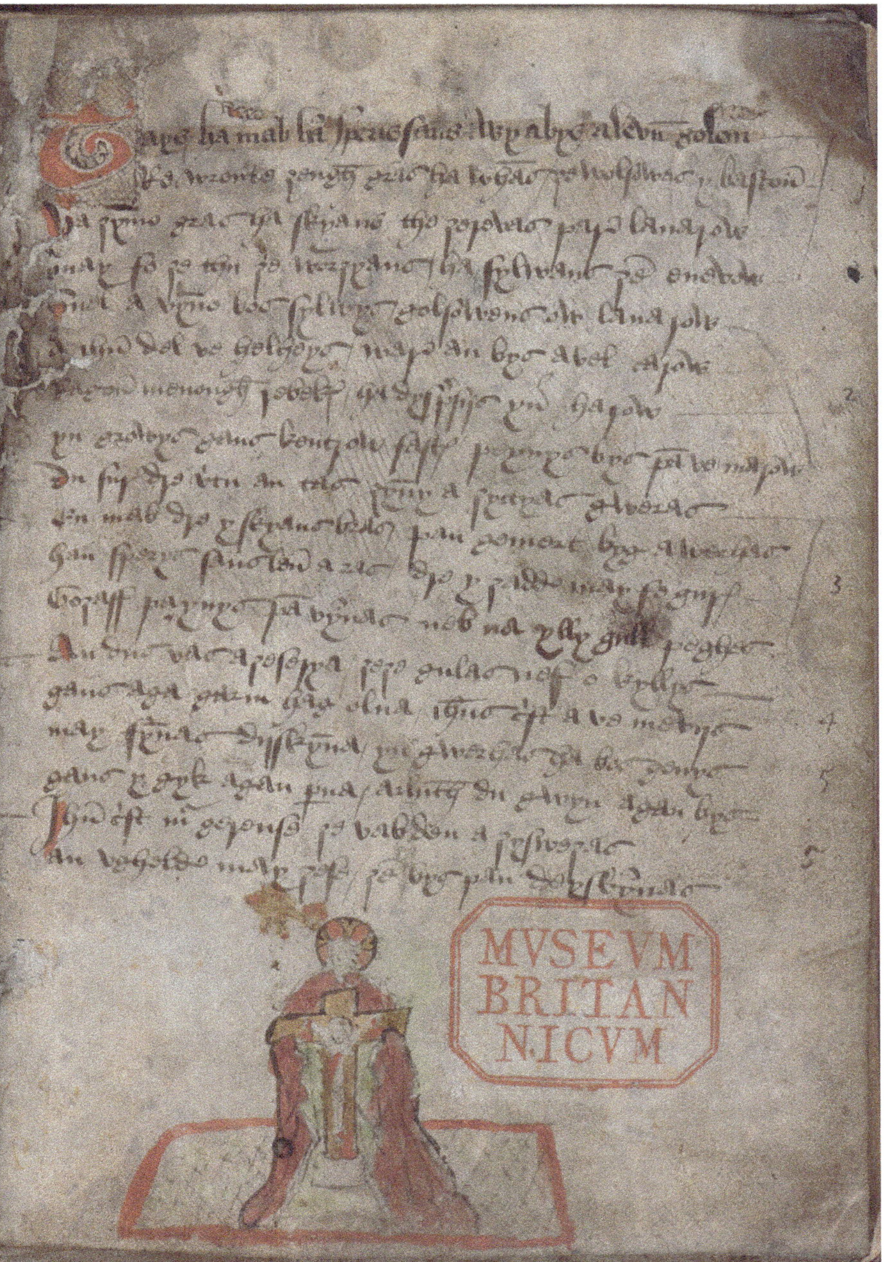

Plate 4. Harley MS 1782, *f.* 1r.

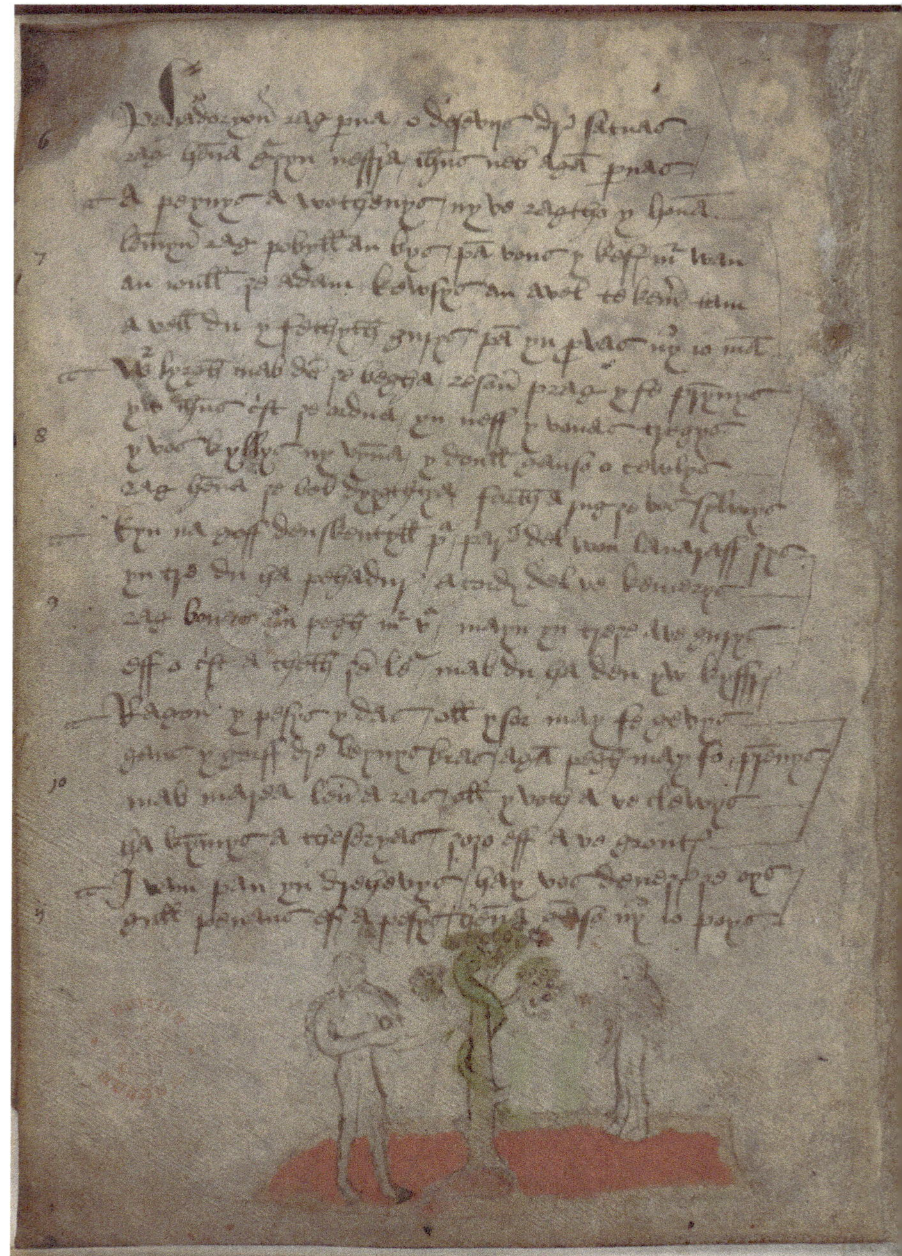

Plate 5. Harley MS 1782, *f.* 1v.

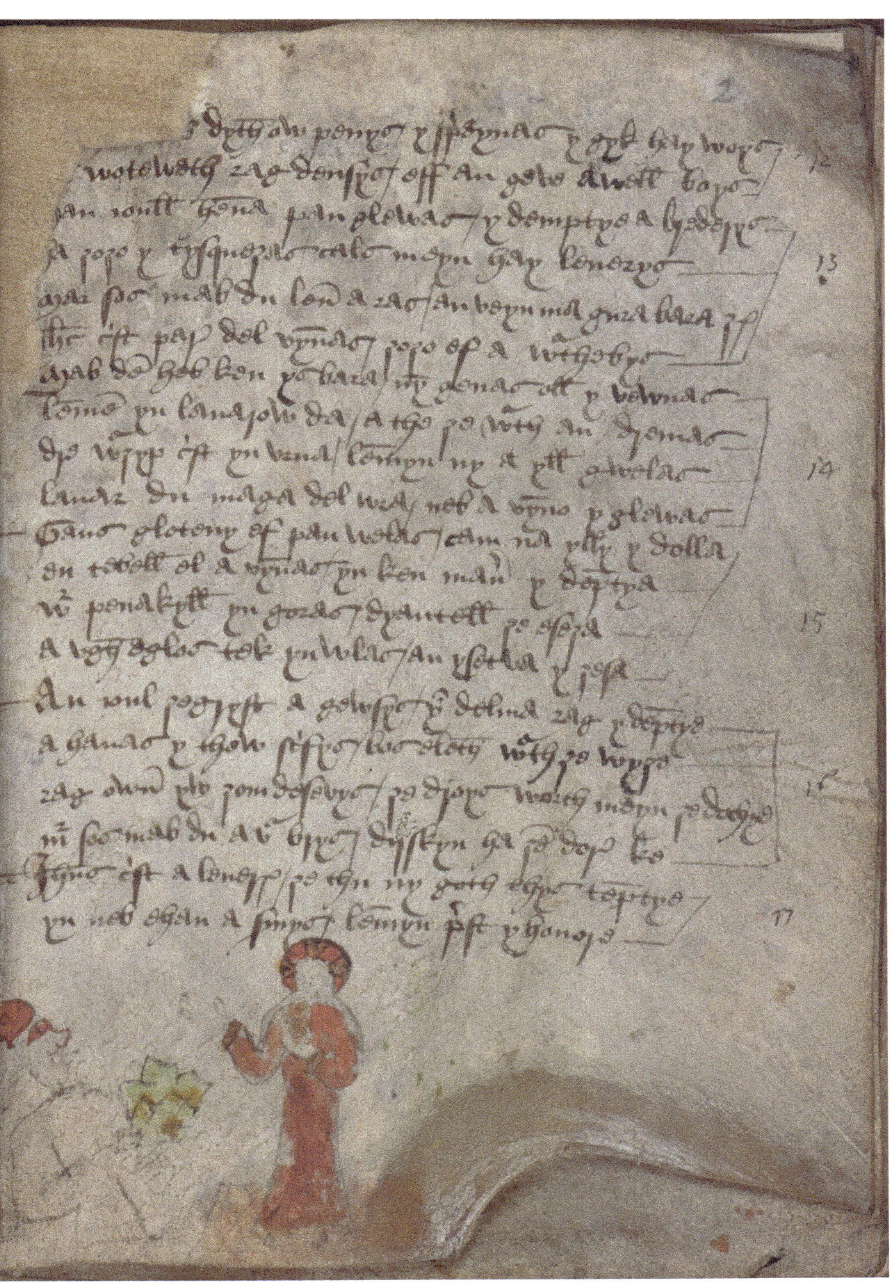

Plate 6. Harley MS 1782, *f.* 2r.

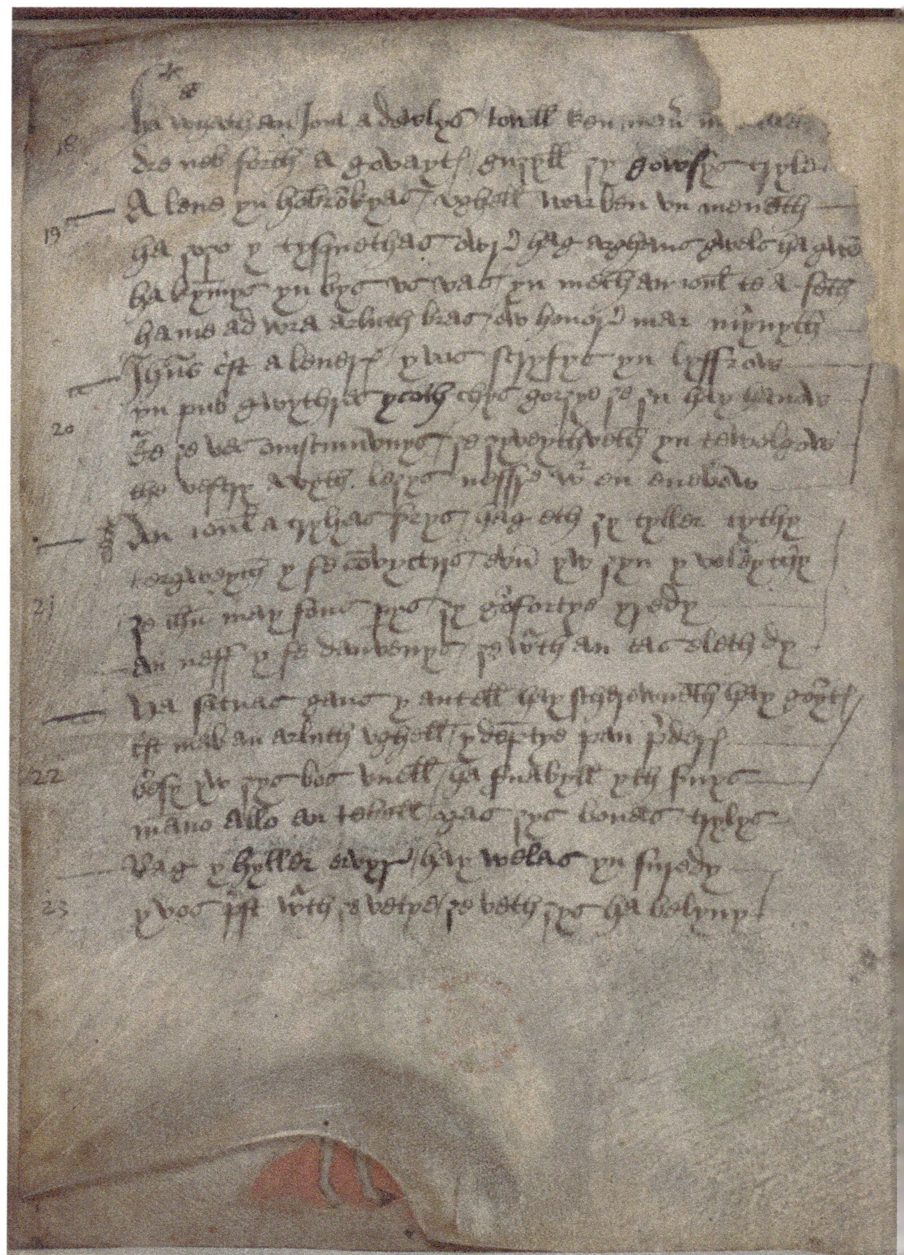

Plate 7. Harley MS 1782, *f*. 2v.

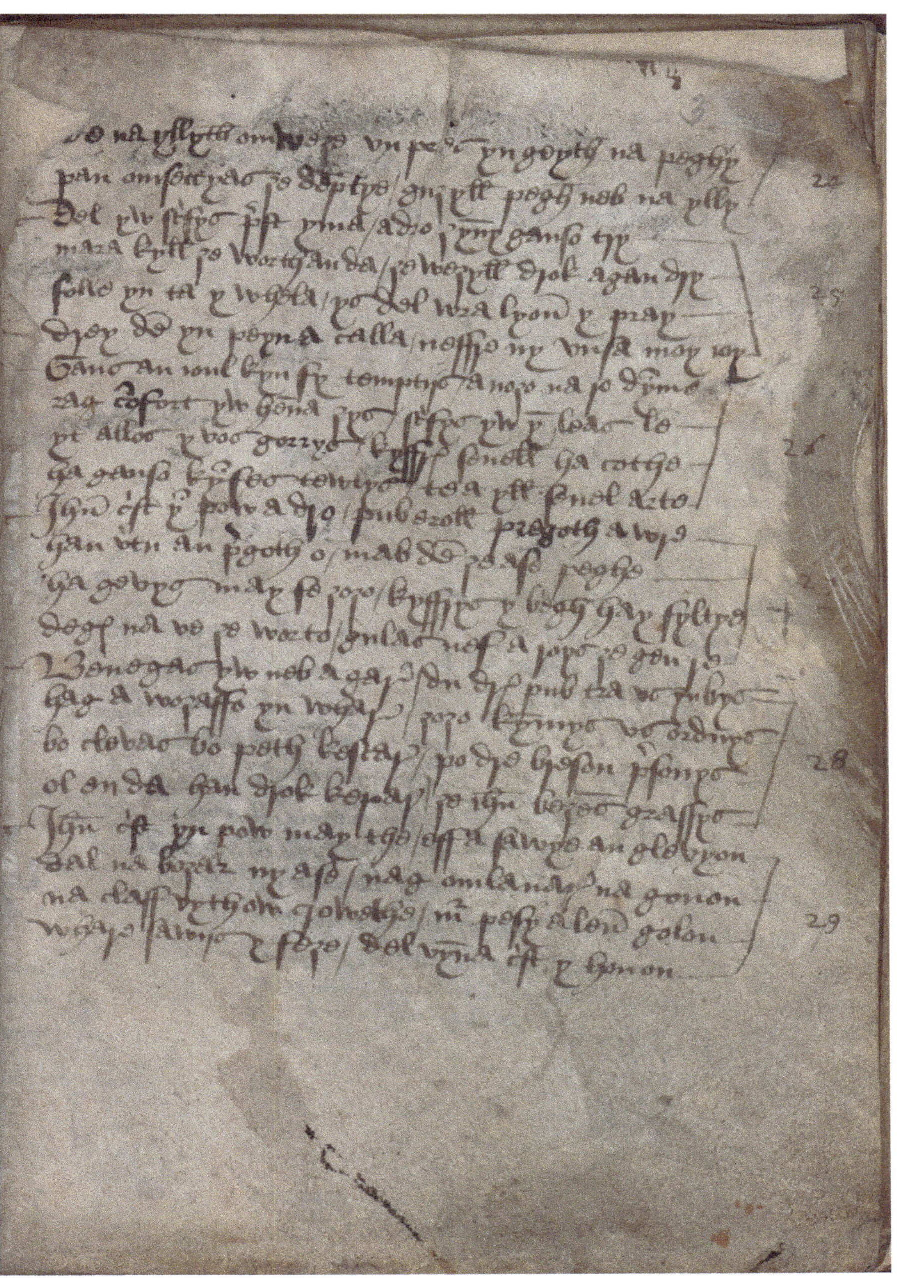

Plate 8. Harley MS 1782, *f.* 3r.

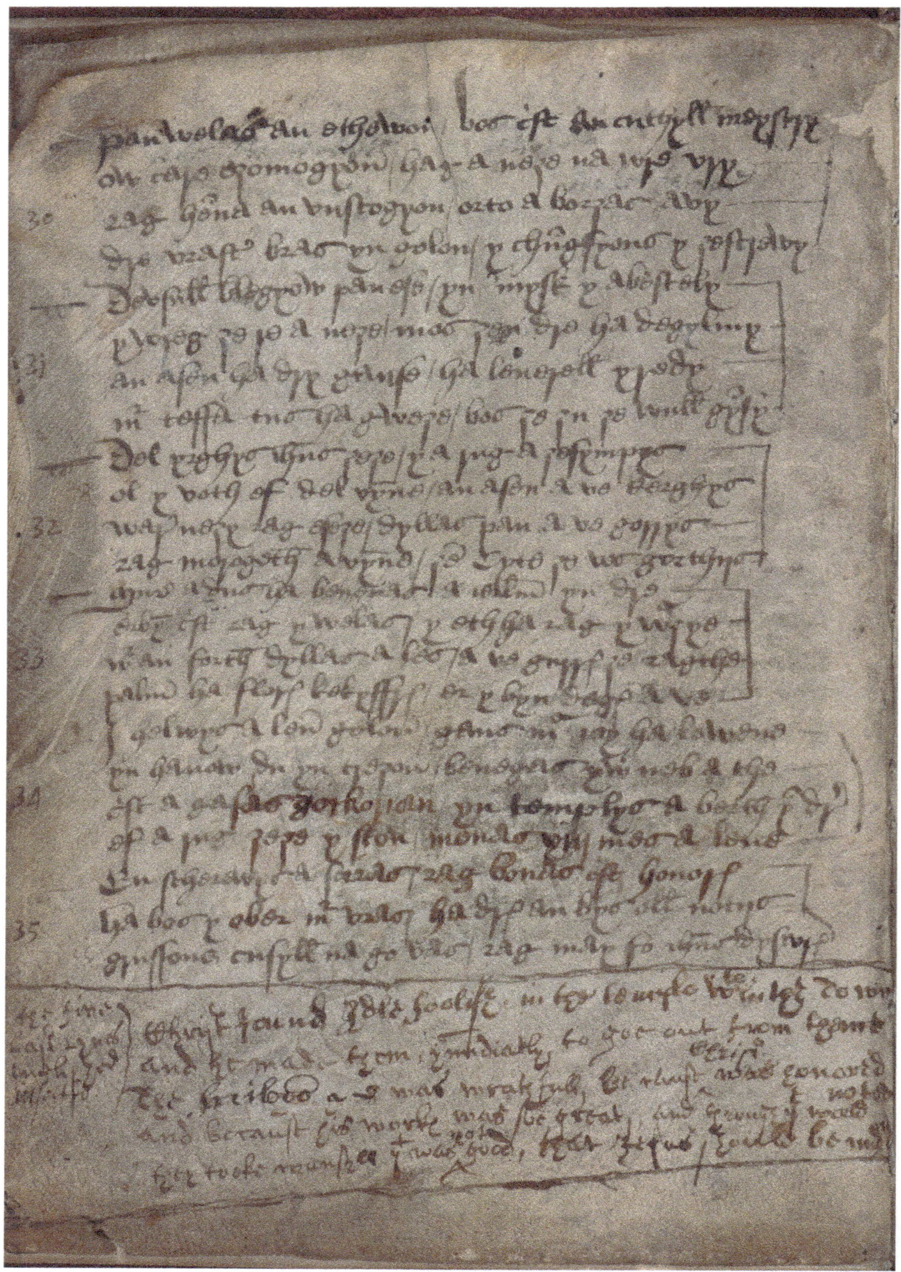

Plate 9. Harley MS 1782, *f.* 3v.

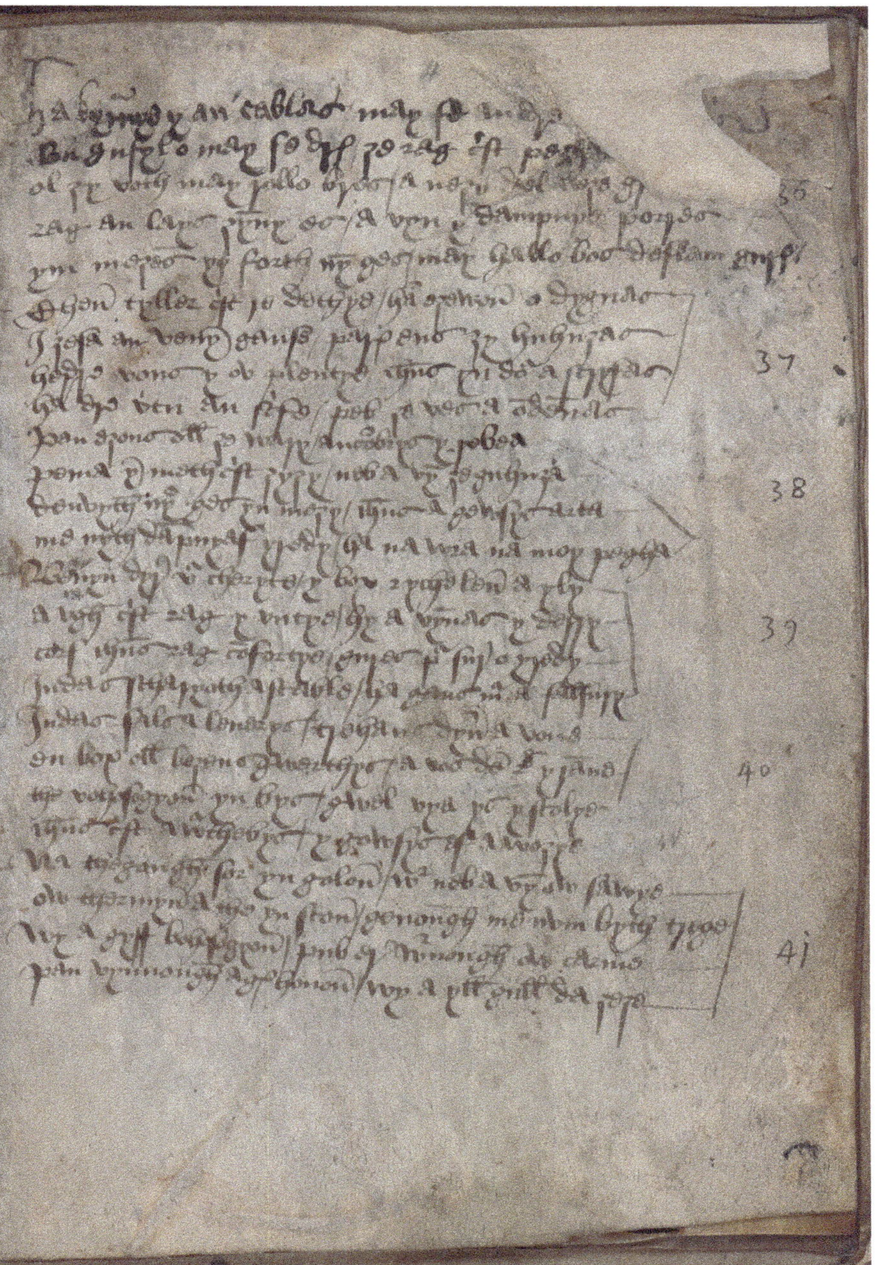

Plate 10. Harley MS 1782, *f.* 4r.

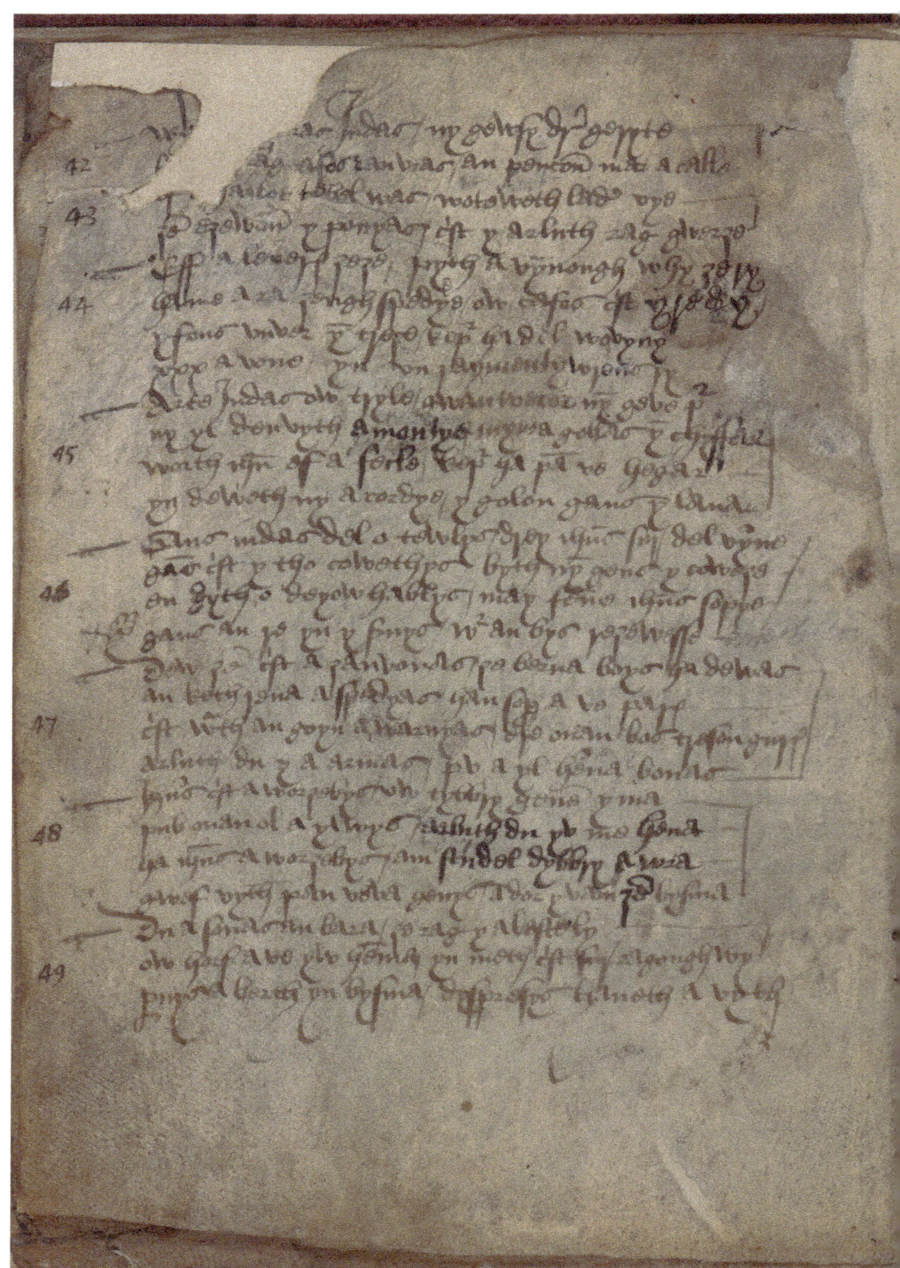

Plate 11. Harley MS 1782, *f*. 4v.

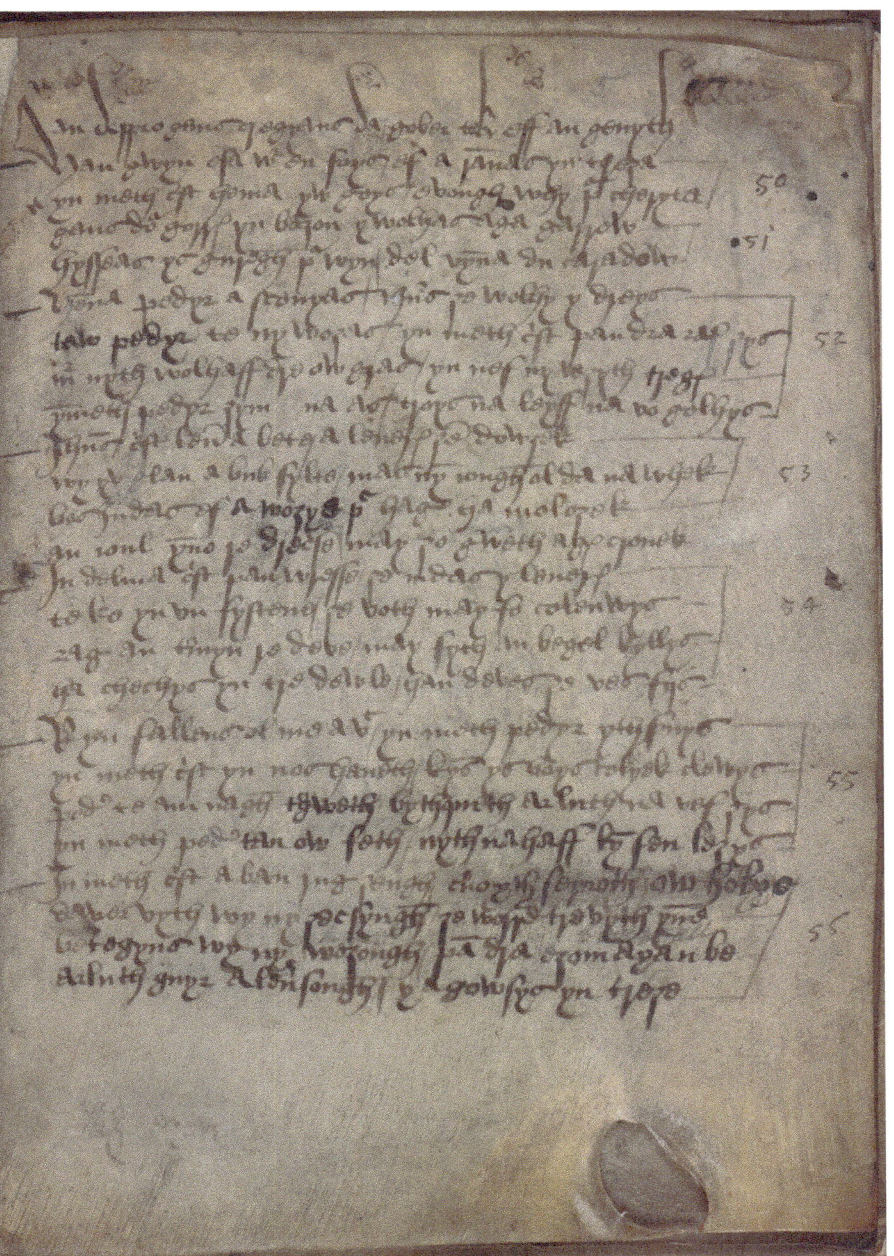

Plate 12. Harley MS 1782, *f*. 5r.

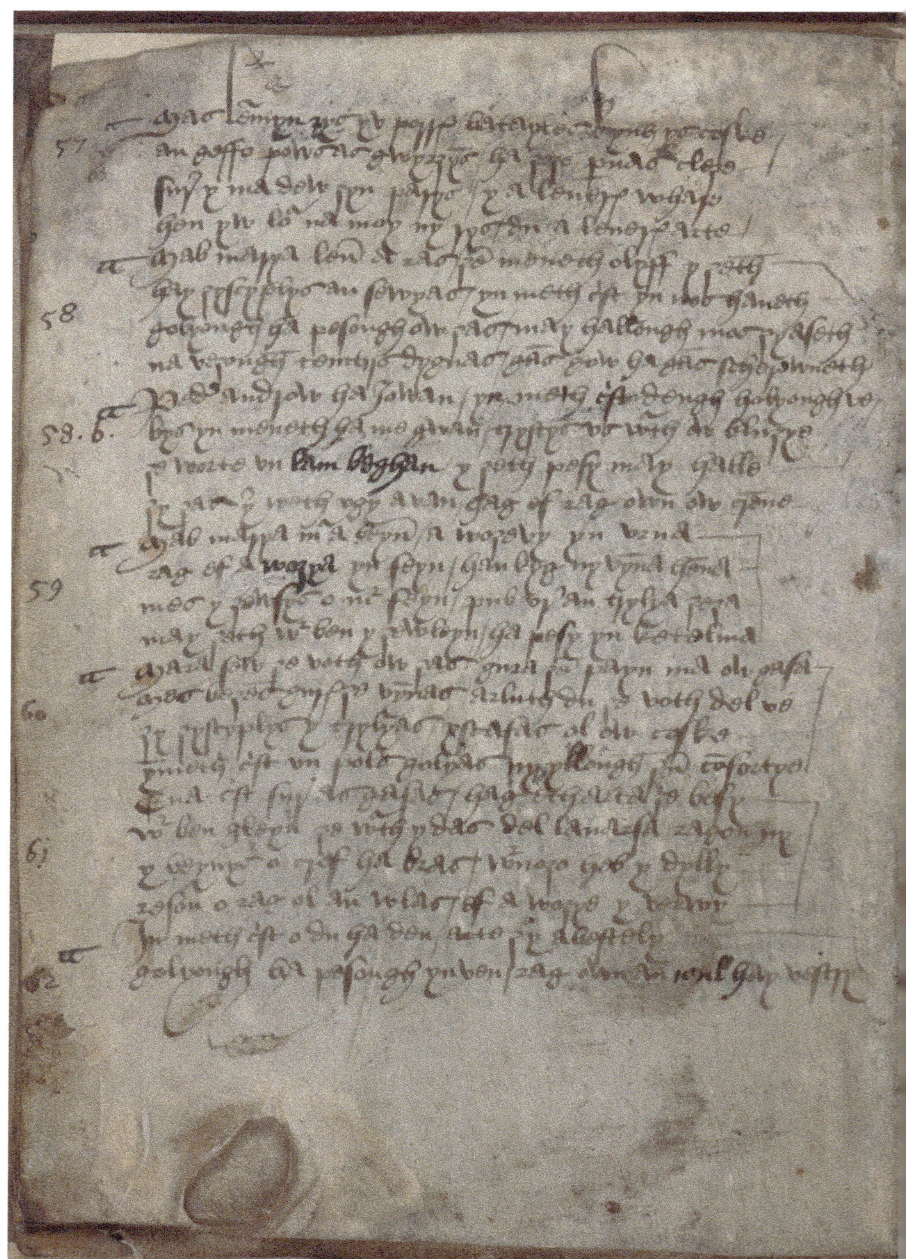

Plate 13. Harley MS 1782, *f*. 5v.

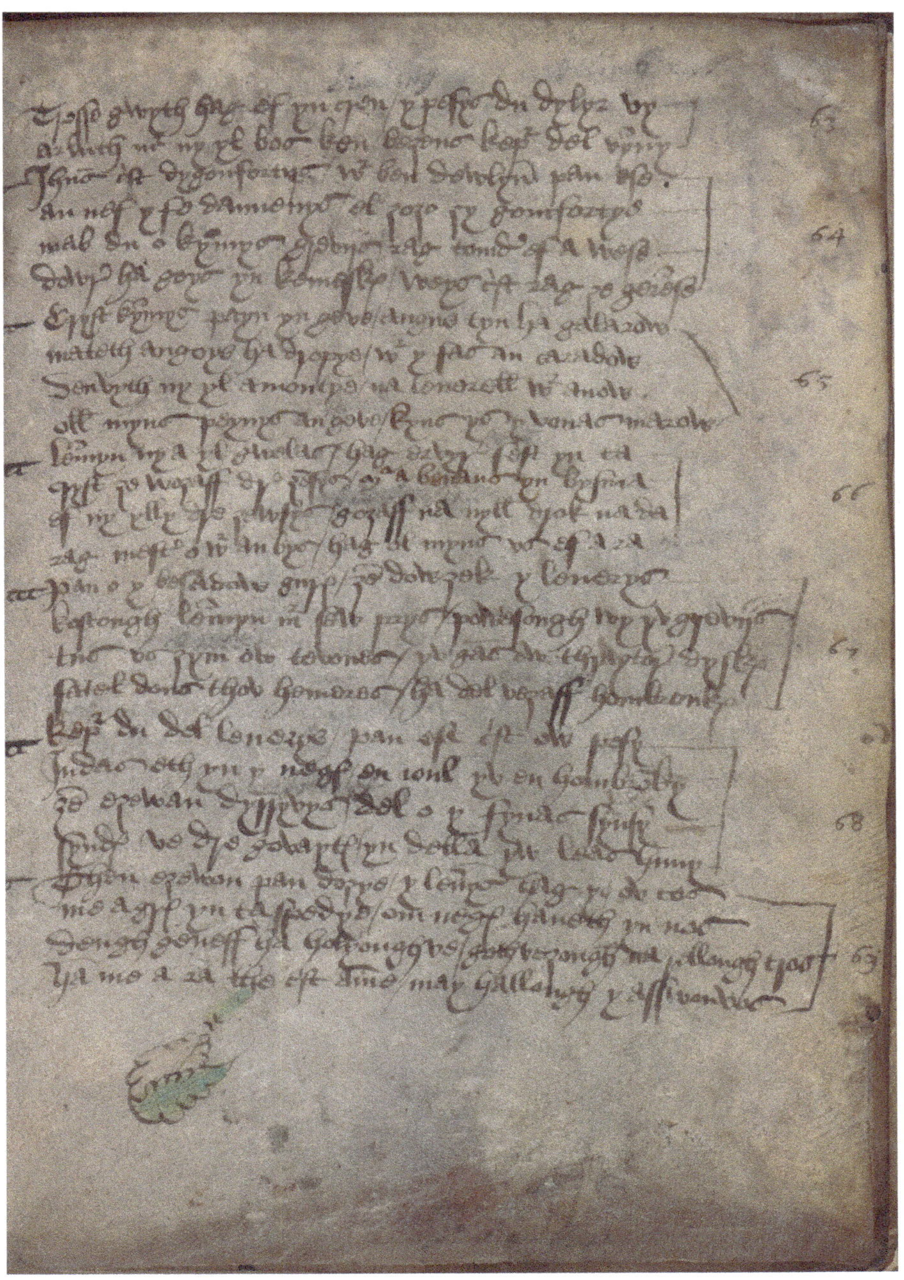

Plate 14. Harley MS 1782, *f.* 6r.

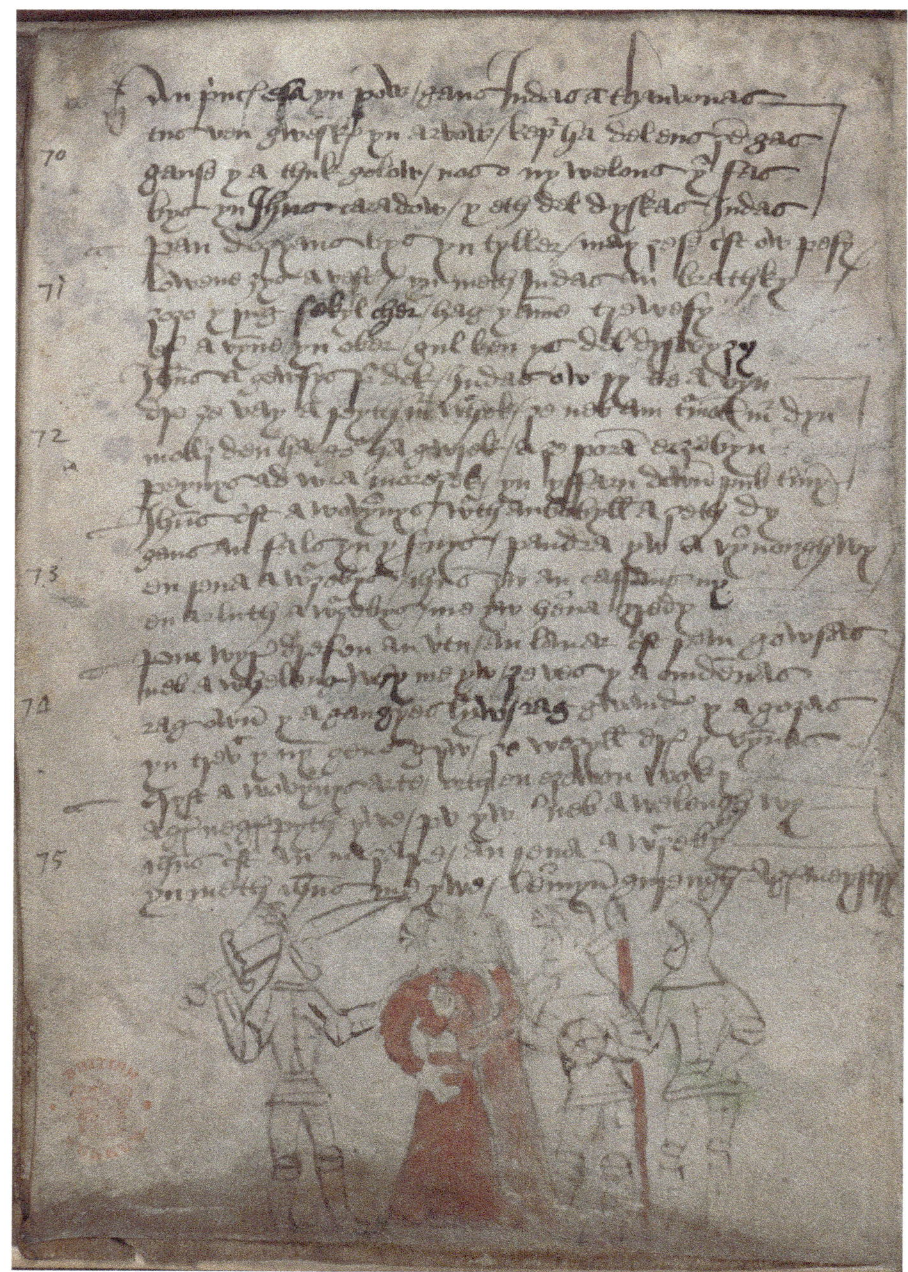

Plate 15. Harley MS 1782, *f.* 6v.

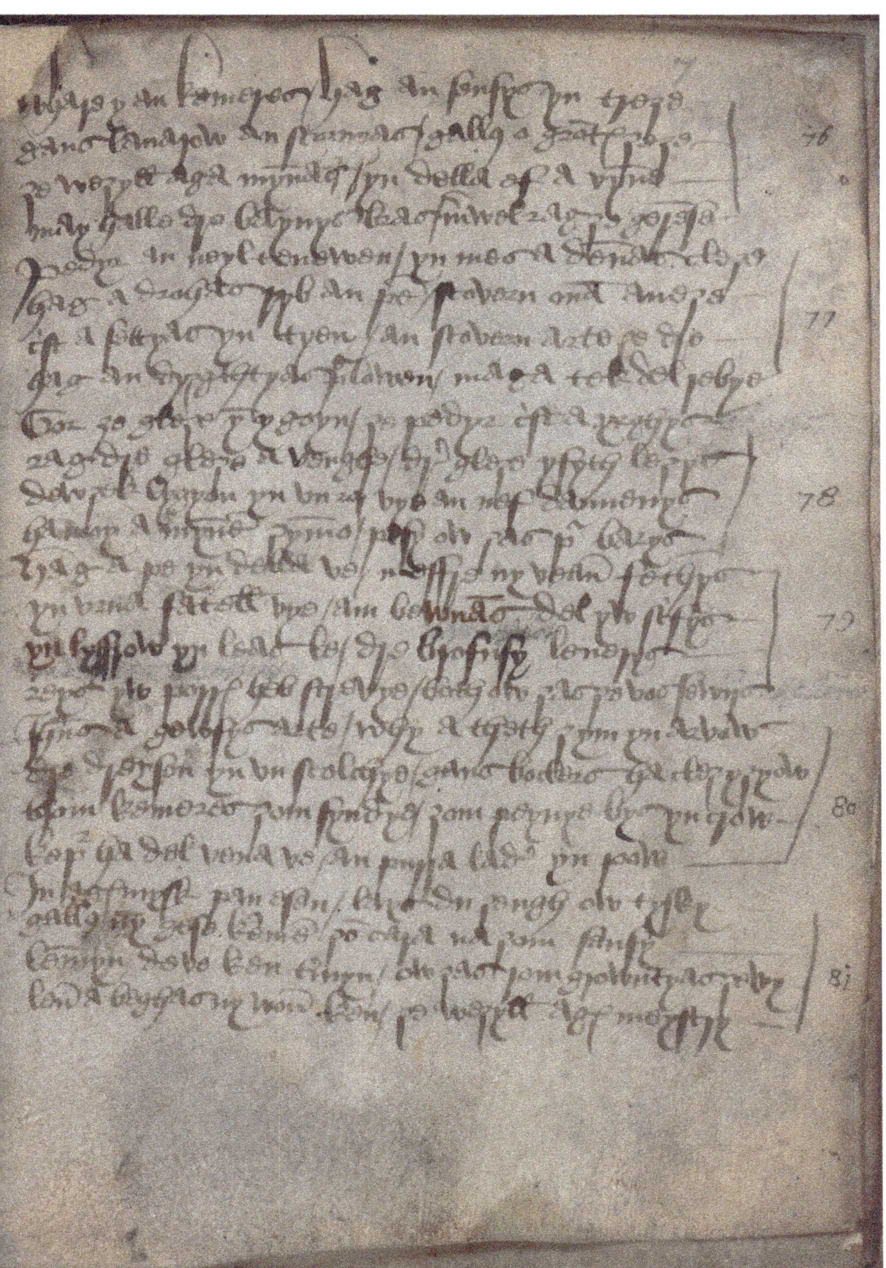

Plate 16. Harley MS 1782, *f.* 7r.

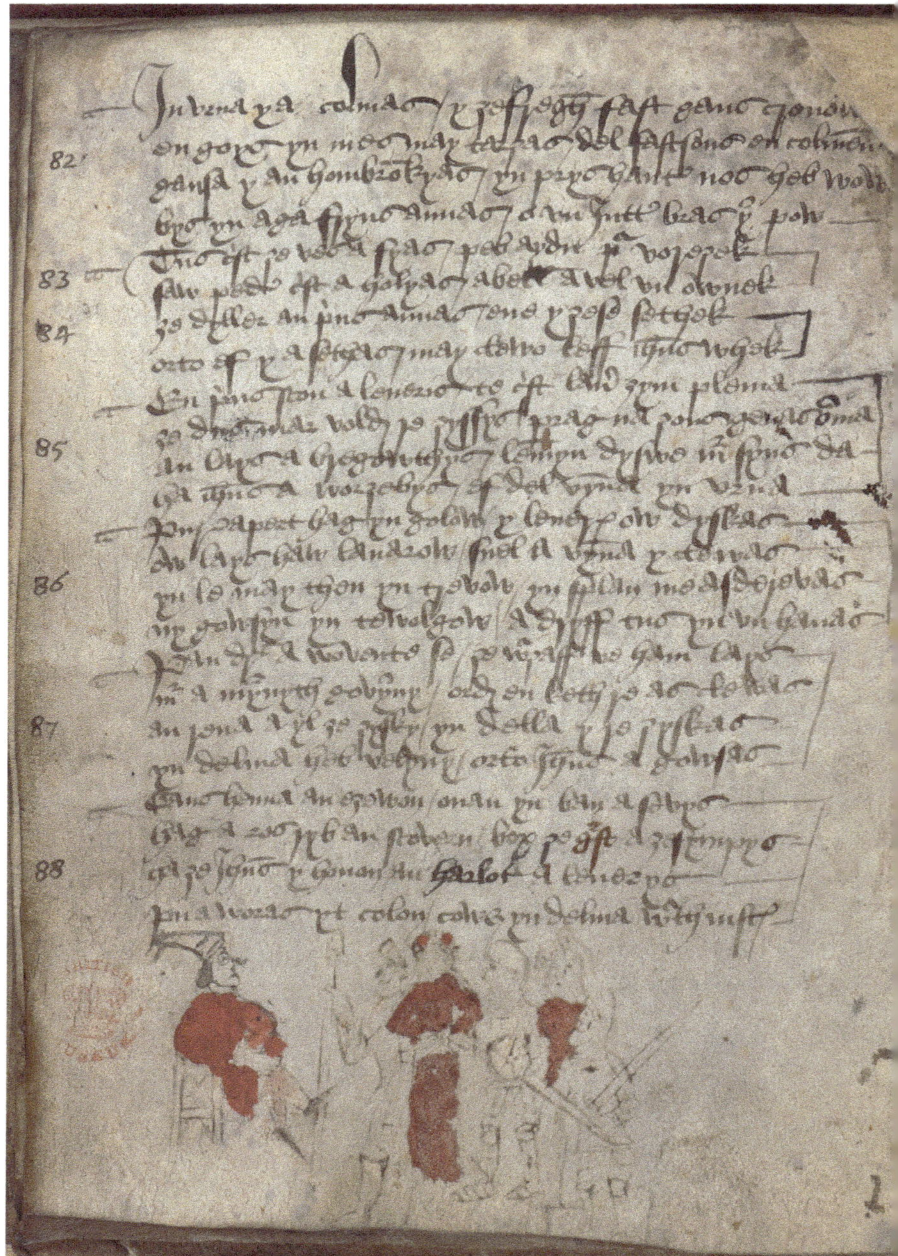

Plate 17. Harley MS 1782, *f.* 7v.

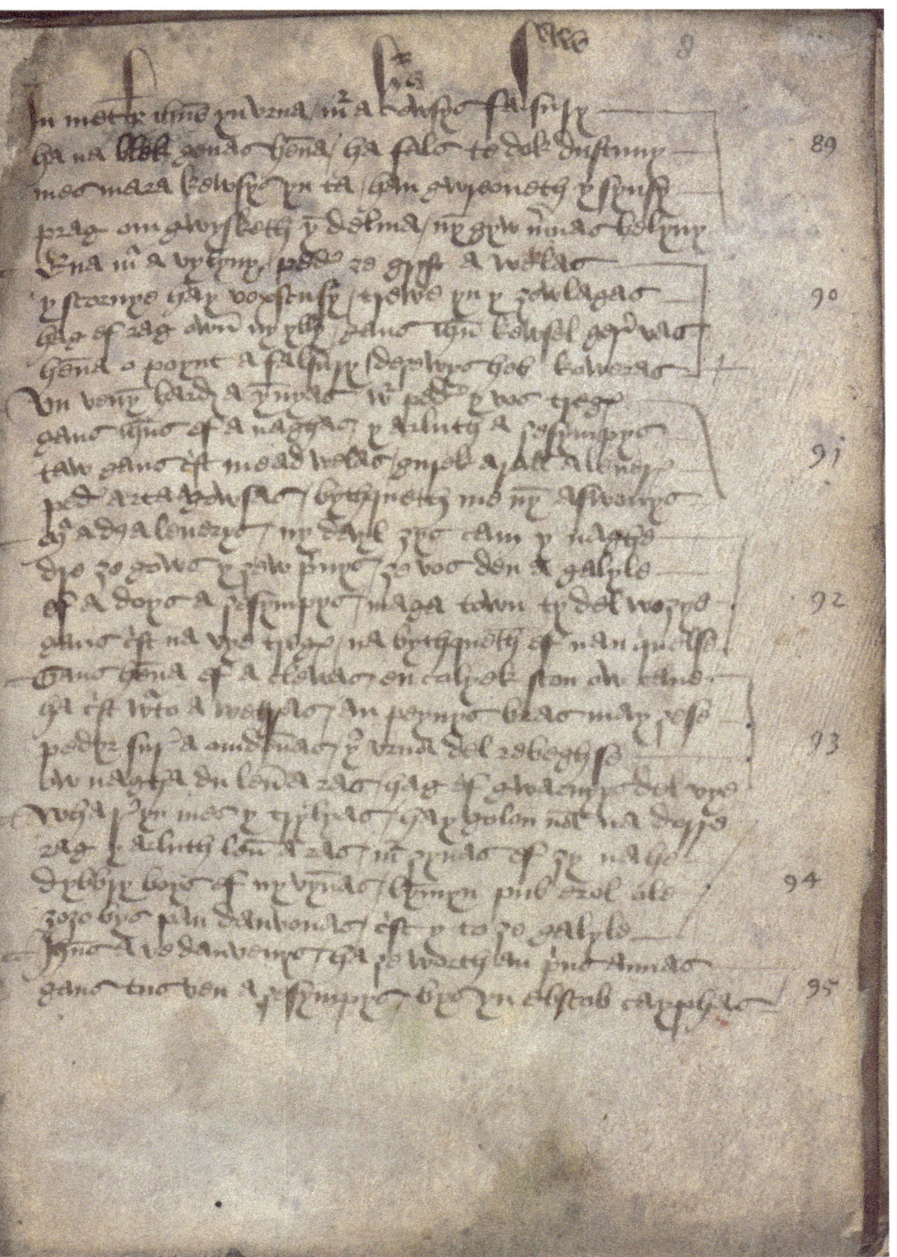

Plate 18. Harley MS 1782, *f.* 8r.

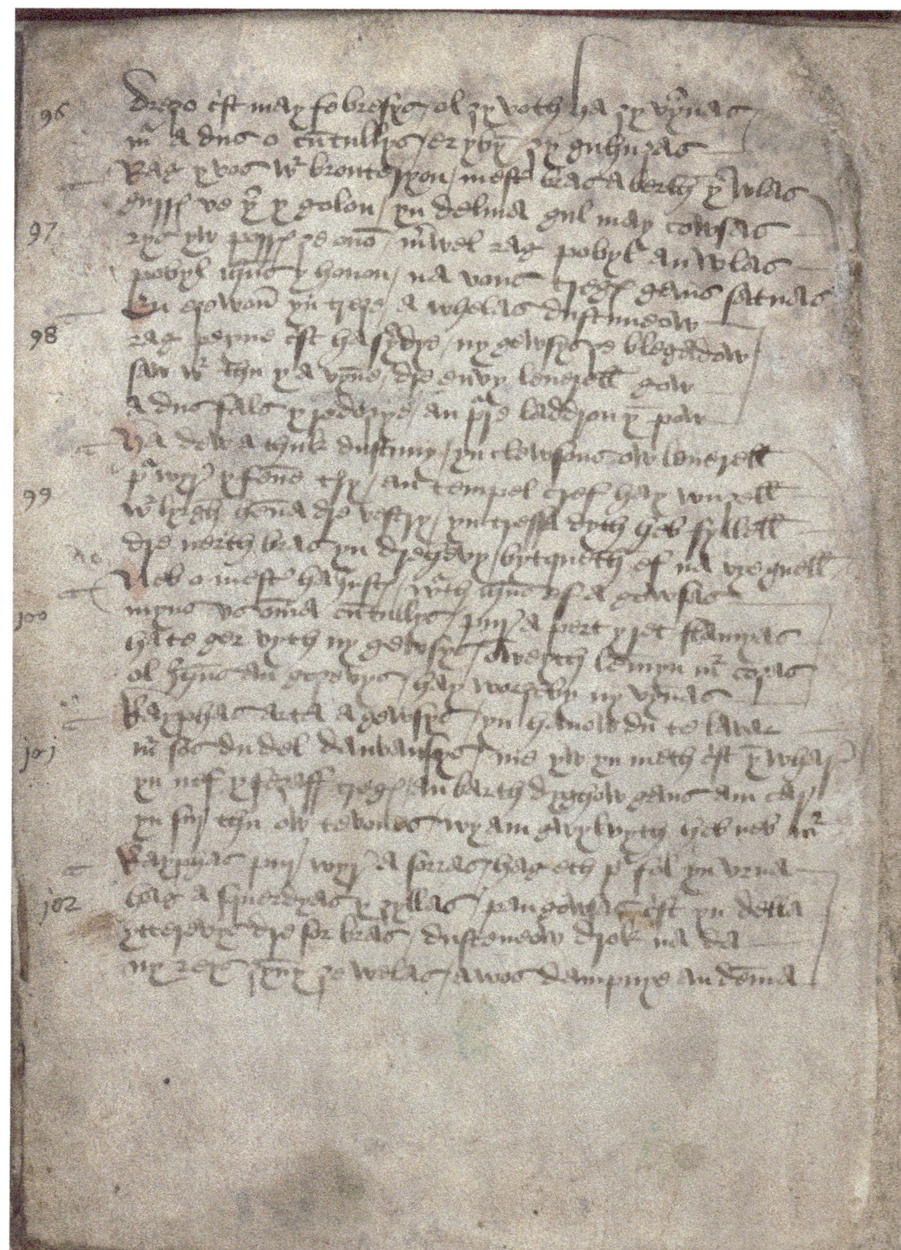

Plate 19. Harley MS 1782, *f.* 8v.

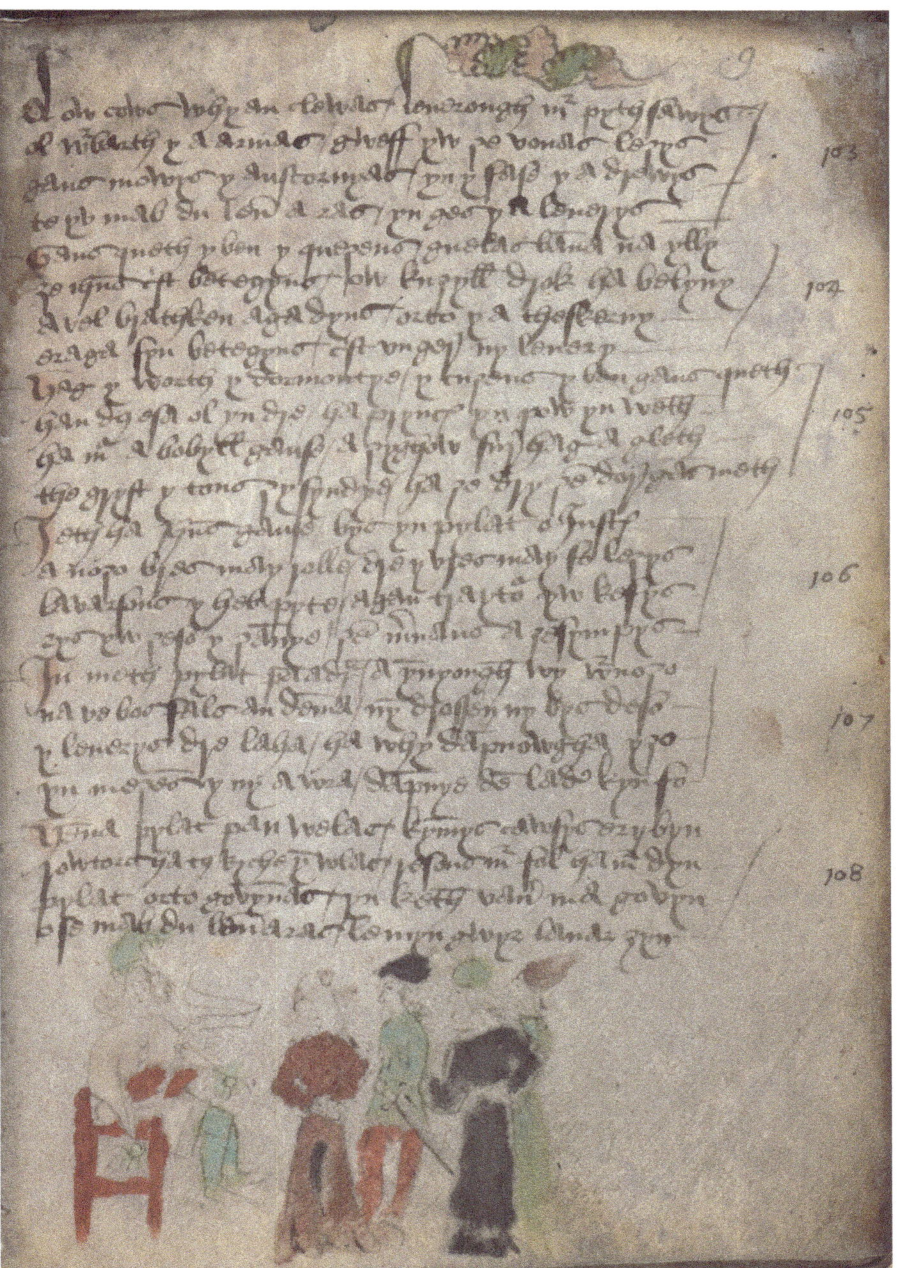

Plate 20. Harley MS 1782, *f.* 9r.

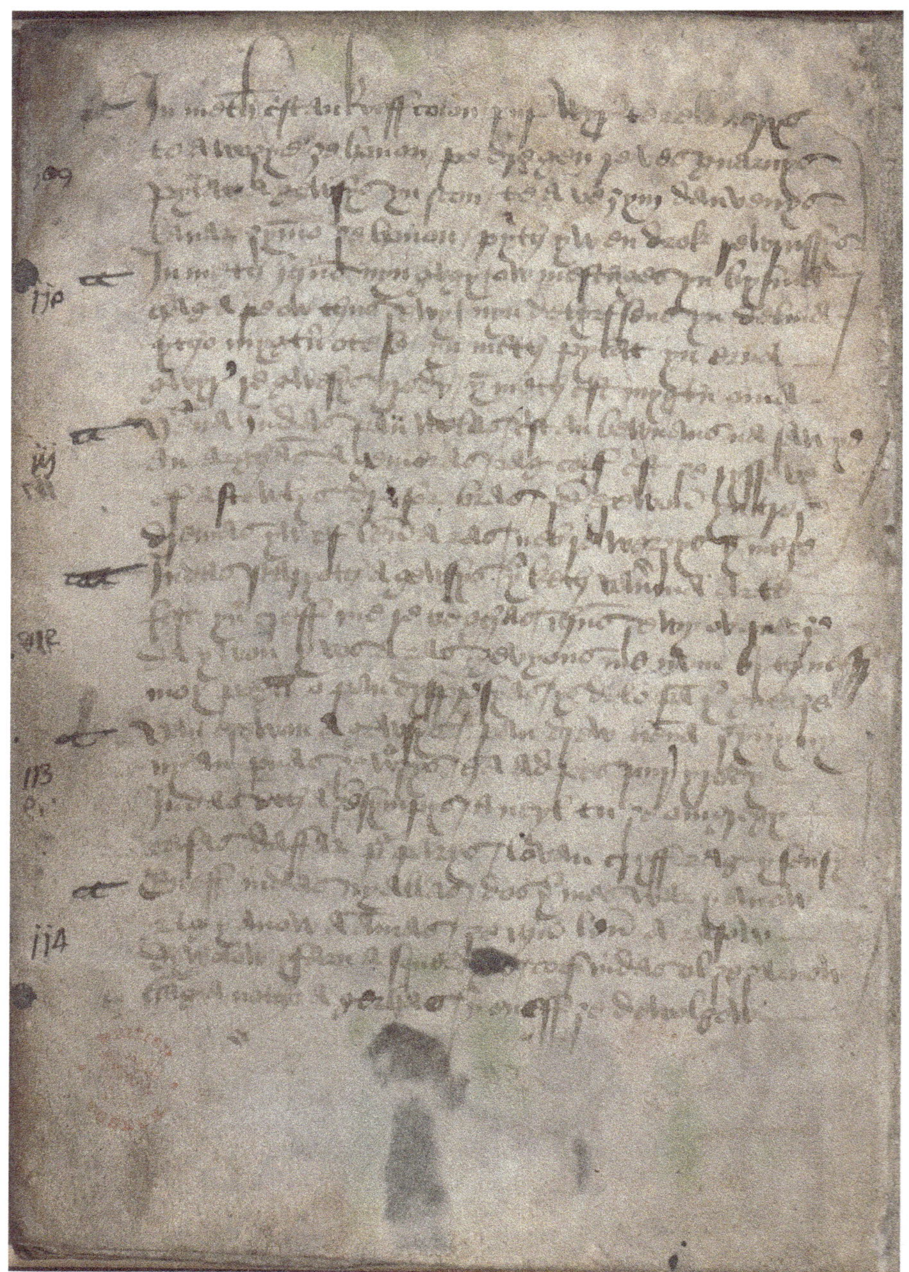

Plate 21. Harley MS 1782, *f.* 9v.

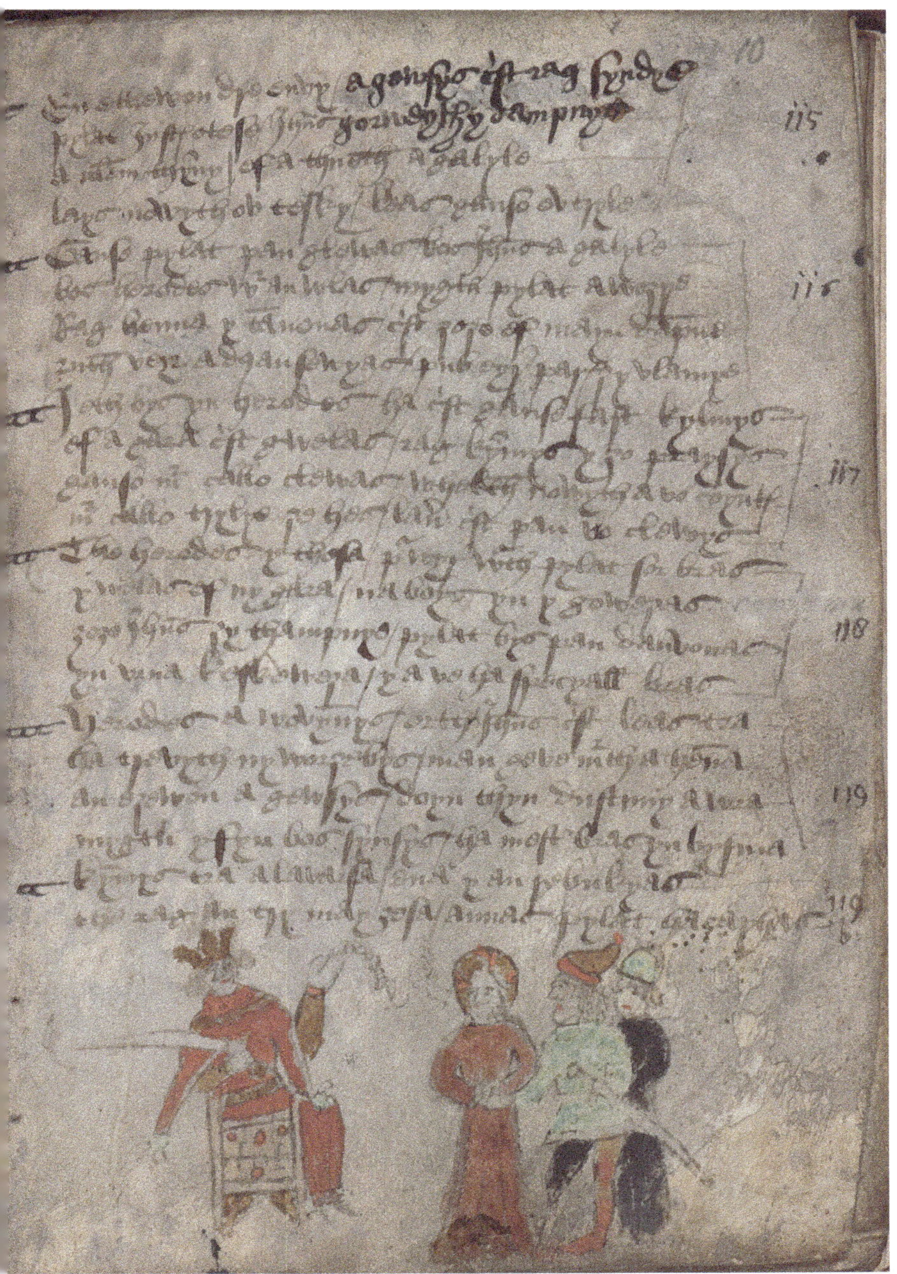

Plate 22. Harley MS 1782, *f.* 10r.

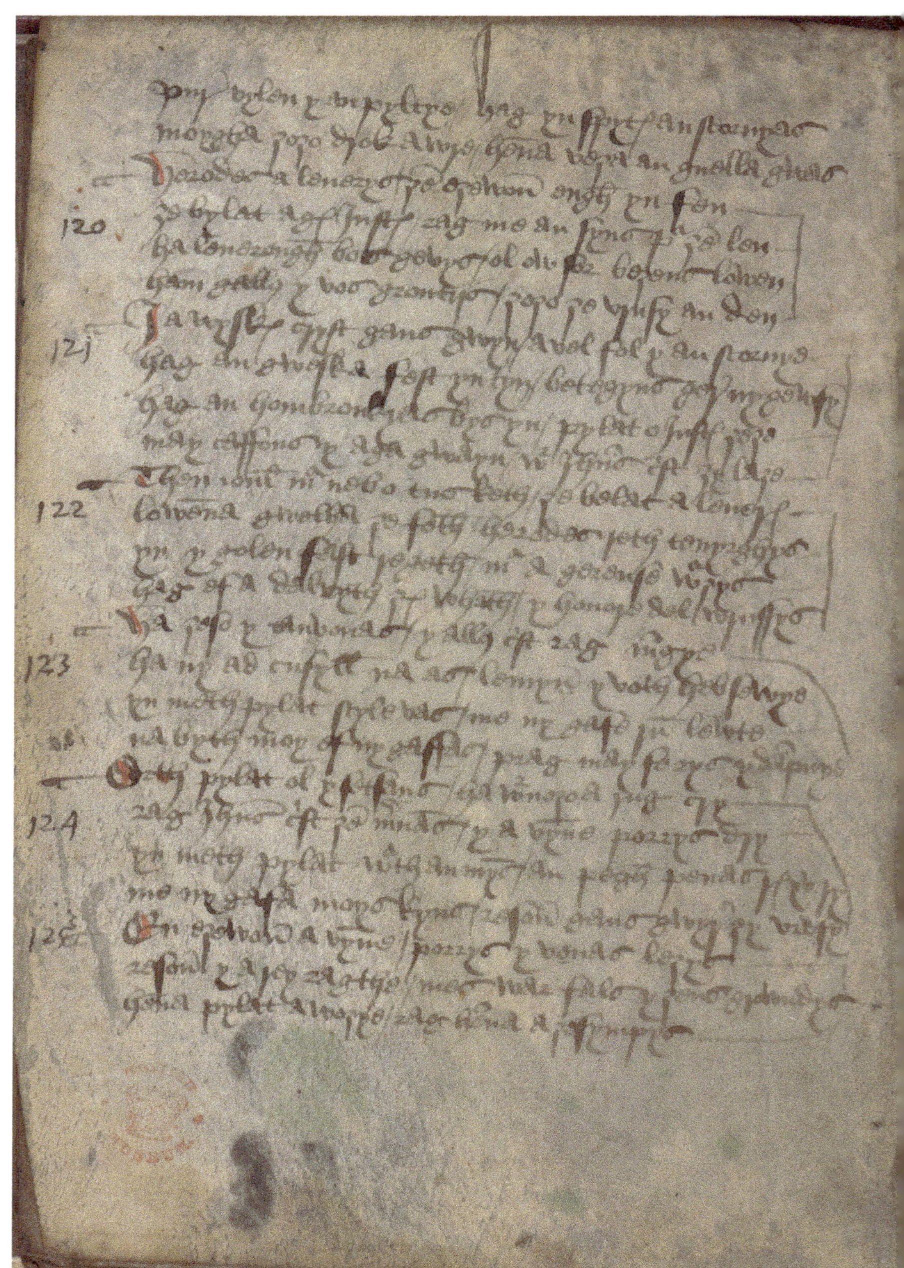

Plate 23. Harley MS 1782, *f.* 10v.

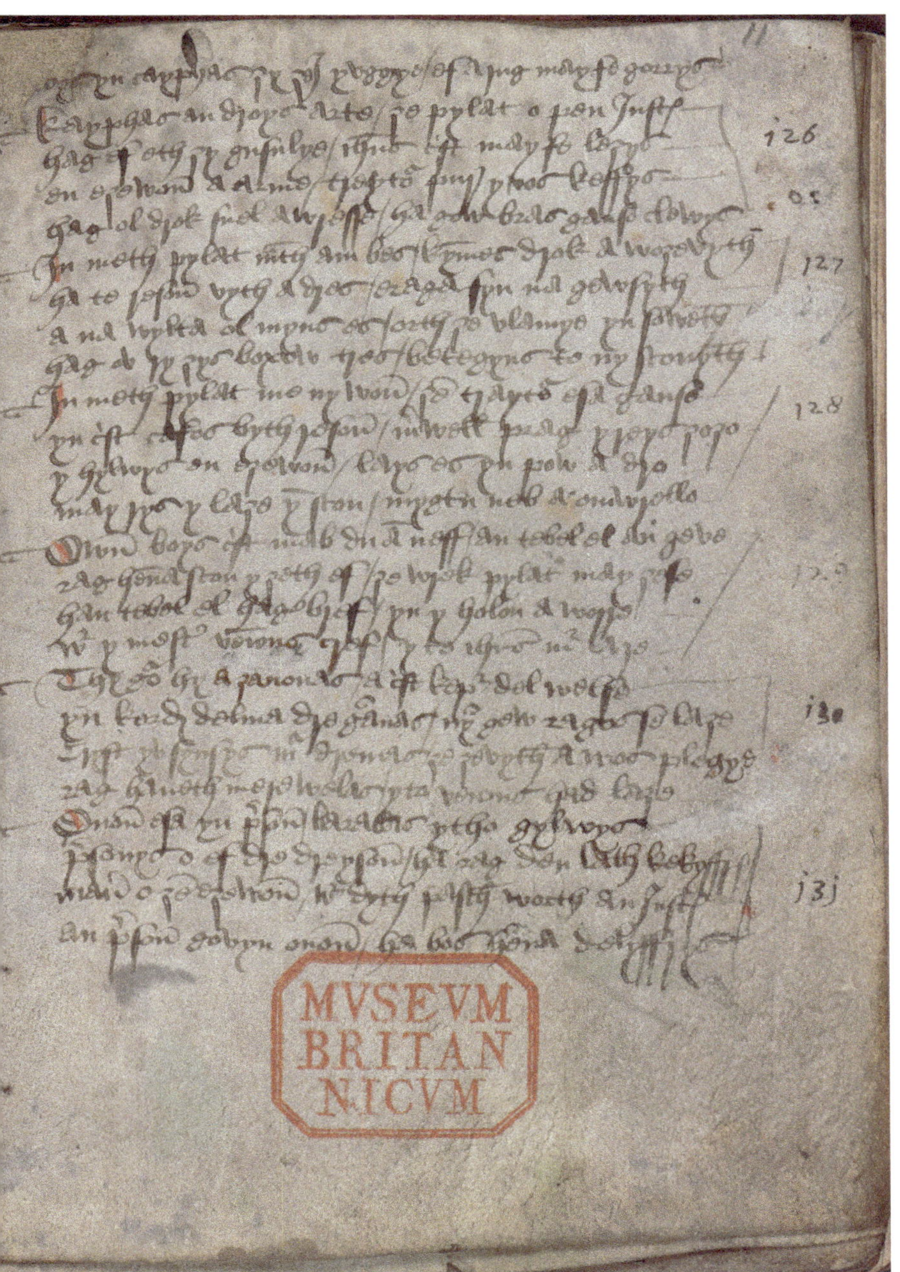

Plate 24. Harley MS 1782, *f.* 11r.

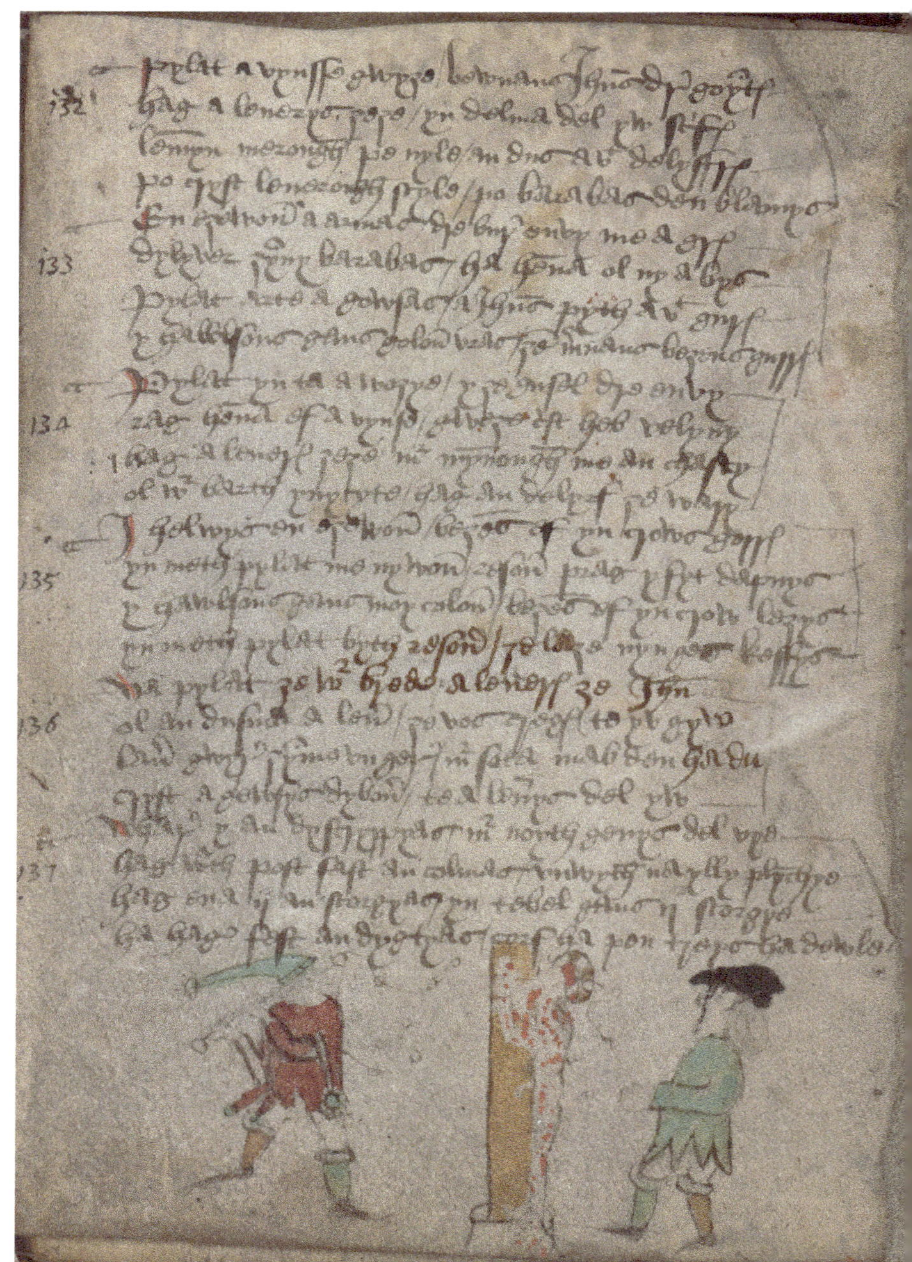

Plate 25. Harley MS 1782, *f.* 11v.

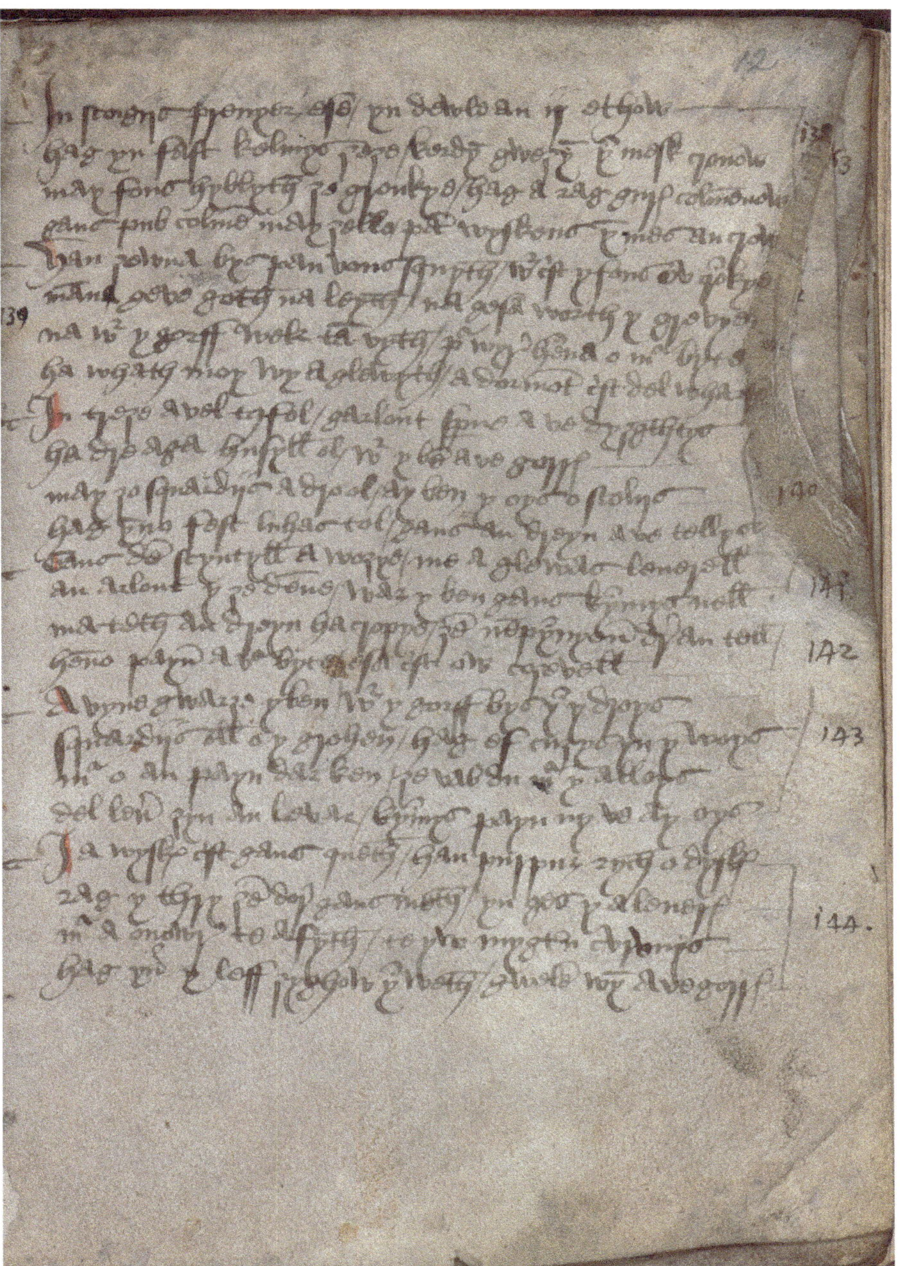

Plate 26. Harley MS 1782, *f.* 12r.

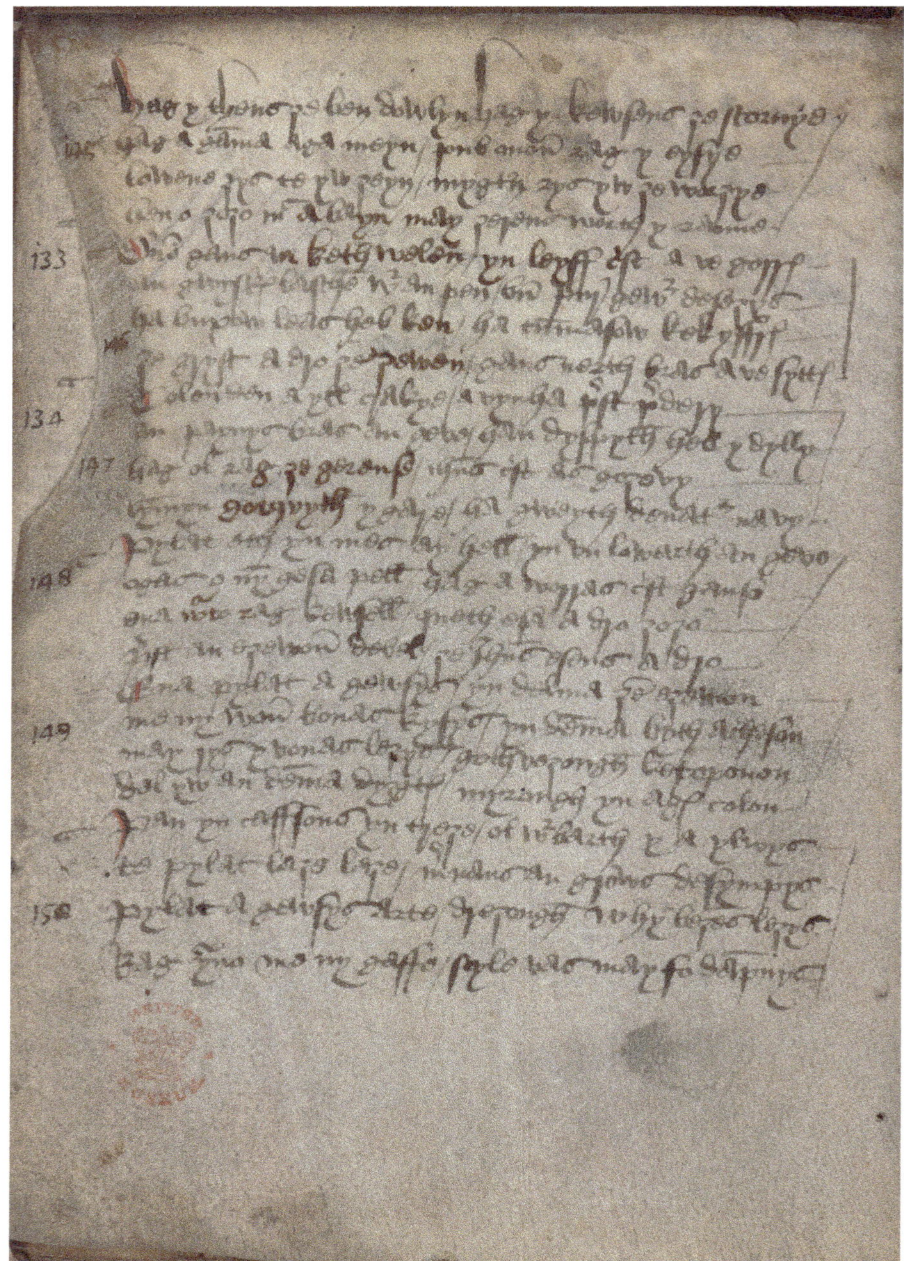

Plate 27. Harley MS 1782, *f.* 12v.

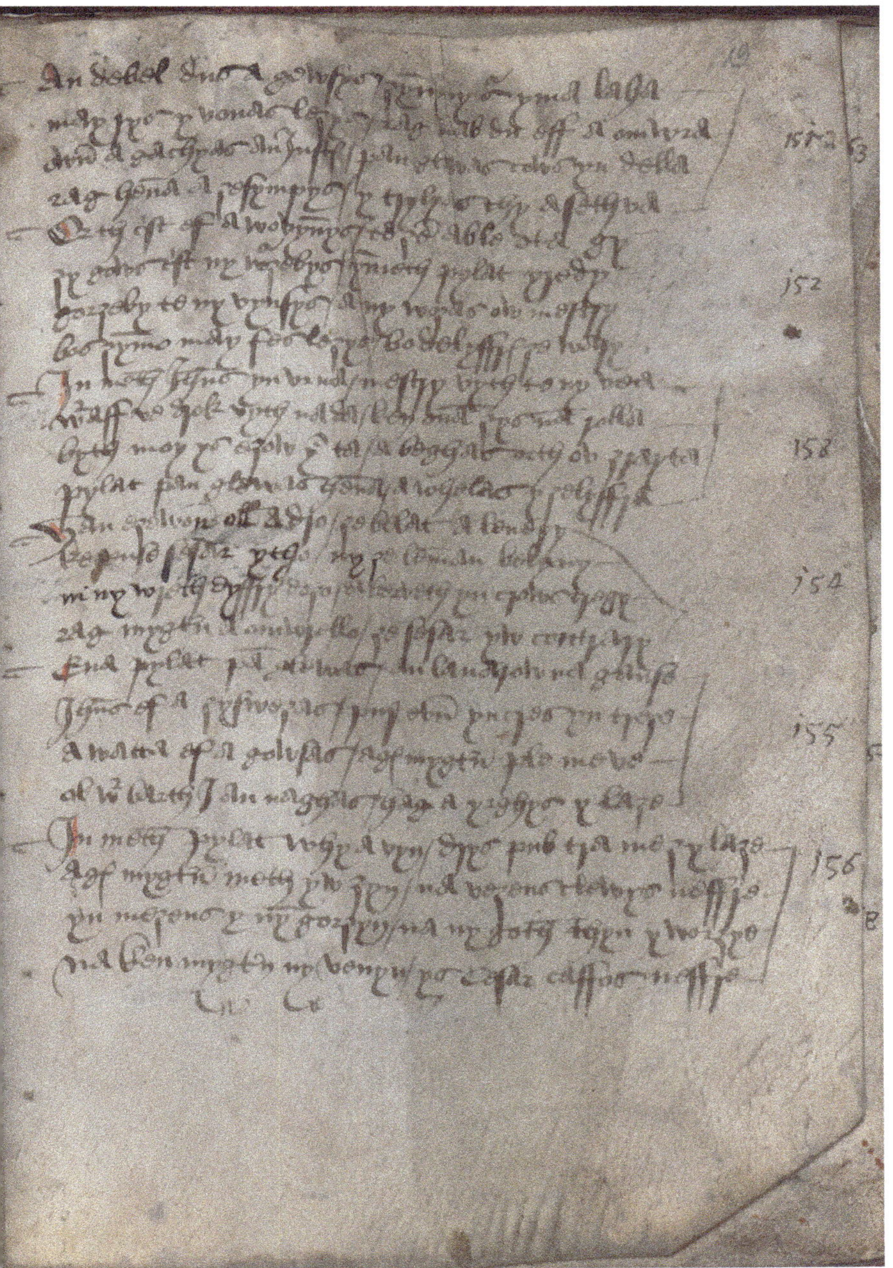

Plate 28. Harley MS 1782, *f.* 13r.

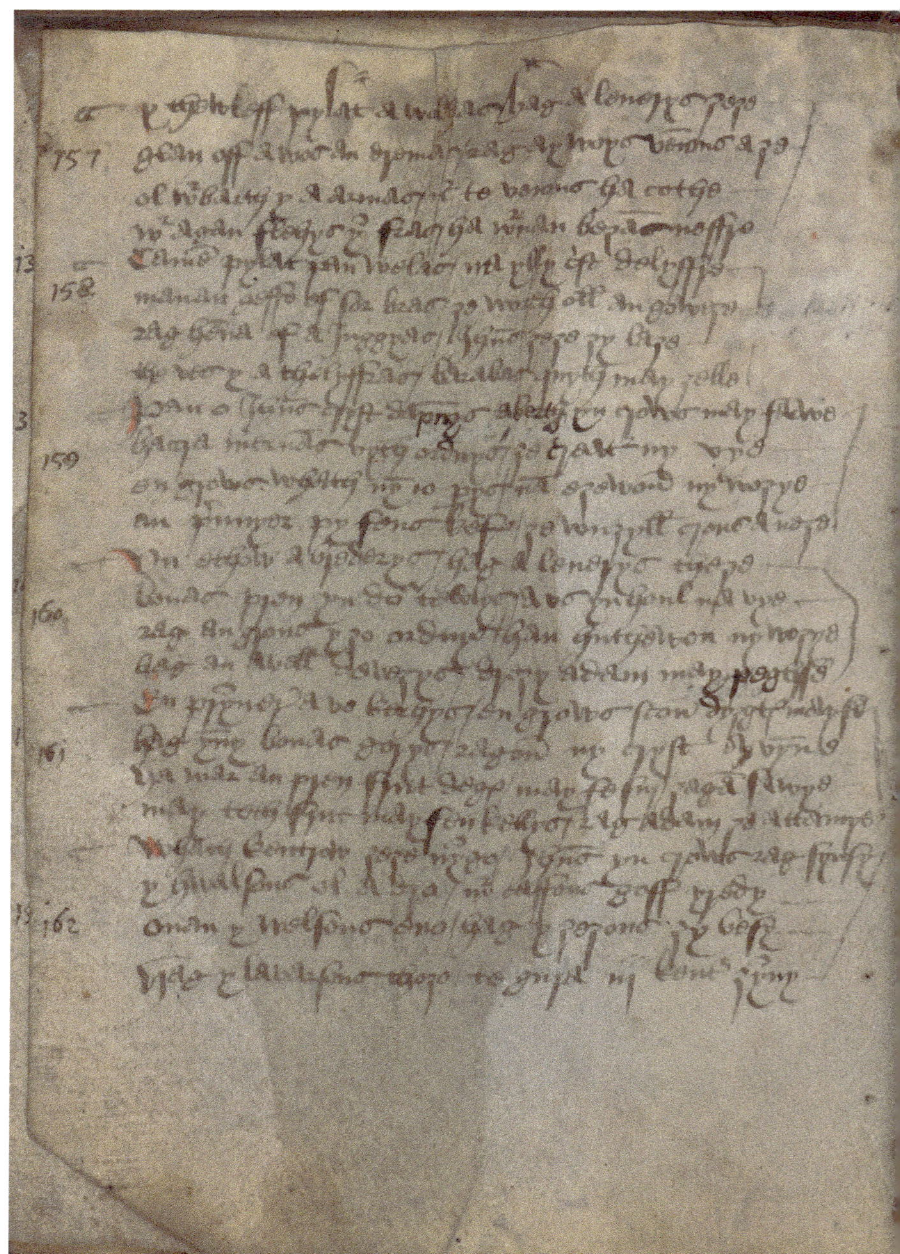

Plate 29. Harley MS 1782, *f.* 13v.

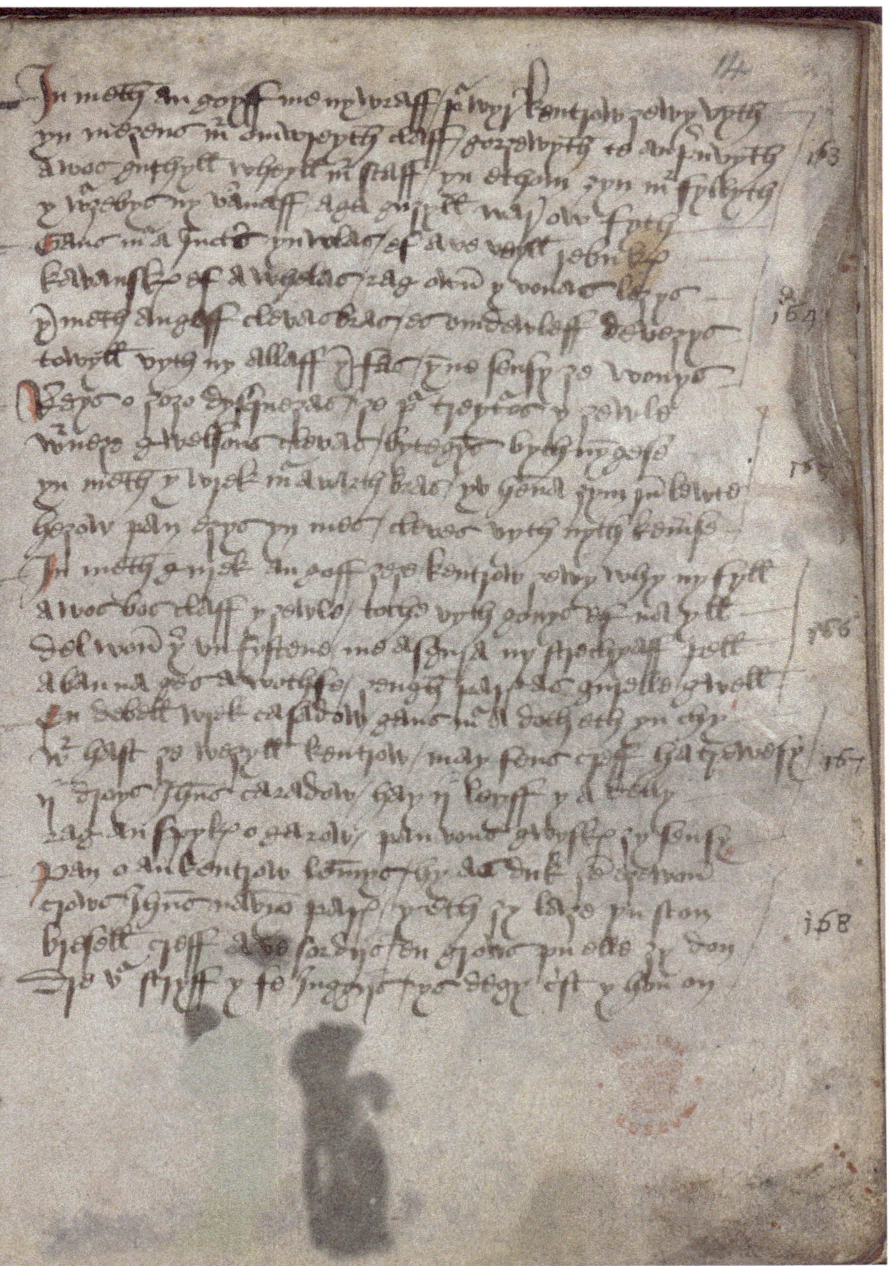

Plate 30. Harley MS 1782, *f*. 14r.

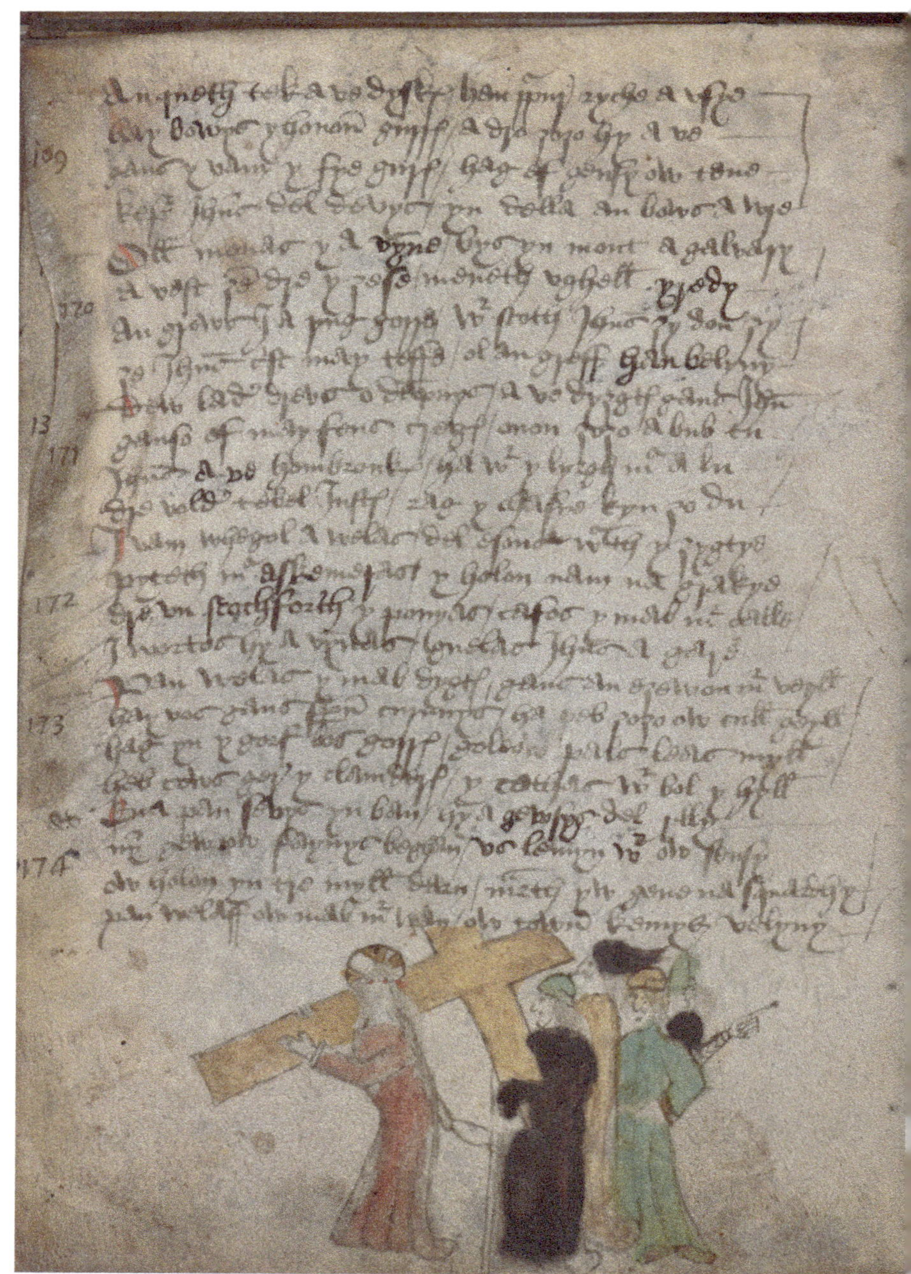

Plate 31. Harley MS 1782, *f*. 14v.

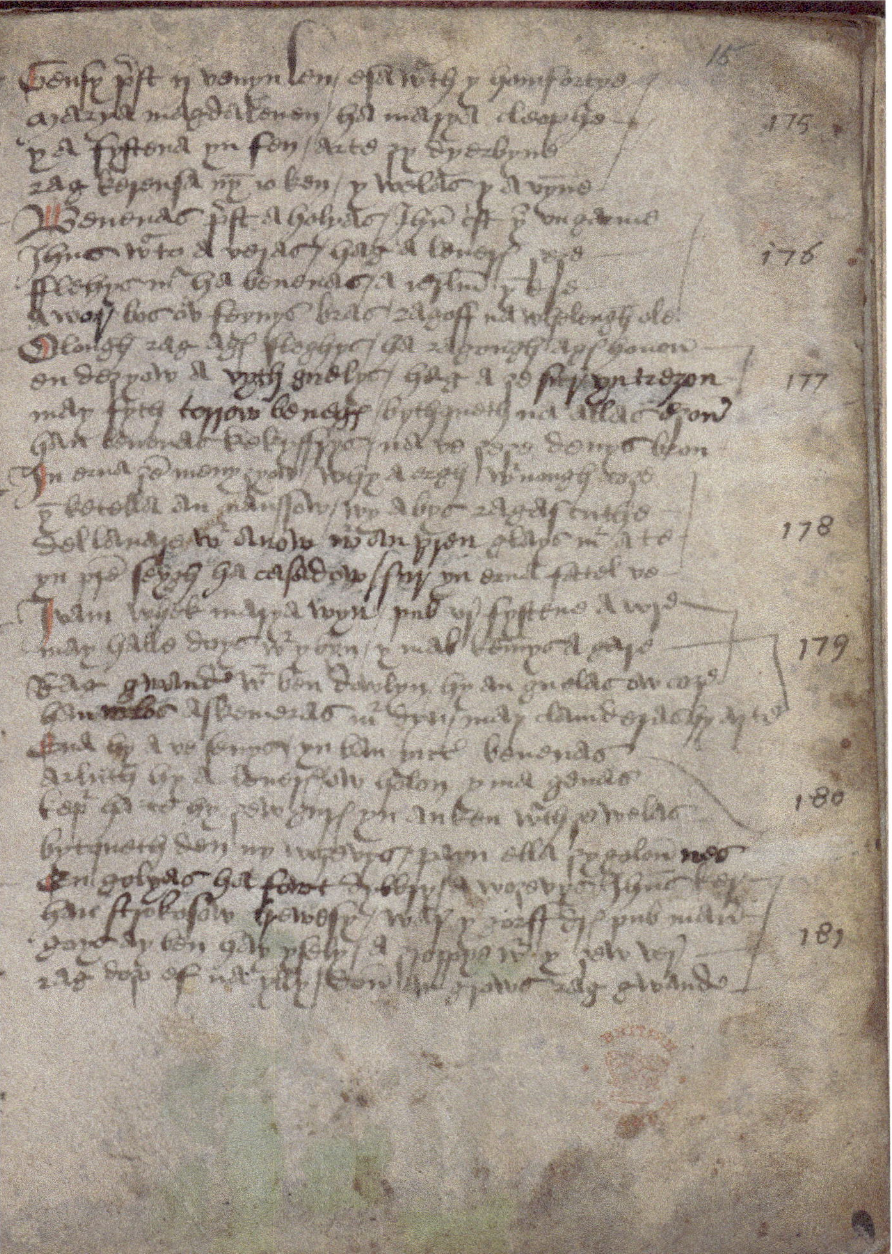

Plate 32. Harley MS 1782, *f.* 15r.

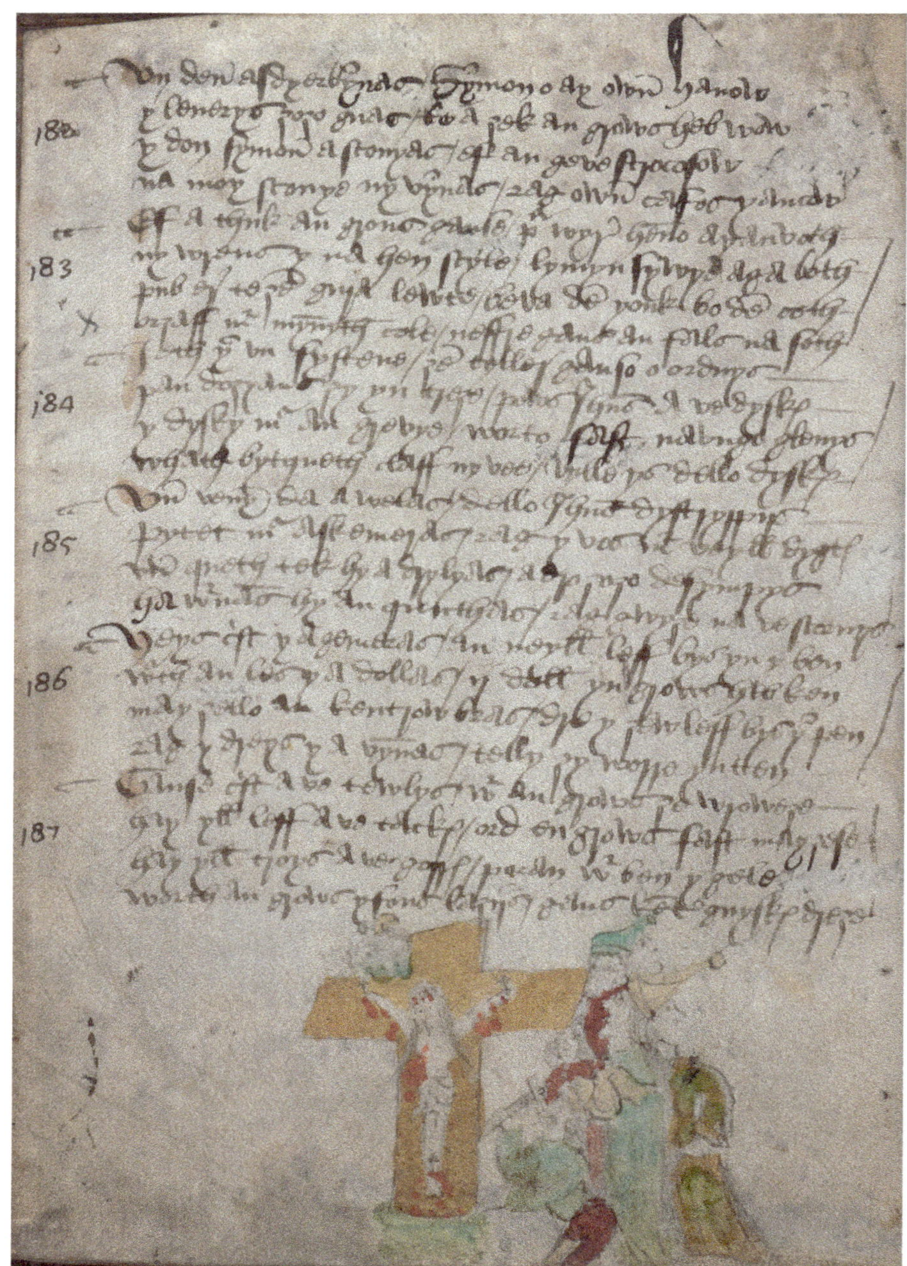

Plate 33. Harley MS 1782, *f.* 15v.

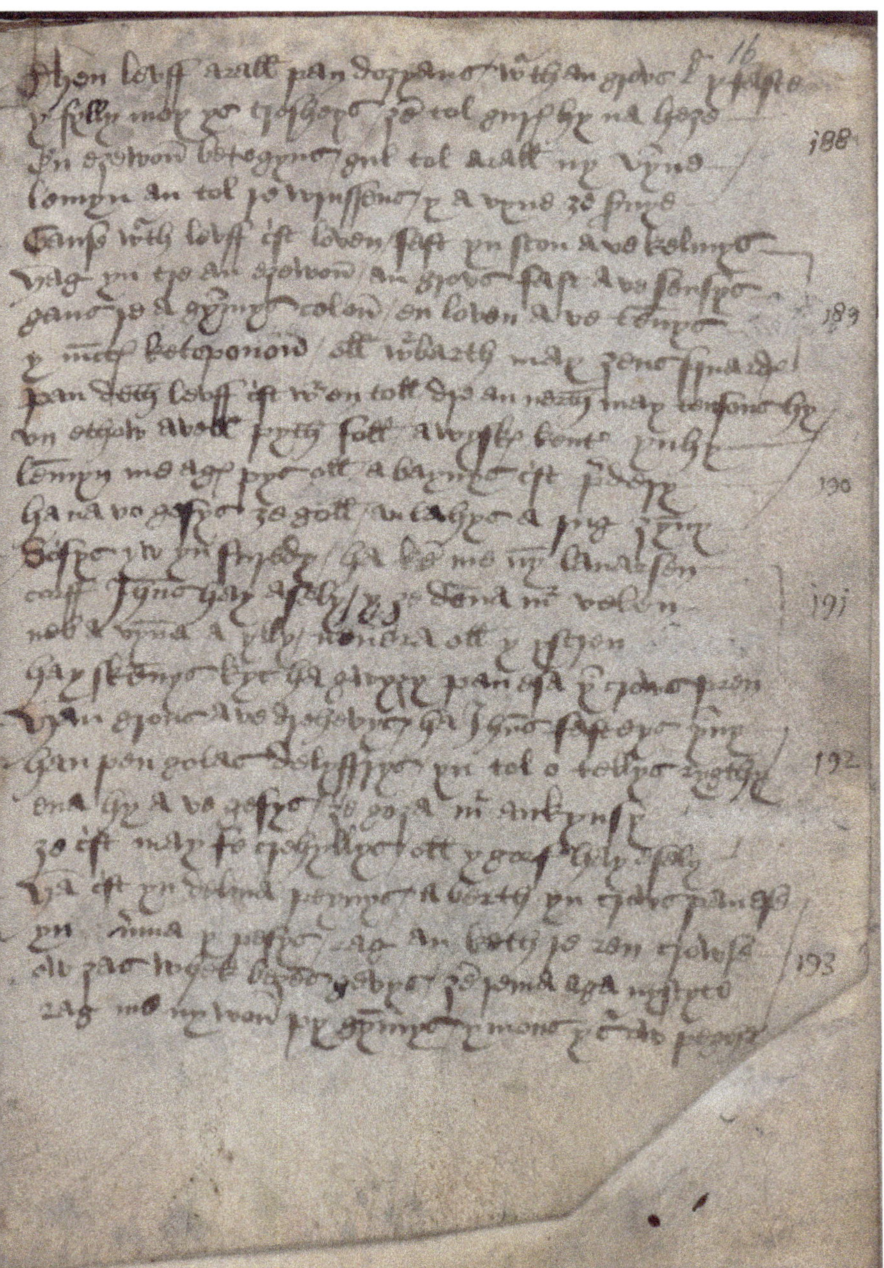

Plate 34. Harley MS 1782, *f*. 16r.

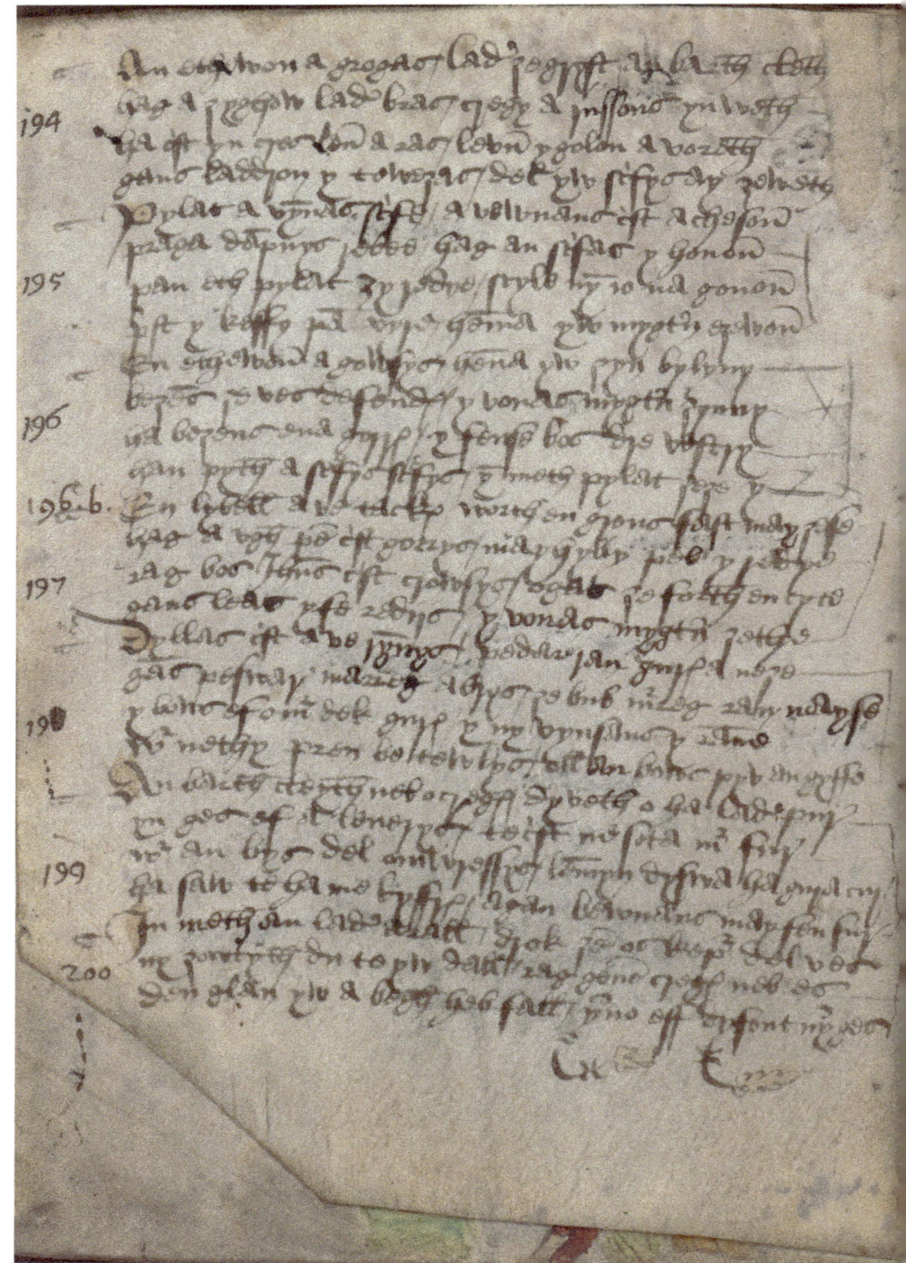

Plate 35. Harley MS 1782, *f*. 16v.

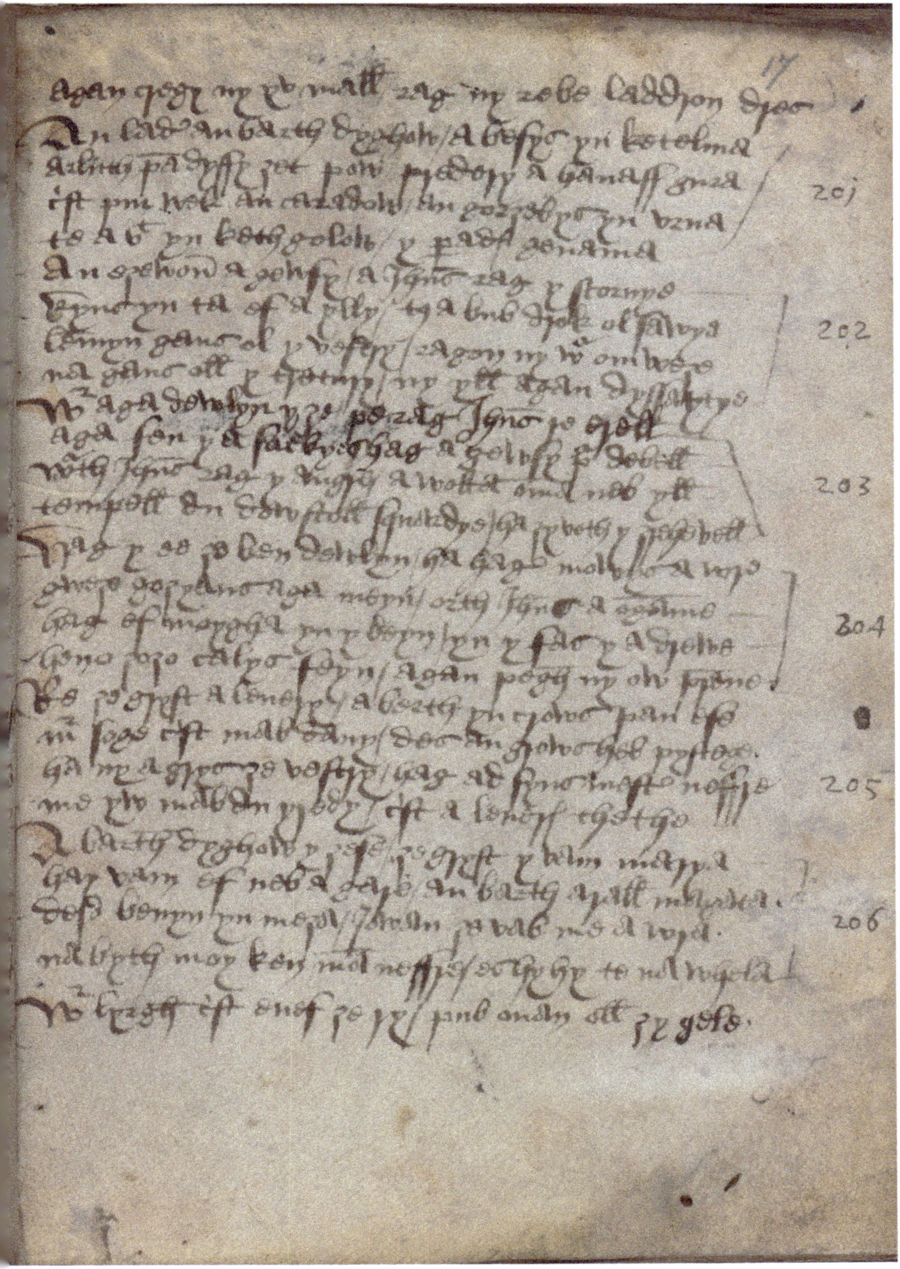

Plate 36. Harley MS 1782, *f*. 17r.

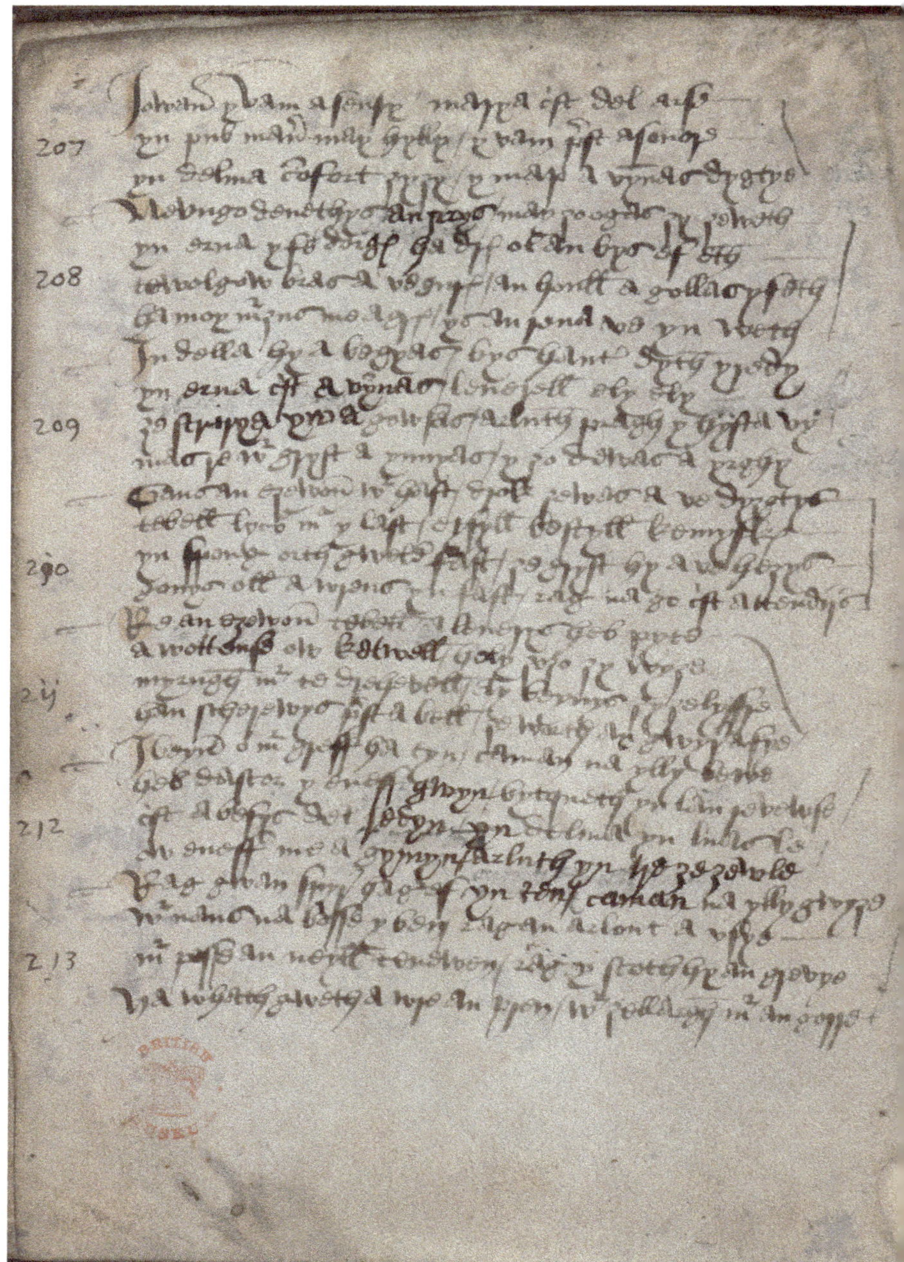

Plate 37. Harley MS 1782, *f.* 17v.

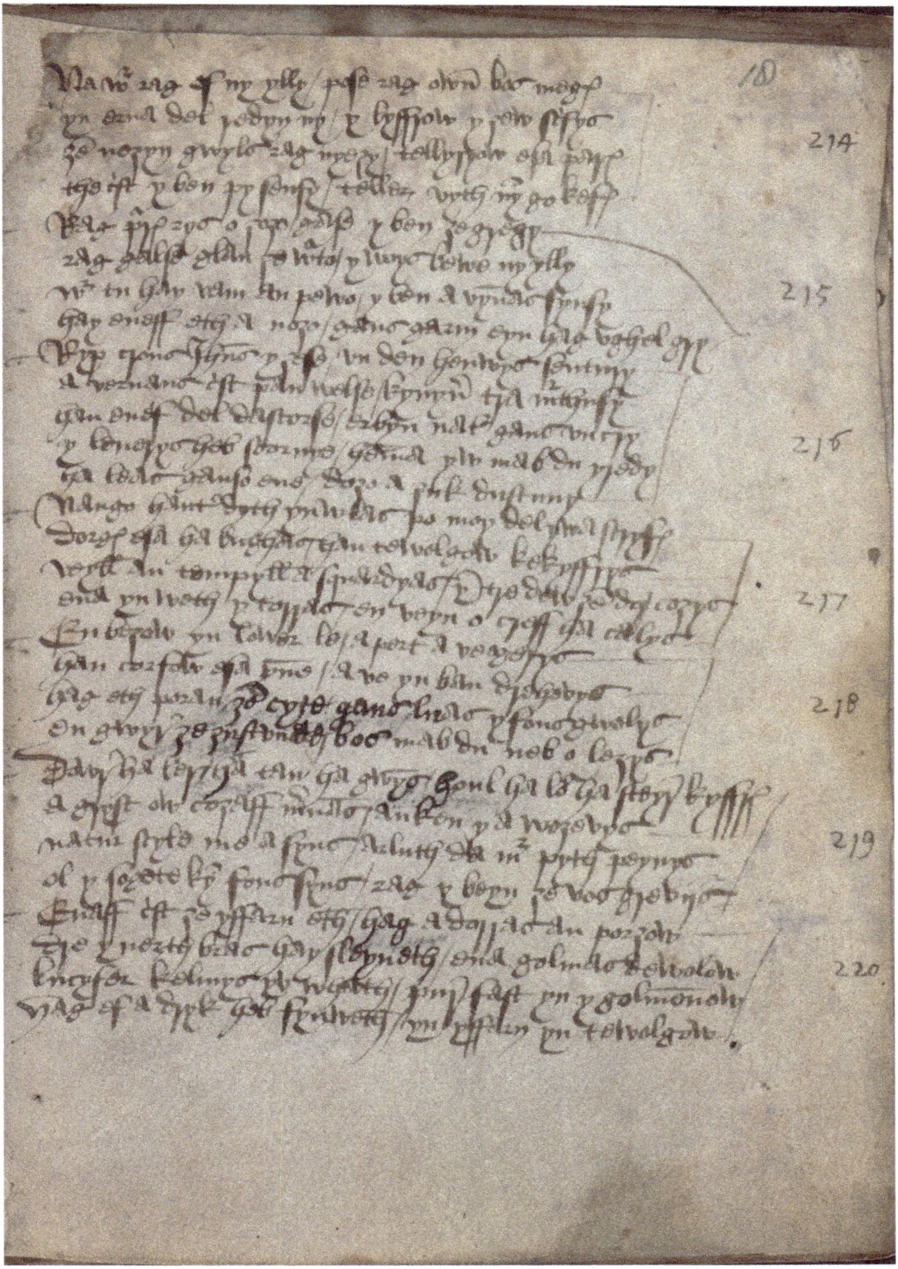

Plate 38. Harley MS 1782, *f*. 18r.

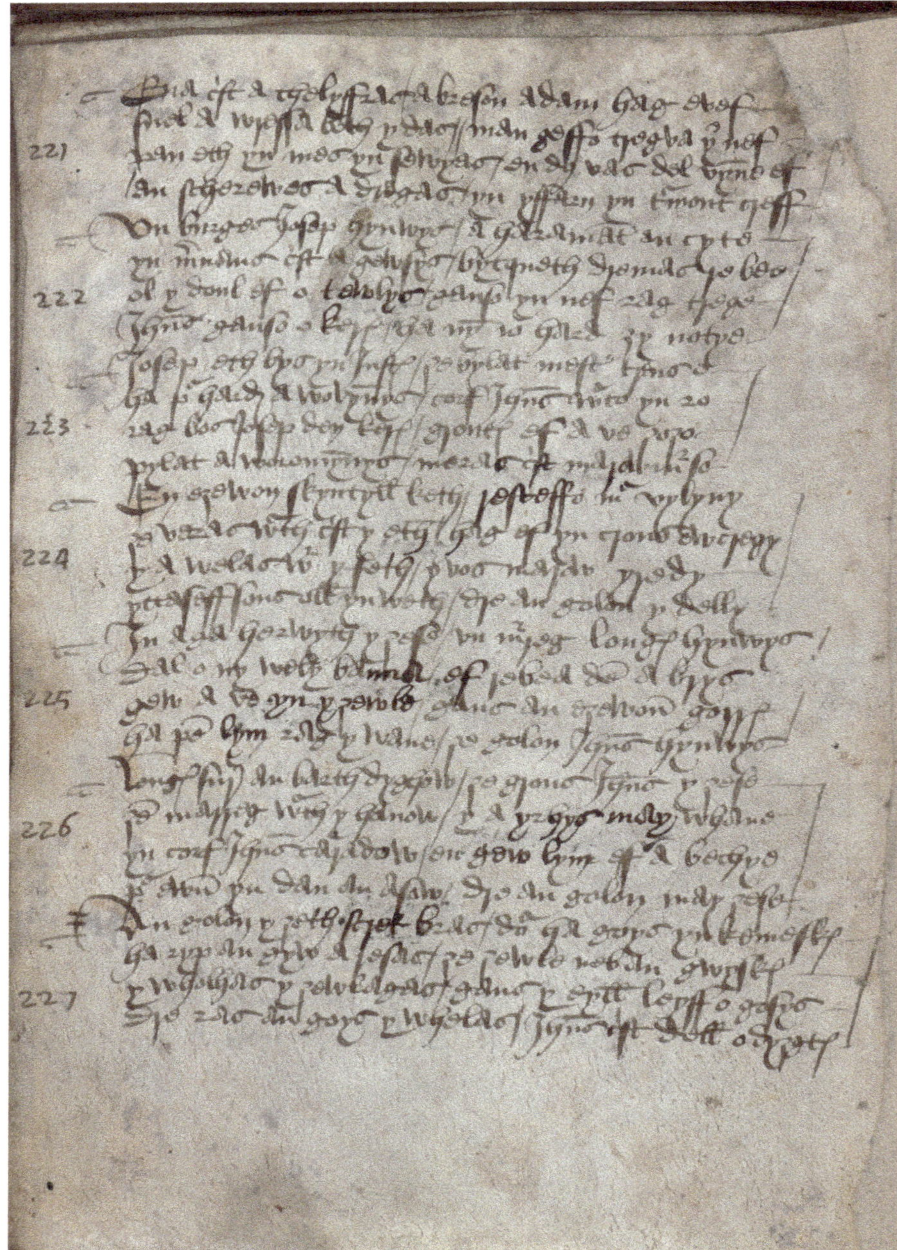

Plate 39. Harley MS 1782, *f.* 18v.

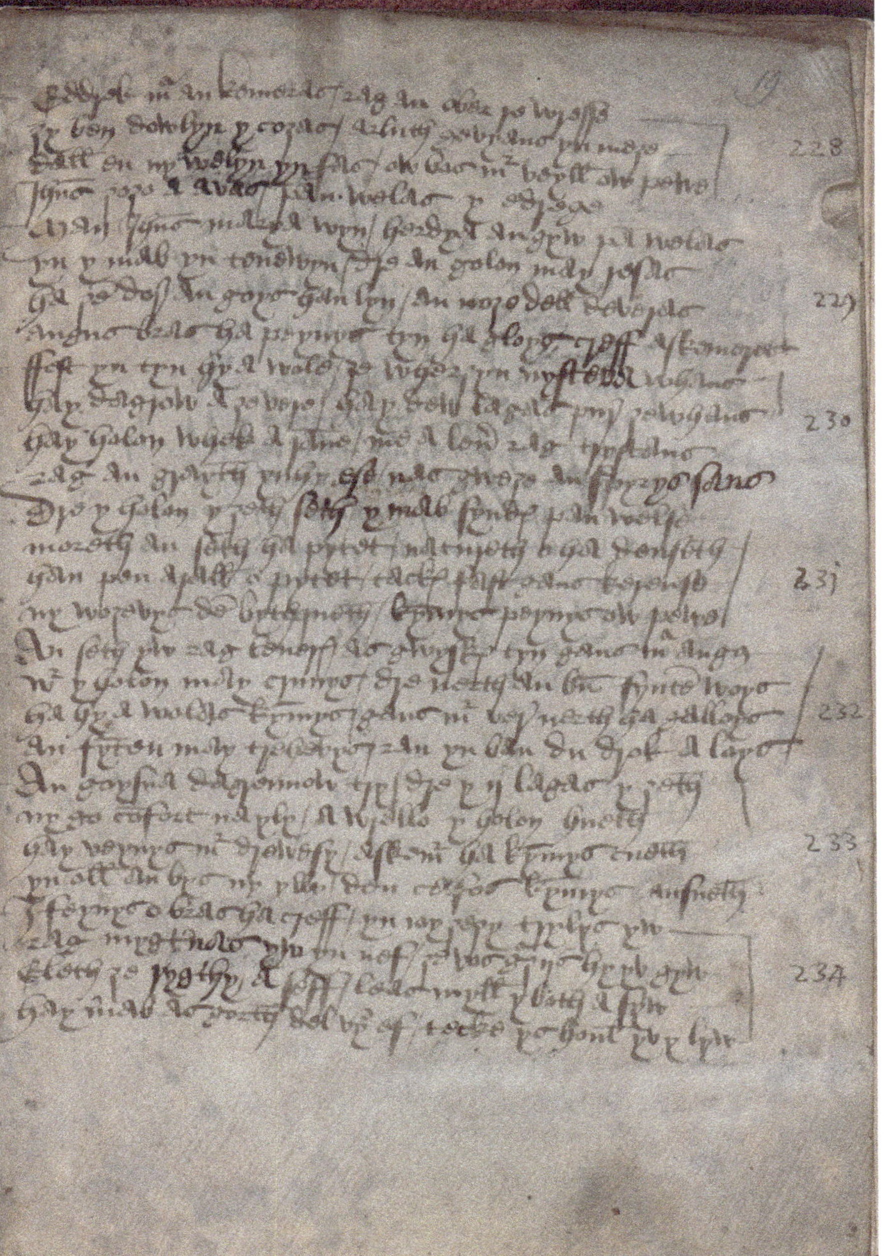

Plate 40. Harley MS 1782, *f*. 19r.

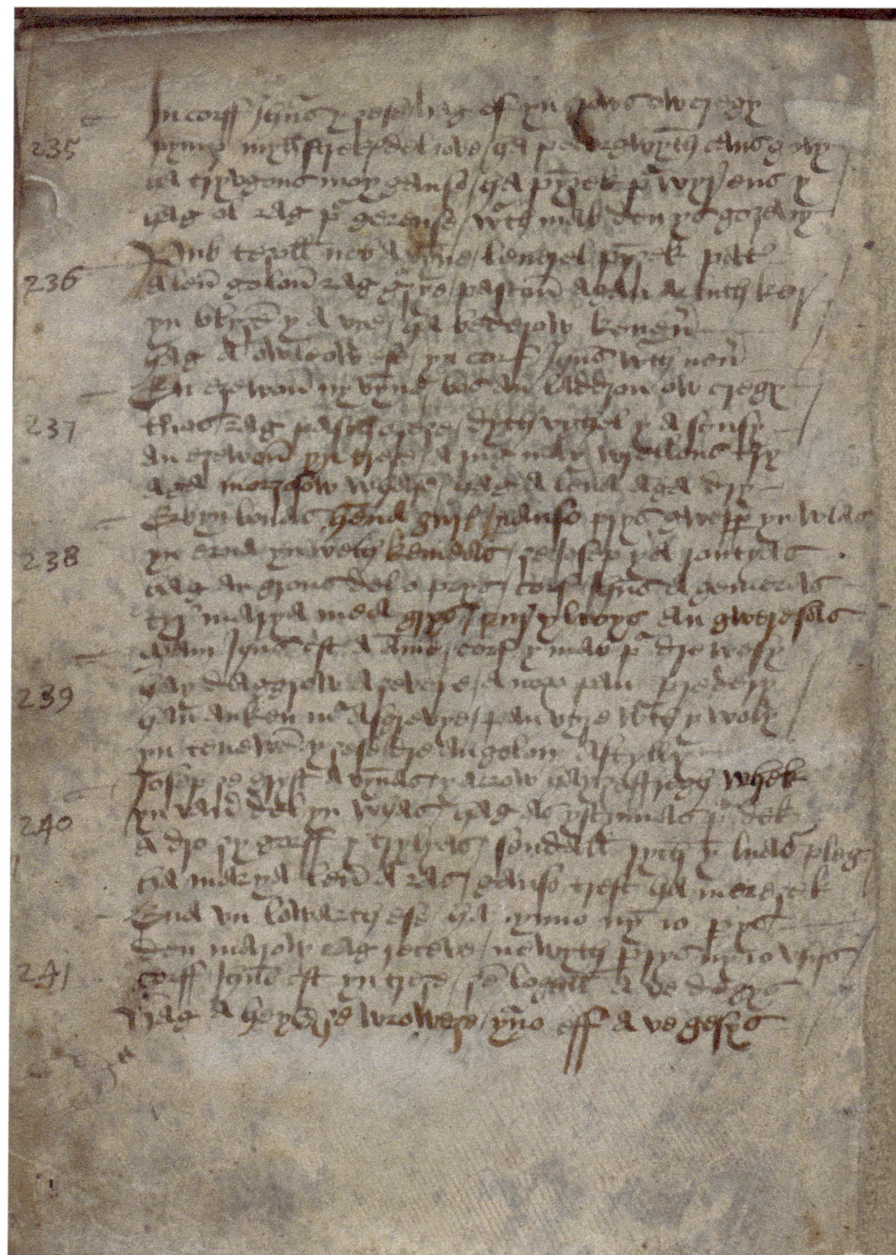

Plate 41. Harley MS 1782, *f.* 19v.

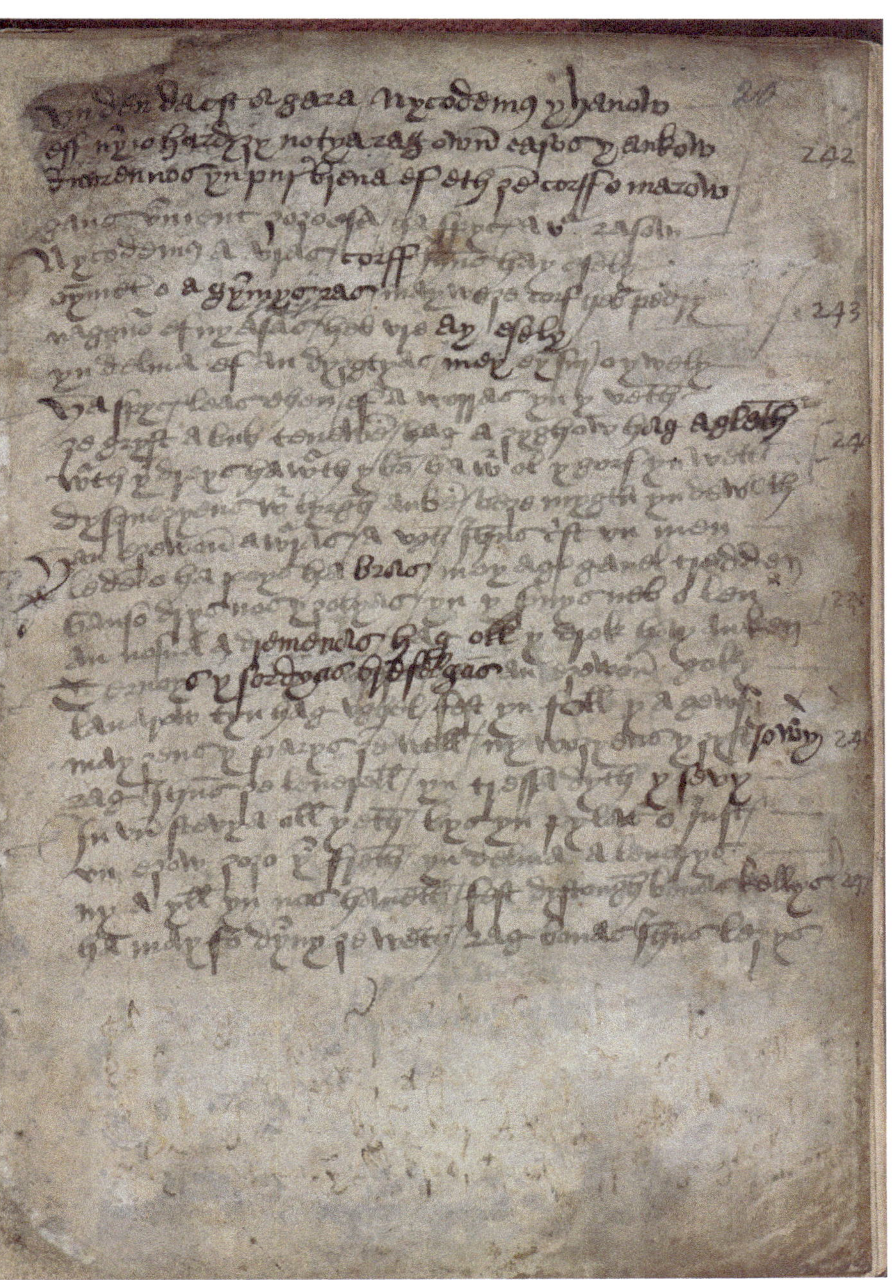

Plate 42. Harley MS 1782, *f*. 20r.

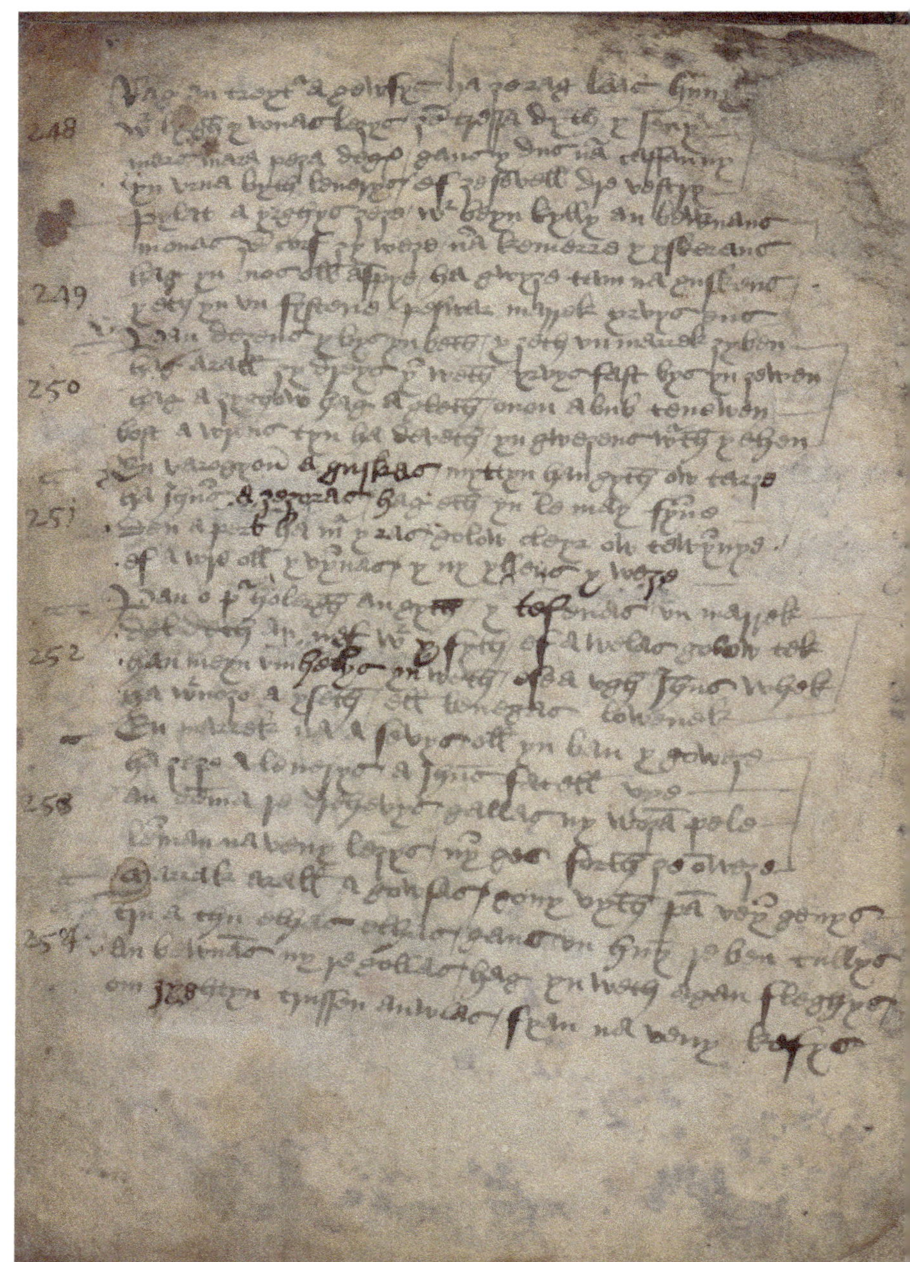

Plate 43. Harley MS 1782, *f.* 20v.

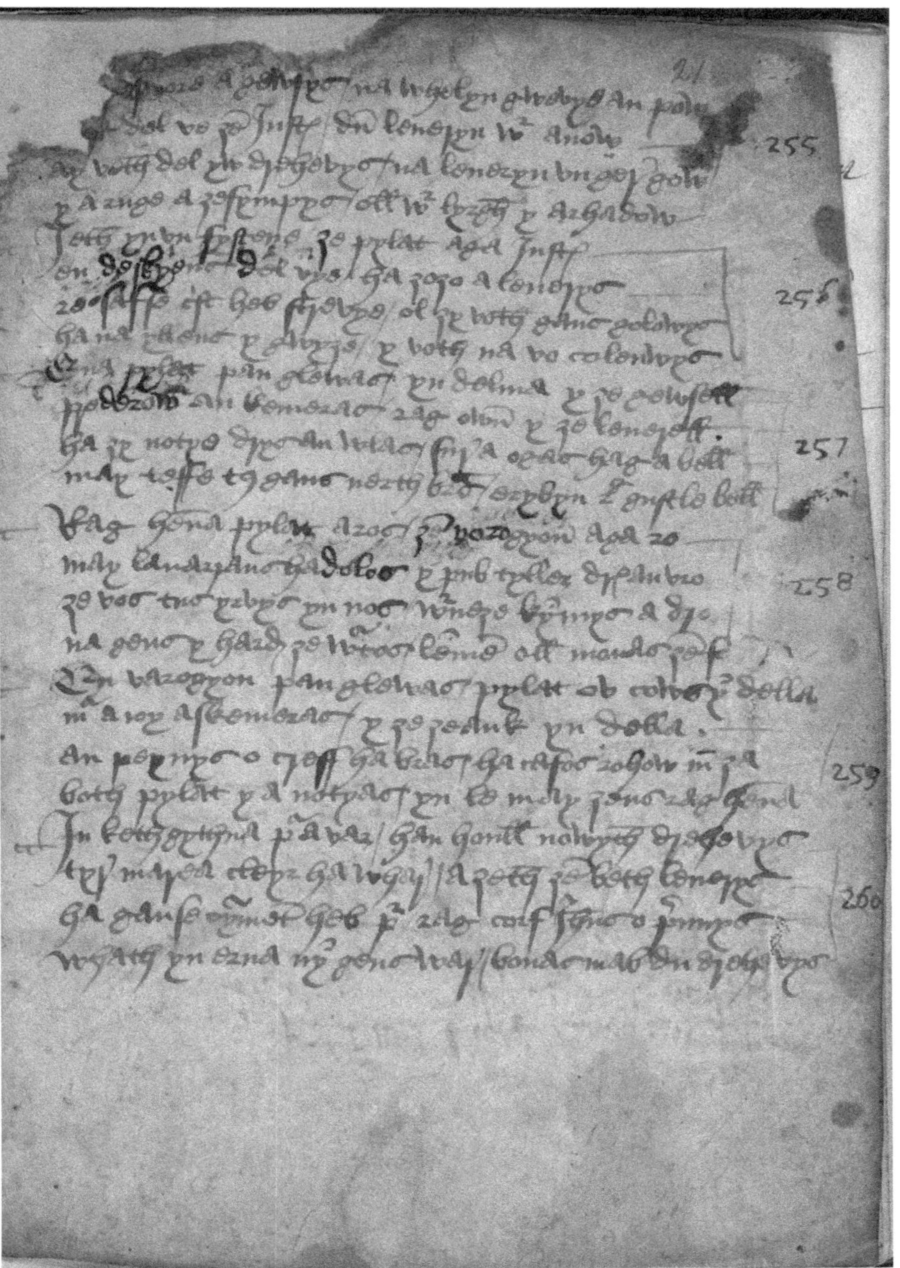

Plate 44. Harley MS 1782, *f*. 21r.

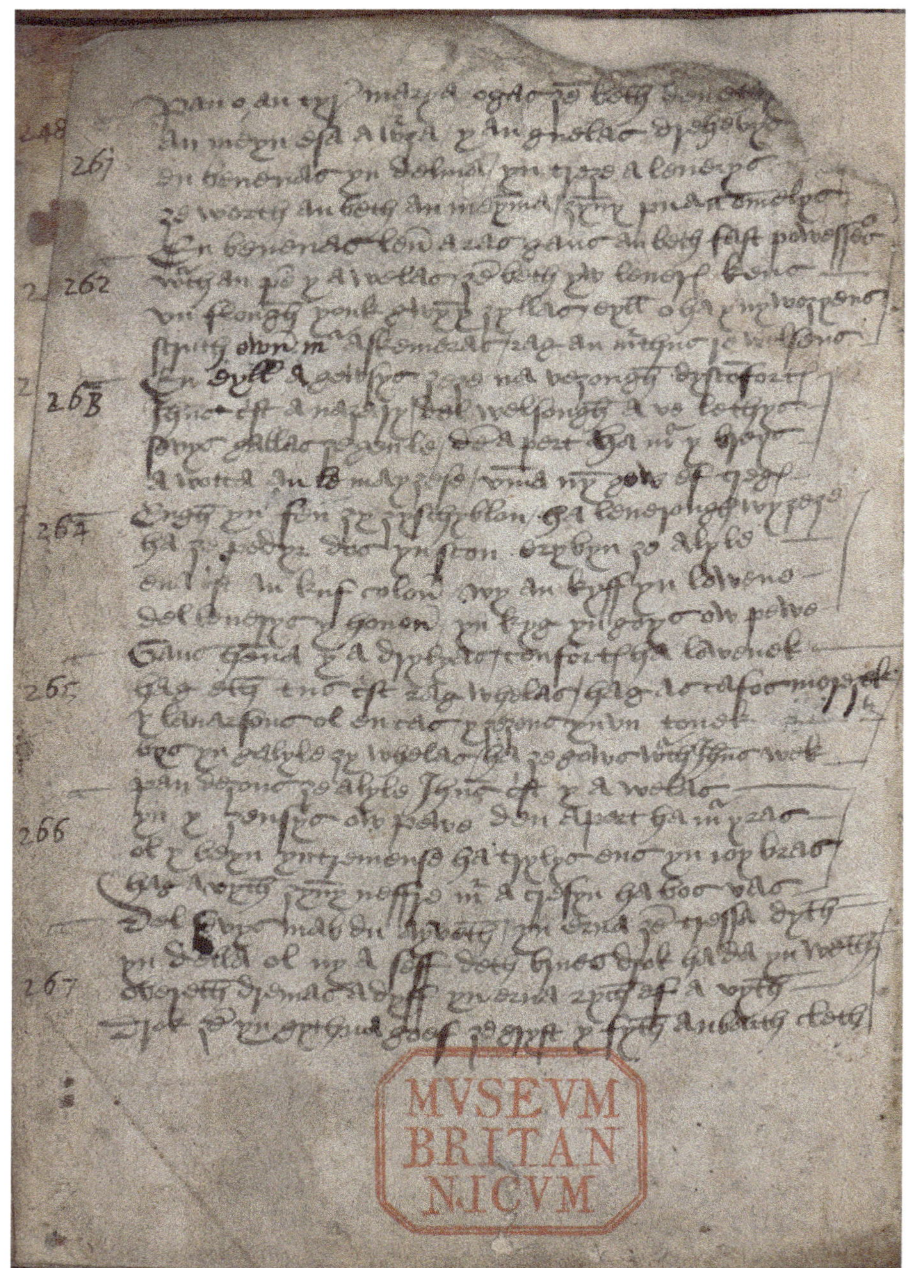

Plate 45. Harley MS 1782, *f.* 21v.

5.2.1 Illustrations in *Pascon agan Arluth*

Harley MS 1782 contains ten coloured drawings some of which have faded and blurred over time. Close-up views of these have been reproduced below, with a description of them as well as of some other ornamentation found, generally in the first or last lines on a manuscript page.

1r Representation of the Trinity with God the Father in a green robe and red mantle on a throne with a sort of carpet beneath, holding the crucified Jesus with the Holy Spirit as a dove above and to their right. Decorated with an elaborate initial insular T (Ꞇ) in red and with initial capitals in red. In the first line the letters *h* in *ha* and *l* in *colon* have high ascenders decorated with leaves.

1v Depiction of the Fall, with Adam and Eve on either side of the Tree with the Serpent, both coloured in green; the ground is red. Adam on the left appears to be holding the apple. In the first line *h* in *Pehadoryon* has a tall ascender and is decorated with two strokes. Initial capitals have rather faded red decoration.

2r Depiction of the Temptation of Christ; Jesus is robed in red and the Devil with red eyes and a red cap is seated, with a pile of stones coloured in green and yellow before him. Initial capitals are coloured in faded red.

2v In the first line *H* in *Ha* has a tall ascender and is decorated with two strokes and a flower. In line 123 the *A* in *An* is decorated with a flower. Initial capitals are coloured in faded red.

3r No particular ornament is found on this page, apart from the colouration of initial capitals in faded red.

3v In the first line the letter *b* in *bos* has a tall ascender. Initial capitals are coloured in faded red. Some text in English in an Elizabethan hand appears at the bottom of the page; it translates lines 237–246 with reasonable accuracy, though the word read here as "*ſcribeȿ* ~ ~" overwrites an original translation which seems to have rendered *ſchezewys* rather differently.[1]

4r In the first line the letter *H* in *Ha* is enlarged somewhat and the abbreviation mark over *kym̃ys* has a tilde-shape. Initial capitals are coloured in faded red.

4v In the first line the letters *h* in *Whare* and *I* in *Iudas* are enlarged; in the last line the final *h* in *vyth* is decorated with two strokes in the right descender. In line 329 the *D* in *Dew* is decorated with a flower. Initial capitals are coloured in faded red.

5r In the first line the letters *d* in *deppzo*, *d* in *da*, *k* in *tek*, and *h* in *geuyth* have high ascenders and are decorated with strokes and flowers. The letter *A* in *An* in the first line is large and a little odd looking. Initial capitals are coloured in red.

5v In the first line the letter *l* in *lẽmyn* has a tilde-shaped abbreviation mark and a tall ascender decorated with strokes and a flower; the letter *k* in *kyns* is enlarged. In the last line the letters *y* and *h* in *golyough* have elongated descenders decorated with leaves. Initial capitals are coloured in faded red.

---

1 One can read perhaps "*...ſchen y..s*", with two tildes erasing the second word; whatever it may have been, it was followed by the singular verb *was*; Gilbert 1826:14 reads the Cornish text as "*Eu sthercwys*" and translated 'The Jews (Scribes)'; Borlase 1769:454 gives "Scherewys, *the Scribes*" which Jago 1887:138 repeats, cross-referencing "See WICKED MEN".

6r In the last line the letter *h* in *the* is elongated and decorated with strokes and a leaf partially coloured green. Initial capitals are coloured in faded red.

6v Depiction of the Betrayal of Jesus with Judas coming from the right to kiss Jesus—both are robed in red—and three armoured soldiers standing by. In the first line the letter *A* in *An* is elongated and decorated with strokes and a leaf; the ascenders of the letters *I* in *Iudas* and *h* in *thanvonas* are elongated. Initial capital rubrication is very faded and hardly to be seen in the last two stanzas.

7r In the first line the letters *h* in *Whare*, *k* in *kemeres*, and *h* in *hag* have tall ascenders. Initial capital rubrication is very faint, almost a brightening in higher stanzas and hardly to be seen in the last two stanzas.

7v Depiction of Jesus in a red robe being brought before the seated prince Annas in a red tunic with by three soldiers accompanied by another red-robed person, perhaps Peter. In the first line the letters *I* in *In* and *l* in *colmas* are elongated. Initial capitals are coloured in faded red, a brown darkening on the lower stanzas.

8r In the first line the letter *h* in *meth̄* is elongated and the letters *k* in *kewſys* and *l* in *falſury* are elongated and decorated with strokes and flowers respectively. Initial capital rubrication is very faint, faded or just a darkening.

8v In the first line the letter *h* in *ha* is elongated. Initial capitals are coloured in red.

9r Depiction of Pilate with a long green cap and hose seated in a red chair, with Jesus in a red robe brought before him by a man with a blue hat, a green tunic, and red hose, a man with a green cap and a blue robe, and a man with a yellow cap and a green robe. Before Pilate there is an S-shaped scroll, perhaps intended to bear his name. (Compare the image on *f.* 10r.) In the first line the ascender of the letter *l* in *Ol* is elongated, and the letter *l* in *leuezough* is elongated and decorated with red and green leaves. Initial capitals are coloured in red.

9v In the first line the letters *I* in *In*, *h* in *meth̄*, and *k* in *kveff* have tall ascenders. Initial capital rubrication has faded to a dull brown.

10r Depiction of Herod, wearing a crown, in a red robe with yellow sleeves seated in a decorated chair, with Jesus in a red robe being brought before him by two men, likely Jews, one wearing a red-trimmed yellow cap, a green tunic, and particoloured hose in blue and red, and the other (perhaps the same who was depicted on *f.* 9r) wearing a green cap and a blue tunic. A scroll between Herod and Jesus has the name *herodes* curving down from Herod's hand; the word next to Jesus is very faint but is perhaps *ihs*. Initial capital rubrication has faded to a dull brown.

10v In the first line the letter *h* in *hag* is elongated. Initial capitals are coloured in bright red.

11r In the first line the ascender of the letter *h* in *cayphas* is elongated. Initial capitals are coloured in red.

11v Depiction of the Scourging of Jesus, who has red wounds and is fixed to a yellow pillar; behind Jesus is a torturer in a green cap, a red tunic, and yellow and green snug boots (hose rolled down over garters); he seems to be holding a scorpion-type scourge, having several knotted thongs. In front of Jesus is another person in a blue cap, a green tunic, and similar boots. In the first line the ascenders of *b* in *bewnans* and *I* in *Ihūs* are elongated. Initial capitals are coloured in red.

12r In the first line the *I* in *In* is enlarged. Initial capitals are coloured in red.

12v In the first line the ascenders of the *h*'s in *Hag*, *thens*, and *hag* are elongated. Initial capitals are coloured in red.

13r In the last line the descenders of the letter *y*'s in *mygh̄* and *ny* are decorated with strokes. Initial capitals are coloured in red.

13v In the first line the ascenders of the letters *l* in *pylat* and *h* in *hag* are elongated and decorated with strokes. Initial capitals are coloured in red.

14r In the first line the *k* in *kentrow* is enlarged. Initial capitals are coloured in red.

14v Depiction of Jesus, robed in red, carrying the cross in the company of four people; one in a green cap and a blue robe is also holding the cross. (Simon of Cyrene, who helps to carry the cross is named later in the text in stanza 174 on folio 15v, and could be this figure; compare the figure with the same clothing in *ff.* 9r and 10r.). Behind are three figures, one in a blue cap and a yellow robe, a bearded man in a yellow cap and a green robe, and another in a green cap pointing away. Initial capitals are coloured in red.

15r In the first line the letter *l* in *len* is elongated. Initial capitals are coloured in red.

15v Depiction of the Crucifixion. Six people appear to be present along with Jesus on the cross, wounded and with clearly visible crucifixion nails. At the bottom left in a green tunic is a man who appears to have a hammer in his hand; above him is a person in a red tunic looking on. To the left of those two is a person in a green cap and red tunic, and a person with a yellow cap and a green tunic. To the right of those seems to be two faces looking away from the scene, the lower of whom is wearing an olive tunic. Perhaps these are two of the Marys. Above and to the left of the cross is a blurry image; perhaps this is the dove representing the Holy Spirit as in *f.* 1r. In the first line the letter *h* in *hanow* is quite tall and boldly drawn. Initial capitals are coloured in red.

16r Initial capitals are coloured in red.

16v In the last line the descenders of the letter *y*'s in *ӯno* and *dyfout* are decorated with strokes and leaves. Initial capitals are coloured in red.

17r Initial capitals are coloured in faded red.

17v In the first line the *n* in *Iowan* and the *v* in *vam* have swash decorations. Initial capitals are coloured in faded red.

18r Initial capitals are coloured in rather faded red.

18v Initial capitals are coloured in rather faded red. In line 1747 the *A* in *An* is decorated with two strokes, also coloured red.

19r In the first line the letter *k* in *kemezas* is enlarged. Initial capitals are coloured in faded red.

19v In the first line the ascender of *h* in *ha* is enlarged. Initial capitals are coloured in rather faded red.

20r In the line 1892 the descender of *H* in *Hag* is decorated with two strokes. The rubrication of initial capitals is hardly to be seen.

20v Initial capital rubrication has bled to brown blotches.

21r Where initial capital rubrication is visible it has bled to brown blotches.

21v Initial capital rubrication is hardly to be seen.

Michael Everson

Plate 46. Closeup of the representation of the Trinity, *f.* 1r.

Plate 47. Closeup of the depiction of the Fall, with Adam and Eve on either side of the Tree with the serpent, *f.* 1v.

Plate 48. Closeup of the depiction of the Temptation of Christ by the Devil, *f*. 2r.

Plate 49. Closeup of the depiction of Judas betraying Christ with a kiss in the presence of soldiers, *f*. 6v.

Plate 50. Closeup of the depiction of Christ before the prince Annas, *f.* 7v.

Plate 51. Closeup of the depiction of Christ before Pilate, *f.* 9r.

Plate 52. Closeup of the depiction of Christ before Herod, *f.* 10r.

Plate 53. Closeup of the depiction of the Scourging at the Pillar, *f.* 11v.

Plate 54. Closeup of the depiction of Jesus carrying his cross, *f.* 14v.

Plate 55. Closeup of the depiction of the Crucifixion, *f.* 15v.

6
TEXTS

6.1 *DARN AN CHARTOUR*

1 Goslow, ty goweth;
byth na borth meth.
  Dieskynn ha powes
ha dhymmo deus nes,
mar codhes dha les
  ha dhis y rov mowes
ha fest onen deg.
Genes mara pleg,
  â, tanha y.
Kemmer hy dhe'th wreg.
Sconya dhis ny vêk,
  ha te a'fÿdh hy.

2 Hy a vÿdh gwreg ty dhâ
dhis dh'y synsy hy.
Pòr wir a lavara'.
Â, govyn worty.

3 Lemmyn i'th torn me a's re
ha wàr an Gres my a'n te
nag eus hy far
a'n barth-ma dhe bons Tamar.

Darn an Chartour

1 Golsoug ty coweȝ [1v]
byȝ na borȝ meȝ
d⟨y⟩yskyn ha po⌜wes⌝
ha ȝymo dus nes
mar coȝes ȝe les
ha ȝys y rof mowe⌜s⌝
ha feſt onan dek
genes mara plek
ha tanha y

6.2 *THE CHARTER FRAGMENT*

{*The older man speaks to the young man*}

1 Listen, you comrade;
never be bashful.
Dismount and rest
and come close to me,
if you know what is good for you,
and I will give you a girl
and a very pretty one.
If she pleases you,
go, take her.
Take her as your wife
She will not presume to refuse you,
and she will be yours.

2 She will be a good wife,
for you to hold her.
I tell you the very truth.
Go, ask her.

3 Now into your hand I place her
and by the Creed I swear
that there is not her equal
from here to the Tamar bridge.

---

kymmerr y ȝoȝ wrek
sconye ȝy⟨s *n*y vek⟩
ha ty a vyȝ hy

2 Hy a vyȝ gwreg ty da • ȝys ȝe synsy⟦ hy⟧
pur wyr a lauara • ha govyn worty

3 Lemen yȝ torn my as re
ha war en greyz my an te
nag vs y far
an barȝ-ma ȝe pons tamar

My a'th pës worty bÿdh dâ,
hag oll dha vodh hy a wra,
rag flogh yw ha gensy doth;
hag a fy dhe gafos hy bodh.
Kyn ès mos dhymmo, emmowgh.
Ewgh alemma ha fystenowgh.

4 Dallath avarr; yn freth darwar
own na bortho,
ev omsettya orthys sy
camm na vetho.

5 Mara'th ergh dhis gul neb tra,
lavar dhesy "Bÿth ny venna'."
Lavar dhodho, "Gwra mar mennyth!"
Awos a allo, na wra tra vÿth.
I'n eur-na y'th sens dhe vos mêstres
hedyr vywy, hag arlodhes.

6 Ras o ganso, ren Oferen.
Cortes yw ha debonêr;
Dhis dregyn ny wra.
Mara'n kefyth in danjer,
sens e fast indella.

---

my ad pes worty byȝ da
ag ol ȝe voȝ hy a wra
rag flog yw ha gensy doȝ
ha⸨g a ffy⸩ ȝe gafus y boȝ
ken es mos ȝymmo ymmyug
eug alema ha fystynyug

4 Dallaȝ avar in freȝ darwar • oun ma ⸢porȝo⸣
ef emfettye worȝe⸨s sy⸩ • kam na veȝo

I beg you be good to her,
and she will do all your will,
for she is a child and well-behaved as well;
and she scorns to get her own way.
Before I go, kiss. {*The older man speaks to them both*}
Go hence and hasten.

{*The older man speaks to the girl*}

4 Begin early; be assiduously careful
that he is not alarmed,
so that he does not dare
in any way to oppose you.

5 If he ask you to do anything,
do you say "I never will."
Say to him, "Do it if you want!"
In spite of all his efforts, do nothing.
Then he will consider you mistress
as long as you live, and lady.

6 He was gracious, by the Mass.
He is polite and good natured;
He will do you no harm.
If you get him in your power,
keep him firmly like that.

---

5 Maraȝ herg ȝys gul nep tra
lauar ȝesy byȝ ny venna
lauar ȝoȝo gwra mar mennyȝ
awos a gallo na wra tra vyȝ
in vr-na yȝ sens ȝe ves meystres
hedyr vywy hag arluȝes

6 Ras o ganso re⟦n ⟧offeren
Curtes yw ha deboner • ȝys dregyn ny ⌜wra⌝
maran kefyȝ in danger
sen⟦s ⟧e fast indella

6.3 *PASSYON AGAN ARLÙTH*

1 Tas ha Mab ha'n Spyrys Sans,
—why a bÿs a leun-golon—
re wrauntyo dhywgh grâss ha whans
dhe wolsowes y Bassyon,
ha dhymmo grâss ha skians
dhe dherivas pàr dell wòn,
may fo dhe Dhuw dh'y wordhyans
ha selwans dhe'n Gristenyon.

2 Seul a vynno bos selwys
golsowens ow lavarow
a Jesu dell veu helhys
wàr an bÿs avell carow;
ragon menowgh rebukys
ha dysprêsys yn harow,
i'n grows gans kentrow fastys,
painys bys pàn veu marow.

3 Duw sur dre vertu an Tas
dhyn ny a dhyghtyas gweres:
an Mab dre y skians brâs
pàn gemert kig an Werhes,
ha'n Spyrys Sans leun a ras
dre y dhader may fe gwrÿs
godhaf painys pàn vynnas,
neb na ylly gul pehas.

Pascon agan Arluth

1 **T**ays ha mab han speris sans ⸗ wy a bys a levn-golon [1r]
Re wronte ʒeugh gras ha whans / ʒe wolsowas y bascon
Ha ʒymmo gras ha skyans • the ʒerevas par ⸨del won⸩
may fo ʒe thu ʒe worʒyans / ha sylwans ʒen ⸨gristenyon⸩

2 **S**uel a vynno bos sylwys / golsowens ow lauarow
a ihesu del ve helheys / war an bys avel carow
Ragon menough rebekys / ha dyspresijs yn harow
yn growys gans kentrow fastys / peynys bys pan ve marow

6.4 *THE PASSION OF OUR LORD*

1 May Father, Son and the Holy Spirit
—you who pray from the bottom of your heart—
grant you grace and yearning
to listen to his Passion,
and to me grace and wisdom
to recount as well as I can,
that it may be for the glory of God
and the salvation of Christians.

2 Whoever wishes to be saved,
let him listen to my words,
of Jesus how he was hunted
on the earth like a stag;
often reproached for us
and cruelly disparaged,
fixed upon the cross with nails,
tormented until he died.

3 God indeed by the Father's power
provided for us assistance:
the Son by his great wisdom
when he assumed the flesh of the Virgin,
and the Holy Spirit, full of grace
by his goodness by which he was made,
when he who was incapable of sin,
decided to suffer torment.

---

3 Du sur dre virtu an tas / ʒyn ny a ʒyttyas gweras
En mab dre y skyans bras / pan gemert kyg a werhas
han sperys sans leun a ras / dre y ʒadder may fe gurys
Goʒaff paynys pan vynnas / neb na ylly gull peghes

4 An dus vas a dhesîrya
dhedha gwlas nev o kellys.
Gans aga garm hag olva
Jesus Crist a veu muvys,
may fynnas dieskynna
in Gwerhes ha bos genys,
gans y gig agan perna;
Arlùth Duw, gwynn agan bÿs!

5 Jesus Crist meur gerensa
dhe vab den a dhyswedhas,
a'n uhelder mayth esa
dhe'n bÿs pàn dhieskynnas
pehadoryon rag perna,
o decêvys dre Satnas.
Rag henna gordhyn nefra
Jesus neb a'gan pernas.

6 An painys a wodhevys
ny veu ragtho y honen,
lemen rag pobel an bÿs,
pàn vowns y kefys mar wann.
An Jowl dhe Adam kêwsys:
"An aval, te, kemmer, tàn;
avell Duw y fedhyth gwrÿs."
Pàn y'n provas, nynj o màn.

---

4 An dus vas a ȝeserya / ȝeȝe gulas nef o kyllys
gans aga garm hag olua / ihesus crist a ve mevijs
may fynnas dijskynna / yn gwerhas ha bos genys
gans y gyk agan perna / Arluth du gwyn agan bys

5 Ihesu crist meur gerense / ȝe vab den a ȝysweȝas
an vghelder mayȝ ese / ȝen bys pan deyskynnas
Pehadoryon rag perna / o desevijs dre satnas [1v]
rag henna gorȝyn neffra / ihesus neb agan pernas

4 Good men desired for themselves
the kingdom of heaven, which had been lost.
By their cries and lamentation
Jesus Christ was moved,
so that he consented to descend
into a Virgin and be born,
to redeem us by his flesh;
Lord God, how happy are we!

5 Jesus Christ showed great love
to mankind, when he descended
from the heights where he was
to this world
to redeem sinners,
who had been deceived by Satan.
Therefore let us forever adore
Jesus who redeemed us.

6 The pains which he suffered
were not for himself,
but for the people of the earth,
since they had been found so weak.
The Devil spoke to Adam:
"The apple, you, pluck it; take it;
you will become like God."
When he tried it, it was not so at all.

---

6 **A** peynys a wotheuys / ny ve ragtho y honan
lemmyn rag pobyll an bys / pan vons y kefys mar wan
an ioull ȝe adam kewsys / an avel te kemer ta((n))
avell du y fethyth gurys / pan yn provas nyni o man

7 Warlergh mab den dhe beha,
rêson prag y feu prenys
yw Jesus Crist dhe ordna
in nev y vones tregys.
Y vos kellys ny vynna;
y dowl ganso o têwlys.
Rag henna dhe bob dyghtya
fordh a wrug dhe vos selwys.

8 Kyn nag ov den skentyl pur,
pàr dell wòn, lavaraf dhis:
intra Duw ha pehador
acord dell veu kemerys.
Rag bones gàn pegh mar veur,
main intredha a veu gwrÿs.
Ev o Crist a dheuth dhe'n leur,
Mab Duw ha den yw kefrÿs.

9 Ragon y pesys y Das
oll y sorr may fe gyvys,
gans y gorf dre bainys brâs
agan pegh may fo prenys.
Mab Maria, leun a ras,
oll y vodh a veu clêwys
ha kemmys a dhesîryas
dhodho ev a veu grauntys.

---

7 **W**arlyrgh mab den ȝe begha / reson prag y fe prynnys
yw ihesus crist ȝe ordna / yn neff y vonas tregys
y vos kyllys ny vynna / y doull ganso o tewlys
rag henna ȝe bob dyȝgthtya / forth a rug ȝe vos sylwys

8 **K**yn nag off den skentyll pur / par del won lauaraff ȝys
yntre du ha pehadur / acord del ve kemerys
rag bonas gonn pegh mar veur / mayn yntreȝe a ve gurys
eff o crist a theth ȝen leur / mab du ha den yw kyffrys

7 After mankind had sinned,
the reason that he was redeemed
is that Jesus Christ decreed
that he should dwell in heaven.
He did not intend that man be lost;
his plan he had determined.
Therefore he provided a way
through which all men could be saved.

8 Though I am not a truly learned man,
I will tell you as best I can:
between God and the sinner
an agreement was adopted.
Because our sin was so great,
he became a mediator between them.
He was Christ who descended to the earth,
the Son of God and man also.

9 He interceded for us with his Father
that all his wrath might be lessened,
that by his body and great torment
our sin should be annulled.
The Son of Mary, full of grace,
all his wish was heard,
and as much as he desired
was granted to him.

---

9 **R**agon y pesys y das / oll y sor may fe gevys
gans y gorff dre beynys bras / agan pegh may fo prennys
mab marea leun a ras / oll y voth a ve clewys
ha kymmys a theseryas / ȝoȝo eff a ve grontys

10 Y vamm, pàn y'n drehevys
ha'y vos devedhys dhe oos,
gul penans ev a besys;
henna ganso nynj o poos.
Dew ugans dÿdh ow penys
y spênas y gig ha'y woos,
ha wotyweth rag densys
ev a'n jeva awel boos.

11 Ha'n Jowl henna pàn glêwas,
y demptya y prederys
ha dhodho y tysqwedhas
cals meyn hag y leverys,
"Mars os Mab Duw, leun a ras,
a'n veyn-ma gwra bara dhis."
Jesus Crist, pàr dell vynnas,
dhodho ev a worthebys:

12 "Mab den heb ken ès bara
ny'n jeves oll y vêwnas,
lemen i'n lavarow dâ
a dheu dhyworth an Dremas."
Dre worthyp Crist i'n eur-na
lemmyn ny a yll gweles
lavar Duw maga dell wra
neb a vynno y glêwes.

---

10 I vam pan yn drehevys / hay vos deueȝys ȝe oys
gull penans ef a pesys / henna ganso nyni o poys
⟨*dew vgon*s⟩ dyth ow penys / y speynas y gyk hay woys [2r]
⟨*ha*⟩ woteweth rag densys / eff an geve awell boys

11 ⟨H⟩an ioull henna pan glewas / y demptye a brederys
⟨h⟩a ȝoȝo y tysqueȝas / cals meyn ha y leuerys
Mar⟦s ⟧os mab du leun a ras / an veyn-ma gura bara ȝys
ihesus crist par del vynnas / ȝoȝo ef a worthebys

10 When his mother reared him
and when he had come to man's estate,
he prayed to do penance;
he was not reluctant to do that.
Fasting for forty days
he spent his flesh and his blood,
and finally for his humanity,
he felt a craving for food.

11 And when the Devil heard that,
he thought to tempt him
and he showed him
a pile of stones and said,
"If you are the Son of God, full of grace,
make bread for yourself from these stones."
Jesus Christ, just as he wished,
answered him:

12 "Man with bread and nothing else
does not have all his life,
but by the good utterances
that come from the Holy One."
By Christ's answer at that time
now we can see
how the word of God nourishes
him who is prepared to hear it.

---

12 **M**ab den heb ken ys bara / nyn geuas oll y vewnas
lemmen yn lauarow da / a the ʒeworth an dremas
dre worʒyp crist yn vr-na / lemmyn ny a yll gwelas
lauar du maga del wra / neb a vynno y glewas

13 Gans glotny ev pàn welas,
camm na ylly y dùlla,
an tebel-el a vynnas
in ken maner y demptya.
Wàr bynakyl y'n gorras
diantell dhe esedha.
A-ugh eglos teg i'n wlas
an esedhva yth esa.

14 An Jowl dhe Grist a gêwsys
indelma rag y demptya:
"Ahanas yth yw screfys
bos eleth worth dha wetha,
rag own yth omdhyseves,
dhe droos worth men dhe dùchya.
Mars os Mab Duw a veur bris,
dieskynn ha dhe'n dor kê."

15 Jesus Crist a leverys,
"Dha Dhuw ny goodh dhis temptya
in neb ehen a servys,
lemen prest y onora."
Ha whath an Jowl a dêwlys
towl ken maner mar calla;
dre neb fordh a goveytys
guthyl dh'y gowsys trailya.

---

13 Gans glotny ef pan welas / cam na ylly y dolla
en tebell-el a vynnas / yn ken maner y demptya
war penakyll yn goras / dyantell ȝe eseȝa
a-vgh eglos tek yn wlas / an ysetva yȝ esa

14 An ioul ȝe gryst a gewsys / yndelma rag y demptye
ahanas yth ew scrifys / bos eleth worth ȝe wyȝe
rag own yȝ omdesevys / ȝe droys worth meyn ȝe dochye
mar((s))os mab du a veur brys / dijskyn ha ȝen dor ke

13 When he perceived that by gluttony he
could in no way deceive him,
the evil angel wished
to tempt him in another way.
He set him upon a pinnacle
sitting precariously.
The seat was above
a fine church in the land.

14 The Devil spoke to Christ
thus to tempt him:
"It has been written of you
that angels guard you,
lest you should stumble
to knock your foot against a stone.
If you are the Son of God, great his worth,
descend and go down."

15 Jesus Christ said,
"You should not tempt your God
in service of any kind,
but honour him always."
And again the Devil intended
a plan otherwise, if he could;
to make his conscience turn aside
through some sort of avarice.

---

15 Ihesus crist a leuerys / ȝe thu ny goth thys temptye
yn neb ehan a seruys / lemmyn prest y honore
Ha whath an Ioul a dewlys / towll ken maner m⟨*ar c*a⟩lle [2v]
dre neb forth a govaytys / guȝyll ȝy gowsys tryle

16 Alena y'n hùmbronkyas
uhel wàr benn unn meneth,
ha dhodho y tysqwedhas
owr hag arhans, gwels ha gwëdh,
ha "Kemmys i'n bÿs eus vas,"
yn medh an Jowl, "te a'fëdh,
ha me a'th wra arlùth brâs,
ow onora mar mynnyth."

17 Jesus Crist a leverys
y vos screfys i'n Lyfrow
"In pùb gwythres y coodh dhis
gordhya dha Dhuw ha'y hanow.
Kê dhe ves, emskemunys
dhe dhyfyth in tewolgow!
Dha vêstry a vëdh lehës
nefra wàr an enevow."

18 An Jowl a drailyas sperys
hag êth dh'y dyller teythy.
Tergweyth y feu convyctys;
ewn yw dhyn y volethy.
Dhe Jesu may fowns parys
dh'y gonfortya iredy
a'n nev y feu danvenys
dhyworth an Tas eleth dy.

---

16 Alene yn hombronkyas / vghell war ben vn meneth
ha ȝoȝo y tysquethas / owr hag arghans gwels ha gwe⟨*th*⟩
ha kymmys yn bys vs vas / yn meth an ioul te a feth
ha me ad wra arluth bras / ow honore mar mynnyth

17 Ihesus crist a leuerys / y vos scryfys yn lyffrow
yn pub gwythres y coth thys / gorȝye ȝe ȝu hay hanow
Ke ȝe ves omscumvnys / ȝe ȝyveyth yn tewolgow
the vestry a vyth leȝys / neffre war an enevow

16 Thence he led him
high upon the summit of a mountain,
and to him he showed
gold and silver, grass and trees,
and "All that is good in the world,"
said the Devil, "you shall have,
and I will make you a great lord,
if you are prepared to worship me."

17 Jesus Christ said
that it was written in the Scriptures,
"In every work it behoves you
to worship God and his name.
Begone, accursed one,
to a wasteland in darkness!
Your power will be lessened
forever over men's souls."

18 The Devil changed his mind,
and went to his proper place.
Three times he had been defeated;
right it is for us to curse him.
To Jesus that they might be ready
to comfort him indeed
from heaven were sent
from the Father angels thither.

---

18 An ioul a trylyas sperys / hag eth ȝy tyller tythy
tergweyth y fe convyctijs / evn yw ȝyn y voleythy
ȝe ihesu may fons parys / ȝy gonfortye yredy
an neff y fe danvenys / ȝeworth an tas eleth dy

19 Ha Satnas gans y antel
ha'y sherewneth ha'y goyntys
Crist mab an Arlùth uhel
y demptya pàn brederys,
bysy yw dhis bos uvel
ha servabyl i'th servys,
ma na allo an tebel
ogas dhis bones trailys.

20 Rag y hyllyr ervira
ha'y weles yn surredy,
y vos prest worth dha vetya
dhe veth dhis ha belyny.
Te ny yllyth omwetha
unn prës i'n jëdh na peghy,
pàn omsettyas dhe demptya
guthyl pegh neb na ylly.

21 Dell yw screfys, prest yma
adro dhyn ny gans outray,
mara kyll dhyworth an dâ
dhe wuthyl drog agan dry.
Folla yn tâ y whela,
ès dell wra lion y bray,
dry den in pain; a calla,
nefra ny yewnsa moy joy.

---

19 **H**a satnas gans y antell / hay scherewneth hay goyntys
crist mab an arluth vghell / y demptye pan prederys
besy yw ȝys bos vuell / ha seruabyll yth seruys
m⟪a ⟫no allo an tebell / ogas ȝys bonas trylys

20 **R**ag y hyller ervyre / hay welas yn suredy
y vos prest worth ȝe vetye / ȝe veth ȝys ha belyny
⟨T⟩e na yllyth omweȝe / vn pres yn geyth na peghy [3r]
pan omsettyas ȝe demptye / guȝyll pegh neb na ylly

19 And Satan with his snares
and his wickedness and subtlety
Christ, the son of the heavenly Lord,
since he thought to tempt him,
it is necessary for you to be humble
and diligent in your service,
so that the evil one
cannot be brought near to you.

20 For it can be concluded
and seen in very truth,
that he continually comes upon you
to your shame and disgrace.
You cannot keep yourself
for any time in the day that you sin not,
since he set about tempting
him who could do no sin.

21 As it is written, he is always
around us with violent attack,
to try if he can lead us
from the good to do evil.
Much more wildly than
a lion its prey, does he seek to bring man
to pain. If he were able,
never would he desire more joy.

---

21 Del yw scrifys prest yma / adro ȝyn ny gan⟦s o⟧try
mara kyll ȝeworth an da / ȝe weȝyll drok agan dry
folle yn ta y whela / ys del wra lyon y pray
drey den yn peyn a calla / neffre ny vnsa moy ioy

22 Gans an Jowl kyn fy temptys,
anodho na ro dema;
rag confort yw henna dhis,
screfys yw in lies le,
i'th allos y vos gorrys
kefrÿs sevel ha codha,
ha ganso kyn fes têwlys,
te a yll sevel arta.

23 Jesu Crist i'n pow adro
pùb eur oll pregoth a wre;
ha vertu an pregoth o
mab den dhe asa peha,
ha gevys may fe dhodho
kefrÿs y begh ha'y fylta,
degys na ve dhyworto
gwlas nev ha rës dhe gen re.

24 Benegys yw neb a gar
Duw dres pùptra eus i'n bÿs,
hag a wodhaffo yn whar
dhodho kemmys eus ordnys,
bò cleves bò pëth kescar,
bò dre bryson prysonys—
oll an dâ ha'n drog kepar
dhe Jesu bedhens grassys.

---

22 Gans an ioul kyn fy temptijs / anoʒo na ro dymme
rag confort yw henna ʒys / scrifys yw yn leas le
yt allos y vos gorrys / kyffrys seuell ha cothe
ha ganso kyn fes tewlys / te a yll seuel arte

23 Ihesu crist yn pow adro / pub er oll pregoth a wre
han virtu an pewgoth o / mab den ʒe ase peghe
ha gevys may fe ʒoʒo / kyffrys y begh hay fyltye
degys na ve ʒeworto / gulas nef a roys ʒe gen re

22 Though you be tempted by the Devil,
do not give a halfpenny for him;
for this is a comfort for you,
it is written in many passages,
it has been put in your power
both to rise and to fall,
and though you be thrown down by him,
you can stand up again.

23 Jesus Christ all around the country
used always to preach;
and the essence of the preaching was
that man should give up sinning,
so that there should be forgiven him
both his sin and his corruption,
to the end that the kingdom of heaven should not
be taken from him and given to others.

24 Blessed is the man who loves
God above everything in the world,
and who should suffer meekly
whatever is ordained for him,
whether sickness or the loss of possessions,
or imprisonment in prison—
for all the good and the evil equally
may Jesus be thanked.

---

24 **B**enegas yw neb a gar / du drys pubtra vs yn bys
hag a woȝaffo yn whar / ȝoȝo kymmys vs ordnys
bo clevas bo peth kescar / po dre breson presonys
ol en da han drok kepar / ȝe ihesu beȝens grassys

25 Jesu Crist i'n pow mayth ê
ev a sawya an glevyon;
dall na bodhar ny asa
nag omlavar nagonen,
na clâv vÿth ow crowedha.
Mar pesy a leun-golon,
whare sawys y fedha,
dell vynna Crist y honen.

26 Pàn welas an Yêdhewon
bos Crist ow cuthyl mêstry,
ow cara ethomogyon,
hag anedha na wre vry,
rag henna an vuscogyon
orto a borthas avy.
Dre vrâster brâs i'n golon
y chauncyons y dhystrêwy.

27 De Sul Blejyow pàn esa
in mesk y abestely,
y whrug dhe re anedha
mos dhe'n dre ha dygelmy
an asen ha dry gansa,
ha leverel iredy,
mar teffa tus ha gwetha,
bos dhe Dhuw dhe wul gensy.

---

25 Ihesu crist yn pow mayth e / eff a sawye an glevyon
dal na boȝar ny ase / nag omlauar nagonon
na claff vyth ow crowethe / mar pesy a leun-golon
whare sawijs y feȝe / del vynna crist y honon

26 Pan welas en ethewon / bos crist au cuthyll meystry [3v]
ow care eȝomogyon / hag aneȝe na wre vry
rag hena an vuscogyon / orto a borȝas avy
dre vraster bras yn golon / y chungsyons y ȝestrewy

25 Jesus Christ, wherever he went in the land,
healed the sick;
he left neither blind nor deaf
nor anyone mute at all,
nor any sick person supine.
If he prayed from the bottom of his heart,
he was healed straightway,
as Christ himself wished.

26 When the Jews saw
that Christ was performing miracles,
caring for the needy,
and that he was not taking account of them,
in consequence the mad ones
bore resentment towards him.
Through great arrogance of heart
they ventured to destroy him.

27 On Palm Sunday when he was
among his apostles,
he had some of them
go to the town and to unbind
an ass and bring her with them,
and indeed to say,
if men should come and prevent them,
that God required to make use of her.

---

27 Dev sull blegyow pan ese / yn mysk y abestely
y wreg ȝe re aneȝe / mos ȝen dre ha degylmy
an asen ha dry ganse / ha leuerell yredy
mar teffa tus ha gweȝe / bos ȝe ȝu ȝe wull gynsy

28 Dell erhys Jesus dhedha,
y a wrug adhesempys
oll y vodh ev, dell vynna;
an asen a veu kerhys;
warnedhy dhe esedha
dyllas pann a veu gorrys,
rag marhogeth a vynna
dhe'n cyta dhe vos gordhys.

29 Mur a dus ha benenes
a Jerùsalem i'n dre
erbynn Crist rag y weles
y êth ha rag y wordhya.
Wàr an fordh dyllas alês
a veu gorrys dhyragtho.
Palm ha flourys kekefrÿs
wàr y bynn degys a veu.

30 Y helwys a leun-golon
gans meur joy ha lowena
"In hanow Duw intredhon
benegys yw neb a dheu!"
Crist a gafas gwycoryon
i'n templys aberth i'n dre.
Ev a wrug dhedha yn scon
mones in mes alena.

---

28 Del yrghys ihesus ȝeȝe / y a rug aȝesympys
ol y voth ef del vynne / an asen a ve kerghys
warneȝy ⟨ȝe⟩ eseȝe / dyllas pan a ve gorrys
rag morogeth a vynne / ȝen Cyte ȝe vos gorthijs

29 Mu⟨r⟩ a dus ha benenas / a ierusalem yn dre
erbyn crist rag y welas / y eth ha rag y worȝye
war an forth dyllas ales / a ve gurrys ȝeragthe
palm ha florys kekyffrys / er y byn degys a ve

28 As Jesus had bidden them,
they did immediately
all his desire, as he wished;
the ass was fetched;
upon her, as a seat
garments of cloth were spread,
for he wished to ride
to the city to be honoured.

29 Many men and women
from Jerusalem, in the city,
towards Christ to see him
they went to do him obeisance.
Upon the road clothes spread out
were placed before him.
Palm and flowers also
were brought to greet him.

30 People called out from the bottom of their heart
with great joy and gladness,
"In the name of God among us
is blessed he who comes!"
Christ found traders
in the temples within the city.
Quickly he caused them
to depart away from there.

---

30 I helwys a leun-golon / gans meur ioy ha lowene
yn hanow du yntreȝon / benegas yw neb a the
crist a gafas gorkorian / yn templys aberth yn dre
ef a rug ȝeȝe y scon / monas yn mes alene

⌞{the five last lynes englished inserted}⌟
⌞Christ found ydle foolish, in the temple within the town
and he made them, ymmidiatly, to goe out from thence
the ⸢...*schen y..s*⸣ ⟪*scribes* ~ ~⟫ was wrathfull, be cause Christ was honored
and because his worke was soe great, and through ye world nown
they tooke counsell yat was not good, that Iesus should be undone⌟

31 An sherewys a sorras
rag bones Crist onorys,
ha bos y ober mar vrâs
ha dres an bÿs oll nôtys.
Gwrussons cùssul nag o vas,
rag may fe Jesus dyswrÿs,
ha kemmys y a'n cablas,
may feu an dre crehyllys.

32 An gùssul o may fe drës
dhyrag Crist pehadores,
oll dh'y vodh may rollo breus
anedhy dell vedha gwrës,
"Rag an lahys dhyn ny eus
a vynn hy dampnya porres,"
yn medhans y, "fordh nynj eus
may hallo bos dyflam gwrës."

33 Dhe'n tyller Crist re dhothya
ha'n Yêdhewon o dygnas.
Th'esa an venyn gansa;
parys êns dh'y hùhudhas.
Hadre vowns y ow plaintya,
Jesus i'n dor a screfas,
ha dre vertu an screfa
pob dhe ves a omdennas.

---

31 En scherewys a sorras / rag bonas crist honorys
Ha bos y ober mar vras / ha drys an bys oll notijs
grussons cusyll nag o vas / rag may fo ihesus dyswrys
Ha kymmys y an cablas / may fe an dre ⟨*crehylly*s⟩ [4r]

32 En gusyl o may fe drys / ȝerag crist peha⟨*dures*⟩
ol ȝy voth may rollo bres / aneȝy del veȝe gr⟨*es*⟩
rag an lays ȝyn ny es / a vyn y dampnye porres
ym meȝens y forth nyng es / may hallo bos deflam gurys

31 The scoundrels were angry
because Christ was honoured,
and that his work was so mighty,
and known throughout the world.
They devised a plan that was not good,
that Jesus might be undone,
and they so maligned him,
that the town was shaken.

32 The plan was that there should be brought
before Christ a sinful woman,
that he might as he wished give judgement on her,
what should be done with her,
"For the laws which we have
will condemn her perforce,"
they said, "there is no way
that she may be rendered guiltless."

33 Christ had come to the place
and the Jews, who were graceless.
The woman was with them;
they were ready to accuse her.
While they were making the complaint,
Jesus wrote in the earth,
and by the power of that writing,
everyone withdrew thence.

---

33 Then tyller crist re dethye / han eȝewon o dygnas
ȝesa an venyn ganse / parys ens ȝy huhuȝas
hedre vons y ov plentye / ihesus yn dor a scryfas
ha dre virtu an scrife / peb ȝe ves a omdennas

34 Pàn êthons oll dhe wary—
ancombrys y re bia—
"Py ma," yn medh Crist dhedhy,
"neb a vynn dha gùhudha?"
"Den vŷth nynj eus," yn medh hy.
Jesus a gêwsys arta,
"Me ny'th dampnyaf iredy,
ha na wra na moy peha."

35 Benyn der veur jeryta
hy box rych leun a ely
a-ugh Crist rag y ùntya
hy a vynnas y derry.
Corf Jesus rag confortya
gwrës pòr sur o iredy.
Jûdas Scaryot a's cabla
ha gans meur a fâlsury.

36 Jûdas fâls a leverys,
"Tryhans dynar a vona
an box oll bedhens gwerthys
awos den rag y ranna
dhe vohosogyon i'n bŷs.
Gwell via ès y scùllya."
Jesus Crist a worthebys
(y gowsys ev a wodhya):

---

34 Pan eȝons oll ȝe wary / ancombrys y re bea
pe ma yn meth crist ȝyȝy / neb a vyn ȝe guhuȝa
denvyth nyng es yn meȝ y / ihesus a gewsys arta
me nyth dampnyaf yredy / ha na wra na moy pegha

35 Benyn dyr veur cheryte / y box rych leun a yly
a-vgh crist rag y vntye / hy a vynnas y derry
corf ihesus rag confortye / gures pur sur o yredy
Iudas scharyoth a((s))cable / ha gans meur a falsury

34 When they had all departed—
they had been embarrassed—
“Where,” said Christ to her,
“are those who wish to condemn you?”
“There is no-one,” she said.
Jesus spoke again,
“I indeed do not condemn you,
and do not sin any more.”

35 A woman with great charity
her rich box full of salve
over Christ to anoint him
wished to break.
To comfort Jesus’ body
it was done indeed very surely.
Judas Iscariot maligned her
and with great falsehood.

36 False Judas said,
“For three hundred pence of money
let all the box be sold
for man’s sake to distribute it
to the poor in the world.
It would be better than to waste it.”
Jesus Christ answered
(he knew his inmost thoughts):

---

36 Iudas fals a leuerys / trehans dynar a vone
en box oll beȝens gwerthys / a vos den rag y ranne
the vohosogyon yn bys / gwel vya ys y scolye
ihesus crist a worthebys / y gowsys ef a woȝye

37 “Na dhegowgh sorr i’n golon
wàr neb a vynn ow sawya.
Ow thermyn a dheu yn scon;
genowgh me ny’m bÿdh trega.
Why a gÿv bohosogyon
pùb eur warnowgh ow carma.
Pàn vynnowgh agas honen,
why a yll gul dâ dhedha.”

38 Whare y sorras Jûdas—
ny gêwsy dre jeryta
lemen rag cafos rann vrâs
a’n pencyon, mara calla.
Ev o harlot, tebel-was;
wotyweth lader via.
Dhe’n Yêdhewon y ponyas
Crist y arlùth dhe wertha.

39 Ev a leverys dhedha,
“Pÿth a vynnowgh why dhe ry
ha me a wra dhywgh spêdya
ow cafos Crist iredy?”
Y fowns unver intredha:
kepar ha dell wovynny,
deg warn ugans a vona
in unn pêmont y whrêns ry.

---

37 **N**a thegough sor yn golon / war neb a vyn ow sawye
ow thermyn a the yn scon / genough me nvm byth trege
Wy a gyff bohosogyon / pub er warnough ow carme
pan vynnough agys honon / wy a yll gull da ʒeʒe

38 **W**⟨h*are y so*⟩ras Iudas / ny gewsy dre geryte [4v]
⟨l*emyn*⟩ rag cafos ran vras / an pencon mara calle
⟨ef *o* h⟩arlot tebel-was / woteweth lader vye
ʒen eʒewon y ponyas / crist y arluth ⦅ʒe⦆ gwerʒe

37 “Bear no anger in your heart
against her who will anoint me.
My time will soon come;
I cannot remain with you.
You will have the poor
calling upon you always.
Whenever you yourselves wish,
you may do good to them.”

38 Immediately Judas became angry—
he did not speak from charity
but to get a large share
of the proceeds, if he could.
He was a scoundrel, an evil man;
at the last he would be a thief.
He ran off to the Jews
to sell Christ, his lord.

39 He said to them,
“What will you give me,
and I will cause you to succeed
in capturing Christ indeed?”
They were of one mind among themselves:
exactly as he was asking,
thirty pieces of money
they would give him as a payment.

---

39 **E**ff a leverys ȝeȝe / pyth a vynnough why ȝe ry
ha me a ra ȝeugh spedye / ow cafos crist yredy
y fons vnver yntreȝe / kepat ha del wovyny
⦅dek warn vgons⦆ a vone / yn vn payment y wrens ry

40 Arta Jûdas ow trailya—
gwann-wycor ny'n jeva par,
ny yll den vÿth amowntya
myns a gollas i'n chyffar—
wàr Jesu ev a fecla,
kepar ha pàn ve hegar.
I'n dyweth ny acordya
y golon gans y lavar.

41 Gans Jûdas dell o têwlys
dry Jesus sur dell vynna,
gans Crist yth o cowethys;
byth nynj êns y cowetha.
An jëdh o De Yow Hablys,
may fynna Jesus sopya
gans an re in y servys
wàr an bÿs re dhêwyssa.

42 Dew dhen Crist a dhanvonas
dhe berna boos ha dewas.
An keth re-na a spêdyas
ha'n soper a veu parys.
Crist worth an gon a warnyas
dre onen bos traison gwrÿs.
"Arlùth Duw," y a armas,
"pyw a yll henna bones?"

---

40 **A**rte Iudas ow tryle / gwan-wecor nyn geve par
ny yl den vyth amontye / myns a gollas yn chyffar
⸨war⸩ ihesu ef a fecle / kepar ha pan ve hegar
yn deweth ny acordye / y golon gans y lauar

41 **G**ans iudas del o tewlys / drey ihesus sur del vynne
gans crist yth o cowethys / byth nyng ens y coweȝe
en gyth o de yow hablys / may fenne ihesus sopye
gans an re yn y seruys / war an bys re ȝewesse

40 Judas turning again—
he had no equal as a poor trader,
no man can calculate
the amount he lost in the transaction—
he pretended to Jesus,
as though he were loving to him.
In the end there was no agreement
between his heart and his utterance.

41 Since it had been planned by Judas,
to hand over Jesus, as he wished,
he had associated with Christ;
never were they companions.
The day was Maundy Thursday
on which Jesus wished to have supper
with those in his service,
whom he had chosen in the world.

42 Christ sent two men
to buy food and drink.
The same men hurried
and the supper was ready.
Christ at the supper warned
that treachery would be committed by one.
"Lord God," they cried,
"who can that be?"

---

42 Dew ȝen crist a ȝanvonas / ȝe berna boys ha dewas
an keth re-na a spedyas / han soper a ve parys
crist worth an goyn a warnyas / dre onan bos treson gurys
arluth du y a armas / pv a yl henna bonas

43 Jesus Crist a worthebys
“Ow tebry genen yma.”
Pùbonen oll a elwys,
“Arlùth Duw yw me henna?”
Ha Jesus a worthebys,
“A’m scudel debry a wra.
Goev vÿth pàn veu genys
a dorr y vamm dhe’n bÿs-ma.”

44 Duw a sonas an bara
dhyrag y abestely.
“Ow horf avy yw hemma,”
yn medh Crist, “sur ragowgh why,
pernys aberth i’n bÿs-ma,
dysprêsys haneth a vÿdh.
A’n deppro gans crejyans dâ,
gober teg ev a’n jevÿdh.”

45 Ha’n gwin esa wàr an voos
ev a rannas intredha.
Yn medh Crist, “Hèm yw ow goos.
Evowgh why par jeryta.”
Gans dowr gorrys in bason
y wholhas aga garrow;
hës ha hës y’s gwrug pòr wynn,
dell vynna Du caradow.

---

43 Ihesus crist a worȝebys / ow tybbry genen yma
pubonan ol a ylwys / arluth du yv me hena
ha ihesus a worȝebys / am scudel dybbry a wra
gwef vyth pan ve genys / a dor y vam ȝen by⸨s⸩-ma

44 Du a sonas an bara / ȝerag y abestely
ow horf ave yw hemma / yn meth crist sur ragough wy
pernys aberth yn by⸨s⸩-ma / dyspresys haneth a vyth
an deppro gans cregyans da / gober tek eff an geuyth [5r]

43 Jesus Christ answered,
"He is eating with us."
Everyone of them all cried,
"Lord God, am I that man?"
And Jesus answered,
"He is eating from my dish.
Woe is him that he was born
of his mother's womb into this world."

44 God blessed the bread
in front of his disciples.
"This is my body,"
said Christ, "surely for you,
redeemed in this world,
it will be despised tonight.
Whoever eats it with sound faith,
will have a fine reward."

45 And the wine that was on the table
he divided among them.
Christ said, "This is my blood.
Drink it in charity."
With water poured into a basin
he washed their feet.
Wholly he made them clean,
as beloved God wished.

---

45 Han gwyn esa war en foys / ef a rannas yntreȝa
yn meth crist ((hem yw ow)) goys / evough why par cheryta
gans dour gorrys yn bazon • y wolhas aga garrow
((heys ha heys)) ys guregh pur wyn / del vynna du caradow

46 Henna Peder a sconyas,
Jesus dhe wolhy y dreys.
"Taw, Peder, te ny wodhes,"
yn medh Crist, "pandra wrav dhis.
Mar ny'th wolhaf dre ow grâss,
in nev ny vedhyth tregys."
Yn medh Peder, "Dhymm na as
troos na leuv na vo golhys."

47 Jesus Crist, leun a byta,
a leverys dhe'n dhôwdhek,
"Why yw glân a bùb fylta,
mès nynj owgh oll dâ na wheg."
Bos Jûdas ev a wodhya
pòr hager ha molothek.
An Jowl ino re dhreksa,
mayth o gweth ages cronek.

48 Indelma Crist pàn wrussa,
dhe Jûdas a leverys,
"Te, kê in unn fystena,
dha vodh may fo colenwys,
rag an termyn re dheuva,
may fÿdh an bugel kefys
ha kechys intra dêwla
ha'n deves dhe ves fies."

---

46 Henna pedyr a sconyas / ihesus ȝe wolhy y dreys
taw pedyr te ny woȝas / yn meth crist pandra raf ȝys
mar nyth wolhaff dre ow gras / yn nef ny veȝyth tregys
yn meth pedyr ȝym na as / troys na leyff na vo golhys

47 Ihesus crist leun a bete / a leuerys ȝen dowȝek
wy yv glan a bub fylte / mas nyni ough ol da na whek
bos Iudas ef a woȝye • pur hager ha moloȝek
an ioul ynno re drecse / mayȝ o gweth agys cronek

46 That deed Peter refused,
that Jesus should wash his feet.
"Silence, Peter, you do not know,"
said Christ, "what I am doing for you.
If I do not wash you by my grace,
you will not dwell in heaven."
Said Peter, "Do not leave on me
any foot or hand that is not washed."

47 Jesus Christ, full of mercy,
said to the twelve,
"You are clean of all filth,
but you are not all good nor sweet."
He knew that Judas was
quite hideous and accursed.
The Devil had taken residence in him,
so that he was worse than a toad.

48 When Christ had done thus,
he said to Judas,
"You, go hurrying,
that your wish may be fulfilled,
for the time has come
when the shepherd will be taken
and seized by hands,
and the sheep will flee away."

---

48 Indelma crist pan wresse / ȝe iudas y leuerys
te ke yn vn fystene / ȝe voth may fo colenwys
rag an termyn re deve / may fyth an begel k⟦ef⟧ys
ha chechys yntre dewle / han deves ȝe ves fijs

49 "Kyn fallens oll, me a vŷdh,"
yn medh Peder, "i'th servys."
Yn medh Crist, "I'n nos haneth,
kyns ès bos colyak clêwys,
Peder, te a'm nagh tergweyth
bythqweth arlùth na veuv dhis."
Yn medh Peder, "Tàn ow fëdh,
ny'th nahaf kyn fen ledhys."

50 Yn medh Crist, "Abàn wrug dhywgh
ternoth, fernoth ow holya,
daffar vŷth why ny dheksowgh
dhe worra tra vŷth ino.
Bytegyns why ny wodhowgh
pandra ethom a'gan beu."
"Arlùth, gwir a leversowgh,"
y a gôwsys intredha.

51 "Mès lemmyn res yw porres
batalyas kyns ès cùsca.
A'n jeffo pows a's gwerthens
ha dhodho pernans cledha."
"Sur yma dhyn dew parys,"
y a leverys whare.
"Hèn yw lowr; na moy ny res,"
Duw a leverys arta.

---

49 Kyn fallens ol me a vyth / yn meth pedyr yth seruys
yn meth crist yn nos haneth / kyns ys boys colyek clewys
peder te am nagh tergweth • bythqueth arluth na vef ȝys
yn meth peder tan ow feth / nyth nahaff kyn fen leȝys

50 In meth crist aban rug ȝeugh / ternoyth fernoth ow holye
daver vyth wy ny ȝecsyugh / ȝe worre tre vyth ynne
betegyns wy ny woȝough / pandra eȝom a⸨g⸩an be
arluth guyr a leuersough / y a gowsys yntreȝe

49 “Though they all fail, I shall be,”
said Peter, “in your service.”
Christ said, “This very night,
before the cock be heard,
Peter, you will deny me three times,
that ever was I your lord.”
Said Peter, “Upon my faith,
I will not deny you, though I be killed.”

50 Said Christ, “Since I caused you
to follow me half-clad and barefoot,
you did not carry any bag at all
in which to put anything.
Nonetheless you do not know
of what we had need.”
“Lord, you have spoken the truth,”
they said among themselves.

51 “But now it is very necessary
to struggle before sleeping.
Let him who has a cloak sell it
and buy himself a sword.”
“Surely we have two ready,”
they said straightway.
“That is enough; no more is necessary,”
God said again.

---

51 **M**as lemmyn rys yv porrys / batayles kyns ys coske [5v]
an geffo pows as gwyrʒyns / ha ʒoʒo pern《an》s cleʒe
sur yma ⦅ʒyn dew⦆ parys / y a leuerys whare
hen yw lour na moy ny rys / du a leuerys arte

52 Mab Maria, leun a ras,
dhe'n Meneth Olyf yth êth,
ha'y dyscyplys a'n sewyas.
Yn medh Crist, "I'n nos haneth
golyowgh ha pesowgh ow Thas,
may hallowgh mos dh'y eseth,
na vedhowgh temptys dygnas
gans gow ha gans sherewneth.

53 "Peder, Androw ha Jowan,"
yn medh Crist, "dewgh, holyowgh vy
bys i'n meneth; ha me gwann
tristans eus worth ow bludhya."
Dhyworta unn lamm bian
yth êth pesy may halla
dh'y Das whath ujy avàn
hag ev rag own ow crena.

54 Mab Maria meur a bain
a wodhevy i'n eur-na,
rag ev a wodhya yn fen,
ha'n kig ny vynna henna,
mès y dhuwsys o mar fin,
pùb eur dhodho a'n trailya,
mayth êth wàr benn y dhêwlin
ha pesy in kettelma:

---

52 Mab marya leun a ras / ȝen meneth olyff yȝ eth
hay ȝyscyplys an sewyas / yn meth crist yn nos haneth
golyough ha pesough ow ȝas / may hallough mos ȝy aseth
na veȝough temtijs dygnas / gans gow ha gans scherewneth

53 Peder androw ha Iowan / yn meth crist deugh holyough ve
bys yn meneth ha me gwan / trystyns vs worth ow bluȝye
ȝeworte vn lam beghan / yȝ eth pesy may halle
ȝy ȝas weth vgy avan / hag ef rag own ow crenne

52 The son of Mary, full of grace,
went to the Mount of Olives,
and his disciples followed him.
Christ said, "Tonight
watch and pray my Father,
in order that you may go to his dwelling,
that you be not wretchedly tempted
by falsehood and wickedness.

53 "Peter, Andrew and John,"
said Christ, "come, follow me
unto the mountain; because I am weak
sorrow is debilitating me."
A short way from them
he went that he might pray
to his Father who is still above
and he was trembling for fear.

54 The Son of Mary was suffering
much pain at that time,
for he knew full well,
and the flesh did not wish it,
but his godhead, which was so fine,
continually turned him to it,
so that he knelt down
and prayed in this way:

---

54 **M**ab marya meur a beyn / a woʒevy yn vr-na
rag ef a woʒya yn feyn / han kyg ny vynna henna
mes y ʒewsys o mar feyn / pub vr ((ʒeʒa an trylya))
mayʒ eth war ben y ʒewleyn / ha pesy yn ketelma

55 “Maras yw dha vodh, ow Thas,
gwra dhe’n pain-ma ow gasa,
mès bedhens gwrÿs dhe vynnas,
Arlùth Duw, dha vodh dell ve.”
Dh’y dhyscyplys y trailyas,
y’s cafas oll ow cùsca.
Yn medh Crist, “Unn pols golyas
’ny yllowgh dhe’m confortya?”

56 Ena Crist sur a’s gasas
hag êth arta dhe besy
wàr benn glin dhyworth y Das,
dell lavarsa, ragon ny.
Y bainys o crev ha brâs
warnodho heb y dylly;
rêson o rag oll an wlas
ev a wodhya y ferwy.

57 Yn medh Crist, o Duw ha den,
arta dh’y abestely,
“Golyowgh ha pesowgh yn fen
rag own a’n Jowl ha’y vêstry.”
Tressa gweyth hag ev yn crèn,
y pesys Duw, “Delyrf vy.
Arlùth, mar ny yll bos ken,
bedhens kepar dell vynny.”

---

55 **M**aras ew ȝe voth ow ȝas / gura ȝen payn-ma ow gasa
Mes beȝens gurys ȝe vynnas / arluth du ȝe voth del ve
ȝy ȝyscyplys y trylyas / y⸨s ⸩cafas ol ow coske
yn meth crist vn pols golyas • ny yllough ȝum confortye

56 **E**na crist sur as gasas / hag eth arta ȝe besy
war ben gleyn ȝeworth y das • del lauarsa ragon ny
y beynys o cref ha bras / warnoȝo heb y dylly
reson o rag ol an wlas / ef a woȝye y verwy

55 "If it is thy will, my Father,
cause this pain to leave me,
but let thy will be done,
Lord God, as your wish may be."
To his disciples he returned,
he found them all sleeping.
Christ said, "To watch a little while
can you not to comfort me?"

56 Then Christ surely left them
and went again to pray
upon his knees from his Father,
as he had said, for our sakes.
His pains were severe and great
upon him, though he did not deserve it;
the reason was that for all the land
he knew he was going to die.

57 Christ, who was God and man,
said again to his apostles,
"Watch and pray assiduously
for fear of the Devil and his power."
The third time, as he was trembling,
he prayed to God, "Deliver me.
Lord, if it cannot be otherwise,
let it be as you wish."

---

57 In meth crist o du ha den / arte ʒy abestely
golyough ha pesough yn ven / rag own an ioul hay vestry
Tresse gwyth hag ef yn cren / y pesys du dylyr«f» vy [6r]
arluth mar ny yl bos ken / beʒens kepar del vynny

58 Jesus Crist dygonfortys
wàr benn dêwlin pan esa,
a'n nev y feu danvenys
el dhodho dh'y gonfortya.
Mab Duw o kemmys grêvys,
rag tomder ev a whesa
dowr ha goos yn kemyskys—
whes Crist rag dha gerensa.

59 Crist kemmys pain a'n jeva,
angùs tynn ha galarow,
may teuth an goos ha droppya
wàr y fâss, an caradow.
Den vÿth ny yll amowntya
na leverel wàr anow
oll myns painys a'n jeva,
kyns ès y vones marow.

60 Lemmyn ny a yll gweles
hag ervira fest yn tâ,
Crist dhe wodhaf dre dhensys
meur a benans i'n bÿs-ma.
Ev ny ylly dre dhuwsys
godhaf naneyl drog na dâ,
rag mêster o wàr an bÿs
hag oll myns eus ev a wra.

---

58 Ihesus crist dygonfortys / war ben dewlyn pan ese
an nef y fe danuenys / el ȝoȝo ȝy gomfortye
mab du o kymmys grevijs / rag tomder ef a wese
dowr ha goys yn kemeskys / weys crist rag ȝe gerense

59 Cryst kymmys payn yn geve / angus tyn ha galarow
ma teth an goys ha dropye / war y fas an caradow
Den vyth ny yl amontye / na leuerell war anow
oll myns peynys an geve / kyns ys y vonas marow

58 Jesus Christ, while he was
distressed upon his knees,
from heaven there was sent
an angel to him to comfort him.
The Son of God was so afflicted,
that he perspired for heat
water and blood mixed—
Christ's sweat for your sake.

59 Christ suffered so much pain,
bitter anguish and affliction,
that the blood actually dropped
upon his face, the beloved one.
No man can reckon
nor describe in words
all the torments he suffered,
before he died.

60 Now we can see
and determine very clearly,
that Christ suffered through manhood
much penance in this world.
He could not in his divinity
suffer either good nor ill,
for he was master of the world,
and he makes everything that there is.

---

60 Lemmyn ny a yl gwelas / hag ervyre fest yn ta
cryst ȝe woȝaff dre ȝensys / Meur a benans yn by((s))-ma
ef ny ylly dre ȝewsys / goȝaff nanyll drok na da
rag mester o war an bys / hag ol myns vs ef a ra

61 Pàn o y besadow gwrës,
dhe'n dôwdhek y leverys,
"Cùscowgh lemmyn, mars yw prÿs;
powesowgh, why yw grêvys.
Tus eus dhymm ow tevones
yw gans ow thraitour deskys,
fatell dhowns dh'ow hemeres
ha dell vedhaf hùmbronkys."

62 Kepar Duw dell leverys,
pàn esa Crist ow pesy,
Jûdas êth in y negys—
an Jowl yw a'n hùmbronky.
Dhe'n Yêdhewon derivys
dell o, y fynnas sensy.
Shyndys veu dre goveytys;
indella yw lies huny.

63 Dhe'n Yêdhewon pàn dhothya,
yn medh ev, hag y ow tos,
"Me a grÿs yn tâ spêdya
i'm negys haneth i'n nos.
Dewgh genef ha holyowgh vy,
godhvedhowgh na wrellowgh tros,
ha me a wra dhe Crist amma,
may hallowgh y aswonvos."

---

61 Pan o y besadow gurys / ȝen dowȝek y leuerys
koscough lemmyn mar((s))ew prys / powesough wy yv grevijs
tus vs ȝym ow tevones / yv gans ow thraytor dyskys
fatel dons thov hemeres / ha del veȝaff hombronkys

62 Kepar du del leuerys / pan esa crist ow pesy
Iudas eth yn y negys / en ioul yv en hombronky
ȝen eȝewan dyrryvys / del o y fynas synsy
syndys ve dre govaytys / yndella yw leas huny

61 When his prayer was finished,
he said to the twelve,
"Sleep now, if it is the time;
rest, you are afflicted.
The men who are coming for me
have been instructed by my betrayer,
how they shall come to arrest me,
and how I shall be led away."

62 Just as God said,
when Christ was praying,
Judas went about his business—
it was the Devil who was guiding him.
To the Jews he declared
as it was, he wished to hold to it.
He was destroyed by avarice;
so is many the one.

63 When he had reached the Jews,
he said, as they were coming,
"I believe I will prosper well
in my business this night.
Come with me and follow me,
be careful not to make a noise,
and I shall kiss Christ,
so that you may recognize him."

---

63 Then eȝewon pan doȝye / ((yn meth ef)) hag y ov tos
me a grys yn ta spedye / om negys haneth yn nos
deugh geneff ha holyough ve / gothveȝough na rellough tros
Ha me a ra the crist amme / may hallough y asswonvos

64 An pryncys esa i'n pow
gans Jûdas a dhanvonas
tus ven gwyskys in arvow,
kepar ha dell êns dhe'n gas.
Gansa y a dhug golow—
nos o, ny welens yn fâs—
bys in Jesus caradow
y êth dell dhescas Jûdas.

65 Pàn dhothyens bys i'n tyller
mayth esa Crist ow pesy,
"Lowena dhis, a vêster,"
yn medh Jûdas, an brathky.
Dhodho y whrug fekyl-cher
hag y amma truesy.
Ev a vynna in ober
gul ken ès dell dhyswedhy.

66 Jesus a gêwsys pòr deg,
"Jûdas, ow ry te a vynn,
dre dha vay a reth mar wheg
dhe neb a'm torment mar dynn.
Mollath den, ha gour ha gwreg
a dheu poran er dha bynn.
Painys a'th wra morethek
in iffarn down pùb termyn."

---

64 An princys esa yn pow / gans Iudas a thanvonas [6v]
tus ven gweskys yn arvow / kepar ha del ens ȝen gas
ganse y a thuk golow / nos o ny welons yn fas
bys yn Ihesus caradow / y eth del dyskas Iudas

65 Pan doȝyans bys yn tyller / mayȝ ese crist ow pesy
lowene ȝys a vester / yn meth Iudas an brathky
ȝoȝo y rug fekyl-cher / hag y amme trewesy
ef a vynne yn ober / gul ken ys del dyswyȝy

64 The princes who were in the land
sent with Judas
strong men dressed in armour,
as though they were going to battle.
With them they carried light—
it was night, they could not see well—
to Jesus, the beloved,
they went as Judas instructed them.

65 When they had come to the place
where Christ was praying,
"Joy to you, O master,"
said Judas, the savage cur.
He gave him a hypocritical greeting
and kissed him fatefully.
He wished in fact
to do other than he appeared to do.

66 Jesus spoke very fairly,
"Judas, you will betray me,
by your kiss, which you give me so sweetly,
to him who will torment me very sharply.
The curse of men, both husband and wife,
will come exactly against you,
Pains will render you wretched
in deep hell forever."

---

66 Ihesus a gewsys pur dek / Iudas ow ry te a vyn
dre ȝe vay a reyth mar whek / ȝe neb am tormont mar dyn
moll《a》ȝ den ha gour ha gwrek / a ȝe poran er ȝe byn
peynys ad wra moreȝek / yn yffarn down pub termyn

67 Jesus Crist a wovynnys
worth an bobel a dheuth dy
gans an fâls in y servys,
"Pandra yw a vynnowgh why?"
An re-na a worthebys,
"Jesus yw, a'n caffen ny."
An Arlùth a worthebys,
"Me yw henna iredy."

68 Pòr wir drefen an vertu
a'n lavar Crist pàn gowsas,
"Neb a whelowgh why me yw,"
dhe ves y a omdennas.
Rag own y a jaunjyas lyw,
rag gwander y a godhas.
In tra vÿth y nynj êns gwyw
dhe wuthyl dres y vynnas.

69 Crist a wovynnas arta
orth an Yêdhewon wocky,
"Agas negys pÿth ywa,
pyw yw neb a whelowgh why?"
"Jesus Crist a Nazare,"
an re-na a wortheby.
Yn medh Jesus, "Me ywa.
Lemmyn gwrewgh agas mêstry."

---

67 Ihesus crist a wovynnys / worth an bobyll a ȝeth dy
gans an fals yn y seruys / pandra yw a vynnough wy
en re-na a worȝebys / ihesus yw an caff⸨en⸩ ny
en arluth a worȝebys / me yw henna yredy

68 Pur wyr drefen an virtu / an lauar crist pan gowsas
neb a wheleugh why me yw / ȝe ves y a omdennas
rag own y a gangyes lyw / rag gwander y a goȝas
yn tre vyth y nyng ens gyw / ȝe weȝyll drys y vynnas

67 Jesus Christ asked
the people who had come there
with the traitor in his service,
"What is it that you want?"
Those men answered,
"It is Jesus, if we could find him."
The Lord answered,
"I am that man indeed."

68 Very truly because of the power
of that utterance when Christ spoke,
"Whom you seek I am,"
they withdrew away.
For fear their colour altered,
for weakness they fell down.
In nothing were they worthy
to do other than his will.

69 Christ inquired again
from the foolish Jews,
"Your errand, what is it,
who is he whom you seek?"
"Jesus Christ of Nazareth,"
those men kept on answering.
Said Jesus, "I am he.
Now exercise your power."

---

69 Cryst a wovynys arte / orth an eȝewon woky
agys negys pyth ywe / pv yw neb a weleugh wy
ihesus crist a nazare / an re-na a worȝeby
yn meth ihesus me ywe / lemmyn gureugh agys meystry

70 Whare y a'n kemeras
hag a'n sensys intredha,
gans lavarow a'n scornyas;
gallos o grauntys dhedha
dhe wuthyl aga mynnas.
Indella ev a vynna,
may halla dre bainys brâs
merwel rag dha gerensa.

71 Peder a'n eyl tenewen
in mes a dennas cledha
hag a drohas ryb an penn
scovarn onen anedha.
Crist a settyas yn tien
an scovarn arta dhe dre
hag a'n dyghtyas pòr lowen,
maga teg dell re bia.

72 "In y won dha gledha dro,"
dhe Peder Crist a erhys,
"rag dre gledha a vêwho
dre gledha y fŷdh ledhys.
Dêwdhek lyjyon in unn rôw
'via a'n nev danvenys,
ha moy a mynnen dhymmo,
pesy ow Thas, pòr barys.

---

70 Whare y an kemeres / hag an sensys yntreʒe [7r]
gans lauarow an scornyas / gallos o grontys ʒeʒe
ʒe weʒyll aga mynnas / yndella ef a vynne
may halle dre baynys bras / merwel rag ʒe gerense

71 Pedyr an eyl tenewen / yn mes a dennas cleʒe
hag a drohas ryb an pen / scovern onan aneʒe
crist a settyas yn tyen / an scovern arte ʒe dre
hag an dyʒgthtyas pur lowen / maga tek del re bye

70 Straightway they took him
and they held him among them,
with speeches that mocked him;
power was granted to them
to do their will.
Thus he wished
that he might by great torments
die for your sake.

71 Peter on the one side
drew out a sword
and cut off near the head
the ear from one of them.
Christ put entirely
the ear back again into its place,
and healed him right gladly,
as fair as he had been.

72 "Put your sword into its sheath,"
Christ bade Peter,
"for whoever shall live by the sword,
by the sword he will be killed.
Twelve legions one after the other
would be sent from heaven,
and more to me if I wanted
to pray my Father, very readily.

---

72 ⸨Yn y goyn ʒe gleʒe dro⸩ / ʒe pedyr crist a yrghys
rag dre gleʒe a veughe / dre gleʒe y fyth leʒys
dewʒek lygyon yn vn ro / vye an nef danuenys
ha moy a mynnen ʒymmo / pesy ow ʒas pur barys

73 “Hag a pe indella, ve,
nefra ny vien fethys.
I’n eur-na fatell via
a’m bêwnans, dell yw screfys
i’n Lyfrow in lies le
dre brofusy leverys?
Res yw porres heb strîvya
bodh ow Thas dhe vos sewys.”

74 Jesus a gêwsys arta,
“Why a dheuth dhymm in arvow
dre draison in unn scolkya
gans boclers ha cledhydhyow
dhe’m kemeres, dhe’m shyndya,
ha dhe’m painya bys in crow,
kepar ha pàn vena vy
an purra lader i’n pow.

75 “In agas mesk pàn esen,
lahys Duw dhywgh ow tesky,
gallos nynj esa cammen
dhe’m cara na dhe’m sensy.
Lemmyn deuva ken termyn;
ow Thas re’m grauntyas dhywgh why,
leun a behas, ny wòn ken,
dhe wuthyl agas mêstry.”

---

73 Hag a pe yndella ve / neffre ny vean fethys
yn vr-na fatell vye / am bewnans del yw scrifys
yn lyffrow yn leas le / dre brofusy leuerys
reys yw porrys heb strevye / both ow ʒas ʒe vos sewijs

74 Ihesus a gewsys arte / why a theth ʒym yn arvow
dre dreyson yn vn scolchye / gans boclers ha cleʒyʒyow
thom kemeres ʒom syndye / «ha» ʒom peynye bys yn crow
kepar ha ⦅pan⦆ vena ve / an purra lader yn pow

73 “And if it were thus, I
never would have been overcome.
Then how would it be
concerning my life, as is written
in the Scripture in many places
told by the prophets?
It is very necessary without opposing
that the will of my Father be obeyed.”

74 Jesus spoke again,
“You have come to me in arms
sneaking up by treachery
with bucklers and swords
to arrest me, to harm me,
and to torture as far as bloodshed,
as though I were
the most out-and-out brigand in the land.

75 “When I was among you,
teaching you the laws of God,
there was no power at all
to kiss me or to imprison me.
Now a different time has come;
my Father has ceded me to you,
full of sin, I do not know the reason,
to exercise your authority.”

---

75 In agys mysk pan esen / lays du ȝeugh ow tysky
gallos nyng ese kemmen • ȝom cara na ȝom sensy
lemmyn deve ken termyn / ow ȝas rom growntyas ȝe wy
leun a beghas ny won ken / ȝe weȝyll agys meystry

76 I'n eur-na y a golmas
y dhywvregh fast gans cronow,
an goos in mes may tardhas
dell fastsens an colmennow.
Gansa y a'n hùmbroncas
in prÿs hanter-nos heb wow
bys in aga fryns Anas,
o unn jùster brâs i'n pow.

77 Tus Crist dhe ves a fias,
pob a'y du pòr vorethek,
saw Peder Crist a holyas
abell avell unn ownek
dhe dyller an pryns Anas.
Ena yth esa sedhek.
Orto ev a esedhas,
may clêwa lev Jesus wheg.

78 An pryns scon a leverys,
"Te, Crist, lavar dhymm ple ma
dha dus mar vold re dhessys?
Prag na dhowns genes omma?
An lahys a bregowthys,
lemmyn dyswa mars yns dâ."
Ha Jesus a worthebys,
ev dell vynna i'n eur-na,

---

76 In vr-na y a colmas / y ȝefregh fast gans crono⟨w⟩ [7v]
en goys yn mes may tarȝas / del fastsens en colmenn⟨*ow*⟩
gansa y an hombronkyas / yn prys hanter-nos heb wow
bys yn aga fryns annas / o vn Iutter bras yn pow

77 Tus crist ȝe ves a fyas / peb ay du pur voreȝek
saw peder crist a holyas / abell avel vn ownek
ȝe dyller an prins annas / ene yȝ ese sethek
orto ef ⸨a e⸩sethas / may clewo leff ihesus whek

76 Then they bound
his two arms fast with thongs,
so that the blood burst forth
when they pulled the knots tight.
They led him off with them
at midnight indeed
to their prince Annas,
who was an important magistrate in the land.

77 Christ's men fled away,
each one his own way very wretchedly,
but Peter followed Christ
from a distance like a coward
to the house of the prince Annas.
There was a tribunal in the place.
He sat down at it
to hear the voice of beloved Jesus.

78 The prince soon said,
"You, Christ, tell me where are
your men, whom you have taught so boldly?
Why do they not come here with you?
The laws which you preached,
reveal now, if they are good."
And Jesus answered,
as he wished at that time,

---

78 **E**n prins scon a leueris / te crist lauar ȝym ple ma
ȝe dus mar vold re ȝyssys / prag na ȝons genas omma
an lays a bregowthys / lemmyn dyswe mar⟦s⟧yns da
ha ihesus a worȝebys / ef del vynna yn vr-na

79 “Pòr apert hag i’n golow
y leverys ow dyscas;
ow lahys ha’w lavarow,
seul a vynna y’s clêwas.
I’n le mayth en i’n trevow
yn splann me a’s derivas.
Ny gôwsyn in tewolgow
adrëv tus in unn hanas.

80 “Pandra a wovynta sy
dhyworthyf vy ha’m lahys?
Mara mynnyth, govyn y
orth an keth re a’s clêwas.
An re-na ’yll dha dhesky;
indella y re dhescas.”
Indelma heb vylyny
orto Jesus a gowsas.

81 Gans henna a’n Yêdhewon
onen in bàn a sevys,
hag a ros ryb an scovarn
box dhe Grist adhesempys,
ha dhe Jesus y honen
an harlot a leverys,
“Pyw a worras i’th colon
cows indelma worth jùstys?”

---

79 Pur apert hag yn golow / y leuerys ow dyskas
ow lays haw lauarow / suel a vynna y《s》 clewas
yn le mayth en yn trevow / yn splan me a⸨s ⸩derevas
ny gowsyn yn tewolgow / adryff tus yn vn hanas

80 Pandra a wovente se / ȝeworȝaff ve ham lays
mara mynnyth gov⸨y⸩n y / ordh en keth re as clewas
an re-na yl ȝe ȝysky / yndella y re ȝyskas
yndelma heb velyny / orto Ihesus a gowsas

79 “Very openly and in broad daylight
I spoke my teaching;
my commandments and my utterances,
whoever wished heard them.
Wherever I went in the towns
clearly I declared them.
I did not speak in darkness,
behind men’s backs whispering.

80 “What are you asking
about me and my commandments?
If you want, ask them
from the very people who heard them.
Those men can teach;
for thus they have learnt.”
In this way without discourtesy
Jesus spoke to him.

81 Thereupon one of the Jews
jumped to his feet,
and dealt a blow to Christ
beside the ear straightway,
and to Jesus himself
the ruffian said,
“Who put it in your heart
to speak thus to a magistrate?”

---

81 **G**ans henna an eȝewon / onan yn ban a sevys
hag a ros ryb an scovern / box ȝe grist aȝesympys
ha ȝe Ihesus y honon / an harlot a leuerys
pu a woras yt colon / cows yndelma worth iustys

82 Yn medh Jesus i'n eur-na,
"Mara kêwsys fâlsury,
ha na blêk genes henna,
ha fâls, te dog dùstuny,
mès mara kêwsys yn tâ
ha'n gwrioneth y sensy,
prag y'm gwyskyth indelma?
Nynj yw marnas bylyny."

83 Ena meur a vylyny
Peder dhe Grist a welas;
y scornya hay voxusy,
trewa in y dhewlagas,
hag ev rag own ny ylly
gans Jesu kêwsel ger vas.
Hèn o poynt a fâlsury,
dedhewys heb keweras.

84 Unn venyn hardh a inyas
worth Peder y vos tregys
gans Jesus. Ev a nahas
y Arlùth adhesempys.
"Taw, gans Crist me a'th welas,"
gwreg aral a leverys.
Peder arta a gowsas,
"Bythqweth me ny'n aswonys."

---

82 In meth ihesus yn vr-na / mara kewsys falsury [8r]
ha na blek genas henna / ha fals te dok dustuny
mes mara kewsys yn ta / han gwreoneth y synsy
prag om gwysketh yndelma / nyng yw marnas belyny

83 Ena meur a vylyny / peder ʒe gryst a welas
y scornye hay voxscusy / trewe yn y ʒewlagas
hag ef rag own ny ylly / gans ihesu kewsel ger vas
⸨hen⸩ o poynt a falsury / deʒewys heb koweras

82 Jesus then said,
"If I spoke falsehood,
and that is not pleasing to you
and false, produce the evidence,
but if I spoke well
and maintained the truth,
why do you thus strike me?
It is nothing but mistreatment."

83 Then Peter saw much mistreatment
meted out to Christ;
mocking him and striking him,
spitting in his eyes;
and he for fear could not
speak a helpful word for Jesus.
That was a matter of treachery,
a promise without fulfilment.

84 A woman boldly insisted
that Peter had resided
with Jesus. Immediately
he denied his Lord.
"Silence, I saw you with Christ,"
another woman said.
Peter again spoke,
"Never did I know him."

---

84 Vn venyn hardh a ynnyas / ⦅worth⦆ peder y vos tregys
gans ihesus ef a naghas / y arluth aȝesympys
taw gans crist me ad welas / gurek arall a leuerys
peder arta a gowsas / bythqueth me nyn aswonys

85 Meur a dus a leverys,
“Ny dal dhis camm y naha.
Dre dha gows yth yw prevys
dha vos den a Alyle.”
Ev a dos adhesempys
maga town ty dell wodhya,
gans Crist na via tregys
na bythqweth ev na’n gwelsa.

86 Gans hemma ev a glêwas
an colyak scon ow cana,
ha Crist worto a whythras
a’n painys brâs mayth esa.
Peder sur a omdennas
i’n eur-na, dell re beghsa,
ow naha Duw, leun a ras,
hag ev gwarnys dell via.

87 Whare in mes y trailyas,
ha’y golon namna dorra,
rag y Arlùth leun a ras
mar dhygnas ev dh’y naha.
Debry boos ev ny vynnas,
lemen pùb eur-oll ola
dhodho bys pàn dhanvonas
Crist y to dhe Alyle.

---

85 **M**eur a dus a leuerys / ny dayl ȝys cam y naghe
dre ȝe gows yȝ ew preuys / ȝe vos den a galyle
ef a doys aȝesympys / maga town ty del woȝye
gans crist na vye tregys / na bythqueth ef nan quelse

86 **G**ans hemma ef a clewas / en colyek scon ow cane
ha crist worto a wetras / an peynys bras mayȝ ese
pedyr sur a omdennas / yn vr-na del re beghse
ow nagha du leun a ras / hag ef gwarnyys del vye

85 Many men said,
"You ought not deny it at all.
By your speech it is shown
that you are a man from Galilee."
Immediately he swore
as deep an oath as he could,
that he had not dwelt with Christ,
nor had he ever seen him.

86 Thereupon he heard
the cock at once crowing,
and Christ looked at him
from the great torments he was enduring.
Peter surely withdrew
at that time, as he had sinned,
denying God, full of grace,
though he had been warned.

87 Quickly he turned away
and his heart was fit to break,
because his Lord, full of grace,
he had denied so perversely.
He did not want to eat food,
but rather weep continually,
until Christ sent word to him
that he would come to Galilee.

---

87 **W**hare yn mes y trylyas / hay golon namna dorre
rag y arluth leun a ras / mar ȝynas ef ȝy nahe
dybbry boys ef ny vynnas / lymmyn pub er-ol ole
ȝoȝo bys pan danvonas / crist y to ȝe galyle

88 Jesus a veu danvenys
adhyworth an pryns Anas
gans tus ven adhesempys
bys an epscop Caÿfas,
dredho Crist may fe brusys
oll dh'y vodh ha dh'y vynnas.
Meur a dus o cùntellys
er y bynn dh'y gùhudhas.

89 Rag y vos wàr brontyryon
mêster brâs aberth i'n wlas,
gorrys veu in y golon
indelma gul, may cowsas:
"Res yw porres dhe onen
merwel rag pobel an wlas,
pobel Jesus y honen,
na vowns tregys gans Satnas."

90 An Yêdhewon intredha
a whelas dùstuniow
rag painya Crist ha'y shyndya.
Ny gêwsens dhe blegadow
saw wàr Dhuw y a vynna
dre envy leverel gow.
A dus fâls y re dhothya,
an purra ladron i'n pow.

---

88 Ihesus a ve danvenys / aʒeworth an prins annas
gans tus ven aʒesympys / bys an ebscob cayphas
Dreʒo crist may fe bresys / ol ʒy voth ha ʒy vynnas [8v]
meur a dus o cuntullys / er y byn ʒy guhuʒas

89 Rag y vos war bronteryon / mester bras aberth yn wlas
gurrys ve yn y golon / yndelma gul may cowsas
rys yw porrys ʒe onon / merwel rag pobyl an wlas
pobyl ihesus y honon / na vons tregys gans satnas

88 Jesus was sent
from the prince Annas
by strong men immediately
to Caiaphas, the bishop,
that Christ might be judged by him
entirely according to his wish and desire.
Many men had been gathered
to make accusations against him.

89 Because he was over priests
a great master in the land,
it was put into his heart
to do thus, so that he spoke:
"It is very necessary that one man
should die for the people of the land,
lest the people of Jesus himself
should dwell with Satan."

90 The Jews among themselves
sought witnesses
to torment Christ and to hurt him.
They did not speak to be agreeable,
but they wished against God
to speak falsehood through envy.
They had come from false men,
the greatest thieves in the land.

---

90 **E**n eʒewon yntreʒe / a whelas dustuneow
rag peyne crist ha⟪y⟫ syndye / ny gews⟦en⟧s ʒe blegadow
saw war thu y a vynne / dre envy leuerell gow
a dus fals y re doʒye / an purre laddron yn pow

91 Ha dew a dhug dùstuny,
y'n clêwsons ow leverel,
pòr wir y fynna terry
an tempel crev ha'y wuthyl
warlergh henna dre vêstry
i'n tressa dÿdh heb fyllel;
dre nerth brâs y'n drehevy,
bythqweth ev na via gwell.

92 Neb o mêster ha jùstys
worth Jesus ev a gowsas,
"Myns eus omma cùntellys
pòr apert y re'th vlamyas,
ha te ger vÿth ny gêwsys.
Omwith lemmyn, mar codhes."
Oll Jesus a'n godhevys
ha'y wortheby ny vynnas.

93 Cayfas arta a gêwsys,
"In hanow Duw te lavar,
mars os Duw dell danvensys."
"Me yw," yn medh Crist yn whar,
"in nev y fedhaf tregys
a'n barth dyhow gans am Car;
yn sur Dhuw ow tevones
why a'm gwelvyth heb neb mar."

---

91 Ha dew a thuk dustuny / yn clewsons ow leuerell
pur wyr y fenne terry / an tempel cref hay wuȝell
warlyrgh henna dre vestry / yn tressa dyth heb fyllell
dre nerth bras yn drehevy / bytqueth ef na vye gwell

92 Neb o mester ha Iustys / worth ihesus ef a gowsas
myns vs omma cuntullys / pur apert y ret flamyas
ha te ger vyth ny gewsys / omweyth lemmyn mar coȝas
ol Ihesus an goȝevys / hay worȝeby ny vynnas

91 And two testified,
that they heard him saying,
very truly that he would break down
the temple and build it
thereafter by power
on the third day without fail;
he would raise it up by great power,
so that never would it have been better.

92 He who was master and a magistrate,
to Jesus he spoke,
"All those who are gathered here
have very publicly condemned you,
and you have not spoken a word.
Defend yourself now, if you can."
Jesus endured it all
and would not answer him.

93 Caiaphas spoke again,
"In God's name say,
if you are God as you have reported."
"I am," said Christ meekly,
"in heaven I shall dwell
on the right hand of my Parent;
as true God coming
you will see me without any doubt."

---

93 Kayphas arta a gewsys / yn hanow du te lavar
mar((s))os du del danvansys / me yw yn meth crist yn whar
yn nef y feȝaff tregys / an barth dyghow gans am car
yn sur thu ow tevones / wy am gwylvyth heb neb mar

94 Cayfas pòr wir a sorras
hag êth pòr fol in eur-na
hag a sqwerdyas y dhyllas,
pàn gowsas Crist indella.
Y terivys dre sorr brâs,
"Dùstuniow drog na dâ
ny res dhyn ny dhe whelas
awos dampnya an den-ma.

95 "Oll ow cows why a'n clêwas.
Leverowgh mar pÿdh sawys."
Oll warbarth y a armas,
"Gwyw yw dhe vones ledhys."
Gans mowys y a'n scornyas,
in y fâss y a drewys.
"Te yw mab Duw, leun a ras!"
in ges y a leverys.

96 Gans qweth y benn y qwethens.
Gweles banna ny ylly.
Dhe Jesus Crist bytegyns
ow cul drog ha bylyny,
avell brathkeun aga dens
orto y a dhaskerny.
Er aga fynn bytegyns
Crist unn ger ny levery.

---

94 Kayphas pur wyr a sorras / hag eth pur fol yn vr-na
hag a squerdyas y ʒyllas / pan gowsas crist yndella
⸨y ⸩terevys dre sor bras / dusteneow drok na da
ny reys ʒyn ny ʒe welas / awos dampnye an den-ma

95 Ol ow cows why an clewas / leuerough mar pyth sawys [9r]
ol warberth y a armas / gweff yw ʒe vonas leʒys
gans mowys y an scornyas / yn y fa⸨s⸩ y a drewys
ty yv mab du leun a ras / yn ges y a leuerys

94 Caiaphas very truly was angered
and he became very mad at that point
and rent his garments,
when Christ spoke thus.
He declared in great anger,
"Witnesses neither evil nor good
we have no need to seek,
in order to condemn this man.

95 "You all have heard him speaking.
Say whether he shall be spared."
All together they shouted,
"He is worthy to be killed."
With grimaces they mocked him,
they spat in his face.
"You are the Son of God, full of grace!"
they said in mockery.

96 With a cloth they covered his head.
He could not see anything.
To Jesus Christ, nevertheless,
doing evil and brutality,
like savage curs their teeth
at him they gnashed.
Against them, however,
Christ was not saying a word.

---

96 **G**ans queth y ben y queȝens / guelas banna na ylly
ȝe ihesus crist betegyns / ow ((kull)) drok ha belyny
avel brathken aga dyns / orto y a theskerny
er aga fyn betegyns / crist vn ger ny leuery

97 Hag y worth y dormentya,
y cudhens y benn gans qweth,
ha'n dus esa oll i'n dre
ha pryncys i'n pow inwedh,
ha meur a bobel gansa
adhyhow sur hag aglêdh,
dhe Grist y towns dh'y shyndya
ha dh'y dhry dhe'n dor gans meth.

98 Y êth ha Jesus gansa
bys in Pilat o jùstys,
anodho breus may rolla,
dre y vreus may fe ledhys.
Lavarsons y heb pyta,
"Agan traitour yw kefys.
Res yw dhyso y dhampnya
dhe'n mernans adhesempys."

99 Yn medh Pilat, "Pana dra
a inyowgh why warnodho?"
"Na ve bos fâls an den-ma,
ny'n drosen ny bys dyso."
Y leverys, "Dre laha
ha why dampnyowgh a ytho."
Yn medhans, "Yêdhow ny wra
dampnya den, lader kyn fo."

---

97 Hàg y worth y dormontye / y cuȝens y ben gans queth
han dus esa ol yn dre / ha pryncys yn pow ynweth
ha meur a bobyll ganse / aȝyghow sur hag agleth
the gryst y tons ȝy syndye / ha ȝe dry ȝen dor gans meth

98 I eth ha Ihesus ganse / bys yn pylat o Iustys
anoȝo bres may rolle / dre y vres may fo leȝys
lavarsons y heb pyte / agan traytour yw kefys
rys yw ȝeso y ȝamnye / ȝen mernans aȝesympys

97 And as they tormented him,
they covered his head with a cloth,
and all the men who were in the town
and the princes of the country also,
and many people with them,
on the right indeed and on the left,
came to Christ to injure him
and to bring him down with shame.

98 They went taking Jesus
to Pilate, who was a magistrate,
so that he might give judgement on him,
so that he might be put to death by his verdict.
They said without pity,
"Our traitor has been caught.
You must condemn him
to death immediately."

99 Pilate said, "What matter
do you urge against him?"
"Had this man not been false,
we should not have brought him to you."
He said, "By law
you then condemn him!"
They said, "A Jew shall not
condemn a man, though he be a robber."

---

99 In meth pylat pan((a))dra / a ynnyough wy warnoʒo
na ve bos fals an den-ma / nyn drossen ny bys deso
y leuerys dre laha / ha why dampnowgh a yʒo
yn meʒens ((eʒow ny)) wra / dampnye den lader kyn fo

100 Henna Pilat pàn welas,
kemmys côwsys wàr y bynn,
rowtours ha tus rych i'n wlas
rêsons mar fol ha mar dynn,
Pilat orto govynnas
i'n keth maner-ma govyn,
"Osa mab Duw, leun a ras?
Lemmyn gwir te lavar dhyn."

101 Yn medh Crist, an cuv colon,
"Pòr wir te re leverys.
Te, a wodhyes dha honen,
pò dre gen re 'veus gwarnys?"
Pilat a gêwsys yn scon,
"Te a veu dhymm danvenys.
Lavar dhymmo dha honen,
pÿth yw an drog re wrussys?"

102 Yn medh Jesus, "Nynj ujy
ow mêstrynjys i'n bÿs-ma,
hag a pe, ow thus dhywgh why
ny'm delyfrens indelma."
"Ytho mytern ota sy?"
yn medh Pilat in eur-na.
"Gwir re gêwsys iredy,"
yn medh Crist, "mytern oma."

---

100 **H**enna pylat pan welas / kymmys cawsys er y byn
rowtors ha tus ⸨rych⸩ yn wlas / resons mar fol ha mar dyn
pylat orto govynnas / yn keth vaner-ma govyn
ose mab du leun a ras / lemyn gwyr 《te》 lauar ȝyn

101 **I**n meth crist an kveff colon / pur wyr te re leuerys [9v]
te a woȝye《s》 ȝe honon / pe dre gen re ves guarnys
pylat a gewsys yn scon / te a ve ȝym danvenys
lauar ȝymmo ȝe honon / pyth yw en drok re wrussys

100 When Pilate saw that,
that so much was spoken against him,
rulers and rich men in the land
speaking matters so foolish and so keen, 796
Pilate asked him
in questioning of this sort,
"Are you the Son of God, full of grace?
Now do you tell me truly." 800

101 Christ said, the beloved,
"Very truly you have spoken.
Did you know yourself
or were you advised by others?" 804
Pilate spoke soon,
"You were sent to me.
Tell me yourself,
what is the evil that you have done?" 808

102 Jesus said, "My dominion
is not of this world,
and if it were, my men would not
have delivered me thus to you." 812
"So you are a king?"
said Pilate then.
"You have spoken truth indeed,"
said Christ, "I am a king." 816

---

102 In meth Ihesus nyng vgy / ow mestrynges yn by⸨s⸩-ma
hag a pe ow thus ʒe wy / ny⸨m⸩ delyrfsens yndelma 812
ytho mygtern ote se / yn meth pylat yn er-na
gwyr re gwesys yredy / yn meth crist mygtern oma 816

103 Henna Jûdas pàn welas,
Crist an bêwnans na sawya,
an arhans a gemeras
rag corf Crist dhe recêva,
ev a's têwlys dre sorr brâs
dhe'n Yêdhewon intredha.
"Dremas yw ev, leun a ras,
neb re werthys," yn medha.

104 Jûdas Scaryot a gêwsys
i'n keth maner-ma arta,
"Fest yn crev me re behas
Jesus dhywgh why ow qwertha.
Dâ y wòn y vos a ras,
gyvyans me ny'm bÿdh nefra."
Moy pegh o pà'n dysprêsyas
ès dell o pàn y'n gwertha.

105 Ha'n Yêdhewon a gêwsys,
"Pandr'yw henna dhyn nyny?
Ny a'n pernas dhyworthys
hag a'th pes pòr iredy."
Jûdas êth adhesempys
a'n eyl tu dhe omgregy.
Cafas daffar pòr barys,
lovan crev rag y sensy.

---

103 **H**enna Iudas pan welas / crist an bewnans na sawye
an arghans a gemeras / rag corf crist ʒe rysseve
ef a⟦s ⟧tewlys dre sor bras / ʒen eʒewon yntreʒe
dremas yw ef leun a ras / neb re werʒys yn meʒe

104 **I**udas scaryoth a gewsys / yn keth vaner-ma arte
fest yn creff me re beghas / ihesus ʒe wy ov querʒe
da y won y vos a ras / gevyons me nvm byth neffr⟨*e*⟩
moy pegh o pan dyspresyas / ys del o pan yn guerʒe

103 When Judas saw that,
Christ would not save his life,
the silver which he got
for their receiving Christ's body,
he threw it in great anger
at the Jews all among them.
"He is a good man, full of grace,
whom I have sold," he said.

104 Judas Iscariot spoke
again in this same way,
"Very seriously I have sinned
by selling Jesus to you.
Well I know that he is of grace,
I shall never have forgiveness."
It was a greater sin when he undervalued him
than when he sold him.

105 And the Jews spoke,
"What is that to us?
We bought him from you
and paid you very truly."
Judas went straightway
apart to hang himself.
He found means very readily,
a strong rope to hold him.

---

105 **H**an eȝewon a gewsys / pandrew henna ȝyn nyny
ny an pernas ȝeworȝys / ha ad pes pur yredy
Iudas eth aȝ⸨e⸩sympys / an eyl tu ȝe omgregy
cafas daffar pur parys / lovan cryff rag y sensy

106 Enef Jûdas ny allas
dos in mes wàr y anow,
rag y anow a ammas
dhe Jesu, leun a rasow.
Dewolow iffarn 'sqwardyas
corf Jûdas oll dhe dharnow,
hag anodho a gerhas
y enef dhe dewolgow.

107 An Yêdhewon dre envy
a gêwsys Crist rag shyndya,
"Pilat, jùstys ota sy;
Jesus gorweyth y dhampnya.
A Jerùsalem dhyn ny
ev a dheuth a Galyle
lahys nowyth ow tesky,
lies ganso ow trailya."

108 Gansa Pilat pàn glêwas
bos Jesus a Galyle,
bos Herodes wàr an wlas
mytern Pilat a wodhya.
Rag henna y tanvonas
Crist dhodho ev may'n dampnya.
Ruth veur a dus a'n sewyas,
pùb eur parys dh'y vlâmya.

---

106 Eneff iudas ny allas / dos yn mes war y anow
rag y anow a ammas / ȝe ihesu leun a rasow
dywolow yfarn squerdyas / corf iudas ol ȝe ȝarnow
hag anotho a gerhas / y eneff ȝe dewolgow

107 En ethewon dre envy / a gewsys crist rag syndye [10r]
pylat Iustys ote se / Ihesus gorweyth y dampnye
a ierusalem thyn ny / ef a thueth a galyle
lays nowyth ov tesky / leas ganso ov tryle

106 The soul of Judas could not
come forth at his mouth,
for his mouth kissed
Jesus, full of grace.
Devils from hell tore
the body of Judas to pieces,
and from it fetched
his soul to darkness.

107 The Jews through malice
spoke in order to hurt Christ,
"Pilate, you are a magistrate;
be sure to condemn Jesus.
To us of Jerusalem
he came from Galilee,
teaching new commandments,
turning many with him."

108 When Pilate heard from them
that Jesus came from Galilee,
Pilate knew that Herod
was king over the kingdom.
Therefore he sent Christ
to him that he might condemn him.
A great crowd of men followed him,
always ready to abuse him.

---

108 Ganse pylat pan glewas / bos Ihesus a galyle
bos herodes war an wlas / mygtern pylat a woȝye
Rag henna y tanuonas / crist ȝoȝo ef mayn dampne
ruth veyr a dus an sewyas / pub eyr parys ȝy vlamye

109 Y êth bys in Herodes,
ha Crist gansa fast kelmys.
Ev a gara Crist gweles,
rag kemmys yth o praisys, 868
ganso mar calla clêwes
wheldh nowyth a ve coyntys,
mar calla trailya dhe hës
lavar Crist pàn ve clêwys. 872

110 Dhe Herodes yth esa
pòr wir worth Pilat sorr brâs.
Y weles ev ny gara
na bos in y gowethas, 876
dhodho Jesus dh'y dhampnya
Pilat bys pàn dhanvonas.
I'n eur-na kescowetha
y a veu ha specyal brâs. 880

111 Herodes a wovynnys
orth Jesus Crist lies tra
ha tra vÿth ny worthebys,
ma'n jeva marth a henna. 884
An Yêdhewon a gêwsys,
"Don dhyn dùstuny a wra,
mytern y fynn bos sensys
ha mêster brâs i'n bÿs-ma." 888

---

109 I eth bys yn herodes / ha crist ganse fast kylmys
ef a gara crist gwelas / rag kymmys yȝ o praysys 868
ganso mar callo clewas / whelth nowyth a vo coyntys
mar callo trylye ȝe hes / lauar crist pan vo clewys 872

110 The herodes yth esa / pur wyr worth pylat sor bras
y welas ef ny gara / na boys yn y goweȝas 876
ȝoȝo Ihesus ȝy thampnye / pylat bys pan danvonas
yn vr-na keskeweȝa / y a ve ha specyall bras 880

109 They went to Herod,
with Christ firmly bound by them.
He wanted to see Christ,
for so greatly had he been praised,
in case he might hear from him
a new story that might be a strange new tale,
if he might twist round
Christ's words when they had been heard.

110 Herod bore towards Pilate
great anger indeed.
He did not want to see him
nor to be in his company,
until Pilate sent to him
Jesus to condemn him.
At that time they became companions,
and specially great ones.

111 Herod asked
Jesus Christ many things
and he answered nothing at all,
so that he was astonished by that.
The Jews spoke,
"He testifies to us,
that he wishes to be considered a king
and a great master in this world."

---

111 **H**erodes a wovynnys / orth Ihesus crist leas tra
ha tre vyth ny worȝebys / man geve marth a henna
an eȝewon a gewsys / doyn thyn dustuny a wra
mygtern y fyn bos synsys / ha mester bras yn by((s))-ma

112 Kemmys tra a lavarsa
ena y a'n rebukyas.
Dhyrag an try mayth esa,
Anas, Pilat ha Cayfas,
pòr vylen y a'n pyltya
hag yn spîtys a'n scornyas.
Moyha dhodho drog a wre,
henna 'vedha'n gwella gwas.

113 Herodes a leverys
dhe'n Yêdhewon, "Ewgh yn fen
dhe Bilat, agas jùstys,
rag me a'n sens pur dhen len,
ha leverowgh bos gyvys
oll ow sorr—bedhens lowen—
ha'm gallos y vos grauntys
dhodho dhe vrusy an den."

114 Y a wyskys Crist gans gwynn,
avell fol y a'n scornya,
hag a'n gwesca fest yn tynn;
bytegyns ger ny gêwsy,
hag y'n hùmbroncas bys in
Pilat, o jùstys dhedha,
may caffens y aga gwain
wàr Jesus Crist dh'y ladha.

---

112 Kymmys tra a lavarsa / ena y an rebukyas
therag an try mayʒ esa / annas pylat ha cayhas
Pur vylen y an pyltye / hag yn spytys an scornyas [10v]
moygha ʒoʒo drok a wre / henna veʒan guella gwas

113 Herodes a leuerys / ʒen eʒewon eugh yn fen
ʒe bylat agys Iustys / rag me an syns pur ʒen len
ha leuerough bos gevys / ol ow sor beʒens lowen
ham gallos y vos grontijs / ʒoʒo ʒe vrusy an den

112 For as many things as he had said
they rebuked him then.
When he was before the three,
Annas, Pilate and Caiaphas,
very vilely they harassed him,
and spitefully they mocked him.
Whoever did the greatest evil to him,
that man was the best fellow.

113 Herod said
to the Jews, "Go speedily
to Pilate, your magistrate,
for I consider him a most honest man,
and tell him that all my anger
has been remitted—let him be joyful—
and my authority is granted
to him to judge the man."

114 They dressed Christ in white.
like a madman they mocked him,
and struck him very sharply;
all the same he spoke no word,
and they led him to Pilate,
who was their magistrate,
that they might get their advantage
over Jesus Christ to kill him.

---

114 I a wyskys cryst gans gwyn / avel fol y an scornye
hag an gweska fest yn tyn / betegyns ger ny gewsy
hag an hombronkyas bys yn / pylat o Iustys ȝeȝe
may caffons y aga gwayn / war Ihesus crist ȝy laȝe

115 Dhe'n Jowl meur neb o tus keth
dhe Bilat a leverys,
"Lowenha! Gwellha dha fëdh!
Herodes re'th tynerhys.
In y golon fast rej êth
meur a gerensa worthys
hag ev a dalvyth dhis whath
y onora dell wrussys.

116 "Ha dhyso y tanvonas
y allos Crist rag jùjya,
ha ny a'th cùssul, na as
lemmyn y vodh heb sewya."
Yn medh Pilat, "Skyla vas
me ny gafaf re'm lewta,"
na bÿth moy ev ny gafas
prag may fe res y dhampnya.

117 Orth Pilat oll y setsons
ha warnodho a wrug cry,
rag Jesus Crist dhe'n mernans
y a vynna porres dry.
Yn medh Pilat, "Worth an myns
a'n pegh pewas res yw ry.
Me ny gafaf moy ès kyns
rêson gans gwir dh'y vrusy."

---

115 Then ioul meur neb o tus keth / ȝe belat a leuerys
lowenna gwelha ȝe feth / herodes reth tenyrghys
yn y golen fast reg eth / meur a gerense worȝys
hag ef a dalvyth ȝys wheth / y honore del wrussys

116 **H**a ȝeso y tanvonas / y allos crist rag iudgye
ha ny ad cusyll na as / lemyn y voth heb sewye
yn meth pylat scyle vas / me ny gafe rum lewte
na byth moy ef ny gaffas / prag may fe rys y dampnye

115 Many who were slaves to the Devil
said to Pilate,
"Rejoice! Cheer up!
Herod has sent greetings to you.
Into his heart has settled
much love for you,
and he will pay you still
for honouring him as you have.

116 "And to you he sent
his authority to judge Christ,
and we advise you, do not omit
now to follow his desire."
Said Pilate, "A good reason
I do not find upon my faith,"
nor did he ever again find
a reason that he should be condemned.

117 They all set upon Pilate
and made an outcry against him,
for to put Jesus Christ to death
they wished urgently.
Said Pilate, "According to the extent
of the offence it is necessary to give reward.
I do not find any more than before
a true reason to condemn him."

---

117 Orth pylat ol y setsans / ha warnoȝo a rug cry
rag Ihesus crist ȝen mernans / y a vynne porrys dry
yn meth pylat worth an myns / an pegh peuas rys yv ry
me ny gafa moy《 e》s kyns / reson gans gwyr ȝy vrvsy

118 An Yêdhewon a vynna
porres y vones ledhys.
Rêsons y a re ragtho,
mès wàr fâls yth êns grôndys. 940
Henna Pilat a wodhya,
rag henna adhesempys
bys in Cayfas dh'y jùjya
ev a wrug may fe gorrys. 944

119 Cayfas a'n dros arta
dhe Pilat o penn-jùstys,
hag ev êth dh'y gùssulya
Jesus Crist may fe ledhys. 948
An Yêdhewon a arma
traitour pur y vos kefys,
hag oll drog seul a wrussa
ha gow brâs ganso clêwys. 952

120 Yn medh Pilat, "Marth a'm beus
kemmys drog a wodhevyth,
ha te rêson vÿth adreus
er aga fynn ny gêwsyth. 956
A ny welta oll myns eus
orth dha vlâmya yn soweth
hag ow ry dhis boxow treus?
Bytegyns te ny sconyth." 960

---

118 **E**n eʒewon a vynne / porrys y vonas leʒys
resons y a rey ragthe / mes war fals yʒ ens growndys 940
henna pylat a woʒye / rag henna aʒesympys
⟨b⟩ys yn cayphas ʒy ⟦Ivggye⟧ / ef a rug may fe gorrys 944 [11r]

119 **K**ayphas an droys arte / ʒe pylat o pen-Iustys
hag ef eth ʒy gusulye / ihesus crist may fe leʒys 948
en eʒewon a arme / treytour pur y vos keffys
hag ol drok suel a wresse / ha gow bras ganso clewys 952

118 The Jews wished
urgently that he should be killed.
They gave reasons for it,
but they were based on falsehood.
That Pilate knew,
therefore immediately
he contrived that he be sent
to Caiaphas to judge him.

119 Caiaphas brought him again
to Pilate, who was the chief magistrate,
and he went to advise him
that Jesus Christ should be killed.
The Jews were crying out
that he had been found to be an utter traitor,
and entirely evil in whatever he had done,
and that great falsehood had been heard from him.

120 Pilate said, "I am astonished,
that you suffer so much evil,
and that no contrary reason
do you speak against them.
Do you not see how many
accuse you wretchedly,
and are giving you adverse blows?
Nevertheless you do not object."

---

120 In meth pylat marth am bes / kymmes drok a woȝevyth
ha te reson vyth adres / er aga fyn na gewsyth
a na wylta ol myns es / orth ȝe vlamye yn soweth
hag ov ry ȝys boxow tres / betegyns te ny sconyth

121 Yn medh Pilat, “Me ny wòn,”
dhe’n traitour esa ganso,
“in Crist cafos bÿth rêson
merwel prag y res dhodho.”
Y helwys an Yêdhewon,
“Lahys eus i’n pow adro,
may res y ladha yn scon
mytern neb a omwrello.”

122 Own bos Crist mab Duw a nev
an tebel-el a’n jeva,
rag henna scon yth êth ev
dhe wreg Pilat mayth esa,
ha’n tebel-el, hager-brëv,
in hy holon a worra
wàr hy mêster venjons crev
y to Jesus mar ladha.

123 Dh’y gour hy a dhanonas
a Grist kepar dell welsa
in kettelma dre gannas,
“Nynj yw ragos sy ladha
Crist, yw sensys meur dremas,
dhe dhen vÿth awos plêgya,
rag haneth me re welas,
y to venjons ha’th ladha.”

---

121 In meth pylat me ny won / ʒen trayteur esa ganso
yn crist cafos byth reson / merwell prag y reys ʒoʒo
y hylwys en eʒewon / lays es yn pow adro
may rys y laʒe yn scon / mygtern neb a omwrello

122 Own boys crist mab du ((a)) neff / an tebel-el an geve
rag henna scon yʒ eth ef / ʒe wrek pylat mayʒ ese
han tebel-el hager-bref / yn y holon a worre
war y mester venions cref / y to ihesus mar laʒe.

121 "I cannot," said Pilate
to the traitor who was with him,
"find any reason in Christ
why he must die."
The Jews cried out,
"There are laws in the country around,
that it is necessary quickly to put to death
any man who claims to be king."

122 The evil angel was afraid
that Christ was the son of the God of heaven,
therefore he went quickly
to Pilate's wife where she was,
and the evil angel, vile reptile,
put it into her heart
that upon her lord a mighty vengeance
would fall, were he to kill Jesus.

123 To her husband she sent word
of what she had seen about Christ
in this manner by a messenger,
"It is not for you to kill
Christ, who is considered a very good man,
for the sake of yielding to anyone,
for tonight I have seen,
that vengeance would come and kill you."

---

123 Thy gour hy a ȝanonas / a crist kepar del welse
yn ke⟦t⟧elma dre gannas / nyng ew ragos se laȝe
Cryst yv synsys meur dremas / ȝe ȝ⟪en⟫ vyth a wos plegye
rag haneth me re welas / y to v⟪en⟫ions had laȝe

124 Onen esa in pryson,
Barabas yth o gelwys.
Prysonys o dre draison
ha rag denladh kekefrÿs.
Maner o dhe'n Yêdhewon
wàr dÿdh Pask worth an Jùstys
a'n pryson govyn onen,
ha bos henna delyfrys.

125 Pilat a vynsa gwetha
bêwnans Jesus dre goyntys
hag a leverys dhedha
indelma, dell yw screfys,
"Lemmyn merowgh, a'n dus-ma
pyneyl a vÿdh delyfrys,
pò Crist—leverowgh skyla—
pò Barabas, den blâmys?"

126 An Yêdhewon a armas,
dre bur envy, me a grÿs,
"Delyrf dhyn ny Barabas,
ha henna ny oll a bÿs."
Pilat arta a gowsas,
"A Jesus pÿth a vÿdh gwrÿs?"
Y hawlsons gans colon vrâs,
"Dhe'n mernans bedhens gorrys!"

---

124 Onon esa yn preson / barabas yth o gylwys
presonys o dre dreyson / ha rag denlath kekyffrys
maner o ȝen eȝewon / war dyth pasch worth an Iustys
an preson govyn onon / ha bos henna delyffrys

125 Pylat a vynsse gwyȝe / bewnans Ihesus dre goyntys [11v]
hag a leuerys ȝeȝe / yndelma del yw scrifys
lemmyn merough ((an dus-ma / penyl)) a vyth delyffrys
po cryst leuerough scyle / po barabas den blamys

124 One that was in prison,
he was called Barabbas.
He had been imprisoned for sedition
and for murder as well.
It was a custom of the Jews
on the day of the Passover from the magistrate
to ask for someone from the prison
and for that man to be released.

125 Pilate would have liked to preserve
the life of Jesus by a stratagem
and he spoke to them
thus, as it is written,
"Now look, of these men
which one shall be released,
either Christ—give the reason—
or Barabbas, a condemned man?"

126 The Jews cried out
through sheer malice, I believe,
"Release to us Barabbas,
and that we all pray."
Pilate again spoke,
"What shall be done with Jesus?"
They called out with great heart,
"Let him be put to death!"

---

126 En eʒewon a armas / dre bur envy me a grys
dyly((rf)) ʒyn ny barabas / ha henna ((ny ol)) a bys
Pylat arte a gowsas / a Ihesus pyth a vyth gurys
y hawlsons gans golon vras / ʒen mernans beʒens gurrys

127 Pilat yn tâ a wodhya
y dhe gêwsel dre envy.
Rag henna ev a vynsa
gwetha Crist heb vylyny,
hag a leverys dhedha,
"Mar mynnowgh, me a'n chasty
oll warbarth in nycyta
hag a'n delyrf dhe wary."

128 Y helwys an Yêdhewon,
"Bedhens ev in crows gorrys!"
Yn medh Pilat, "Me ny wòn
rêson prag y fydh dampnys."
Y hawlsons gans moy colon,
"Bedhens ev in crows ledhys!"
Yn medh Pilat, "Bÿth rêson
dh'y ladha nynj eus kefys."

129 Ha Pilat dhe war breder
a leverys dhe Jesu,
"Oll an dus-ma a lever:
dhe vos cregys te yw gwyw.
Lavar gwir dhymmo unn ger,
mars ota mab den ha Duw."
Crist a gêwsys debonêr,
"Te a leverys dell yw."

---

127 Pylat yn ta a woȝye / y ȝe gusel dre envy
rag henna ef a vynse / gweȝe crist heb velyny
hag a leuerys ȝeȝe / mar mynnough me an chasty
ol warbarth 《yn》 nycyte / hag an delyrf ȝe wary

128 I helwys en eȝewon / beȝens ef yn crows gorrys
yn meth pylat me ny won / reson prag y fyt d《am》pnys
y hawlsons gans moy colon / beȝens ef yn crow《s》 leȝys
yn meth pylat byth reson / ȝe laȝe nyng es keffys

127 Pilate knew full well
that they were speaking out of malice.
Therefore he would have wished
to preserve Christ from mistreatment,
and he said to them,
"If you wish, I will chastise him
in utter ignorance of his crime,
and will let him go free."

128 The Jews cried out,
"Let him be crucified!"
Pilate said, "I do not know
any reason for him to be condemned."
They cried out with more vigour,
"Let him be crucified!"
Pilate said, "No reason at all
has been found to put him to death."

129 And Pilate after careful thought
said to Jesus,
"All these men say
that you deserve to be hanged.
Tell me truly one word,
if you are man and God."
Christ spoke courteously,
"You have said the way it is."

---

129 Ha pylat ȝe war breder / a leuerys ȝe Ihesu
ol an du((s))-ma a leuer / ȝe vos cregys te yv gyw
lauar gwyr ȝymmo vn ger / mar((s))ota mab den ha du
cryst a gewsys dyboner / te a leuerys del yw

130 Whare y a'n dystryppyas
mar noth genys dell via,
hag orth post fast a'n colmas,
unweyth na ylly plynchya;
hag ena dew a'n scorjyas
yn tebel gans dew scorja,
ha hager fest a'n dyghtyas,
corf ha penn, treys ha dêwla.

131 I'n scorjys prennyer esa
in dêwla an dhew Yêdhow,
hag yn fast kelmys dhedha
kerdyn gwethyn mesk cronow,
may fowns heblyth dhe gronkya;
hag arag gwrÿs colmennow,
gans pùb colmen mayth ella,
pàn wyskens in mes an crow.

132 Ha'n dhew-na bys pàn vowns sqwith,
wàr Crist y fowns ow cronkya,
ma na'n jeva gooth na lith
nag esa worth y grêvya,
na wàr y gorf wheg tra vÿth.
Pòr wir hèn o meur byta
ha whath moy why a glêwvyth
a dorment Crist dell wharva.

---

130 Whare y an dystryppyas / mar noyth genys del vye
hag ((orth)) post fast an colmas / vnwyth na ylly plynchye
hag ena ((dew)) an scorgyas / yn tebel gans ((dew)) scorgye
ha hager fest an dygtyas / corf ha pen treys ha dewle

131 In scorgijs prenyer ese / yn dewle an ((ʒew)) ethow [12r]
hag yn fast kelmys ʒeʒe / kerdyn gweʒyn mesk cronow
may fons hyblyth ʒe gronkye / hag arag gurys colmennow
gans pub colmen mayʒ elle / pan wyskens yn mes an crow

130 Straightway they stripped him
as naked as he had been born,
and they tied him fast to a post
so that he might not flinch at all; 1036
and then they flogged him
dreadfully with two scourges,
and very hideously they treated him,
body and head, feet and hands. 1040

131 As scourges there were sticks
in the hands of the two Jews,
and firmly tied onto them
supple cords among the thongs, 1044
so that they might be pliable to strike;
and at the front knots were made,
so that when they struck with every knot
the blood might pour out. 1048

132 And those two men until they were tired
continued to beat,
so that he had neither vein nor sinew
that was not painful for him, 1052
nor any part of his sweet body.
In very truth that was a great shame,
and still more you shall hear
of Christ's torment as it happened. 1056

---

132 Han ȝew-na bys pan vons squyth / war crist y fons ov cronkye
⸨ma nan⸩ geve goth na leyth / nag esa worth y grevye 1052
na war y gorff wek tra vyth / pur wyr ⸨hen⸩ o meur byte
ha whath moy wy a glewyth / a dormont crist del wharfe 1056

133 Intredha avell tus fol
garlont spern a veu dyghtys,
ha dre aga hùssul oll
wàr y benn a veu gorrys,
mayth o sqwardys adro oll;
a'y benn y woos o scùllys,
hag ino fest lies toll
gans an dreyn a veu tellys.

134 Gans den skentyl a wodhya,
me a glêwas leverel,
an arlont y dhe denna
wàr y benn gans kemmys nell,
ma teuth an dreyn ha crôpya
dhe'n empynyon dre an tell.
Hèn o pain a veur pyta
esa Crist ow codhevel.

135 A finna gwartha y benn
wàr y gorf bys in y droos
sqwardys oll o y grohen,
hag ev cudhys in y woos.
Meur o an pain adar ken
dhe vab Duw, meur y allos;
dell lever dhyn an Lyver
kemmys pain ny veu a'y oos.

---

133 Intreȝe avel tus fol / garlont spern a ve dyȝgthtys
ha dre aga husyll ol / war y ben a ve gorrys
mayȝ o squardijs adro ol / ay ben y oys o scolijs
hag ynno fest luhas tol / gans an dreyn a ve tellys

134 Gans den scyntyll a woȝye / me a glewas leuerell
an arlont y ȝe denne / war y ben gans kymmys nell
ma teth an dreyn ha cropye / ȝen empynnyon dre an tell
henn o payn a veur byte / esa crist ow coȝevell

133 Among them like madmen
a garland of thorns was prepared
and by the counsel of them all
was placed upon his head,
so that it was torn all around;
from his head his blood was spilt,
and in it very many holes
were pierced by the thorns.

134 From a learned man who knew,
I have heard it said,
that they pulled the garland
onto his head with such force,
that the thorns actually penetrated
the brain through the holes.
That was pain of great pity
that Christ was enduring.

135 From the very top of his head
to his foot on all his body
all his skin was torn
and he was covered in his blood.
Great was the pain beyond any other
to the Son of God, great his power;
as the Scripture tells us,
so much pain there never was before.

---

135 **A** vyne gwarʒe y ben / war y gorff bys yn y droys
squardijs oll o y grohen / hag ef cuʒys yn y woys
meur o an payn «a»dar ken / ʒe vab du meur y alloys
del leuer ʒyn an levar / kymmys payn ny ve ay oys

136 Y a wyscas Crist gans qweth,
a'n pùrpur rych o dyghtys;
rag y dhry dhe'n dor gans meth
in ges y a leverys,
"Meur a onour te a'fÿdh,
te yw mytern cùrunys,"
hag in y leuv dhyhow inwedh
gwelen wynn a veu gorrys.

137 Hag yth êns dhe benn dôwlin
hag y kêwsens dh'y scornya,
hag a gamma aga min,
pùbonen rag y êsya,
"Lowena dhis, te yw dhyn
mytern; res yw dha wordhya."
Hèn o dhodho meur a bain,
mayth esens worth y ranna.

138 Onen gans an keth welen,
i'n leuv Crist a veu gorrys,
a'n gwyskys lash wàr an penn,
bomm pòr gewar desedhys;
ha boxow lies heb ken,
ha tomasow kekefrÿs
dhe Grist adro dh'y dhywen
gans nerth brâs a veu settys.

---

136 **I** a wyskys crist gans queth / an purpur rych o dy((ʒgt))ys
rag y thry ʒen dor gans meth / yn ges y a leuerys
meur a onour te a fyth / te yw mygtern cvrvnys
hag yn y leff ʒyghow ynweth / gwelen wyn a ve gorrys

137 **H**ag yth ens ʒe ben dowlyn • hag y kewsens ʒe scornye [12v]
hag a gamma aga meyn / pubonon rag y eysye
lowene ʒys te yw ʒeyn / mygtern rys yw ʒe worʒye
hen o ʒoʒo meur a bayn / mayʒ e((s))ens worth y ranne

136 They clothed Christ in a garment
which had been made of rich purple;
in order to bring him down with shame
in mockery they said,
"Much honour you will have,
you are a crowned king,"
and in his right hand also
a white staff was put.

137 And they went on bended knee
and spoke to mock him,
and they twisted their mouths,
everyone to make fun of him,
"Hail to you, you are our king;
we needs must worship you."
That was to him much pain,
which they were dealing out to him.

138 One with the same staff
which had been put in Christ's hand,
struck him a lash upon the head,
a blow very accurately aimed;
and many blows without reason
and buffets likewise
on Christ about his jaws
were landed with great force.

---

138 **O**non gans an keth welen / yn leyff crist a ve gorrys
an gwyskys lasch war an pen / bum pur gewar deseȝys
ha buxow leas hep ken / ha tummasow kekyffrys
ȝe gryst adro ȝe ȝewen / gans nerth bras a ve syttys

139 Colon den a yll crackya,
a vynha prest predery
an painys brâs a'n jeva
ha despît heb y dylly,
hag oll rag dha gerensa
Jesus Crist a's godhevy.
Lemmyn gorqwyth y gara
ha gwait dynatur na vy.

140 Pilat êth in mes a'y hel
in unn lowarth a'n jevo.
Ogas o, nynj esa pell
hag a worras Crist ganso
ena worto rag kêwsel;
qweth esa adro dhodho;
prest an Yêdhewon debel
dhe Jesus esens adro.

141 Ena Pilat a gêwsys
indelma dhe'n Yêdhewon,
"Me ny wòn bones kefys
i'n den-ma bÿth achêson,
may res y vones ledhys.
Godhvedhowgh kettep onen
dell yw an den-ma dyghtys;
merowgh in agas colon."

---

139 Colon den a yll crakye / a vynha prest predery
an paynys bras an geve / han dyspyth heb y dylly
hag ol rag ʒe gerense / ihesus crist as goʒevy
lymmyn gorqvyth y gare / ha gweyth denatur na vy

140 Pylat eth yn mes ay hell / yn vn lowarth an gevo
ogas o nyng esa pell / hag a worras crist ganso
ena worto rag kewsell / queth esa adro ʒoʒo
prest an eʒewon debel / ʒe Ihesus esens adro

139 A man's heart could crack,
who would ever consider
the great pains he endured,
and the contempt that he did not deserve,
and all for your sake
Jesus Christ suffered it.
Now be sure to love him
and be careful not to be ungrateful.

140 Pilate went out from his hall
into a garden he possessed.
It was near, it was not far
and he brought Christ with him
thither to talk.
There was a garment about him;
always the evil Jews
were around Jesus.

141 Then Pilate spoke
thus to the Jews,
"I do not know that there has been found
in this man any cause
that he should be killed.
Be aware every one of you
how this man is treated;
look into your hearts."

---

141 Ena pylat a gewsys / yndelma ȝen eȝewon
me ny won bonas kyfys / yn den-ma byth acheson
may rys y vonas leȝys / gothveȝough ketop onon
del yw an den-ma dyȝgtys / myrough yn agys colon

142 Pàn y'n cafsons intredha,
oll warbarth y a elwys,
"Te, Pilat, ladh e, ladh e!
Mernans an grows desempys!"
Pilat a gêwsys arta,
"Dredhowgh why bedhens ledhys,
rag ino me ny gafa'
skyla vas may fo dampnys."

143 An debel-dus a gêwsys,
"Dhyn ny sur yma laha,
may res y vones ledhys,
rag Mab Duw ev a omwra."
Own a gachyas an jùstys,
pàn glêwas cows indella.
Rag henna adhesempys
y trailyas dh'y esedhva.

144 Orth Crist ev a wovynnys,
"Te dhen, able ota jy?"
Dh'y gows Crist ny worthebys.
Yn medh Pilat iredy,
"Gortheby te ny vynsys.
A ny wodhes ow mêstry
bos dhymmo may fes ledhys
pò delyfrys dhe wary?"

---

142 Pan yn caffsons yntreʒe / ol warbarth y a ylwys
te pylat laʒ e laʒ e / mernans an grows desympys
Pylat a gewsys arte / dreʒough why beʒens leʒys
Rag ynno me ny gaffe / scyle vas may fo dampnys

143 An debel-dus a gewsys / ʒynn ny sur yma laha [13r]
may rys y vonas leʒys / rag mab du eff a omwra
own a gachyas an Iustys / pan glewas cows yndella
rag henna aʒesympys / y trylyas thy asethva

142 When they had him among them,
they all cried together,
"You, Pilate, kill him, kill him!
Death straightway by crucifixion!"
Pilate spoke again,
"Let him be killed by you,
for in him I do not find
a good reason to condemn him."

143 The evil men spoke,
"Indeed we have a law,
that he must be killed,
for he claims to be the Son of God."
Fear seized the magistrate,
when he heard that spoken.
Therefore without delay
he returned to his bench.

144 From Christ he asked,
"You man, whence do you come?"
Christ did not answer his speech.
Pilate said indeed,
"You would not answer.
Do you not know that I possess the authority
to have you put to death
or released free to go?"

---

144 Orth crist ef a wovynnys / te ʒen able ota gy
ʒy gows crist ny worʒebys / yn meth pylat yredy
gorʒeby te ny vynsys / a ny woʒas ow mestry
bos ʒymmo may fes leʒys / bo delyffrys ʒe wary

145 Yn medh Jesus i'n eur-na,
"Mêstry vÿth te ny via
warnaf vy drog vÿth na dâ,
ken onen dhis na'n rolla,
bÿth moy ès Yêdhow yn tâ
a behas orth ow thraita."
Pilat, pàn glêwas henna,
a whelas y dhelyfra.

146 Ha'n Yêdhewon oll adro
dhe Bilat a levery,
"Kerensa Cesar ytho
ny'th fe lemen bylyny,
mar ny wreth defry dodho
aberveth in crows cregy,
rag mytern a omwrello
dhe Cesar yw contrary."

147 Ena Pilat pàn glêwas
an lavarow-na gansa,
Jesus ev a dhyswedhas
pòr ewn i'n cres intredha.
"Awotta," ev a gowsas,
"agas mytern ple ma va."
Oll warbarth y a'n nahas
hag a yrhys y ladha.

---

145 In meth Ihesus yn vr-na / mestry vyth te ny vea
war《n》aff ve drok vyth na da / ken onan ȝys nan rolla
byth moy ys eȝow yn ta / a beghas orth ov ȝrayta
pylat pan glewas henna / a whelas y ȝelyffra

146 Han eȝewon oll adro / ȝe belat a leuery
kerense sesar ytho / ny⦅ȝ fe⦆ lemman belyny
mar ny wreth dyffry doȝo / aberveth yn crows cregy
rag mygtern a omwrello / ȝe sesar yw contrary

145 Then Jesus said,
"You would not have any authority
over me evil or good,
if another had not given it to you,
any more than a Jew indeed
who sinned when he betrayed me."
When Pilate heard that,
he sought to release him.

146 And the Jews all around
said were saying to Pilate,
"You would not have Caesar's love,
but only reproach,
if indeed you do not have him
hanged on a cross,
for whoever makes himself a king
is an enemy of Caesar's."

147 Then Pilate, when he heard
these words from them,
showed Jesus
in the middle among them,
"Behold," he said,
"your king where he is."
All together they rejected him
and commanded that he be killed.

---

147 **E**na pylat pan glewas / an lauarow-na ganse
Ihesus ef a ȝysweȝas / pur evn yn cres yntreȝe
awatta ef a gowsas / agys mygtern ple me ve
ol warbarth I an naghas / hag a yrghys y laȝe

148 Yn medh Pilat, “Why a vynn
dres pùb tra me dh’y ladha
agas mytern.” “Meth yw dhyn.
Na vedhens clêwys nefra!”
Yn medhans y, “Ny’n gordhyn
na ny goodh dhyn y wordhya,
na ken mytern ny vynnyn
ès Cesar cafos nefra.”

149 Y dhewla Pilat a wolhas
hag a leverys dhedha,
“Glân ov a woos an dremas
rag a’y woos venjons a dheu.”
Oll warbarth y a armas,
“Mar teu venjons ha codha
wàr agan flehes yn frâs
ha warnan, bedhens nefra!”

150 Cammen Pilat pàn welas
na ylly Crist delyfra,
ma na’n jeffa ev sor brâs
dhyworth oll an gowetha,
rag henna ev a’n jùjyas,
Jesus dhedha dh’y ladha.
Dhe ves y a dhelyfras
Barabas qwît mayth ella.

---

148 In meth pylat why a vyn / drys pub tra me ȝy laȝe
agys mygtern meth yw ȝyn / na veȝens clewys neffre
yn meȝens y nyn gorȝyn / na ny goth thyn y worȝye
Na Ken mygtern ny venyn / ys Cesar caffos neffre

149 Y thewleff pylat a wolhas / hag a leuerys ȝeȝe [13v]
glan off a wos an dremas / rag ay woys venions a ȝe
ol warbarth y a armas / mar te v《en》ions ha cothe
war agan flehys yn fras / ha warnan beȝans neffre

148 Pilate said, "You wish
above all things that I should kill him—
your king." "It is a disgrace to us.
Let it never be heard!"
they said, "We will not revere him
nor should we revere him,
nor will we have a king
other than Caesar ever."

149 Pilate washed his hands
and said to them,
"I am innocent of the blood of the good man,
for from his blood vengeance will come."
All together they cried,
"If vengeance happens to fall
upon our children greatly
and upon us, let it be so forever!"

150 When Pilate saw
that he could not set Christ free,
without incurring the wrath
from all his companions,
therefore he ruled,
Jesus to be given to them to be killed.
They released
Barabbas that he might go free.

---

150 Camen pylat pan welas / na ylly crist delyffre
ma nan geffo ef sor bras / ȝeworth oll an goweȝe
rag henna ef ((an)) Iuggyas / Ihesus ȝeȝe ȝy laȝe
the ves y a thelyffras / barabas quyth mayȝ elle

151 Pàn o Jesus Crist dampnys
aberth in crows may farwa—
hackra mernans bÿth ordnys
dhe greatur ny via—
an grows whath nynj o parys,
ha'n Yêdhewon ny wodhya
an prennyer py fêns kefys
dhe wuthyl crows anedha.

152 Unn Yêdhow a brederys
hag a leverys dhedha,
bones prenn i'n dowr tôwlys
a'y oos i'n howl na via.
Rag an grows yth o ordnys—
ha'n Yêdhewon ny wodhya—
hag a'n aval devedhys
dredhy Adam may pehas.

153 An prynnyer a veu kerhys,
an grows scon dyghtys may fe,
hag inhy bones gorrys
ragon ny Crist, a vynna,
ha wàr an prenn frût degys
may fe sur dh'agan sawya,
may teuth frût may feun kellys,
rag Adam dh'y attamya.

---

151 **P**an o Ihesus cryst dampnys / aberth yn crows may farwe
haccra mernans vyth ordnys / ʒe creatur ny vye
en grows whath nyni o parys / ⸨h⸩an eʒewon ny woʒye
an prennyer py fens kefys / ʒe wuʒyll crous aneʒe

152 **V**n ethow a brederys / hag a leuerys theʒe
bonas pren yn dowr tewlys / a《y》 vs yn houl na vye
rag an grous yʒ o ordnys / han ⸨e⸩thewon ny woʒye
hag an avell deveʒys / dreʒy adam may pegh⸨es⸩

151 When Jesus Christ had been condemned
to die upon the cross,
—there had not been a nastier death
ever prescribed for any creature—
the cross was not yet ready,
and the Jews did not know
where the planks would be found
to make a cross of them.

152 One Jew considered
and told them,
that there was a tree cast into the water,
which had never been in the sun.
It had been predetermined for the cross—
and the Jews did not know—
and it derived from the apple
through which Adam sinned.

153 The timbers were fetched,
that the cross might soon be prepared
and upon it Christ put
for us, who was willing,
and that there might be borne a fruit
indeed to save us,
whence a fruit came by which we were lost,
for Adam took the first bite of it.

---

153 **E**n prynner a ve kerhys / en grows scon dyȝgtys may fe
hag ynny bonas gorys / ragon ny cryst a vynne
ha war an pren frut degys / may fe sur ȝagan sawye
may teth frut may fen kellys • rag adam ȝe attamye

154 Whath kentrow dhedha nynj o
Jesus i'n grows rag sensy.
Y hawlsons oll adro
mar caffens gov iredy.
Onen a welsons eno
hag yth êthons dh'y besy,
hag y lavarsons dhodho,
"Te, gwra teyr henter dhyn ny."

155 Yn medh an gov, "Me ny wrav
pòr wir kentrow dhywgh why vÿth."
Yn medhans, "Mar omwreth clâv,
gordhyweth te a'n prenvyth,
awos guthyl whel mar scav
in ethom dhyn mar fyllyth."
Y whorthebys, "Ny vanaf
aga guthyl wàr ow fÿdh."

156 Gans meur a jùsters i'n wlas
ev a veu vil rebukys.
Cavanskes ev a whelas
rag own y vones ledhys.
Yn medh an gov, "Cleves brâs
eus i'm dêwla devedhys.
Toul vÿth ny allaf yn fas
inha sensy dhe wonys."

---

154 Whath kentrow ȝeȝe nyng o / Ihesus yn crows rag synsy
y h((aw))lsons ol adro / mar caffons goff yredy
onan a welsons eno / hag yȝ eȝons ȝy besy
Hag y lauarsons thoȝo / te gura ((tyr)) kenter ȝyn ny

155 In meth an goyff me ny wraff / pur wyr kentrow ȝe wy vyth [14r]
yn meȝens mar omwreyth claff / gorȝewyth te an prenvyth
awos guthyll wheyll mar scaff / yn ethom ȝyn mar fyllyth
y worȝebys ny vannaff / aga guȝyll war ow fyth

154 Still they had no nails
to hold Jesus upon the cross.
They cried all around
to see if they could find a smith indeed.
One they saw there
and they went to ask him,
and they said to him,
"You, make three nails for us."

155 The smith said, "I will not make
any nails for you right truly."
They said, "If you pretend to be ill,
in the end you will pay for it,
if you fail us in our need
concerning doing such a light job."
He answered, "I will not
make them upon my faith."

156 He was vilely rebuked
by many magistrates in the land.
He tried to make an evasion
for fear of being killed.
The smith said, "A great sickness
has come upon my hands.
I can hardly hold any tool
in them in order to work."

---

156 **G**ans meur a Iucters yn wlas / ef a ve veyll rebukys
kavanskys ef a whelas / rag own y vonas leȝys
yn meth an goff clevas bras / es om dewleff deveȝys
towyll vyth ny allaff yn fas / ynno sensy ȝe wonys

157 Res o dhodho dysqwedhes
dhe bur traitours y dhewla.
Warnedha gwelsons cleves,
bytegyns bÿth nynj esa.
Yn medh y wreg, "Meur varth brâs
yw henna dhymm re'm lewta.
Hedhyw pàn êthys in mes,
cleves vÿth ny'th kemersa."

158 Yn medh gwreg an gov dhedha,
"Kentrow dhywgh whywhy ny fyll,
awos bos clâv y dhewla.
Tùch vÿth gonys ev ny yll,
dell wòn; in unn fystena
me a's gwra, ny strechyaf pell,
abàn nag eus a wothfa,
dhywgh parys a's gwrella gwell."

159 An debel-wreg gasadow
gans meur a doth êth i'n chy
wàr hast dhe wuthyl kentrow,
may fêns crev ha truesy.
Dewdros Jesus caradow
ha'y dhewla y a delly,
rag an spîkys o garow,
pàn vowns gweskys dh'y sensy.

---

157 Reys o ȝoȝo dysqueȝas / ȝe pur treytours a ȝewle
warneȝe gwelsons clevas / bytegyns byth nyng ese
yn meth y wrek meur varth bras / yv henna ȝym rum lewte
heȝow pan eȝys yn mes / cleves vyth nyth kemerse

158 In meth gurek an goff ȝeȝe / kentrow ȝe wywhy ny fyll
awos bos claff y ȝewle / toche vyth gonys ef na yll
del won yn vn fystene / me a((s))gura ny strechyaff pell
aban nag es a wothfe / ȝeugh parys as gurelle gwell

157 He was compelled to show
his two hands the utter traitors.
Upon them they saw leprosy,
nonetheless there was none at all.
His wife said, "That is a great astonishment
to me upon my word.
Today when you went out,
no sickness had seized you."

158 The smith's wife said to them,
"You shall not lack for nails,
because there a disease on his hands.
He cannot do any work at all,
as I can see; I will hurry
and make them, I shall not linger long,
since there is no one who could,
who would get them ready for you better."

159 The hateful wicked wife
entered the house hurriedly
with great speed to make nails,
so that they would be strong and painful.
They would pierce the two feet of beloved Jesus
and his two hands,
for the spikes were rough to hold him,
when they were driven in.

---

159 **E**n debell-wrek casadow / gans meur a doth eth yn chy
war hast ȝe weȝyll kentrow / may fens creff ha trewesy
((dew))droys Ihesus caradow / hay ((ȝew))leyff y a delly
rag an spykys o garow / pan vons gwyskys ȝy sensy

160 Pàn o an kentrow lemmys,
hy a's dug dhe'n Yêdhewon.
Crows Jesus naunj o parys;
y êth dh'y ladha yn scon.
Bresel crev a veu sordys,
an grows pyw ella dh'y dhon.
Dre veur strif y feu jùjys
y's degy Crist y honen.

161 An gweth deg a veu diskys
ha'n pùrpur rych a ûsya,
ha'y bows y honen gorrys
adro dhodho hy a veu.
Gans y vamm y fia gwrÿs,
hag ev gensy ow tena.
Kepar Jesus dell devys,
indella an bows a wre.

162 Oll mones y a vynna
bys i'n mownt a Galvary.
A-west dhe'n dre yth esa,
meneth uhel iredy.
An grows y a wrug gorra
wàr scooth Jesus dh'y don dhy,
dhe Jesus Crist may teffa
oll an grêf ha'n bylyny.

---

160 Pan o an kentrow lemmys / hy as duk ʒen eʒewon
crows Ihesus navn⟦g ⟧o parys / y eth ʒy laʒe yn scon
bresell creff a ve sordijs / en grows pu elle ʒy don
Dre veur stryff y fe Iuggijs / ys degy crist y honon

161 An queth tek a ve dyskys / han purpur rych a vsye [14v]
hay bows y honon gurrys / adro ʒoʒo hy a ve
gans y vam y fye gurys / hag ef gensy ow tene
kepar Ihesus del devys / yndella an bows a wre

160 When the nails had been sharpened,
she carried them to the Jews.
Now the cross of Jesus was ready;
they went to kill him quickly.
A strong dispute arose
about the cross, who should carry it.
After much dispute it was decided
that Christ himself would bear it.

161 The fair garment was removed
and the rich purple he was wearing,
and his own coat was put
about him.
It had been made by his mother,
when he was being suckled by her.
As Jesus grew,
so did the coat.

162 They all wanted to go
to the hill of Calvary.
It was to the west of the town,
a high mountain indeed.
They put the cross
upon the shoulder of Jesus to carry it thither,
so that Jesus Christ might endure
all the pain and infamy.

---

162 Oll monas y a vynne / bys yn mont a galvary
a-vest ʒen dre yʒ ese / meneth vghell yredy
an grows I a rug gorre / war scoth Ihesus ʒy don ʒy
ʒe Ihesus crist may teffe / ol an greff han belyny

163 Dew lader dreus o dampnys
a veu dyghtys gans Jesu,
ganso ev may fêns cregys,
onen dhodho a bùb tu.
Jesus a veu hùmbronkys
ha wàr y lergh meur a lu
dre volder tebel-jùstys
rag y jacya, kynth o Duw.

164 Y vamm whegoll a welas
dell esons worth y dhyghtya.
Pyteth meur a's kemeras,
hy holon namna grackya.
Der unn scochfordh y ponyas
cafos hy mab, mar calla.
Y wortos hy a vynnas,
gweles Jesus, a gara.

165 Pàn welas hy mab dyghtys
gans an Yêdhewon mar vil,
ha'y vos gans spern cùrunys
ha pùb dhodho ow cul gil,
hag in y gorf bos gorrys
goliow pals, lies mil,
heb cows ger y clamderys,
y codhas wàr bol y hil.

---

163 Dew lader drevs o dampnys / a ve dyȝgtys gans Ihesu
ganso ef may fens cregys / onon ȝoȝo a bub tu
Ihesus a ve hombronkys / ha war y lyrgh meur a lu
dre volder tebel-Iustys / rag y chasye kynȝ o du

164 I vam whegol a welas / del esons worth y ȝygtye
pyteth meur a⸨s⸩kemeras / y holon namna grakye
dre vn scochforth y ponyas / cafos y mab mar calle
I wortos hy a vynnas / guelas Ihesus a gare

163 Two wicked robbers who had been condemned
were dealt with alongside Jesus,
so that they might be hanged,
one on either side of him. 1300
Jesus was led
and after him a great crowd,
through the temerity of an evil magistrate,
to persecute him, though he was God. 1304

164 His most beloved mother saw
how they were treating him.
She was overwhelmed with compassion,
her heart nearly broke. 1308
She ran down a short-cut
to find her son, if she could;
she wished to wait for him,
to see Jesus whom she loved. 1312

165 When she saw her son treated
so vilely by the Jews,
and that he was crowned with thorns
and that everyone was tricking him, 1316
and that in his body had been made
numerous wounds, many thousands,
without speaking a word she fainted,
she fell backwards. 1320

---

165 **P**an welas y mab dygtys / gans an eȝewon mar veyll
hay vos gans spern curunys / ha peb ȝoȝo ow cull geyll 1316
hag yn y gorf bos gorrys / goleow pals leas myll
heb cows ger y clamderys / y cothas war bol y hyll 1320

166 Ena pàn sevys in bàn,
hy a gêwsys dell ylly:
"Nynj yw ow fainys bian
eus lemmyn worth ow sensy.
Ow holon intre mil dharn
marth yw genef na sqward hy,
pàn welaf ow Mab mar wann
ow ton kemmys vylyny."

167 Gensy prest dyw venyn len
esa worth y homfortya,
Maria Magdalenen
ha Maria Cleofa.
Y a fystena yn fen
arta dh'y dierbyna;
rag kerensa (nynj o ken)
y weles y a vynna.

168 Benenes prest a holyas
Jesu Crist in unn arma.
Jesus orta a veras
hag a leverys dhedha,
"Flehes meur ha benenes
a Jerùsalem i'n dre,
a wor bos ow fainys brâs,
ragof na whelowgh ola.

---

166 Ena pan sevys yn ban / hy a gewsys del ylly
nyng ew ow faynys beghan / vs lemyn ((worth)) ow sensy
ow holon yntre myll darn / marth yw gene na squard hy
pan welaff ow mab mar wan / ow town kemys velyny

167 Gensy prest ((dyw)) venyn len / esa worth y homfortye [15r]
Marya magdalenen / ha marya cleophe
y a fystena yn fen / arte ȝy dyerbyne
rag kerensa nyni o ken / y welas y a vynne

166 Then, when she stood up,
she spoke as best she could:
"Not small are my pains,
that are now seizing me.
I am amazed that my heart
does not split into a thousand pieces,
when I see my son so weak,
bearing such ill-treatment."

167 Constantly two loyal women,
were comforting her,
Mary Magdalene
and Mary wife of Cleophas.
They hurried eagerly
to meet him again;
for love (it was nothing else)
they wished to see him.

168 Women continually followed
Jesus Christ crying out.
Jesus looked at them
and said to them,
"You many children and women
from Jerusalem in the town,
who know my pains are great,
do not seek to weep for me.

---

168 **B**enenas prest a holyas / Ihesu crist yn vn garme
Ihesus worto a veras / hag a leuerys ȝeȝe
Flehys meur ha benenas / a ierusalem yn dre
a wor bos ov feynys bras / ragoff na wheleugh ole

169 “Olowgh rag agas flehes
ha ragowgh agas honen.
An dedhyow a vÿdh gwelys
hag a dheu sur intredhon,
may fÿdh torrow benegys
bythqweth na allas omdhon,
ha benenes kekefrÿs
na veu dhedha denys bronn.

170 “I’n eur-na dhe’n menydhyow
why a ergh warnowgh codha;
in kettella an nansow
why a bÿs ra’gas cudha.
Dell lavaraf wàr anow,
wàr an prenn glas mara teu,
i’n prenn sëgh ha casadow
sur i’n eur-na fatel ve?”

171 Y vamm wheg, Maria Wynn,
pùb eur fystena a wre,
may halla dos wàr y bynn,
hy Mab kemmys a gara.
Wàr gwander wàr benn dôwlin
hy a’n gwelas ow codha,
ha’n wlos a’s kemeras mar dynn,
may clamderas hy arta.

---

169 Olough rag agys fleghys / ha ragough agys honon
en deʒyow a vyth guelys / hag a ʒe sur yntreʒon
may fyth torrow benegys / bythqueth na allas ⸨om⸩ʒon
han benenas kekyffrys / na ve ʒeʒe denys bron

170 In er-na ʒen menyʒyow / why a ergh warnough coʒe
yn ketella an nanssow / wy a bys ragas cuthe
del lavare war anow / war an pren glays mara te
yn pren seygh ha casadow / sur yn er-na fatel ve

169 "Weep for your children
and for yourselves.
The day will be seen
and is coming surely among us,
when blessed will be wombs
that could never conceive,
and women also
whose breast were never sucked.

170 "In that hour you will bid
the mountains to fall upon you;
in like manner the valleys
you will pray to cover you.
As I say openly,
if it comes upon the green tree,
how would it be in that our
on the hateful dried-up tree?"

171 His sweet mother, Blessed Mary,
was always hastening,
that she might meet him,
her Son whom she loved so much.
For weakness upon his knees
she saw him falling,
and the pain overcame her so sharply,
that she fainted again.

---

171 I vam whek marya wyn / pub vr fystene a wre
may halle doys war y byn / y mab kemmys a gare
Rag gwander war ben dowlyn / hy an guelas ow coȝe
han wlos a⸨s⸩kemeras mar dyn / may clamderas hy arte

172 Ena hy a veu sevys
in bàn intra benenes.
"Arlùth," hy a leverys,
"ow holon yma genes
kepar ha te hedhyw gwrÿs
in anken worth dha weles."
Bythqweth den ny wodhevys
pain ella dh'y golon nes.

173 An golyas ha fowt debry
a wodhevys Jesus ker
ha'n strocosow truesy
wàr y gorf dres pùb maner,
goos a'y benn ha'y esely
a dhroppya wàr y dhywverr,
rag dodho ev na ylly
don an grows rag gwander.

174 Unn den a's dierbynnas,
Simon o a'y ewn hanow.
Y leverys dhodho gwas,
"Te a dheg an grows heb wow."
A'y dhon Simon a sconyas—
ev a'n jeva strocosow—
na moy sconya ny vynnas,
rag own cafos y ancow.

---

172 Ena hy a ve seuys / yn ban yntre benenas
arluth hy a leuerys / ow holon yma genas
kepar ha te hyȝew gurys • yn anken worth ȝe welas
bytqueth den ny woȝevys / payn ella ȝy golon nes

173 En golyas ha fowt dybbry / a woȝevys Ihesus ker
han strokosow trewesy / war y gorff drys pub maner
goys ay ben hay ysely / a ȝroppye war y ȝewver
rag doȝo ef na ylly / don an grows rag gwander

172 Then she was raised
up among some women.
"Lord," she said,
"my heart is with you,
made even like you today
seeing you in misery."
Never did a man suffer
pain that might go closer to his heart.

173 The staying awake and the lack of food
which beloved Jesus suffered
and the painful blows
upon his body in every way,
the blood of his head and his limbs
dropped upon his legs,
that because of it he could not
carry the cross for weakness.

174 A man met them,
his own name was Simon.
A fellow said to him,
"You will carry the cross without a lie."
Simon refused to carry it—
he received blows—
no more was he ready to refuse,
for fear of being killed.

---

174 **V**n den a⦅s ⦆dyerbynnas / Symmon o ay own hanow [15v]
y leuerys ȝoȝo guas / te a ȝek an grows heb wow
⟪a⟫y don symon a sconyas / ef an geve strocosow
na moy sconye ny vynnas / rag own cafos y ancow

175 Ev a dhug an grows gansa.
Pòr wir hèn o a'y anvodh.
Ny wrêns y na hen skyla
lemen sewya aga bodh.
Pùb eur, te dhen, gwra lewta,
be va den yonk bo den coth.
Orthyf mar mynnyth cola,
nefra gans an fâls na soodh.

176 Y êth in unn fystena
dhe'n tyller kyns o ordnys.
Pàn dhothyens dhy, intredha
pows Jesus a veu diskys.
Y dhisky meur a'n grêvya;
worto fast naunj o glenys.
Whath bythqweth clâv ny via
villa ès dell o diskys.

177 Unn venyn dhâ a welas
dell o Jesus dystryppys.
Pyteth meur a's kemeras,
rag y vos mar vil dyghtys.
Unn gweth deg hy a drailyas
adro dhodho desympys,
ha wàr nans hy a'n qwethas,
rag gwetha na ve storvys.

---

175 Ef a thuk an grous ganse / pur wyr henn o ay anvoth
ny wrens y na hen scyle / lymyn sywye aga both
pub er te ȝen gura lewte / be va den yonk bo den coth
orȝaff mar mynnyth cole / neffre gans an fals na soth

176 I eth yn vn fystene / ȝen tyller ((kyns)) o ordnys
pan doȝyans ȝy yntreȝe / pows Ihesus a ve dyskys
y dysky meur an grevye / worto fast navng o glenys
whath bytqueth claff ny vee / vylle ys dell o dyskys

175 He carried the cross with them.
In truth that was against his will.
They gave no other reason
than to follow their wish. 1396
Always, you man, be loyal,
whether he be a young man or old.
If you will harken to me,
never take service with the false. 1400

176 They went hastening
to the place that had been pre-arranged.
When they had arrived there,
between them Jesus' coat was taken off him. 1404
To take it off hurt him;
it was by now stuck fast to him.
Never yet had a leper been
stripped more vilely than he. 1408

177 A good woman saw
that Jesus had been stripped.
Great pity overcame her,
that he was treated so cruelly. 1412
She wound around him
a fair cloth immediately,
and downwards she clad him,
to prevent his dying with cold. 1416

---

177 Vn venyn da a welas / dell o Ihesus dystryppijs
pytet meur a⸨s ⸩kemeras / rag y vos mar veyll dygtys 1412
vn queth tek hy a drylyas / adro ȝoȝo desympys
ha war nans hy an quuthas / rag gwyȝe na ve storuys 1416

178 Hës Crist y a gemeras
a'n eyl leuv bys in hy ben.
Worth an les y a dollas,
dew doll in an grows heb ken,
mayth ella an kentrow brâs
dre y dhewla bys i'n prenn;
rag y dreys y a vynnas
telly, dh'y worra yn ten.

179 Gansa Crist a veu têwlys
wàr an grows dhe wrowedha,
ha'y eyl leuv a veu tackys
orth an grows fast mayth esa,
ha'y eyl troos a veu gorrys
poran wàr benn y gela;
worth an grows y fowns lathys
gans kenter gweskys dredha.

180 Dhe'n leuv aral pàn dhothyens
worth an grows rag hy fastya,
y fylly moy ès tros'hës,
dhe'n toll gwrës hy na hedha.
An Yêdhewon bytegyns
gul toll aral ny vynna,
lemen an toll re wrussens
y a vynna dhe servya.

---

178 **H**eys crist y a gemeras / an eyll lef bys yn y ben
worth an les y a dollas / ⦅dew⦆ doll yn 《an》 grows heb ken
mayȝ ello an kentrow bras / dre y ȝewleff bys yn p《r》en
rag y dreys y a vynnas / telly ȝy worre ⦅yn ⦆ten

179 **G**anse crist a ve tewlys / war an grows ȝe wroweȝe
hay yll leff a ve tackys / ord en grows fast mayȝ ese
hay yll troys a ve gorrys / poran war ben e gele
worth an grows y fons laȝijs / gans kenter guyskys dreȝe

178 They measured the breadth of Christ
from one hand to the other.
According to the width they bored
two holes in the cross without another,
so that the great nails
might go through his hands into the wood;
for his feet they wished
to make a hole, to set him outstretched.

179 By them Christ was thrown down
upon the cross to lie,
and his one hand was nailed
firmly to the cross where it was,
and one of his feet was placed
exactly over the other;
upon the cross they were fastened
with a nail struck through them.

180 When they had come to the other hand
to fasten it to the cross,
more than a foot was lacking,
so that it would not reach to the hole they had made.
The Jews notwithstanding
were unwilling to make another hole,
but the hole which they had made,
they wished for it to do service.

---

180 Then levff arall pan doȝyans / worth an grovs rag y faste [16r]
y fylly moy ys tresheys / ȝen tol gurys hy na heȝe
En eȝewon betegyns / gul tol arall ny vynne
lemyn an tol re wrussens / y a vyne ȝe seruye

181 Gansa worth leuv Crist lovan
fast yn scon a veu kelmys,
hag intra an Yêdhewon
an grows fast a veu sensys.
Gans re a gemmys colon
an lovan a veu tennys,
y jùntys ketep onen
oll warbarth mayth êns sqwardys.

182 Pàn dheuth leuv Crist wàr an toll,
dre an nerth may tensons hy,
unn Yêdhow avell pÿth fol
a weskys kenter inhy.
Lemmyn me a'gas pÿs oll
a bainys Crist predery,
ha na vo gesys dhe goll
an lahys a wrug dhyn ny.

183 Screfys yw yn surredy
ha ken me ny'n lavarsen,
corf Jesus ha'y esely
y dhe denna mar vylen,
neb a vynna a ylly
nyvera oll y eskern,
ha'y skennys, kig ha gwythy,
pàn esa ev i'n growsprenn.

---

181 **G**anse worth levff crist loven / fast yn scon a ve kelmys
Hag yntre an eȝewon / an grovs fast a ve sensys
gans re a gymmys colon / en loven a ve tennys
y iunctys ketop onon / oll warbarth mayȝ ens squardys

182 **P**an deth levff crist war en toll / dre an nerth may tensons hy
vn ethow avell pyth foll / a wyskys kenter ynhy
lemmyn me agys pys oll / a baynys crist predery
ha na vo gesys ȝe goll / an lahys a rug ȝyn ny

181 A rope on Christ's hand
was tied fast by them,
and among the Jews
the cross was held firm. 1444
By some the rope was pulled
with so much vigour,
that all his joints, every one,
all together were torn. 1448

182 When Christ's hand came to the hole
by the force with which they pulled it,
a Jew like a mad thing
struck a nail into it. 1452
Now I would pray you all
to consider Christ's pains,
and that the laws he made for us
may not go to waste. 1456

183 It is written in very truth
and otherwise I should not say it,
that they pulled so viciously
Jesus' body and limb, 1460
that whoever wished could
number all his bones,
his sinews, flesh and veins,
when he was on the cross. 1464

---

183 **S**crifys yw yn suredy / ha ken me nyn lauarsen
corff Ihesus hay asely / y ȝe denna mar velen 1460
neb a vynna a ylly / neuera oll y yscren
hay skennys kyc ha gwyȝy / pan esa yn crow((s))pren 1464

184 Ha'n grows a veu drehevys
ha Jesus fast'hës inhy,
ha'n penn goles delyfrys
i'n toll o tellys rygthy.
Ena hy a veu gesys
dhe godha mar ankensy
dhe Grist, may feu crehyllys,
oll y gorf ha'y esely.

185 Ha Crist indelma painys
aberth i'n grows pàn esa,
i'n vaner-ma y pesys
rag an keth re re'n crowssa,
"Ow Thas wheg, bedhens gevys
dhe'n re-ma gà nycyta,
rag ny wodhons pygemmys
ymowns y sur ow peha."

186 An Yêdhewon a grogas
lader dhe Grist a'n barth cledh
hag adhyhow lader brâs
cregy a wrussons inwedh,
ha Crist i'n cres leun a ras,
leun y golon a voreth.
"Gans ladron y tewedhas,"
dell yw screfys a'y dhyweth.

---

184 **H**an grous a ve drehevys / ha Ihesus fasteys ynny
han pen golas delyffrys / yn tol o tellys rygthy
ena hy a ve gesys / ȝe goȝa mar ankynsy
ȝe crist may fe crehyllys / oll y gorf hay esely

185 **H**a crist yndelma peynys / aberth yn crows pan ese
yn ⟨*va*⟩ner-ma y pesys / rag an keth re ren crowse
ow ȝas whek beȝens gevys / ȝen re-ma ga nyscyte
rag ⟦ny woȝons⟧ pygymmys / ymons y sur ow peghe

184 And the cross was lifted up
with Jesus fastened to it,
and the bottom end was let go
into the hole made for it.
Then it was allowed
to fall so grievously
for Christ, so that was shaken
all his body and his limbs.

185 When Christ was thus being pained
while he was on the cross,
he prayed in this manner
for the very men who had crucified him,
"My dear Father, let these men's
ignorance be forgiven,
for they do not know how greatly
they are sinning indeed."

186 The Jews hanged
a robber on Christ's left hand
and on the right a great robber
they hanged also,
and Christ in the middle, full of grace,
his heart full of sorrow.
"With thieves he ended,"
as has been written of his death.

---

186 **A**n ethewon a grogas / lader ʒe gryst an barth cleth [16v]
hag aʒyghow lader bras / cregy a russons ynweth
ha crist yn cres leun a ras / levn y golon a voreth
gans laddron y teweʒas / del yw scrifys ay ʒeweth

187 Pilat a vynnas screfa
a vernans Crist achêson,
praga dampnys re bia,
hag a'n screfas y honen. 1492
Pàn êth Pilat dh'y redya
skyla nynj o nagonen.
Prest y kefy pàn vera,
"Hèm yw mytern Yêdhewon". 1496

188 An Yêdhewon a gôwsys,
"Henna yw dhyn bylyny.
Bedhens dhe ves dyfendys,
y vones mytern dhyn ny, 1500
ha bedhens ena gorrys,
'Y fynsa bos dre vêstry'."
"An pÿth a screfys, screfys,"
yn medh Pilat dhedha y. 1504

189 An lîbel a veu tackys
worth an grows fast mayth esa,
hag a-ugh penn Crist gorrys,
may hylly pob y redya. 1508
Rag bos Jesus Crist crowsys
ogas dhe fordh an cyta,
gans lies y feu redys
y vones mytern dhedha. 1512

---

187 Pylat a vynnas scrife / a vewnans crist acheson
praga dampnys re bee / hag an scrifas y honon 1492
pan eth pylat ȝy redye / scyle nyni o nagonon
prest y keffy pan vyre / ((hem)) yw mygtern eȝewon 1496

188 En ethewon a gowsys / henna yw ȝyn bylyny
beȝens ȝe ves defendys / y vonas mygtern ȝyn ny 1500
ha beȝens ena gorrys / y fense bos dre vestry
han pyth a screfys screfys / yn meth pylat ȝeȝe y 1504

187 Pilate wished to write
the reason for Christ's death,
why he had been convicted,
and he wrote it himself.
When Pilate went to read it
there was no reason at all.
When he looked he always found,
"This is the king of the Jews".

188 The Jews spoke:
"This is an insult to us.
Let it be removed,
that he is a king to us,
and let be put in its place,
'He had wanted to be by domination'."
"What I have written, I have written,"
said Pilate to them.

189 The charge was firmly fixed
to the cross where he was,
and put above Christ's head,
so everyone might read it.
Because Jesus Christ was crucified
beside the road into the city,
it was read by many
that he was their king.

---

189 **E**n lybell a ve tackys / worth en grous fast mayȝ ese
hag a-vgh pen crist gorrys / may hylly peb y redye
rag bos Ihesus crist crowsys / ogas ȝe forth an cyte
gans leas y fe redijs / y vonas mygtern ȝethe

190 Dyllas Crist a veu rynnys,
peder rann gwrÿs anedha
gans peswar marhek a bris
dhe bùb marhek rann may fe.
Y bows ev o mar deg gwrÿs,
y ny vynsens hy ranna.
Warnedhy prenn beu têwlys
oll an bows pyw a'n jeffo.

191 A'n barth clêdh neb o cregys
dyveth o ha lader pur.
In ges ev a leverys,
"Te, Crist mars ota mar fur,
wàr an bÿs dell omwrussys,
lemmyn dyswa ha gwra cur
ha saw te ha me kefrÿs,
a'gan bêwnans may fen sur."

192 Y'n medh an lader aral
"Drog-dhen os kepar dell veus.
Ny dhowtyth Duw; te yw dall;
rag genen cregys neb eus
den glân yw a begh heb fall.
Ino ev defowt nynj eus;
agan cregy ny yw màl,
rag ny re beu ladron dreus."

---

190 Dyllas crist a ve rynnys / pedar ran gurys aneȝe
gans peswar marreg a brys / ȝe bub marreg ran ⸨m⸩ay ⸨f⸩e
y bous ef o mar dek gurys / y ny vynsans y ranne
warnethy pren be tewlys / oll an bows pyv an gyffe

191 An barth cleyth neb o cregys / dyveth o ha lader pur
yn ges ef a leuerys / te crist mar⸨s ⸩ota mar fur
war an bys del omwressys / lemmyn dyswa ha gura cur
ha saw te ha me kyffrys / agan bewnans may fen sur

190 Christ's clothes were divided,
four shares were made of them
by four important soldiers,
so that each soldier might have a share.
His coat was made so beautifully,
they did not wish to divide it.
For it lots were cast
as to whomever might get the whole coat.

191 The man crucified on the left
was shameless and an utter thief.
In mockery he said,
"You, Christ, if you are as wise,
as you claimed to be in the world,
now demonstrate and do a remedy
and save yourself and me also,
so that we may be assured of our life."

192 The other robber said,
"You are an evil man as you have been.
You do not fear God; you are blind;
for he who is hanged with us
is a man pure of sin without fail.
There is no fault in him.
It is right to hang us,
for we have been perverse brigands."

---

192 In meth an lader arall / drok-ȝen os kepar del ves
ny ȝowtyth du te yw dall / rag genen cregys neb es
den glan yw a begh heb fall / ynno eff dyfout nyng es
agan cregy ny yv mall / rag ny re be laddron dres [17r]

193 An lader a'n barth dyhow
a besys in kettelma,
"Arlùth, pàn dhyffy dhe'th pow,
predery ahanaf gwra."
Crist pòr wheg, an caradow,
a'n gorthebys i'n eur-na,
"Te a vÿdh i'n keth golow
in paradîs genama."

194 An Yêdhewon a gêwsy
a Jesus rag y scornya,
"Kyns yn tâ ev a ylly
tus a bùb drog oll sawya,
lemmyn gans oll y vêstry
ragon ny wor omwetha,
na gans oll y draitury,
ny yll agan dysseytya."

195 Wàr aga dêwlin yth ê
dhyrag Jesus re erel;
aga fenn y a shakya
hag a gêwsy pòr debel
worth Jesus rag y angra,
"Awot omma neb a yll
tempel Duw doust oll sqwardya
ha dh'y vodh y dhrehevel."

---

193 An lader an barth dyghow / a besys yn ketelma
arluth pan dyffy ȝet pow / predery ahanaff gura
crist pur wek an caradow / an gorȝebys yn vr-na
te a vyth yn keth golow / yn paradys genama

194 An eȝewon a gewsy / a Ihesus rag y scornye
kyns yn ta ef a ylly / tus a bub drok ol sawye
lemmyn gans ol y vestry / ragon ny wor omweȝe
na gans oll y tretury / ny yll agan dyssaytye

193 The robber on the right hand side
prayed him thus,
"Lord, when you come into your land,
do think of me."
Very sweetly, Christ, the beloved,
answered him then,
"You will be on this same day
in paradise with me."

194 The Jews spoke
of Jesus to mock him,
"Before he could well
heal men of all ill,
now with all his power
he cannot protect himself from us,
nor with all his treachery
can he deceive us."

195 Others went down upon their knees
in front of Jesus;
they shook their heads
and spoke very spitefully
against Jesus to annoy him,
"Look here is someone who can
break down the temple of God to dust,
and raise it according to his will."

---

195 War aga dewlyn yȝ e / ⸨ȝ⸩erag Ihesus re erell
aga fen y a sackye • hag a gewsy pur debell
worth Ihesus rag y angre / awott omma neb ⟪a⟫ yll
tempell du dowst oll squardye / ha ȝe voth y ȝrehevell

196 Hag y ê dhe benn dêwlin
ha hager-mowys a wre;
gwetha godhyens aga min
orth Jesus a omgamma,
hag ev moyha in y bain,
in y fâss y a drewa.
Hèn o dhodho cales fin
agan pegh ny ow prena.

197 Re dhe Grist a levery,
aberth i'n grows pàn esa,
"Mars oja Crist, mab Davy,
deus a'n grows heb pystyga,
ha ny a grÿs dha vêstry
hag a'th sens mêster nefra."
"Me yw mab Duw iredy,"
Crist a leverys dhedha.

198 Abarth dyhow yth esa
dhe Grist y vamm Maria,
ha'y vaw ev neb a gara
a'n barth aral magata.
"Dyso, benyn," yn medh e
"Jowan dha vab me a wra —
na bÿth moy ken mamm nefra
ès hyhy te na whela."

---

196 **H**ag y ee ȝe ben dewlyn / ha hager-mowys a wre
gweȝe goȝyans aga meyn / orth Ihesus a omgame
hag ef moygha yn y beyn / yn y fas y a drewe
hen o ȝoȝo calys feyn / agan pegh ny ow prenne

197 **R**e ȝe gryst a leuery / aberth yn crows pan ese
mar((s))oge crist mab dauy / des an grows heb pystege.
ha ny a grys ȝe vestry / hag ad syns mester neffre
me yw mab du yredy / crist a leuerys thethe

196 And they went down on their knees
and pulled ugly faces,
as badly as they could they twisted
their mouths at Jesus,
while he was in the greatest pain,
they spat in his face.
That was for him a harsh end,
redeeming our sins.

197 Some said to Christ,
while he was on the cross,
"If you are Christ, the son of David,
come down from the cross unharmed,
and we will believe in your power
and will hold you forever our master."
"I am indeed the Son of God,"
Christ said to them.

198 On the right side of Christ
was his mother Mary,
and his servant whom he loved
on the other side as well.
"To you, woman," he said,
"I make John your son—
and never again other than her
seek a mother."

---

198 **A**barth dyghow yʒ ese / ʒe gryst y vam marya
hay vam ef neb a gare / an barth arall magata.
deso benyn yn meʒ a / Iowan ʒe vab me a wra.
na byth moy ken mam neffre / es hyhy te na whela

199 Warlergh Crist enef dhe ry,
pùb onen oll dh'y gela,
Jowan y vamm a sensy
Maria, Crist dell arghsa.
In pùb maner may hylly
y vamm prest a's onora.
Indelma comfort dhedhy
hy mab a vynnas dyghtya.

200 Naunj o devedhys an prÿs
mayth o ogas dh'y dhyweth.
I'n eur-na y feu dorgis
ha dres oll an bÿs ev êth.
Tewolgow brâs a veu gwrÿs,
an howl a gollas y feth,
ha moy marthus, me a grÿs,
ès an re-na veu inwedh.

201 Indella hy a bêjyas
bys hanter-dÿdh iredy.
I'n eur-na Crist a vynnas
leverel "Ely, Ely";
dhe styrya yw a gowsas,
"Arlùth, prag y hysta vy?"
mès re wàr Grist a inyas,
yth o dewas a erhy.

---

199 Warlyrgh crist enef ʒe ry / pub onan oll ʒy gele.
Iowan y vam a sensy / marya crist del arse [17v]
yn pub maner may hylly / y vam prest a((s))onore
yndelma confort ʒyʒy / y map a vynnas dygtye

200 Nevng o deuethys an prys / mayʒ o ogas ʒy ʒeweth
yn er-na y fe dorgys / ha drys ol an bys ef eth
tewolgow bras a ve gurys / an houll a gollas y feth
ha moy marʒus me a grys / ys an re-na ve ynweth

199 After Christ had given up his spirit,
they both the one and the other,
John considered as his mother
Mary, as Christ had bidden him.
In every way as he could
he honoured her as his mother.
Thus a comfort to her
her Son wanted to provide.

200 Now had come the time
when his death was near.
At that hour there was an earthquake
and it went through all the earth.
A great darkness occurred,
the sun lost his face,
and further miracles, I believe,
happened more than those.

201 Thus it lasted
until midday indeed.
Then Christ wished
to say "Eli, Eli":
what he said means,
"My God, why have you forsaken me?"
but some urged against Christ,
that it was a drink that he was asking.

---

201 Indella hy a begyas / bys hanter-dyth yredy
yn er-na crist a vynnas / leuerell ely ely
ȝe strirya yw a gowsas / arluth pragh y hysta vy
mas re war gryst a ynnyas / yȝ o dewas a yrghy

202 Gans an Yêdhewon wàr hast
drog-dhewas a veu dyghtys,
tebel-lycour meur hy last,
eysel bestyl kemyskys.
In unn spong orth gwelen fast
dhe Grist hy a veu hedhys.
Gonys oll a wrêns in hast,
rag nag o Crist attendys.

203 Re a'n Yêdhewon tebel
a leverys heb pyta,
"Awottensa ow kelwel
Hely dhodho dh'y wetha.
Merowgh mar teu drehevel,
a'y bainys dh'y dhelyfra."
Ha'n sherewys prest abell
dhyworth an gwir a via.

204 Y bain o mar grev ha tynn,
cammen ny ylly bêwa
heb dascor y enef gwynn,
bythqweth yn lân re vêwsa.
Crist a besys, dell redyn
indelma in lies le,
"Ow enef me a gemyn,
Arlùth, intra dha dhewla."

---

202 **G**ans an eʒewon war hast / drok-ʒewas a ve dyʒgtys
tebell-lycour meur y last / eysyll bestyll kemyskys
yn ⸨vn⸩ spong orth gwelen fast / ʒe gryst hy a ve heʒys
gonys oll a wrens yn ⸨h⸩ast / rag nag o crist attendijs

203 **R**e an eʒewon tebell • a leuerys heb pyte
awottense ow kelwell / hely ʒoʒo ʒy wyʒe
myrugh mar te drehevell / ay beynys ʒy ʒelyffre
han scherewys prest abell / ʒeworth an gwyr a fye

202 By the Jews in haste
an evil drink was prepared,
a horrible liquor of great nastiness,
vinegar and gall mixed.
In a sponge fixed on a rod
it was held up to Christ.
They all were working in haste,
because they did not understand Christ.

203 Some of the evil Jews
said without pity,
"Look, he is calling
Elijah to him to preserve him.
Look to see whether he will come to raise him
from his pains to release him."
And the villains always
had been far from the truth.

204 His pain was so great and sharp
that he could not live at all
without relinquishing his blessed soul,
that had always lived purely.
Christ prayed, as we read,
thus in many places,
"My soul I commend,
Lord, into your hands."

---

204 I beyn o mar greff ha tyn / caman na ylly bewe
heb dascor y eneff gwyn / bytqueth yn lan re vewse
crist a besys del redyn / yndelma yn luas le
ow eneff me a gymyn / arluth yntre ȝe ȝewle

205 Rag gwan spern hag ev yn tenn
cammen ny ylly gwetha
wàr nans na bossa y benn
rag an arlont a ûsya.
Mar possa 'neyl tenewen,
rag y scoodh hy a'n grêvya,
ha whath gweth a wre a'n prenn
wàr dhelergh mara'n gorra.

206 Na wàr rag ev ny ylly
posa rag own bos megys.
I'n eur-na, dell redyn ny,
i'n Lyfrow yth yw screfys,
dhe'n ÿdhyn gwyls rag neythy
tyleryow esa parys.
Dhe Crist y benn py sensy,
tyller vÿth nynj o kefys.

207 Rag porres rÿs o dhodho
gasa y benn dhe gregy,
rag galsa glân dhyworto
y woos; bêwa ny ylly.
Wàr tu ha'y vamm a'n pewo
y benn a vynnas sensy,
ha'y enef êth anodho
gans garm yêyn hag uhel gry.

---

205 **R**ag gwan spyrn hag ef yn ten / caman na ylly gwyȝe
war nans na bosse y ben / rag an arlont a vsye
mar posse neyll tenewen / rag y scoth hy an grevye
Ha whath gweth a wre an pren / war ȝellargh maran gorre

206 **N**a war rag ef ny ylly / pose rag own bos megys [18r]
yn er-na del redyn ny / «yn» lyffrow yȝ ew scrifys
ȝen eȝyn gwyls rag nyeȝy / tellyryow esa parys
the crist y ben py sensy / teller vyth nyng o kefys

205 For thorn pricks as he was stretched out
he could in no way prevent
his head from leaning down
because of the crown he was wearing.
If he leant it to one side,
it would hurt him because of his shoulder,
and the wood would hurt him all the worse
if he put it backwards.

206 Nor could he lean it forwards
for fear of being stifled.
Then, as we read,
in the Scriptures it is written,
there were ready to make their nests
places for the wild birds.
For Christ, where to hold his head,
no place was found.

207 For it was very necessary for him
to let his head hang down,
for completely had gone from him
his blood; he could not live.
Towards his mother who possessed him
he wished to hold his head,
and his soul went from him
with a shrill scream and a loud cry.

---

207 **R**ag porrys rys o ȝoȝo / gase y ben ȝe gregy
rag galse glan ȝeworto / y woys bewe ny ylly
war tu hay vam an pewo / y ben a vynnas synsy
hay eneff eth anoȝo / gans garm eyn hag vghel gry

208 Ryb crows Jesus yth esa
unn den henwys Century.
A vernans Crist pàn welsa
kenyver tra marthusy
ha'n enef dell dascorsa,
erbynn natur gans unn cry
y leverys heb scornya,
"Hèm yw Mab Duw iredy,"
(ha lies ganso ena
dodho a dhug dùstuny).

209 Nanj o hanter-dÿdh i'n wlas
pò moy dell yma screfys.
Dorgîs esa ha luhes
ha'n tewolgow kekefrÿs.
Veyl an tempel a sqwardyas
intra dew dhe'n dor codhys.
Ena inwedh y torras
an veyn, o crev ha cales.

210 An bedhow in lower le
apert a veu egerys
ha'n corfow esa inha
a veu in bàn drehevys,
hag êth poran dhe'n cyta;
gans lies y fowns gwelys
in gwir dhe dhùstunia
bos mab Duw neb o ledhys.

---

208 **R**yp crous Ihesus yʒ ese / vn den henwys sentury
a vernans crist pan welse / kynyuer tra marthusy
han enef del dascorse / erbyn natur gans vn cry
y leuerys heb scornye / ((hem)) yw mab du yredy
ha leas ganso ene / doʒo a ʒuk dustuny

209 **N**ang o hanter-dyth yn wlas • po moy del yma scryfys
dorgys esa ha lughas / han tewolgow kekyffrys
veyll an tempyll a squardyas / yntre dew ʒen dor coʒys
ena ynweth y torras / en veyn o creff ha calys

208 By the cross of Jesus there was
a man called Centurion.
When he had seen all the wonders
at the death of Christ,
and that he had given up his spirit,
contrary to nature with a cry
he said without mockery,
"This is the Son of God indeed."
(and many with him there
bore witness to it.)

209 Now it was midday in the country
or later, as is written.
There was an earthquake and lightning
and darkness also.
The veil of the temple tore
in two, fallen to the ground.
There also broke
the stones, which were mighty and hard.

210 The graves in many places
were clearly opened
and the bodies which were in them
were raised up,
and went straight to the city;
by many they were seen
to witness to the truth
that it was the Son of God who was killed.

---

210 **E**n beȝow yn lower le / apert a ve egerys
han corfow esa ynne / a ve yn ban drehevys
hag eth poran ȝen cyte / gans luas y fons gwelys
en gwyr ȝe ȝustvnee / bos mab du neb o leȝys

211 Dowr ha leur ha tan ha gwyns,
howl ha loor ha ster kefrÿs,
a Grist ow codhaf mernans
anken y a wodhevys.
Natur skyla me a syns,
arlùth dâ mar pÿdh painys,
oll y sojet kyn fowns syns
rag y bain dhe vos grêvys.

212 Enef Crist dhe iffarn êth
hag a dorras an porthow;
dre y nerth brâs ha'y sleyneth
ena 'golmas dewolow.
Lûcyfer kelmys yw whath
pòr fast in y golmennow
hag ev a drig heb finweth
in iffarn in tewolgow.

213 Ena Crist a dhelyfras
a bryson Adam hag Ev,
seul a wrussa bodh y Das
ma'n jeffa trigva in nev.
Pàn êth in mes, y'n sewyas
an dus vas dell vynna ev;
an sherewys a dregas
in iffarn in torment crev.

---

211 Dowr ha ler ha tan ha gwyns / houl ha lour ha steyr kyffrys
a gryst ow coȝaff mernans / anken y a woȝevys
natur scyle me a syns / arluth da mar pyth peynys
ol y soget kyn fons syns / rag y beyn ȝe vos grevijs

212 Enaff crist ȝe yffarn eth / hag a dorras an porȝow
dre y nerth bras hay sleyneth / ena golmas dewolow
lucyfer kelmys yv whath / pur fast yn y golmennow
Hag ef a dryk heb fynweth / yn yffarn yn tewolgow

211 Water and earth and fire and wind,
sun and the moon and the stars also,
suffering at the death of Christ
they endured misery.
Nature is the cause, I consider,
if a good lord is pained,
all his subject though they be saints,
for his pain to be aggrieved.

212 The soul of Christ went to hell
and broke the gates;
by his great power and his skill
there he bound devils.
Lucifer is still bound
very firmly in his bonds
and he will dwell forever
in hell in darkness.

213 Then Christ released
Adam and Eve from prison,
that whoever should do the will of his Father
should have his dwelling in heaven.
When he went out, there followed him
the good people as he wished;
the scoundrels remained
in hell in bitter torment.

---

213 **E**na crist a thelyffras / a breson adam hag ef [18v]
suel a wressa both y das // man geffo tregva yn nef
pan eth yn mes yn sewyas / en dus vas del vynne ef
an scherewes a dregas / yn yffarn yn tormont creff

214 Unn bùrjes Josep henwys
a Baramat, an cyta,
in mernans Crist a gêwsys,
"Bythqweth dremas re bia."
Oll y dowl ev o têwlys
ganso in nev rag trega.
Jesus ganso o kerys
ha nynj o hardh dh'y nôtya.

215 Josep êth bys i'n jùstys,
dhe Bilat, mêster treus o,
ha pòr hardh a wovynnys
corf Jesus worto yn ro.
Rag bos Josep den kerys,
grauntys ev a veu dhodho.
Pilat a worhemynnys
meras Crist marow mars o.

216 An Yêdhewon skentyl keth—
re's teffo meur vylyny!—
dhe veras worth Crist y êth
hag ev in crows ow cregy.
Y a welas worth y feth
y vos marow iredy:
y tesefsons oll inwedh
dre an golon y delly.

---

214 Vn burges Iosep hynwys / a ⟦b⟧aramat an cyte
yn mernans crist a gewsys / bytqueth dremas re bee
ol y doul ef o tewlys / ganso yn nef rag trege
Ihesus ganso o kerys / ha nyni o hard ȝy notye

215 Iosep eth bys yn Iustys / ȝe bylat mester treus o
ha pur hardh a wovynnys / corf Ihesus worto yn ro
rag bos Iosep den kerys / grontys ef a ve ȝoȝo
pylat a woromynnys / meras crist marow mar⟦s ⟧o

214 A citizen called Joseph
from Arimathea, the city, 1708
at the death of Christ spoke,
"Always he had been a good man."
All his intention was planned
to dwell with him in heaven. 1712
Jesus was loved by him
and he was not brave enough to display it.

215 Joseph went to the justice,
to Pilate, he was a tricky master, 1716
and very vigorously he asked
from his as a gift the body of Jesus.
Because Joseph was loved,
it was granted to him. 1720
Pilate commanded
to look to see whether Christ was dead.

216 The crafty servile Jews—
may they receive much reproach!— 1724
they went to examine Christ
while he was hanging on the cross.
They saw from his face
that he was dead indeed: 1728
they all presumed as well
to pierce him through the heart.

---

216 **E**n eȝewon skyntyll keth / re((s))teffo meur vylyny 1724
ȝe veras worth crist y eth / hag ef yn crous ow cregy
y a welas ((worth)) y feth / y vos marow yredy 1728
((y))taseffsons oll ynweth / dre an golon y delly

217 I'gà herwyth yth esa
unn marhek, Longys henwys. 1732
Dall o, ny wely banna,
ev re bia den a bris.
guw a veu in y dhewla
gans an Yêdhewon gorrys 1736
ha penn lymm rag y wana
dhe golon Jesus gwynnvÿs.

218 Longys sur a'n barth dyhow
dhe grows Jesus yth esa. 1740
Dhe'n marhek worth y hanow
y a erhys may whanha
in corf Jesus caradow;
an guw lymm ev a bychya 1744
pòr ewn in dann an asow
dre an golon mayth êth e.

219 A'n golon yth êth streth brâs,
dowr ha goos yn kemeskys, 1748
ha ryb an guw a resas
dhe dhewla neb a'n gweskys;
y wholhas y dhewlagas
gans an eyl leuv o gosys. 1752
Dre ras an goos y whelas
Jesus Crist dell o dyghtys.

---

217 ⦅I⦆ga herwyth yȝ ese / vn marreg longys hynwys 1732
dal o ny wely banna / ef re bea den a brys
gew a ve yn y ȝewle / gans an eȝewon gorrys 1736
ha pen lym rag y wane / ȝe golon Ihesus ⦅gw⦆ynwys

218 Longys sur an barth dyghow / ȝe grous Ihesus yȝ ese 1740
ȝen marreg worth y hanow / y a yrhys may whane
yn corf Ihesus caradow / en gew lym ef a bechye 1744
pur ewn yn dan an asow / dre an golon mayȝ e⦅th ⦆e

217 In their company there was
a soldier, called Longius.
He was blind, he could see nothing,
he had been a man of importance.
A spear was put into his hands
by the Jews
with a sharp point to thrust
into the heart of blessed Jesus.

218 Longius indeed was
on the right of the cross of Jesus.
They bade the soldier
by his name that he should thrust
into the body of beloved Jesus;
he thrust the sharp spear
exactly under the ribs
so that it went through the heart.

219 From the heart there went forth a great stream,
water and blood mixed,
and along the spear it ran
to the hands of him who struck;
He wiped his two eyes,
with the one hand that had been bloodied.
By the virtue of the blood he saw
how Jesus Christ had been treated.

---

219 An golon yȝ eth stret bras / dowr ha goys yn kemeskys
ha ryp an gyw a resas / ȝe ȝewle neb an gwyskys
y wholhas y ȝewlagas / gans y eyll leyff o gosys
dre ras an goys y whelas / Ihesus crist dell o dyȝgtys

220 Edrek meur a'n kemeras
rag an ober re wrussa.
Dhe benn dôwlin y codhas.
"Arlùth, gyvyvans!" yn medh e.
"Dall en, ny welyn yn fâs
ow bos mar vil ow pêwa."
Jesus dhodho a avas,
pàn welas y edrega.

221 Mamm Jesus, Maria Wynn,
herdhya an guw pàn welas
in hy mab i'n tenewen,
dre an golon may resas
ha dhe'n dor an goos ha'n lynn,
anodho dell dheveras,
angùs brâs ha painys tynn,
ha gloos crev a's kemeras.

222 Fest yn tynn hy a ola,
dhe wherthyn ny's teva whans,
ha'y dagrow a dhevera
a'y dewlagas pòr dhewhans,
ha'y holon wheg a ranna,
me a lever, rag tristans,
rag an grath inhy esa
na's gwetha an Spyrys Sans.

---

220 **E**ddrek meur an kemeras / rag an ober re wresse [19r]
ȝy ben dowlyn y coȝas / arluth gevyans yn meȝ e
dall en ny welyn yn fas / ow bos mar veyll ow pewe
Ihesus ȝoȝo a avas / pan welas y edrege

221 **M**am Ihesus marya wyn / herdya an gyw pan welas
yn y mab yn tenewyn / dre an golon may resas
ha ȝen dor an goys han lyn / annoȝo dell deveras
angus bras ha peynys tyn / ha gloys creff a((s))kemeres

220 Great repentance overcame him
for the deed he had done.
He fell upon his knees.
"Lord, forgiveness!" he said.
"I was blind, I did not see properly
that I was living so vilely."
Jesus forgave him,
when he saw his repentance.

221 The mother of Jesus, Blessed Mary,
when she saw the spear thrust
into her son, into his side,
so that it penetrated his heart
and that the blood and water
dripped down from him,
great anguish and keen torment
and mighty pain overcame her.

222 Very bitterly she was weeping,
she had no desire to laugh,
and her tears dropped
from her eyes very fast,
and her sweet heart was splitting,
I tell you, for sorrow,
if by the grace which was in her
the Holy Spirit had not protected her.

---

222 **F**est yn tyn hy a wole / ȝe wherȝyn ny((s))teva whans
hay dagrow a ȝevere / ay dewlagas pur ȝewhans
hay holon whek a ranne / me a leuer rag trystans
rag an grayth ynhy ese / nas gweȝe an spyrys sans

223 Dre hy holon yth êth seth,
hy mab shyndys pàn welsa,
moreth an seth ha pyteth,
natureth o ha denseth,
ha'n penn aral o pyteth
tackys fast gans kerensa.
Ny wodhevys den bythqweth
kemmys painys ow pêwa.

224 An seth yw ragleverys
a's gweskys gans meur angùs
wàr hy holon may crunys
dre nerth an bomm fenten woos;
ha hy a olas kemmys
gans mar veur nerth ha gallos,
a'n fenten may trehevys
rann in bàn—Duw drocka loos!

225 A'n goos-na dagrennow try
dre hy dewlagas yth êth.
Nynj o confort na ely
a wrello hy holon heuth,
ha'y fainys mar druesy
a's kemeras, kemmys keuth;
in oll an bÿs ny ylly
den cafos kemmys anfeuth

---

223 Dre y holon yȝ eth seth / y mab syndys pan welse
moreth an seth ha pytet / natureth a ha denseth
han pen arall o pytet / tackys fast gans kerense
ny woȝevys den bythqueth / kymmys peynys ow pewe

224 An seth yw ragleuerys / as gwyskys gans meur angus
war hy holon may crunys / dre nerth an bum fynten woys
ha hy a wolas kymmys / gans meur ver nerth ha galloys
an fynten may trehevys / ran yn ban du droka loys

223 Through her heart an arrow went,
when she had seen her son injured,
grief was the arrow and pity,
it was natural feeling and humanity,
and the other end was pity
closely attached to love.
No man ever has suffered
so many pains while alive.

224 The aforementioned arrow
struck her with great anguish
upon her heart so that there was gathered
by dint of the blow a well of blood,
and she wept so much
with great power and strength,
that from the well there rose
part upwards—God, what torment!

225 Of that blood three drops
went through her eyes.
It was not a comfort nor salve
that would make her heart joyful,
and her pains so wretched
overcame her, so much misery,
that in the world nobody
could endure so much misfortune.

---

225 An goy⸨s⸩-na dagrennow try / dre y ⸨dew⸩lagas yȝ eth
n《yn》g o confort na yly / a wrello y holon hueth
hay veynys mar drewesy / ⸨as kemeras⸩ kymmys cueth
yn oll an bys ny ylly / den cafos kymmys anfueth

226 Hy fainys o brâs ha crev
yn joy dhedhy trailys yw;
rag myternes yw in nev,
dhe vos gordhys hy yw gwyw.
Eleth dhyrygthy a sev,
lies mil hy bodh a sew,
ha'y Mab a's gordh dell vynn ev.
Tecka ès howl yw hy lyw.

227 In corf Jesus yth esa
hag ev in crows ow cregy
pymp mil strocas, dell joue
ha pedergweyth cans goly
ha try ugans moy gansa,
ha pymthek pòr wir êns y,
hag oll rag pur gerensa
worth mab den y's godhevy.

228 Pùptëdh oll neb a vynna
leverel pymthek pater
a leun-golon rag gordhya
passyon agan Arlùth ker,
in bledhen y a via
a bederow kenyver
hag a woliow esa
in corf Jesus worth nyver.

---

226 I feynys o bras ha creff / yn ioy ȝeȝy trylys yw
rag mygternas yw yn nef / ȝe vos gorȝijs hy yv gyw
Eleth ȝerygthy a seff / leas myll y both a syw
hay mab as gorth del vyn ef / tecke ys houl yv y lyw

227 In corff Ihesus yȝ ese / hag ef yn crows ow cregy [19v]
pymp myll strekys del iove / ha pedergwyth cans goly
ha try vgons moy ganse / ha pymȝek pur wyr ens y
hag ol rag pur gerense / worth mab den ys goȝevy

226 Her pains which were great and strong
have been turned for her into joy;
for she is queen in heaven,
she is worthy to be adored.
Angels stand before her,
many thousands do her will,
and her Son adores her as he will.
Brighter than the sun is her appearance.

227 There were in the body of Jesus
as he hung upon the cross
five thousand weals, as I have heard,
and four times a hundred wounds,
and three score more in addition,
and fifteen very truly they were,
and all for sheer love
of mankind did he suffer them.

228 Whoever wishes every day
to say fifteen paternosters
sincerely to adore
the passion of our dear Lord,
in a year there would be
as many prayers by number
as there were wounds
in the body of Jesus.

---

228 **P**ubteȝ oll neb a vynne / leuerel pymȝek pater
a leun-golon rag gorȝye / pascon agan arluth ker
yn blyȝen y a vye / ha bederow keneuer
hag a ⦅wo⦆leow ese / yn corf Ihesus worth neuer

229 An Yêdhewon ny vynna
bos an ladron ow cregy
ternos, rag Pask o dhedha,
dÿdh uhel y a sensy.
An Yêdhewon intredha
a wrug may whrellens terry
aga mordhosow whare
hag alena aga dry.

230 Erbynn bones henna gwrÿs,
nans o prÿs gwesper i'n wlas.
I'n eur-na inwedh cumyas
dhe Josep y a rauntyas
hag a'n growsprenn dell o prÿs
corf Jesus a gemeras.
Teyr Maria, me a grÿs,
p'eur hylwys a'n gweresas.

231 Mamm Jesus Crist a amma
corf hy mab pòr druesy,
ha'y dagrow a dhevera
anodho pàn bredery,
ha'n anken meur a's grêvya,
pàn vera worth y woly;
i'n tenewen yth esa,
dre an golon a's tylly.

---

229 En eȝewon ny vynne / bos an laddron ow cregy
ternos rag pasch o ȝeȝe / dyth vghel y a sensy
an eȝewon yntreȝe / a rug may wrellons terry
aga morȝosow whare / hag alena aga dry

230 Erbyn bonas henna gurys / nan⦅s ⦆o prys gwesper yn wlas
yn er-na ynweth kemeas / ȝe Iosep y a rontyas
hag an grou⦅s⦆《pren》 del o prys / corf Ihesus a gemeras
tyr marya me a grys / pur ylwys an gweresas

229 The Jews did not wish
that the robbers should be hanging
on the next day, for it was their Passover,
they kept it as a high day.
The Jews among themselves
decided that they should break
their thighs without delay
and take them thence.

230 By the time that had been done,
it was already evening in the land.
At that point permission
they granted to Joseph
and from the cross, as it was time,
he took down the body of Jesus.
The three Marys, I believe,
when he called, helped him.

231 The Mother of Jesus Christ kissed
her Son's body very sadly,
and her tears fell
as she thought of him,
and the misery greatly grieved her,
when she looked upon his wound;
it was in the side,
it pierced her in the heart.

---

231 **M**am Ihesus crist a amme / corf y mab pur drewesy
hay daggrow a ȝevere / anoȝo pan predery
han anken meur a((s))grevye / pan vyre worth y woly
yn tenewen yȝ ese / dre an golon a((s))tylly

232 Josep dhe Grist a ewnas
y arrow ha'y dhywvregh wheg
i'n vaner ev dell vêwas,
hag a's istynnas pòr deg.
Adro dh'y gorf y trailyas
sendal rych in lies pleg
ha Maria leun a ras
ganso trist ha morethek.

233 Ena unn lowarth esa
hag ino bedh o parys
den marow rag recêva,
nowyth o, nynj o ûsys.
Corf Jesus Crist intredha
dhe'n logel a veu degys
hag ahës dhe wrowedha
ino ev a veu gesys.

234 Unn den dâ Crist a gara,
Nycodêmus y hanow,
ev nynj o hardh dh'y nôtya
rag own cafos y ancow;
dworennos yn pur brena
ev êth dhe'n corf o marow
gans oynment dhodho esa
ha spîcys a veur rasow.

---

232 Iosep ȝe gryst a ⦅ew⦆nas / y arrow hay ȝeffregh whek
yn vaner ⟪ef⟫ del ⦅vew⦆as / hag as ystynnas pur dek
adro ȝy gorff y trylyas / sendall rych yn luas pleg
ha marya leun a ras / ganso trest ha moreȝek

233 Ena vn lowarth ese / ha ynno ⦅beth o⦆ parys
den marow rag receve / newyth ⦅o⦆ nyni o vsijs
corff Ihesus crist yntreȝe / ȝen logell a ve degys
Hag aheys ȝe wroweȝe / ynno eff a ve gesys

232 Joseph straightened Christ's
legs and his two sweet arms
as though he were living
and stretched them out very nicely.
About his body he wound
a rich linen cloth in many folds
and Mary full of grace,
was with him, sad and woeful.

233 There was there a garden
and in it a tomb was ready
to receive a dead body,
newly made, it had not been used.
The body of Jesus Christ between them
was carried to the sepulchre,
and to lie at length
it was left in it.

234 A good man loved Christ,
his name Nicodemus,
he was not brave enough to declare it
for fear of being put to death;
as night fell, purely for expiation,
he went to the body, which was lifeless,
with ointment which he had
and spices of great virtue.

---

234 Vn den da ⟪cri⟫st a gara / Nycodemus y hanow [20r]
eff nyni o hardh ʒy notya / rag own cafos y ankow
dworennos yn pur brena / ef eth ʒen corff o marow
gans vnment ʒoʒo esa / ha spycys a veur rasow

235 Nycodêmùs a uras
corf Jesus ha'y esely.
Oynment o a gemmys ras
may whetha corf heb pedry.
Nagonen ev ny asas
heb ura a'y esely.
Indella ev a'n dyghtyas.
Meyn yêyn sur o y wely.

236 A spîcys lies ehen
ev a worras in y vedh
dhe Grist a bùb tenewen
hag adhyhow hag aglêdh,
worth y dreys hag orth y benn
ha worth oll y gorf inwedh—
dysqwedhyans warlergh anken,
bedha mytern i'n dyweth.

237 Ha'n Yêdhewon a worras
a-ugh Jesus Crist unn men;
ledan o ha poos ha brâs,
moy ages gavel tredden.
Ganso dres nos y wholyas
in y servys neb o len.
An nos-na a dremenas
hag oll hy drog ha'y anken.

---

235 **N**ycodemus a vras / corff Ihesus hay esely
oynment o a gymmys ras / may weʒe corf heb pedry
nagonon ef ny asas / heb vre ay esely
yndel⸨l⸩a ef an dyʒgtyas / mey eyn sur o y wely

236 ⸨**A**⸩ spycys leas ehen / ef a worras yn y veth
ʒe gryst a bub tenewen / hag aʒyghow hag agleth
worth y dreys ha worth y ben / ha ⸨worth⸩ ol y gorf ynweth
dysqueʒyens warlyrgh anken / beʒe mygtern yn deweth

235 Nicodemus anointed
the body of Jesus and his limbs. 1876
It was ointment of such efficacy,
that it would keep a body from decomposing.
He left not one of his limbs
without anointing it. 1800
Thus he treated him.
Cold stones indeed were his bed.

236 Many kinds of spices
he put in his tomb 1884
on both sides of Christ,
both on the right and on the left,
at his feet and at his head
and over all his body also— 1888
an indication after suffering,
that he would be a king in the end.

237 And the Jews placed
over Jesus Christ a stone; 1892
it was wide and heavy and large,
more than three men could grasp.
There watched with him overnight
someone who was faithful in his service. 1896
That night passed away,
and all its evil and misery.

---

237 **H**an eȝewon a worras / a-vgh Ihesus crist vn men 1892
leden o ha poys ha bras / moy agys gauel tredden
Ganso drys nos y ⦅g⦆olyas / yn y seruys neb o len 1896
an no⦅s⦆-na a dremenas / hag oll y drok hay anken

238 Ternos y sordyas bresel
gans an Yêdhewon wocky.
Lavarow tynn hag uhel
fest yn fol y a gêwsy,
may fêns y parys dhe well.
Ny wodhyens y dhystrôwy,
rag Jesus dhe leverel
i'n tressa dÿdh y sevy.

239 In unn stêvya oll y êth
bys in Pilat o jùstys.
Unn Yêdhow dhodho yn freth
indelma a leverys,
"Ny a yll i'n nos haneth
fest dystowgh bones kellys
ha may fo dhyn ny dhe weth
rag bones Jesus ledhys.

240 "Rag an traitour a gêwsys,
ha dhyrag lies huny,
warlergh y vones ledhys
dhe'n tressa dÿdh y sevy,
mès mara pedha degys
gans y dus na'n caffen ny,
i'n eur-na bÿdh leverys
ev dhe sevel dre vêstry."

---

238 Ternoys y sordyas bresel / gans an eȝewon goky
lauarow tyn hag vghel / fest yn foll y a gewsy
may ((f))ens y parys ȝe well / ny woȝyens y ȝystrowy
rag Ihesus ȝe leuerell / yn tressa dyth y sevy

239 In vn stevya oll y eth / bys yn pylat o Iustys
vn eȝow ȝoȝo yn freth / yndelma a leuerys
ny a yll yn nos haneth / fest dystough bonas kellys
ha may fo dyn ny ȝe weth • rag bonas Ihesus leȝys

238 On the next day a dispute arose
among the foolish Jews.
Utterances sharp and loud
very wildly they were speaking,
that they might the better be prepared.
They were not able to destroy him,
for Jesus had said,
he would on the third day rise again.

239 They all went hurrying
to Pilate, who was a magistrate.
A Jew eagerly to him
spoke thus,
"We can this night
very suddenly be lost,
and thus it may be the worse for us
that Jesus has been put to death.

240 "For the traitor said
and in the presence of many,
after his being killed,
he would rise on the third day,
but if he is removed
by his men so that we can't find him,
then it will be said,
that he rose by miraculous power."

---

240 **R**ag an treytour a gewsys / ha ȝerag leas huny [20v]
warl⟨yr⟩gh y vonas leȝys / ȝen tressa dyth y seuy
mars mara peȝa degys / gans y dus nan caffan ny
yn vr-na byth leuerys / ef ȝe sevell dre vestry

241 Pilat a erhys dhedha,
wàr bain kelly an bêwnans,
mones dhe'n corf dh'y wetha,
na kemerra eskerens,
hag i'n nos oll aspia
ha gwetha tamm na gùskens.
Y êth in unn fystena
peswar marhek; ervys êns.

242 Pàn dheuthons y bys i'n bedh,
yth êth unn marhek dh'y benn
hag aral dh'y dreys inwedh
ervys fest bys i'n dhywen,
hag adhyhow hag aglêdh
onen a bùb tenewen.
Bost a wrêns tynn ha dyveth
y'n gwethens worth y ehen.

243 An varhogyon a gùscas
myttyn ha'n jÿdh ow tardha;
ha Jesus a dhassorhas
hag êth i'n le may fynna;
Duw apert ha meur y ras,
golow cler ow tewynya,
ev a wre oll y vynnas.
Y ny yllens y wetha.

---

241 Pylat a yrghys ȝeȝe / war beyn kylly an bewnans
monas ȝen corf ȝy weȝe / n((a)) kemerre yskerans
hag yn nos oll aspye / ha gwyȝe tam na guskens
y eth yn vn fystene / peswar marrek yrvys ens

242 Pan deȝens y bys yn beth / yȝ eth vn marrek ȝy ben
hag arall ȝy dreys ynweth / yrvys fast bys yn ȝewen
hag aȝyghow hag agleth / onon a bub tenewen
bost a wrens tyn ha deveth / yn gweȝens worth y ehen

241 Pilate commanded them,
on pain of losing their life,
to go to the body to guard it,
that enemies should not take it,
and to watch out all night long
and to be careful not to sleep a wink.
Four soldiers went
in a hurry; they were armed.

242 When they came to the tomb,
one soldier went to his head
and another also to his feet,
fully armed to the jaws,
and both on the right and on the left
one on both sides.
They made a bitter and shameless boast,
that they would guard him in spite of his utmost.

243 The soldiers fell asleep
in the morning, as the day dawned;
and Jesus rose again
and went whither he wished;
manifestly God and great in grace,
a bright light shining,
he did exactly as he wished.
They could not prevent him.

---

243 En varogyon a guskas / myttyn han gyth ow tarʒe
ha Ihesus a ʒeʒo⸨rh⸩as / hag eth yn le may fynne
Deu apert ha meur y ras / golow cleyr ow tewynnye
ef a wre oll y vynnas / y ny yllens y weʒe

244 Pàn o pòr holergh an jëdh,
y tyfunas unn marhek.
Dell dheuth a'n nev wàr y feth,
ev a welas golow teg
ha'n men omwhelys inwedh,
esa a-ugh Jesus wheg,
ha warnodho a'y eseth
el benegys lowenek.

245 An marhek-na a sevys
oll in bàn y gowetha,
ha dhedha y leverys,
a Jesus fatell via:
"An den-ma re dhrehevys.
Gallas ny wodhon pyle.
Lemmyn na ven ny ledhys,
nynj eus fordh dhe omwetha."

246 Marhek aral a gowsas,
"Gony vÿth pàn veun genys!
Tru, a Dhuw, elhas, elhas!
Gans an hun re beun tùllys.
An bêwnans ny re gollas
hag inwedh agan flehes.
Omdhyghtyn, trussen a'n wlas!
Fien na ven ny kefys."

---

244 **P**an o pur holergh an gyth / y tefenas vn marrek
del deth an nef war y fyth / ef a welas golow tek
han meyn vmhelys ynweth / ese a-vgh Ihesus whek
ha warnoʒo a«y» yseth / ell benegas lowenek

245 **E**n marrek-na a sevys / oll yn ban y goweʒe
ha ʒeʒe a leuerys / a Ihesus fatell vye
an den-ma re drehevys / gallas ny woʒan pele
lemman na ven« n»y leʒys / nyng es forth ʒe omweʒe

244 When it was very late morning,
one soldier awoke.
As it came from heaven upon his face
he saw a beautiful light,
and the stone overturned also,
which was over beloved Jesus,
and sitting upon it
a joyful blessed angel.

245 That soldier aroused
all his companions
and to them he said
what had happened to Jesus:
"This man has risen up.
He has gone we know not where.
Now for us not to be killed,
there is no way for us to guard ourselves."

246 Another soldier spoke,
"Alas that we were ever born!
Woe, O God, alas, alas!
We have been seduced by sleep.
We have forfeited our life
and also our children.
Let us get ready, let's pack off from the country.
Let's flee so that we are not caught."

---

246 **M**arrak arall a gowsas / gony vyth pan veyn genys
tru a thu elhas elhas / gans vn huyn re ben tullys
an bewnans ny re gollas / hag ynweth agan fleghys
omʒyghtyn trussen an wlas / fyan na ven《 n》y kefys

247 An peswora a gêwsys,
“Na whelyn gwêvya a’n pow.
Kepar dell veu dhe’n jùstys,
deun, leveryn wàr anow—
A’y vedh dell yw drehevys.
Na leveryn unn ger gow.”
Y a wrug adhesempys
oll warlergh y arhadow.

248 Y êth in unn fystena
dhe Bilat aga jùstys;
y’n dyskens y dell via,
ha dhodho a leverys,
re safsa Crist heb strîvya,
oll a’y vodh gans golowys
ha na yllens y wetha
y vodh na vo colenwys.

249 Ena Pilat pàn glêwas
indelma y dhe gêwsel,
prederow a’n kemeras
rag own y dhe leverel
ha dh’y nôtya dres an wlas
sur a-ogas hag abell,
may teffa tus gans nerth brâs
er y bynn rag gùstla bell.

---

247 ⟨***An*** p⟩eswore a gewsys / na whelyn gwevye an pow [21r]
⟨*k*⟩epar del ve ȝen Iustys / dun leueryn war anow
ay veth del yw drehevys / na leueryn vn ger gow
y a ruge aȝesympys / oll warlyrgh y arhadow

248 I eth yn vn fystene / ȝe pylat aga Iustys
en deskyens ⟪y⟫ del vye / ha ȝoȝo a leuerys
re safse crist heb strevye / ol ⸨a⸩y voth gans golowys
ha na yllens y gwyȝe / y voth na vo colenwys

247 The fourth spoke:
"Let us not try to leave the country.
Come, let us admit by word of mouth
to the magistrate exactly as it happened—
that he has been raised from his tomb.
Let us not speak any false word."
They did immediately
all according to his command.

248 They went hurrying
to Pilate, their magistrate;
they informed him how it had been,
and they told him,
that Christ had risen without effort,
entirely at his will in splendour,
and that they could not prevent
his wish from being fulfilled.

249 Then when Pilate heard
that they spoke thus,
he was overcome with concern,
lest they should say
and declare it throughout the kingdom
surely near and far,
so that men would come with a great force
against him to wage war.

---

249 **E**na pylat pan glewas / yndelma y ȝe gewsell
prederow an kemeras / rag own y ȝe leuerell
ha ȝy notye drys an wlas / sur a-ogas hag abell
may teffe tus gans nerth bras / ((er y byn)) rag gustle bell

250 Rag henna Pilat a ros
dhe'n varhogyon aga ro,
may lavarsens ha dolos
in pùb tyller dres an vro
dhe vos tus ervys i'n nos,
warnedha kemmys adro
nag êns y hardh dhe wortos,
lemen oll mones dhe'n fo.

251 An varhogyon pàn glêwas
Pilat ow cows indella,
meur a joy a's kemeras
y dhe dhiank indella
a'n painys o crev ha brâs,
ha cafos rohow mar dhâ.
Bodh Pilat y a nôtyas
in le mayth êns rag henna.

252 I'n keth jÿdh-na pòr avarr
ha'n howl nowyth drehevys
teyr Maria clor ha whar
a dheuth dhe'n bedh leverys
ha gansa oynment heb par,
rag corf Jesus o prenys.
Whath i'n eur-na nynj êns war
bones Mab Duw drehevys.

---

250 **R**ag henna pylat a ros / ȝen vorogyon aga ro
may lavarsans ha dolos / yn pub tyller drys an vro
ȝe vos tus yrvys yn nos / warneȝe kymmys adro
nag ens y hardh ȝe wortos / lemmen oll monas ȝen fo

251 **E**n varogyon pan glewas / pylat ov cows yndella
meur a ioy a⸨s ⸩kemeras / y ȝe ȝeank yndella
an peynys o creff ha bras / ha cafos rohow mar ȝa
both pylat y a notyas / yn le mayȝ ens rag henna

250 Therefore Pilate gave
to the soldiers their gratuity,
that they should say and pretend
everywhere throughout the country,
that so many armed men in the night
came upon them round about,
that they were not able to resist them,
but they all departed in flight.

251 When the soldiers heard
Pilate speaking thus,
they were overcome with great joy,
that they had in that way escaped
from the pains, which were strong and great,
and had received such fine gifts.
They therefore declared what Pilate wished
wherever they went.

252 On that same day very early
when the sun was newly up,
the three Marys, meek and mild,
came to aforesaid tomb
and brought with them peerless ointment,
which had been bought for the corpse of Jesus.
Still at that time they did not know
that the Son of God had arisen.

---

252 In keth gyth-na pur avar / han houll nowyth drehevys
tyr marea cleyr ha whar / a ȝeth ȝen beth leuerys
ha ganse oynment heb par / rag corf Ihesus o prennys
whath yn er-na nyng ens war / bonas mab du drehevys

253 Pàn o an Teyr Maria
ogas dhe'n bedh devedhys,
an men esa awartha,
y a'n gwelas drehevys.
An benenes indelma
intredha a leverys,
"Dhyworth an bedh an men-ma
dhyn ny pyw a'n omwhelys?"

254 An benenes leun a ras
gans an bedh fast powesens.
Worth an penn y a welas
dhe'n bedh yw leverys kyns
unn flogh yonk, gwynn y dhyllas;
el o ha y ny wodhyens.
Scruth, own meur a's kemeras
rag an marthus re welsens.

255 An el a gêwsys dhedha,
"Na vedhowgh dysconfortys.
Jesus Crist a Nazare,
dell welsowgh, a veu ledhys,
sevys, gallas dhe gen le,
Duw apert ha meur y bris.
Awot an le mayth esa.
Omma nynj yw ev tregys.

---

253 **P**an o an tyr marya • ogas ȝen beth deueth⟨*ys*⟩ [21v]
an meyn esa awarȝa / y an guelas drehevys
en benenas yndelma / yntreȝe a leuerys
ȝeworth an beth an meyn-ma / ȝyn ny pu an ommelys

254 **E**n benenas leun a ras / gans an beth fast powessens
worth an pen y a welas / ȝen beth yw leuerys kens
vn flough yonk gwyn y ȝyllas / eyll o ha y ny woȝyens
scruth own meur a⸨s ⸩kemeras / rag an marthus re welsens

253 When the Three Marys had
come near to the tomb,
the stone which was on top,
they saw had been lifted.
So the women
among themselves said,
"From the tomb this stone
who has overturned it for us?"

254 The women, full of grace,
rested right at the tomb.
At the head of the tomb,
mentioned previously, they saw
a young child, in white raiment;
he was an angel and they did not know.
Terror, great fear overcame them,
because of the marvel they had seen.

255 The angel spoke to then,
"Do not be alarmed.
Jesus Christ of Nazareth,
as you saw, was put to death,
he has risen, he has gone to another place,
God manifest and of great worth.
Lo, here is the place where he was.
Here he does not abide.

---

255 **E**n eyll a gewsys ȝeȝe / na veȝough dysconfortys
Ihesus crist a nazary / del welsough a ve lethys
sevys gallas ȝe gen le / dew apert ha meur y breys
awott an le mayȝ ese / vmma nyng ew ef tregys

256 “Ewgh yn fen dh’y dhyskyblon
ha leverowgh why dhedha
ha dhe Peder dos yn scon
er y bynn dhe Alyle.
Ena Crist, an cuv colon,
why a’n kÿv in lowena,
dell leverys y honen,
in kig, in goos ow pêwa.”

257 Gans henna y a drailyas
confortys ha lowenek
hag êth tus Crist rag whelas
hag a’s cafas morethek.
Y lavarsons oll an câss.
Yth êthons in unn tonek
bys Galyle dh’y whelas
ha dhe gows worth Jesus wheg.

258 Pàn dheuthons dhe Alyle,
Jesus Crist y a welas
in y dhensys ow pêwa,
Duw apert ha meur y ras.
Oll y bain y’n tremensa
ha trailys êns in joy brâs,
hag a vÿdh dhyn ny nefra,
mara cresyn ha bos vas.

---

256 **E**ugh yn fen ȝy ȝyschyblon / ha leuerough wy ȝeȝe
ha ȝe pedyr dos yn scon / ((er y byn)) ȝe alyle
ena crist an kuf colon / wy an kyff yn lowene
del leuerys y honon / yn kyg yn goys ow pewe

257 **G**ans henna y a drylyas / confortys ha lowenek
hag eth tus crist rag whelas / hag as cafos moreȝek
y lauarsons ol an cas / yȝ eȝons yn vn tonek
bys galyle ȝy whelas / ha ȝe gows worth Ihesus wek

256 "Go quickly to his disciples
and do you tell them
and to Peter to come quickly
to meet him to Galilee.
There Christ, the beloved,
you will find in joy,
as he said himself,
alive in flesh and blood."

257 Thereupon they turned,
comforted and happy,
and went to seek Christ's men,
and found them sorrowful.
They told all the matter.
They went as a crowd
to Galilee to seek him
and to speak to dear Jesus.

258 When they came to Galilee,
they saw Jesus Christ
alive in his human form,
God manifest and of great grace.
All his pains had passed from him
and they had been turned to great joy,
and it will be ours forever,
if we believe and are good.

---

258 **P**an deȝons ȝe alyle / Ihesus crist y a welas
yn y ȝensys ow pewe / deu apert ha meur y ras
ol y beyn yn tremense / ha trylys ens yn ioy bras
hag a vyth ȝyn ny neffre / mara cresyn ha bos vas

259 Dell sevys Mab Duw a'y vedh
i'n eur-na dhe'n tressa dëdh,
indella oll ny a sev,
dëdh breus, drog ha dâ inwedh.
Obereth dremas a dëv;
i'n eur-na rych ev a vëdh;
drog-dhen i'n jÿdh-na goev!
Dhe Grist y fÿdh a'n barth cledh.

---

259 Del sevys mab du ay veth / yn er-na ʒen tressa dyth
yndella ol ny a seff / deth brues drok ha da ynweth
obereth dremas a dyff / yn er-na rych ef a vyth
drok-ʒen yn gyth-na goef • ʒe gryst y fyth an barth cleth

259 As the Son of God rose from the tomb
at that time on the third day, 2068
so we all shall rise,
on the day of judgement, evil and good also.
The works of a good man will grow;
at that hour he will be rich; 2072
woe betide the wicked man on that day!
He will be on the left side of Christ.

7
INDEXES

7.1 *THE CHARTER FRAGMENT*

7.1.1 Index verborum

There are 149 unique wordforms in *The Charter Fragment*, though some of them are, as expected, slightly different spellings for the same word. Seven begin with a capital letter (see comments in § 3.4 above). The figure given in square brackets below is the number of times the word occurs in the text; the figures thereafter indicate the lines in which the words appear. The list shown here gives the alphabetical order used, with each letter separated by a semicolon, and letters considered variants for the purposes of sorting (here under *e*, *l*, *r*, *s*, and *y*) separated by commas.

(◌̇, ◌̄, ◌̑, ◌᷎); a, ◌ᷓ; b; c; d; e, ɘ; f; g; h; i; k; l, ƚ;
m; n; o; p; r, ꝛ, ◌͛; s, ſ; t; u; v; ɓ; ꝩ; y, ẏ, ŷ; ʒ; z

Of the diacritical marks, only FLATTENED OPEN A ABOVE ◌ᷓ and ZIGZAG ABOVE ◌͛ are meaningful in this text. The OVERCURL ◌᷎ in *The Charter Fragment* is only a decorative feature on final *-r*, and is ignored except for tie-breaking in *mar/mar᷎*; the DOT ABOVE ◌̇ and INVERTED BREVE ◌̑ are likewise decorative on *y*, as is the OVERLINE ◌̄ on *L* and *l*. The editorial marks ⌜ ⌝, ⟨ ⟩, and ⟦ ⟧ are not given in the wordlist, but are given surrounding the line number where applicable (see the note on punctuation in § 3.5 above).

a [6] 12, 13, 15, 22, ⟦24⟧, 34
ad [1] 21
ag [1] 22
aƚema [1] 26
an [2] 18, 20
arluʒes [1] 36
aſ [1] 17
avar᷎ [1] ⟦27⟧
aꝩos [1] 34
barʒ [1] 20
boꝛʒ [1] 2
boʒ [1] 24
bẏʒ [1] 32
bŷʒ [2] 2, 21
coꝩeʒ [1] 1
coʒes [1] 5
Curtes [1] 38
da [2] 13, 21
Dallaʒ [1] 27
danger᷎ [1] 40
dar᷎ꝩar᷎ [1] 27
deboꝛ͛ [1] 38
dek [1] 7
della [1] 41
doʒ [1] 23
dregŷn [1] 39

dus [1] 4
dyŷſkẏn [1] ⟨3⟩
ə [1] ⟪41⟫
ef [1] 29
emſettẏə [1] 29
en [1] 18
es [1] 25
eug [1] 26
faȓ [1] 19
faſt [1] 41
feſt [1] 7
ffŷ [1] ⟪24⟫
flog [1] 23
freʒ [1] 27
fŷſtŷnŷug [1] 26
gafus [1] 24
gallo [1] 34
ganſo [1] 37
genes [1] 8
genſÿ [1] 23
Golſoug [1] 1
govŷn [1] 16
greẏz [1] 18
gul [1] 31
gvɜra [1] 33
gvɜreg [1] 13
ha [11] 3, 4, 6, 7, 9, 12, 16, 18, 23, 26, 38
hag [2] ⟪24⟫, 36
hedẏȓ [1] 36
herg [1] 31
hy [2] 12, ⟪14⟫
Hŷ [1] 13
hŷ [1] 22
in [4] 27, 35, 40, 41
kam [1] 30
kefÿʒ [1] 40
ken [1] 25
kŷmmerr [1] 10
lauara [1] 15
lauaȓ [2] 32, 33
Ꝉemen [1] 17
les [1] 5
ma [1] 28
-ma [1] 20
mar [1] 33
maȓ [1] 5
maȓa [1] 8
maȓan [1] 40
Maȓaʒ [1] 31
mennŷʒ [1] 33
meŷſtres [1] 35
meʒ [1] 2
movɜes [1] ⌜6⌝
mẏ [1] 21
mŷ [2] 17, 18
na [3] 2, 30, 34
-na [1] 35
nag [1] 19
nep [1] 31
nes [1] 4
ny [2] ⟨11⟩, 39
nŷ [1] 32
o [1] 37
offeren [1] ⟪37⟫
ol [1] 22
onan [1] 7
oun [1] 28
pes [1] 21
plek [1] 8
pons [1] 20
poꝛʒo [1] ⌜28⌝
povɜes [1] ⌜3⌝
puȓ [1] 15
rag [1] 23
Ras [1] 37
rə [1] 17
rən [1] ⟪37⟫
rof [1] 6
sconye [1] 11
sens [2] 35, ⟪41⟫

7.1.2 Index literarum

Here is given a frequency count of the 42 characters in *The Charter Fragment*. The first figure gives the count of letters in the set of words given in the list above; the second figure gives the count in the entire manuscript. The hyphen is listed first as it appears in this edition, though it does not occur in the original manuscript.

(◌̇, ◌̄, ◌̂, ◌̑); a, ◌̈; b; c; d; e, ɘ; f; g; h; i; k; l, ƚ; m; n; o; p; r, ꝛ, ◌; s, ſ; t; u; v; 6; vɞ; y, ẏ, ŷ; ȝ; z

- 2, 2	**c** 3, 3	**h** 7, 19	**p** 7, 7	**v** 11, 12
◌̇ 17, 18	**D** 1, 1	**i** 1, 4	**R** 1, 1	**6** 1, 1
◌̄ 2, 2	**d** 12, 13	**k** 9, 9	**r** 40, 44	**vɞ** 16, 19
◌̂ 23, 32	**e** 52, 54	**L** 1, 1	**ꝛ** 3, 3	**y** 51, 64
◌̑ 15, 16	**ɘ** 7, 10	**l** 16, 17	◌ 1, 1	**ȝ** 34, 43
a 57, 81	**f** 14, 14	**M** 1, 1	**s** 25, 30	**z** 1, 1
◌̈ 1, 1	**G** 1, 1	**m** 25, 26	**ſ** 14, 14	
b 6, 7	**g** 23, 24	**n** 37, 45	**t** 15, 18	
C 1, 1	**H** 1, 1	**o** 36, 37	**u** 13, 14	

7.1.3 Index signorum diacriticorum

Here is given a frequency count of the 6 diacritical marks used in *The Charter Fragment*. The full count is given in § 7.1.2 above; here each of the letters bearing a diacritical mark are counted.

◌̇	◌̄	◌̑	◌᷎	◌ᷱ	◌ᷣ
ẏ 18	**L̄** 1	**y̑** 32	**r᷎** 16	**tᷱ** 1	**nᷣ** 1
	Ī 1				

7.2 *PASCON AGAN ARLUTH*

7.2.1 Index verborum

There are 2732 unique wordforms in *Pascon agan Arluth*, though many of them are, as expected, slightly different spellings for the same word. A relatively small number of those—134—begin with a capital letter (see comments in § 3.4 above). The figure in square brackets below is the number of times the word occurs in the text; the figures thereafter indicate the lines in which the words appear. The list below gives each of them in alphabetical order. That order is given here, with each letter separated by a semicolon, and letters having variants for the purposes of sorting (here under *a*, *d*, *e*, *g*, *i*, ◌̄, *r*, *s*, *t*, and *w*) separated by commas.

The list shown here gives the alphabetical order used, with each letter separated by a semicolon, and letters considered variants for the purposes of sorting (here under *a*, *d*, *e*, *g*, *i*, ◌̄, *r*, *s*, *t*, and *w*) separated by commas.

(◌́; ◌̇); a, ◌ᷱ; b; c; d, ◌ͩ; đ; e, ◌ͤ; f; g, ᵍ; h; i, ◌ͥ, j; k;
l; m; ◌̃, ◌͒, ◌̄, ◌̑, ◌᷎; n; o; p; ꝑ; ꝓ; q; r, ꝛ, ◌ᷣ, ◌ꝰ, ◌̃;
s, ſ; ẜ; t, ᵗ, ꞇ; u; v; w, ꝡ; x; y; ȝ; z; ꝭ; ꝯ

Of the diacritical marks, DOT ABOVE ◌̇ and ACUTE ACCENT ◌́ are not meaningful in this text, and TILDE ◌̃, FERMATA ◌͒, OVERLINE ◌̄, and INVERTED BREVE ◌̑ are polyvalent. These, and the OVERCURL ◌᷎, are sorted as a separate letter between *m* and *n* along with when they can be read as *m* or *n* (or as *e*, *nt*, *s*, or *w*), but are ignored in sorting when used decoratively in *c̄h*, *ḡh*, *t̄h*, *t̄t*, or as abbreviation marks as in *ih̄us*, *ihūs*, *ihȗs*, *ihu͒s*, or *ihũs* (since in these they are neither *m* and *n*). The OVERCURL however is not ignored because it may be otiose or it may stand for *m*, *n*, or *e*. The editorial marks ⟨ ⟩, ⟪ ⟫, and ⦅ ⦆ are not given in the wordlist, but are given surrounding the page number where applicable (see the note on punctuation in § 3.5 above). Roman numerals have been expanded and so a number of instances of *i*, *j*, and *x* are not listed here; they are given however in § 7.2.4 below.

fallens [1] 385
fals [7] 281, 531, 652, 719, 787, 940, 1400
falſury [3] 280, 650, 663
faꝛwe [1] 1202
fas [6] 468, 510, ⦅758⦆, 1247, 1566, 1759
faſt [15] 602, 866, 917, 1035, 1043, 1406, 1428, 1442, 1444, 1506, 1613, 1696, 1784, 1934, 2028
faſte [1] 1434
faſteys [1] 1466
faſtſens [1] 604
faſtƒ [1] 15
fatel [2] 487, 1360
fateꝉꝉ [2] 579, 1958
faynys [1] 1323
fe [21] 22, 50, 66, 139, 143, 181, 248, 249, 459, 701, 928, 944, 948, ⦅1164⦆, 1218, 1222, 1279, 1471, 1511, ⦅1516⦆, 1595
fecle [1] 317
fekyl-cheꝛ [1] 517
fēne [2] 326, 723
fen [7] 392, 898, 1223, 1333, 1528, 1555, 2043
fens [4] 1207, 1268, 1299, ⦅1903⦆
fenſe [1] 1502
fernoth [1] 394
fes [2] 175, 1151
Feſt [1] 1771
feſt [7] 474, 827, 907, 1039, 1063, 1902, 1912
feth [2] 391, 1727
feth̄ [3] 126, 915, 1598
fethys [1] 578
fethyth̄ [1] 47
feyn [3] 427, 429, 1567
feynys [2] 1343, 1803
feȝaff [1] 741
feȝe [1] 199
fijs [1] 384
flamyas [1] 732
fleghys [2] 1345, 1968
Flehys [1] 1341
flehys [1] 1191
florƒ [1] 231
flough̄ [1] 2031
fo [9] 7, 68, 246, 380, 780, 792, 1136, 1913, 2002
fol [4] 746, 796, 906, 1057
foꝉꝉ [2] 1451, 1902
folle [1] 165
fons [7] 141, 309, 1045, 1050, 1431, 1680, 1689
foꝛth [1] 255
foꝛth̄ [5] 56, 119, 229, 1510, 1962
fowt [1] 1377
foys [1] 353
fꝛas [1] 1191
freth̄ [1] 1909
frut [2] 1221, 1223
fryns [1] 607
fur̃ [1] 1524
fy [1] 169
fyan [1] 1970
fyas [1] 609
fye [2] 1285, 1624
fyꝉꝉ [1] 1258
fylleꝉꝉ [1] 726
fylly [1] 1435
fyllyth [1] 1238
fylte [1] 371
fyltye [1] 182
fy̅nas [1] 29
fŷne [1] 1942
fy̅ten [1] 1793
fyn [3] 767, 887, 956
fynas [1] 494
fynte̊ [1] 1790
fynweth̄ [1] 1697
fyſtena [1] 1333

leuerough [1] 2044
leueꝛough [1] 754
leueꝛough̄ [2] 901, 999
leuery [2] 1162, 1569
leueꝛy [1] 768
leueryn [1] 1974
leueꝛyn [1] 1976
leuerys [14] 582, 760, 802, 1186, 1210, 1523, 1618, 1663, 1910, 1921, 1957, 1982, 2014, 2049
leueꝛys [11] 84, 281, 482, 489, 646, 673, 789, 897, 995, 1387, 2024
leuerꝭ [16] 113, 129, 370, 378, 406, 408, 626, 670, 914, 1013, 1026, 1084, 1340, 1371, 1576, 2030
leū [1] 691
leũ [14] 21, 85, 274, 369, 409, 599, 687, 759, 799, 823, 844, 1485, 1857, 2027
leû [1] 69
leũ-golon [1] 198
leũ-goloñ [2] 233, 1821
leuꝰ [3] 1027, 1079, 1776
leuꝰfough̄ [1] 399
leuꝰys [1] 1032
levaꝛ [1] 1079
leverꝭ [1] 305
levff [3] 1433, 1441, 1449
levñ [1] 1486
levn̄-golon [1] 2
lewte [3] 926, 1254, 1397
leyff [3] 368, 1098, 1752
leyth̄ [1] 1051
leʒys [17] 135, 392, 572, 756, 780, 938, 948, 1022, 1125, 1134, 1139, 1151, 1244, 1682, 1914, 1917, 1961
logell̄ [1] 1864
Longꝭ [1] 1739
longꝭ [1] 1732
lõ [2] 407, 1684
lovan [1] 840
loven [2] 1441, 1446
lowaꝛth [2] 1114, 1859
lowēna [1] 915
lowen [2] 567, 902
lowene [4] 234, 515, 1093, 2048
lowenek [2] 1954, 2052
loweꝛ [1] 1675
loys [1] 1794
lu [1] 1302
luas [3] 1630, 1680, 1856
lucyfeꝛ [1] 1695
lughas [1] 1669
luhas [1] 1063
lybell̄ [1] 1505
lyffrow [2] 581, 1644
lyffꝛovꝭ [1] 130
lygyon [1] 573
lym [2] 1737, 1744
lymyn [1] 1396
lȳmyn [2] 694, 1111
lyn [1] 1767
lyoñ [1] 166
lyꝛgh [1] 1302
lyw [2] 541, 1810
ma [7] ⸨151⸩, 267, 467, 618, ⸨1051⸩, 1069, 1195
-ma [19] 86, ⸨344⸩, ⸨349⸩, 434, ⸨476⸩, 752, 787, 798, ⸨81ō⸩, 826, ⸨888⸩, ⸨997⸩, ⸨1027⸩, 1124, 1127, 1475, 1478, 1959, 2025
Mab [3] 89, 409, 425
mab [30] 1, 19, 49, 64, 69, 85, 111, 147, 180, 461, 759, 799, 969, 1030, 1140, 1310, 1313, 1327, 1364, 1571, 1575, 1664, 1682, 1765, 1780, 1809, 1818, 1844, 2018, 2067
maga [3] 95, 568, 678
magata [1] 1580
magdalenen [1] 1331

purpuꝛ [1] 1082
purra [1] 592
pv [2] 336, 548
py [2] 1207, 1647
pygȳmys [1] 1479
Pylat [7] 993, 1005, 1009, 1113, 1133, 1489, 1923
pylat [41] 778, 785, 793, 797, 805, 814, 851, 857, 860, 874, 878, 892, 910, 925, 929, 933, 941, 946, 953, 961, 972, 1019, 1023, 1025, 1121, 1131, 1148, 1159, 1169, 1177, 1185, 1193, 1493, 1504, 1721, 1908, 1980, 1987, 1995, 2004, 2009
pyltye [1] 893
pymp [1] 1813
pȳʒek [2] 1816, 1820
pys [1] 1453
pyſtege [1] 1572
pyte [2] 781, 1618
pytet [3] 1411, 1781, 1783
pyteth [1] 1307
pyth [6] 306, 547, 754, 808, 1006, 1688
pyth̄ [2] 1451, 1503
pyv [1] 1520
ꝑadſ [1] 1544
ꝑna [2] 31, 37
ꝑnās [1] 《404》
ꝑnas [2] 40, 835
ꝑnys [1] 349
ꝑys [3] 141, 1205, 1860
ꝓvas [1] 48
quelſe [1] 680
queꝛʒe [1] 828
queth [4] 761, 770, 1118, 1413
queth̄ [2] 1081, 1281
queʒens [1] 761
quuthas [1] 1415
quyth̄ [1] 1200
ꝛa [3] 307, 480, 503
ꝛaf [1] 364
Rag [9] 153, 705, 861, 1135, 1365, 1633, 1649, 1915, 1995
ꝛag [105] 37, 39, 43, 55, 61, 79, 106, 109, 171, 205, 223, 227, 228, 242, 246, 253, 275, 277, 299, 381, 424, 427, 447, 452, 462, 464, 479, 541, 542, 560, 571, 661, 691, 710, 715, 820, 840, 843, 850, 868, 900, 922, 931, 942, 971, 983, 988, 1011, 1083, 1092, 1109, 1117, 1140, 1143, 1167, 1188, 1197, 1213, 1224, 1226, 1244, 1271, 1304, 1335, 1345, 1383, 1384, 1392, 1412, 1416, 1423, 1476, 1479, 1509, 1532, 1536, 1546, 1557, 1616, 1636, 1638, 1641, 1642, 1645, 1651, 1690, 1712, 1719, 1737, 1756, 1776, 1777, 1805, 1817, 1821, 1829, 1861, 1870, 1905, 1914, 1990, 2010, 2016, 2034, 2053
ꝛagaf [1] 1356
ꝛagleuerſ [1] 1787
ꝛagoff [1] 1344
ꝛagon [2] 444, 1550
Ragon̄ [2] 13, 65
ꝛagon̄ [1] 1220
ꝛagos [1] 980
ꝛagough [1] 348
ꝛagough̄ [1] 1346
ꝛagthe [1] 939
ꝛagtho [1] 42
rānas [1] 354
rāne [2] 284, 1775
ꝛāne [1] 1518
ran [1] 1514
ꝛan [3] 299, 1516, 1794
ꝛanne [1] 1096

7.2.2 Index literarum

Here is given a frequency count of the 76 characters used in *Pascon agan Arluth*. The first figure gives the count of letters in the set of words given in the list above in § 7.2.1; the second figure gives the count in the entire manuscript. The hyphen is listed first as it appears in this edition, though it does not occur in the original manuscript. Of the diacritical marks, only ◌̇ and ◌́ are not meaningful in this text; the marks ◌̅ and ◌̑ may or may not be meaningful, but all are counted together here.

(◌́; ◌̇); *a*, ◌̃; *b*; *c*; *d*, ◌ᵈ; *ꝺ*; *e*, ◌ᵉ; *f*; *g*, ᵍ; *h*; *i*, ◌ⁱ, *j*; *k*;
l; *m*; ◌̃, ◌̂, ◌̅, ◌̂, ◌̑; *n*; *o*; *p*; *ꝑ*; *ꝓ*; *q*; *r*, *ꝛ*, ◌ᷣ, ◌ᷣ, ◌̃;
s, *ſ*; *ẜ*; *t*, ᵗ, *ꞇ*; *u*; *v*; *w*, *ꝡ*; *x*; *y*; *ʒ*; *z*; *ꝭ*; *ꝯ*

- 26, 84
◌́ 40, 46
◌̇ 5, 6
A 6, 21
a 1030, 3763
◌̃ 5, 5
B 3, 3
b 202, 593
C 5, 7
c 231, 506
D 10, 15
d 352, 824
◌ᵈ 1, 1
ꝺ 5, 7
E 10, 39
e 1732, 4169
◌ᵉ 1, 2
F 2, 2
f 312, 693
G 5, 16
g 544, 1290
ᵍ 1, 3
H 7, 32
h 592, 1577
I 28, 158
i 53, 106
◌ⁱ 11, 152
j 26, 29
K 6, 9
k 185, 334
L 2, 2
l 748, 1613
M 10, 14
m 271, 806
◌̃ 7, 8
◌̂ 61, 103
◌̅ 607, 1163
◌̂ 10, 16
◌̑ 136, 328
N 5, 8
n 869, 2785
O 7, 8
o 893, 1959
P 9, 28
p 221, 536
ꝑ 9, 13
ꝓ 2, 2
q 23, 35
R 5, 16
r 492, 1047
ꝛ 407, 865
◌ᷣ 32, 156
◌ᷣ 66, 133
◌̃ 39, 142
S 3, 3
s 708, 1795
ſ 479, 996
ẜ 4, 9
T 3, 4
t 668, 1500
ᵗ 1, 5
Ꞇ 7, 7
u 333, 758
V 2, 6
v 260, 680
W 6, 7
w 504, 1192
Ꝡ 2, 2
ꝡ 31, 39
x 4, 6
Y 2, 2
y 1224, 3578
ʒ 300, 959
z 3, 3
ꝭ 76, 196
ꝯ 6, 15

7.2.3 Index signorum diacriticorum

Here is given a frequency count of the 14 diacritical marks used in *Pascon agan Arluth*. The full count is given in § 7.2.2 above; here each of the letters bearing a diacritical mark are counted. At the end of the list the punctuation characters used are given; the last of these is the editorial bullet • which was supplied where a verse divider was missing (see § 3.3.3 above).

◌́
í 23
ȷ́ 23

◌̏
m̏ 2
ȑ 2
z̏ 1

◌ͩ
uͩ 1

◌ͤ
cͤ 2

◌ͥ
cͥ 142
gͥ 2
pͥ 4
vͥ 4

◌̃
ã 1
ẽ 1
õ 1
ũ 2
ỹ 3

◌̂
â 6
ê 13
ô 9
û 3
v̂ 1
ŷ 73

◌̄
ā 66
c̄ 5
ē 92
ḡ 55
h̄ 233
ī 353
n̄ 1
ō 18
t̄ 132
ū 61
v̄ 2
ȳ 145

◌̑
ȇ 3
ȗ 3
y̑ 10

◌ꝰ
aꝰ 2
eꝰ 85
mꝰ 3
nꝰ 113
rꝰ 84
sꝰ 2
tꝰ 5
uꝰ 27
yꝰ 7

◌ꝰ + ◌̇
ėꝰ 2
ṅꝰ 3
u̇ꝰ 1

◌ᷣ
mᷣ 65
pᷣ 13
tᷣ 3
Wᷣ 2
wᷣ 72
Wʒᷣ 1

◌̉
d̉ 24
g̉ 4
m̉ 12
n̉ 11
p̉ 23
r̉ 4
t̉ 44
ủ 11

◌͌
e͌ 2
g͌ 3
m͌ 35
o͌ 12
p͌ 30
s͌ 2
t͌ 3
v͌ 6
w͌ 49

⸗ 1
/ 1019
// 1
. 5
• 16

7.2.4 Index numerorum

Here is given a list of the Roman numerals in *Pascon agan Arluth*. In the list in § 7.2.1 above, these are expanded as shown in italics here.

ííȷ́ [1] 1232 *tyr*
íȷ́ [8] 1037 *dew*, 1038 *dew*, 1042 *ȝew*, 1269 *dew*, 1270 *ȝew*, 1329 *dyw*, 1420 *dew*, 1796 *dew*
xxx [1] 311 *dek wazn vgons*

www.ingramcontent.com/pod-product-compliance
Lightning Source LLC
Chambersburg PA
CBHW040406110426
42812CB00011B/2474
* 9 7 8 1 7 8 2 0 1 1 8 2 8 *